Palgrave Studies in the History of Finance

The study of the history of financial institutions, markets, instruments and concepts is vital if we are to understand the role played by finance today. At the same time, the methodologies developed by finance academics can provide a new perspective for historical studies. Palgrave Studies in the History of Finance is a multi-disciplinary effort to emphasise the role played by finance in the past, and what lessons historical experiences have for us. It presents original research, in both authored monographs and edited collections, from historians, finance academics and economists, as well as financial practitioners.

Christiaan van Bochove · Juliette Levy
Editors

Beyond Banks

A Global History of Credit Markets and Intermediation

palgrave
macmillan

Editors
Christiaan van Bochove
Department of History and Art History
Utrecht University
Utrecht, The Netherlands

Juliette Levy
Department of History
University of California, Riverside
Riverside, USA

ISSN 2662-5164 ISSN 2662-5172 (electronic)
Palgrave Studies in the History of Finance
ISBN 978-3-031-75818-8 ISBN 978-3-031-75819-5 (eBook)
https://doi.org/10.1007/978-3-031-75819-5

Cover credit: Bank van lening or (municipal) pawn shop, drawing by Willem de Keyser dated 1657–1692. Rijksmuseum, object number RP-T-1913-25

This Palgrave Macmillan imprint is published by the registered company Springer Nature Switzerland AG
The registered company address is: Gewerbestrasse 11, 6330 Cham, Switzerland

Preface

This edited volume concludes a long collaboration on the topic of non-bank credit markets. It started in 2009, when we were connected by Oscar Gelderblom, with whom one of us had shared an office at UCLA and the other was carrying out a postdoc. Oscar was right that since we were both working on the role of notaries in private credit markets—one of us in Mexico, the other one in the Netherlands—we might have some things to talk about. Oscar's introduction resulted in the off-program session "Alternative financial institutions and non-traditional intermediaries" at the World Economic History Congress (Utrecht, 2009). It was followed by two workshops and another session at a World Economic History Congress: "Intermediaries and intermediation in capital markets: A global historical approach" (Utrecht, 2010)[1], "Information, intermediation and financial markets" (Riverside, 2012)[2], and "Banking before banks: Financial markets, intermediaries and networks in a global historical perspective" (Boston, 2018).

At these and other meetings we met scholars working on (intermediation in) non-bank credit markets. It increasingly became clear to us that

[1] With financial support from Oscar Gelderblom and Joost Jonker's EURYI project and the Professor Van Winter Foundation.

[2] In collaboration with Jean-Laurent Rosenthal at the California Institute of Technology, Ghislaine Lydon at UCLA, Jan Luiten van Zanden at Utrecht University, the Utrecht University Seminar Series, and the All-UC Economic History seminar.

while we were all researching roughly the same topics, differences in our disciplinary backgrounds embedded our research in different literatures, and we formulated our research questions slightly differently, and—more confusingly—used different terminologies for similar concepts. And worse, we did not know of each other's work to begin with. This is something we wanted to remedy, and this volume is the outcome of more than a decade of conversations exploring the nature of non-bank credit markets as such—not as an alternative to banks. This led us to consider not merely credit markets and intermediaries before the existence of banks, but also credit markets and intermediaries that existed alongside banks, since across the globe and across history, most people did not have access to banks. This project thus had to go *beyond* banks—ergo the title of this volume.

We had two objectives with this volume. First, to produce an extensive review of the literature and to produce a set of questions (and range of answers) that researchers working on credit markets across time (modern and pre-modern) and place (whether it be Africa, Asia, Europa, or North or South America) could share. We wanted to move beyond a society/economy in one particular historical era and facilitate meaningful comparison between different contexts. We do this in the Introduction, which we hope will help others situate their work, turn to useful parallels, and conduct comparative research. Second, we wanted to bring scholars together who were working on widely differing cases and cross the boundaries that so often separate us. We did this by inviting contributions that address noteworthy aspects of non-bank credit markets worldwide that are occasionally quite unique and in other cases closely similar to practices seen elsewhere. While this volume focuses on private credit markets from the early modern period onwards, we are aware that similar mechanisms and intermediaries operate on public credit markets as well as in other time periods.

We are exceedingly grateful to all the contributors to this volume, and the ones that joined us at previous workshops and sessions. Everyone of those interactions has impacted how we think about credit markets and intermediation beyond banks. We also want to thank our mentors, all of whom will see their influence reflected here. Oscar Gelderblom, Joost Jonker, Naomi Lamoreaux, and Jean-Laurent Rosenthal—they guided our thinking on the issues at hand. As mentors and scholars they have always shown the sort of intellectual acuity and generosity we both aspire to.

We are grateful to Pleun Hendrikx for copy editing the manuscript, Roelof Meijer for compiling the index and generating the alt texts, the team at Palgrave, the series editors, as well as David and Erica, and Julia, Thomas, and Enzo. This volume may have eaten more than a few hours of family time, vacations, and ball-throwing.

Ultimately, *Beyond Banks: A Global History of Credit Markets and Intermediation* is the outcome of the work of a community, but whatever mistakes remain are ours alone. We hope they are few.

Utrecht, The Netherlands — Christiaan van Bochove
Riverside, USA — Juliette Levy

Contents

Notes on Contributors

Elise M. Dermineur is an associate professor of Economic History at Stockholm University. She specializes in financial history and gender history. She is the authors of several books and articles. In 2017, she published *Gender and Politics in Eighteenth-Century Sweden*, a political biography of the Swedish queen Lovisa Ulrika (1720–1782) with Routledge. In 2018, she published a collection of essays titled *Women and Credit in Preindustrial Europe* and she co-edited *Revisiting Gender in European History, 1400–1800*. And in 2024, she co-edited *Credit Networks in The Preindustrial World* with Palgrave and she published the monograph *Before Banks, The Making of Credit and Debt in Preindustrial France* with Cambridge University Press.

Konstantinos Giakoumis is associate professor of history, arts, and their didactics at LOGOS University College, Tirana, Albania. His expertise and training are on the medieval and early modern political, social, cultural, and economic history of the Balkans. He is interested in the development of the guilds and has written a number of contributions in collective volumes and journals, among others, in *The Turkish Historical Review*. His latest book, co-authored with Katerina Korre on the guild of tailors of Voskopoja is currently in preparation.

Philip T. Hoffman (California Institute of Technology) combines economic theory and historical evidence to explain long-term changes in politics, society, and the economy—in particular, economic growth and political development. He has worked on why the West grew rich before other parts of the world, why it became a dominant military power, how financial and political institutions develop, and how to establish causality with historical data. Hoffman was president of the Economic History Association in 2013–2014 and president of the Social Science History Association in 2019–2020. He has been a visiting professor at the Ecole des Hautes Etudes en Sciences Sociales in France, a visiting researcher at the Paris School of Economics (2011), and a visiting professor at the Hong Kong University of Science and Technology (2013). In addition to numerous articles, he has written six books, edited two, and won numerous prizes for his publications.

J. Howard M. Jones is a senior research fellow at the Institute of Commonwealth Studies, School of Advanced Study, University of London. Howard's research on rural informal finance in India is based on access to a moneylender's records over time, these data being analyzed in the context of related research on local social structures, livelihood change and diversification, including migration. A particular interest, addressed in a number of his journal papers and book chapters, is in exploring insights from the moneylender's loan records for the theory and practice of financial inclusion and microfinance.

Juliette Levy is an associate professor of history at the University of California, Riverside and affiliated faculty at Centro de Investigación y Docencia Económica (CIDE) in Mexico, where she co-directs MX.digital, a data digitization project of historical Mexican statistics. Her research explores pre-banking forms of finance and credit in Latin America. Her book *The Making of a Market: Credit, Henequen, and Notaries in Yucatán, 1850–1900* was published by Pennsylvania State University Press in 2012.

Cyril Milhaud holds a Ph.D. in economic history from the Paris School of Economics. His fields of interest are the economic history of Spain and Latin America, financial history, and long-term issues. His research examines the influence of jurisdictional barriers and the role of ecclesiastical institutions in capital market integration in early modern Europe.

Matthew Mitchell is an assistant professor of religion at High Point University in North Carolina. He has written articles and book chapters on gender, finances, law, and popular practices in early modern and modern Japanese religions. His current monograph project is on the social, legal, and financial activities of the nuns affiliated with Zenkōji's Daihongan Convent in the early modern period. He received his BA from Illinois Wesleyan University, MA from the University of Hawai'i at Mānoa, and his Ph.D. from Duke University.

Clemente Penna is a research fellow at the Fundação de Amparo à Pesquisa e Inovação do Estado de Santa Catarina and the Universidade Federal de Santa Catarina, Brazil. His research examines the relationship between peer-to-peer credit and slavery and its impact on Brazilian financial markets and banking. He was awarded the 2020–2021 Best Dissertation Prize by both the Brazilian and Latin American Associations of Economic History. His book, *Economias Urbanas: Capital, Créditos e Escravidão na Cidade do Rio de Janeiro, c.1820–1860*, was published by Editora Hucitec in 2023.

Matteo Pompermaier is an assistant professor of economic history at the University of Brescia. He specializes in the history of finance, particularly preindustrial credit markets. His research centers on Italy and Sweden between the fifteenth and twentieth centuries. He is the author of a monograph on the Venetian credit market and several scientific articles.

Gilles Postel-Vinay is professor emeritus at the Paris School of Economics. His research interests focused on Economic and Social Mobility, Wealth inequality, Money, Credit, Finance in the long run. He co-authored with Philip T. Hoffman and Jean-Laurent Rosenthal *Priceless Markets: the political economy of credit in Paris, 1662–1869* (2000) and *Dark Matter Credit. The development of peer-to-peer lending and banking in France* (2019).

Jean-Laurent Rosenthal (California Institute of Technology) is trying to understand what institutions encourage long-term economic growth and wealth formation. He has studied changes in property rights at the time of the French Revolution, credit markets in Europe, law and the organization of enterprises (in France, Germany, the United States, and the United Kingdom), and wealth inequality. Rosenthal is the author or co-author of several books including *Before and Beyond Divergence: The Politics of Economic Change in China and Europe* (with R. Bin Wong,

Harvard University Press, 2011) and *Dark Matter Credit: The Development of Peer-to-Peer Lending and Banking in France* (with Philip T. Hoffman and Gilles Postel-Vinay, Princeton University Press, 2019).

Christie Swanepoel is an associate professor of economics at the University of the Western Cape. Her main research interests are in the South Africa financial markets and their historical development. She has published in various journals including *Economic History of Developing Regions* and *Journal of Southern African Studies.*

Christiaan van Bochove is an associate professor of economic and social history at Utrecht University. He is interested in how financial markets provided their functions when banks were either absent or not serving the majority of society. His research focuses on early modern and modern financial markets in the Netherlands and has been published, among others, in *The Journal of Economic History* and *The Economic History Review*.

Martín L. E. Wasserman is scientific researcher at the National Scientific and Technical Research Council (CONICET), República Argentina. His work on credit and monetary social history was recognized by the Spanish Economic History Association with the Ramon Carande Prize (2013) and by the Argentinian Economic History Association with the Best Doctoral Thesis in Argentinian Economic History (2016). His book *Las obligaciones fundamentales. Crédito y consolidación económica durante el surgimiento de Buenos Aires* was published by Prometeo in 2018.

List of Figures

The Decline of a Great Financial Intermediary: Notaries in France, 1851–1934

Financial Intermediation in Colonial Seventeenth- and Eighteenth-Century Buenos Aires: Credit, Trust, and Asymmetric Information

A Network Analysis of Credit Transactions at the Cape Colony During the Eighteenth Century

An Enslaved Credit Market: Slavery, Deeds, and Litigation in Nineteenth-Century Rio de Janeiro's Financial Landscape

From Peer-to-Peer Credit to Banks: A Study of Credit Networks in Uppsala (1810–1910)

Consumer Credit in Early Modern Venice: The Lending Activity of Innkeepers and *Bastioneri*

List of Tables

The Decline of a Great Financial Intermediary: Notaries in France, 1851–1934

Financial Intermediation in Colonial Seventeenth- and Eighteenth-Century Buenos Aires: Credit, Trust, and Asymmetric Information

A Network Analysis of Credit Transactions at the Cape Colony During the Eighteenth Century

An Enslaved Credit Market: Slavery, Deeds, and Litigation in Nineteenth-Century Rio de Janeiro's Financial Landscape

From Peer-to-Peer Credit to Banks: A Study of Credit Networks in Uppsala (1810–1910)

Lender Classifications and Contracts: Categorization in the All-India Surveys (1951–2012) and Evidence From the Account Books of a Moneylender in Rajasthan (1982–2015)

Sacré Crédit! The Rise and Fall of Ecclesiastical Credit in Early Modern Spain

Ottoman Guilds as Credit-Providing Institutions from the Late 17th to the Early 19th Century

Beyond Banks: An Introduction

Christiaan van Bochove and Juliette Levy

1 The Historiographical Relationship Between Banks and Economic Growth

One of the oldest debates in economic history explores the origins and regional variations in long-term economic growth.[1] In this perspective, the Industrial Revolution takes center stage since it is largely considered to have allowed first Europe and then the United States to pull ahead of the rest of the world. Large-scale industrialization certainly fostered economic growth and since this required significant and often long-term

[1] See, among many others, Joel Mokyr, *The Lever of Riches: Technological Creativity and Economic Progress* (Oxford, 1990); Kenneth Pomeranz, *The Great Divergence: China, Europe, and the Making of the Modern World Economy* (Princeton, 2000); Robert C. Allen, *The British Industrial Revolution in Global Perspective* (Cambridge, 2009).

C. van Bochove (✉)
Department of History and Art History, Utrecht University, Utrecht, The Netherlands
e-mail: C.J.vanBochove@uu.nl

J. Levy
Department of History, University of California, Riverside, USA
e-mail: juliette.levy@ucr.edu

C. van Bochove and J. Levy (eds.), *Beyond Banks*, Palgrave Studies in the History of Finance,
https://doi.org/10.1007/978-3-031-75819-5_1

investments in capital goods and infrastructure, a large strand of literature has focused on how these investments were mobilized; and thus the focus on banks. Banks became a prime focus of the financial engines of the Industrial Revolution because they so visibly played that role. Banks, in their simplest form, were and are for-profit financial institutions that take funds (such as equity, debt, and deposits) and lend them out at their own account. The intermediation between the two generates their profit. This is how banks aggregate excess funds of one sector of the economy and direct that excess into investments that generate income, (indirectly) bringing together groups who might otherwise not transact with each other. Embedded in this intermediation are a series of processes by which banks screen loan applicants, determine appropriate ways of securing loans, and develop instruments that attract funding. The apparent emergence of banks with the economic growth generated by the Industrial Revolution, generated the impression that banks were the key to the financing of the Industrial Revolution. This led to banks being seen as a sort of ***deus ex machina*** in the economic history literature. It became dogma that economic growth and modernization of credit markets could only occur if and when banks were present.

The bias in the literature privileging the role of banks among any other credit system or institution has reputable origins. In Joseph Schumpeter's words "[t]he banker [...] has either replaced private capitalists or become their agent; he has himself become the capitalist par excellence. [...] He stands between those who wish to form new combinations and the possessors of the productive means."[2] This perspective on the banker as the handmaiden of innovation extended to all banks as mobilizers of savings, managers of risks, and facilitators of transactions. Seeing banks as essential for technological innovation and economic growth became a paradigm that has been hard to break. In 1962, Alexander Gerschenkron, in speaking on the differences between industrialized economies and those needing to "catch-up," commented on the role of banking in speeding up the industrial transformation of continental Europe. There, where retained earnings and money from family and friends could not mobilize sufficient funds, the "money creating"[3] activities of banks shaped

[2] Joseph Schumpeter, *The Theory of Economic Development: An Inquiry into Profit, Capital, Credit, Interest and the Business Cycle* (Abingdon, 2021), 62.

[3] Alexander Gerschenkron, *Economic Backwardness in Historical Perspective: A book of essays* (Cambridge [MA], 1962), 14.

a process which supported the speedy industrialization and economic growth in countries such as Germany.[4]

This is how the role of finance in innovation and industrialization in countries that others aspired to replicate became defined by banks. The systemic alternative in this historical chapter was the large state enterprise, best represented by the centralized Soviet model, which the literature has rarely invoked as an example worth replicating. In developed economies, decreasing transaction costs—a process driven by a rise of salaried labor (which made income streams predictable and more practical to use in credit transactions), assets that could be collateralized, and technology (including credit ratings)—further cemented the role of banks during the twentieth century.[5]

In the meantime, the banking literature flourished.[6] A specific part of that literature focused on collecting time series evidence on financial structure and depth, and on using advanced statistical techniques to analyze the nexus between (bank) finance and growth.[7] All of this perpetuated the notion that banks were *the* institution through which to borrow

[4] See Christiaan van Bochove, Christopher L. Colvin, and Oscar Gelderblom, 'Detecting the Function of Finance through History: An Essay in Celebration of the Work of Joost Jonker', in: *The Low Countries Journal of Social and Economic History* 18:3 (2021), 125–166 for a more elaborate discussion.

[5] Lucy Newton, 'Trust and Virtue in English Banking: The Assessment of Borrowers by Bank Managements at the Turn of the Nineteenth', in: *Financial History Review* 7:2 (2000), 177–199; Rowena Olegario, 'Credit Reporting Agencies: A Historical Perspective', in: Margaret J. Miller (ed.), *Credit Reporting Systems and the International Economy* (Cambridge [MA], 2003), 115–159; Allen N. Berger and Gregory F. Udell, 'A More Complete Conceptual Framework for SME Finance', in: *Journal of Banking & Finance* 30:11 (2006), 2945–2966; Rowena Olegario, *A Culture of Credit: Embedding Trust and Transparency in American Business* (Cambridge [MA], 2006); Josh Lauer, *Creditworthy: A History of Consumer Surveillance and Financial Identity in America* (New York, 2017); Oskar Broberg and Anders Ögren, 'Names, Shares and Mortgages: The Formalization of Swedish Commercial Bank Lending, 1870–1938', in: *Financial History Review* 26:1 (2019), 81–108.

[6] L.S. Pressnell, *Country Banking in the Industrial Revolution* (Oxford, 1956); Rondo Cameron, *Banking in the Early Stages of Industrialization: A Study in Comparative Economic History* (Oxford, 1967); Michael Collins, *Money and Banking in the UK: A History* (London, 1988); Richard S. Grossman, *Unsettled Account: The Evolution of Banking in the Industrialized World since 1800* (Princeton, 2010); Youssef Cassis, Richard S. Grossman, and Catherine R. Schenk (eds.), *The Oxford Handbook of Banking and Financial History* (Oxford, 2016).

[7] Raymond W. Goldsmith, *Financial Structure and Development* (New Haven, 1969); Robert C. King and Ross Levine, 'Finance and Growth: Schumpeter Might be Right',

and lend in a developed or developing market, which in turn internalized a series of assumptions about the role of banks, and the lesser role of non-bank institutions. While the literature has since evolved to recognize that economic growth was more gradual and had early modern and even medieval roots,[8] the original focus on the Industrial Revolution and on banks has had a long-lasting impact on the field of financial history. This is why credit interactions and markets that have existed for almost as long as humanity and have been integral to the existence, survival, and success of businesses and households[9]—continue to be seen in much of the literature as too small, too inefficient, too risky, and too expensive to support or foster meaningful investments or growth.

Any scholar of non-bank credit should be uncomfortable with these conclusions. This volume relies on a significant and rich literature on bank and non-bank credit markets that spans multiple academic fields, uses different terminologies, and focuses on many different times and places to counter the prevailing narrative. That being said, the wealth of research has produced a new problem: the literature remains unclear about what the nature of non-bank credit was and is.

Non-bank credit is routinely referred to as informal despite the fact that much of the credit observed outside of banks was exceedingly formal—if formal means that the agreement is recorded, that it is regulated, and that it has consequences. Non-bank credit is often also referred to as

in: *The Quarterly Journal of Economics* 108:3 (1993), 717–737; Ross Levine, 'Financial Development and Economic Growth: Views and Agenda', in: *Journal of Economic Literature* 35:2 (1997), 688–726; Richard Sylla, 'Financial Systems and Economic Modernization', in: *The Journal of Economic History* 62:2 (2002), 277–292; Peter L. Rousseau and Richard Sylla, 'Financial Systems, Economic Growth, and Globalization', in: Michael D. Bordo, Alan M. Taylor, and Jeffrey G. Williamson (eds.), *Globalization in Historical Perspective* (Chicago, 2003), 373–415; Ross Levine, 'Finance and Growth: Theory and Evidence', in: Philippe Aghion and Steven N. Durlauf (eds.), *Handbook of Economic Growth* 1A (Amsterdam, 2005), 865–934; Stephan Heblich and Alex Trew, 'Banking and Industrialization', in: *Journal of the European Economic Association* 17:6 (2019), 1753–1796.

[8] See, for instance, Bas J.P. van Bavel and Jan Luiten van Zanden, 'The Jump-Start of the Holland Economy during the Late-Medieval Crisis, c.1350–c.1500', in: *The Economic History Review* 57:3 (2004), 503–532; Jan Luiten van Zanden and Bas van Leeuwen, 'Persistent But Not Consistent: The Growth of National Income in Holland 1347–1807', in: *Explorations in Economic History* 49:2 (2012), 119–130; Stephen Broadberry et al., *British Economic Growth 1270–1870* (Cambridge, 2015).

[9] David Graeber, *Debt: The First 5,000 Years* (New York, 2011) offers a sweeping and occasionally pessimistic view on debt in human history.

alternative—which is an unhelpful term, since in many cases this does not explain what non-bank credit is an alternative to. The implication is that it is an alternative to bank credit, which it rarely is. The literature also often confuses peer-to-peer lending with informal arrangements and ignores the intermediaries and norms that regulate those arrangements. There are too many examples that trouble the established monodirectional storyline about financial modernization and economic growth, and beg for a global and multi-disciplinary exploration of the issue.

This introductory chapter summarizes the literature on credit markets—it is a historiographical review of mostly English language publications and is thereby definitionally incomplete. It provides a review of the broad, fascinating, and idiosyncratic literature that has deeply influenced our thinking and this volume. Sections 2, 3, and 4 review the historiographies on the Western and non-Western worlds of credit. We find that once we move beyond established terminologies (such as formal and informal or alternative), it becomes possible to focus on how these credit markets actually functioned. In Sect. 5 we propose that how the demand for and supply of loanable funds meet, whose funds change hands, what form loans are recorded in, and what mechanisms secure and enforce repayment, should be central to the study of bank and non-bank credit markets alike. Section 6 introduces the contributors to this volume and how they operationalize our perspectives on non-bank credit.

2 Reversing the Trend: Reaching Beyond Banks

Since Schumpeter and Gerschenkron published their seminal works, an abundance of research on Western economies has—often indirectly—questioned aspects of their ideal-type bank. The literature questions whether banks actually presented a radical break with the past, and suggests that merchant bankers and their firms had their origins in trade and regularly provided credit to trading partners or raised it for others, including foreign sovereigns. In Europe, such firms had been around since medieval times and remained important into the nineteenth and twentieth centuries. While they did not typically label themselves as banks, merchant bankers provided functions essential to banks. The Amsterdam firm of Hope & Co is a famous but exceptional case in that it was founded during the eighteenth century, became part of ABN AMRO bank after World War II following various mergers, and was involved in large-scale (sovereign) lending operations.[10] Many other smaller merchant firms were important to the financial landscapes not only of the Netherlands but many other countries as well.[11]

Just as old firms and ways of mobilizing funds remained important, personal relationships continued to matter for solving information asymmetries. This applied to modern banks,[12] but also to the non-standard banks that emerged and became popular during the nineteenth century, such as credit cooperatives and cosignatory lending institutions.[13] Both types of institutions used personal relationships to gather information

[10] Marten G. Buist, *At Spes Non Fracta: Hope & Co. 1770–1815* (The Hague, 1974); J.P.B. Jonker, *MeesPierson. Schakel tussen verleden en toekomst. 275 jaar traditie en vernieuwing in het Nederlands bankwezen* (Amsterdam, 1997); Joh. de Vries, Wim Vroom, and Ton de Graaf (eds.), *Worldwide Banking: ABN AMRO Bank 1824–1999* (Amsterdam 1999).

[11] Joost Jonker and Keetie Sluyterman, *At Home on the World Markets: Dutch International Trading Companies from the Sixteenth Century until the Present* (The Hague, 2000). See Anders Perlinge, 'International Mercantile Networks and Financial Intermediation in Nineteenth Century Scania (Sweden): Foreign Private Capital Imports and Informal Credit Market Imbalances', in: *Business History* 63:6 (2021), 1030–1047 for a Swedish example.

[12] Naomi Lamoreaux, *Insider Lending: Banks, Personal Connections and Economic Development in Industrial New England* (Cambridge, 1996); Newton, 'Trust and Virtue'; Gabriele B. Clemens and Daniel Reupke, 'Challenging the Institutional Revolution of Credit Markets in the Nineteenth Century', in: Marcella Lorenzini, Cinzia Lorandini, and D'Maris Coffman (eds.), *Financing in Europe: Evolution, Coexistence and Complementarity of Lending Practices from the Middle Ages to Modern Times* (Cham, 2018), 267–288; Broberg and Ögren, 'Names, Shares and Mortgages'.

[13] See Abhijit V. Banerjee, Timothy Besley, and Timothy W. Guinnane, 'Thy Neighbor's Keeper: The Design of a Credit Cooperative with Theory and a Test', in: *The Quarterly Journal of Economics* 109:2 (1994), 491–515; Maitreesh Ghatak and Timothy W. Guinnane, 'The Economics of Lending with Joint Liability: Theory and Practice', in: *Journal of Development Economics* 60:1 (1999), 195–228; Timothy W. Guinnane, 'Cooperatives as Information Machines: German Rural Credit Cooperatives, 1883–1914', in: *The Journal of Economic History* 61:2 (2001), 366–389 for rural credit cooperatives; Christopher L. Colvin, 'Organizational Determinants of Bank Resilience. Explaining the Performance of SME Banks in the Dutch Financial Crisis of the 1920s', in: *Business History Review* 92:4 (2018), 661–690; Amaury De Vicq, 'Caught Between Outreach and Sustainability: The Rise and Decline of Dutch Credit Unions', in: *Business History* 66:6 (2022), 1524–1551 for urban credit cooperatives; Amaury De Vicq and Christiaan van Bochove, 'Historical Diversity in Credit Intermediation: Cosignatory Lending Institutions in Europe and North America, 1700s–1960s', in: *Social Science History* 47:1 (2023), 95–119; Amaury De Vicq and Christiaan van Bochove, 'Lending a Hand: Help Banks in the Netherlands, 1848–1898', in: *European Review of Economic History* 28:2 (2024), 163–192 for cosignatory lending institutions.

about loan applicants and to secure loans. The latter involved different levels of joint liability, usually more in tight-knit rural villages and less in urban environments. Interestingly, many of these financial institutions carried the word bank in their name. Yet, maximizing profit was not the chief objective of these institutions.

This all points to the fact that the banking landscape itself was much more diverse than suggested by Schumpeter and Gerschenkron. Interestingly, this also applies to the regular banks themselves. These, and the banking systems they belonged to, could assume fundamentally different shapes (with differing effects on financial as well as economic stability).[14]

The scholarship on stock markets also revealed that stock markets became an important alternative and complementary source of funding.[15] Where such markets were large and liquid, investors could borrow and collateralize loans with securities, reducing the demand for bank lending.[16] While data for bank lending was published by banks themselves or collected by governments, data on peer-to-peer credit was much less systematically available. Evidence of successful (i.e., repaid) loans tends to disappear, often leaving historians to deduce from probate inventories and insolvency files what might have been.[17] Governments only exceptionally collected encompassing information on segments of the peer-to-peer

[14] Caroline Fohlin, 'Universal Banking in Pre-World War I Germany: Model or Myth?', in: *Explorations in Economic History* 36:4 (1999), 305–343; Caroline Fohlin, *Finance Capitalism and Germany's Rise to Industrial Power* (Cambridge, 2007); Michael D. Bordo, Angela Redish, and Hugh Rockoff, 'Why Didn't Canada have a Banking Crisis in 2008 (or in 1930, or 1907, or…)?', in: *The Economic History Review* 68:1 (2015), 218–243.

[15] Ross Levine and Sara Zervos, 'Stock Markets, Banks, and Economic Growth', in: *The American Economic Review* 88:3 (1998), 537–558; Asli Demirgüç-Kunt, Erik Feyen, and Ross Levine, 'The Evolving Importance of Banks and Securities Markets', in: *The World Bank Economic Review* 27:3 (2013), 476–490; Stefano Ugolini, 'The Coevolution of Banks and Corporate Securities Markets: The Financing of Belgium's Industrial Take-Off in the 1830s', in: *Business History* 63:6 (2021), 892–913.

[16] Joost Jonker, 'Competing in Tandem: Securities Markets and Commercial Banking Patterns in Europe During the Nineteenth Century', in: Douglas J. Forsyth and Daniel Verdier (eds.), *The Origins of National Financial Systems: Alexander Gerschenkron Reconsidered* (London, 2003), 64–86.

[17] Håkan Lindgren, 'The Modernization of Swedish Credit Markets, 1840–1905: Evidence from Probate Records', in: *The Journal of Economic History* 62:3 (2002), 810–832; Sheilagh Ogilvie, Markus Küpker, and Janine Maegraith, 'Household Debt in Early Modern Germany: Evidence from Personal Inventories', in: *The Journal of Economic History* 72:1 (2012), 134–167; Christiaan van Bochove and Heleen Kole, 'Uncovering

credit market.[18] There is enough evidence that credit played an important role in the lives of poor and rich households alike, representing a survival strategy to some and a source of investment funds for others. The work of Craig Muldrew and Laurence Fontaine showed that funding was often mobilized without the assistance of banks or stock markets. This research moved the field of non-bank credit forward in several significant ways. First, by demonstrating the ubiquity of peer-to-peer lending among ordinary people before and alongside banks; and second, by focusing on the people that facilitated the connection between the supply of finance and the demand for loans.[19]

These non-bank credit markets were large. They were also often quite formal: contracts were cast in the right legal formulas and were embedded in a legal framework that enabled parties to go to court.[20] Funds were provided by individuals and, perhaps surprisingly to a contemporary observer, a broad range of institutions. The municipal pawn shops that were funded specifically for providing small loans are perhaps the most

Private Credit Markets: Amsterdam, 1660–1809', in: *The Low Countries Journal of Social and Economic History* 11:3 (2014), 39–72.

[18] Daan Verwaaij and Christiaan van Bochove, 'Credit without Banks: the Amsterdam Water Bailiff's Ledger of 1856', in: *Financial History Review* 26:2 (2019), 171–195.

[19] Craig Muldrew, *The Economy of Obligation: The Culture of Credit and Social Relations in Early Modern England* (Basingstoke, 1998); Laurence Fontaine, *The Moral Economy: Poverty, Credit, and Trust in Early Modern Europe* (Cambridge, 2014) (translation of the 2008 original in French). Also see Jürgen Schlumbohm (ed.), *Soziale Praxis des Kredits 16.–20. Jahrhundert* (Hannover, 2007); Gabriele B. Clemens (ed.), *Schuldenlast und Schuldenwert: Kreditnetzwerke in der europäischen Geschichte (1300–1900)* (Trier, 2008); Antonio Giuffrida, Roberto Rossi, and Gaetano Sabatini, *Informal Credit in the Mediterranean Area (XVI–XIX Centuries)* (Palermo, 2016); Elise M. Dermineur (ed.), *Women and Credit in Pre-Industrial Europe* (Turnhout, 2018); Marcella Lorenzini, Cinzia Lorandini, and D'Maris Coffman (eds.), *Financing in Europe: Evolution, Coexistence and Complementarity of Lending Practices from the Middle Ages to Modern Times* (Cham, 2018); Stephan Nicolussi-Köhler (ed.), *Change and Transformation of Premodern Credit Markets: The Importance of Small-Scale Credits* (Heidelberg, 2021); Pavla Slavíčková (ed.), *A History of the Credit Market in Central Europe: The Middle Ages and Early Modern Period* (Abingdon, 2021).

[20] Ogilvie, Küpker, and Maegraith, 'Household debt'; Van Bochove and Kole, 'Uncovering Private Credit Markets'.

well-known example of the latter.[21] But there were many more institutions that for a variety of reasons, accumulated funds. Institutions with religious affiliations or beneficent missions, such as churches, convents, deaconries, guilds, and orphanages, often received donations above their operating needs. These surplus funds would find their way to the market, investing in public debt if it was deemed safe and liquid, or to private borrowers—in a similar way as institutional investors do nowadays with the pensions and funds of their clients.[22]

[21] Paul Soetaert, *De Bergen van Barmhartigheid in de Spaanse, de Oostenrijkse en de Franse Nederlanden (1618–1795)* (s.l., 1986); H.A.J. Maassen, *Tussen commercieel en sociaal krediet: De ontwikkeling van de Bank van Lening in Nederland van Lombard tot Gemeentelijke Kredietbank 1260–1940* (Hilversum, 1994); Montserrat Carbonell-Esteller, 'Montes de piedad and Savings Banks as Microfinance institutions on the Periphery of the Financial System of Mid-Nineteenth-Century Barcelona', in: *Business History* 54:3 (2012), 363–380; Guillaume Pastureau and Bertrand Blancheton, 'The Success of the Bordeaux Mont-de-Piété, 1801–1913', in: *Financial History Review* 21:3 (2014), 281–299; Mauro Carboni and Massimo Fornasari, 'The 'Untimely' Demise of a Successful Institution: The Italian Monti di pietà in the Nineteenth Century', in: *Financial History Review* 26:2 (2019), 147–170. Private pawn shops, of course, also existed. See Melanie Tebbutt, *Making Ends Meet: Pawnbroking & Working-Class Credit* (Leicester, 1983); John P. Caskey, *Fringe Banking: Check-Cashing Outlets, Pawnshops, and the Poor* (New York, 1994); Eoin Mclaughlin and Rowena Pecchenino, 'Fringe Banking and Financialization: Pawnbroking in Pre-famine and Famine Ireland', in: *The Economic History Review* 75:3 (2022), 903–931.

[22] Oscar Gelderblom and Joost Jonker, 'With a View to Hold: The Emergence of Institutional Investors on the Amsterdam Securities Market During the Seventeenth and Eighteenth Centuries', in: Jeremy Atack and Larry Neal (eds.), *The Origins and Development of Financial Markets and Institutions: From the Seventeenth Century to the Present* (Cambridge, 2009), 71–98; Harm Zwarts, 'Institutional Investors in the Countryside of the Dutch Republic: An Analysis of the Investment Portfolios of Reformed Deaconries in the Countryside of the Dutch Republic, c.1750–1800' (unpublished thesis, Utrecht University, 2015); Enno Bünz, 'Kredit bei den Heiligen: Die Dorfkirche als Geldinstitut in Spätmittelalter und Frühneuzeit', in: Kurt Andermann and Gerhard Fouquet (eds.), *Zins und Gült: Strukturen des Ländlichen Kreditwesens in Spätmittelalter und Frühneuzeit* (Epfendorf, 2016), 41–67; Hans-Jörg Gilomen, 'Klöster und Spitäler als Kreditgeber der ländlichen Gesellschaft: Hilfe oder Ausbeutung', in: Kurt Andermann and Gerhard Fouquet (eds.), *Zins und Gült: Strukturen des Ländlichen Kreditwesens in Spätmittelalter und Frühneuzeit* (Epfendorf, 2016), 69–92; Håkan Lindgren, 'Parish banking in informal credit markets: the business of private lending in early nineteenth-century Sweden', in: *Financial History Review* 24:S1 (2017), 83–102; Alistair Mutch, 'The Business of Religion: Lending and the Church of Scotland in the Eighteenth Century', in: *Journal of Scottish Historical Studies* 37:2 (2017), 136–154; Cyril Milhaud, 'Interregional Flows of Capital and Information in Spain: A Case Study of the Theresian Carmelite Order', in: *Revista de Historia Económica* 37:1 (2019), 81–110.

Non-bank credit markets relied on several forms of intermediation and several types of intermediaries. These financial intermediaries rarely identified themselves as such—because their primary function and occupation were not that of intermediaries on credit markets and their activity on credit markets was a small part of their normal line of work—which makes them harder to recognize. Some of these intermediaries, like shopkeepers and peddlers, were not primarily lenders, but their business relied on advancing credit to their clients. They essentially operated like bankers did, taking in funds in one form and lending those out in another form. The records show, for instance, that bakers obtained supplies from wholesale merchants on credit and allowed their clients to run up a tab in turn.[23] Specialized purchasers of seafarers' IOUs in eighteenth-century Amsterdam provide another example, borrowing large amounts of money on short terms from local elites and lending them out in small sums on longer terms to seafarers.[24] These intermediaries displayed many similarities with payday lenders active in the United States at the turn of the twentieth century.[25] And orphan chambers similarly were institutions that managed the assets of underage orphans, lending out funds on behalf of them and sometimes pooling funds from several orphans' accounts in the process.[26]

Shopkeepers operated on their own account, but there were also intermediaries who only matched demand and supply. This type of involvement is more difficult—but not impossible—to establish and the challenge is to find and use qualitative and quantitative evidence in such a way to unequivocally establish the intermediary's activities. Philip Hoffman, Gilles Postel-Vinay, and Jean-Laurent Rosenthal's work on France has, more than anyone else, familiarized us with one such

[23] Laurence Fontaine, *History of Pedlars in Europe* (Durham, 1996); Bart Willems, *Leven op de pof: Krediet bij de Antwerpse middenstand in de achttiende eeuw* (Amsterdam, 2009).

[24] Christiaan van Bochove and Ton van Velzen, 'Loans to Salaried Employees: The Case of the Dutch East India Company, 1602–1794', in: *European Review of Economic History* 18:1 (2014), 19–38.

[25] Michael Edward Easterly, 'Your Job Is Your Credit: Creating a Market for Loans to Salaried Employees in New York City, 1885–1920' (unpublished dissertation, Los Angeles, 2008); Michael Easterly, 'Your Job is Your Credit: Creating a Market for Loans to Salaried Employees in New York City, 1885–1920', in: *Enterprise & Society* 10:4 (2009), 651–660.

[26] J.W. Schnitzeler, 'In Loco Parentis: Holland's orphan chambers in a European context', in: *The History of the Family* 27:2 (2022), 243–267.

intermediary: the notary.[27] In Roman law countries and among those that adopted the Napoleonic code, notaries played an important role in civil contracting. The civil contracting obligation of notaries guaranteed that their contracts were recorded and carefully kept in ledgers, and notarial archives provide scholars with an endless trove of material. The work of Hoffman, Postel-Vinay, and Rosenthal used these sources to show that occasionally some notaries took deposits and provided loans on their own account, but most of them were involved in matching lenders and borrowers. Notaries could do so because they knew the potential lenders who had cash to spare as well as the potential borrowers who owned unencumbered real estate that could be posted as collateral. The French notaries exploited this information, and even worked together in this, to intermediate as many matches between lenders and borrowers as possible. Hoffman, Postel-Vinay, and Rosenthal's longitudinal analysis of the French mortgage markets showed that notaries provided this service for centuries, that they were complementary to banks for a long time once they arose, and only finally yielded to banks during the twentieth century.

This work on the French notaries has inspired many others to explore this institution and its role in the financial market.[28] In fact, Hoffman, Postel-Vinay, and Rosenthal's work has been so influential that the field now has a new paradigm, one in which notaries are assumed to have acted as intermediaries always and everywhere and in which they are the only ones to have done so. It cannot be precluded that no other intermediaries matched lenders and borrowers on non-bank credit markets, and a more nuanced assessment of notaries beyond the foundational example is in order. Various systematic studies have provided evidence of large

[27] Philip T. Hoffman, Gilles Postel-Vinay, and Jean-Laurent Rosenthal, *Priceless Markets: The Political Economy of Credit in Paris, 1660–1870* (Chicago, 2000); Philip T. Hoffman, Gilles Postel-Vinay, and Jean-Laurant Rosenthal, 'Entry, Information, and Financial Development: A Century of Competition between French Banks and Notaries', in: *Explorations in Economic History* 55 (2015), 39–57; Philip T. Hoffman, Gilles Postel-Vinay, and Jean-Laurent Rosenthal, *Dark Matter Credit: The Development of Peer-to-Peer Lending and Banking in France* (Princeton, 2019).

[28] See among others: Marcella Lorenzini, 'The Credit Market and Notaries in Verona in the Second Half of the Seventeenth Century', in: *The Journal of European Economic History* 44:1 (2015), 123–148; Oscar Gelderblom, Mark Hup, and Joost Jonker, 'Public Functions, Private Markets: Credit Registration by Aldermen and Notaries in the Low Countries, 1500–1800', in: Marcella Lorenzini, Cinzia Lorandini, and D'Maris Coffman (eds.), *Financing in Europe: Evolution, Coexistence and Complementarity of Lending Practices from the Middle Ages to Modern Times* (Cham, 2018), 161–192.

differences in the size and type of notarial activity, which must surely have affected the secondary activities notaries could build on.[29] Other work has emphasized that in other locations, public cadastral systems had been established long before notaries appeared on the scene. Notaries do not always possess exclusive information about ownership of and liens on real estate therefore, and as a consequence, all notaries did not always have an informational advantage or play an intermediary role in mortgage credit.[30] In France, the notaries' unique informational advantage dissipated once a functional public cadastral system was established. Title and liens no longer were valuable private information and the notaries' role in mortgage markets could, but only gradually, be taken over by banks.[31]

The story of bank credit is much less straightforward than the one suggested in Sect. 1. The financial system is complex enough to accommodate multiple sources of credit, of which banks are just one element. Banks are significant, but there are many circumstances in which credit—or more generally: funding—was not provided by banks, but mobilized in other ways. Credit was creative and flexible, could take many shapes, and was more malleable than banks. This credit market was also inclusive, serving not only the elites but also those who were relatively poor.[32] That non-bank credit was replaced neither fully nor swiftly as a source of funding with the creation of banks is further testimony to their success. Non-bank credit was resilient and sometimes even got a second lease on

[29] Gelderblom, Hup, and Jonker, 'Public Functions'; Claire Lemercier and Francesca Trivellato, '1751 and Thereabout: A Quantitative and Comparative Approach to Notarial Records', in: *Social Science History* 46:3 (2022), 555–583.

[30] Christiaan van Bochove, Heidi Deneweth, and Jaco Zuijderduijn, 'Real Estate and Mortgage Finance in England and the Low Countries, 1300–1800', in: *Continuity and Change* 30:1 (2015), 9–38; Gelderblom, Hup, and Jonker, 'Public Functions'. The former also show that in the English case, scattered information about ownership and liens left room for yet other types of intermediaries. Also see Julia Rudolph, 'A Broker's Advice: Credit Networks and Mortgage Risk in the Eighteenth-Century Empire', in: Michael Lobban and Ian Williams (eds.), *Networks and Connections in Legal History* (Cambridge, 2020), 185–209.

[31] Hoffman, Postel-Vinay, and Rosenthal, *Priceless Markets*; Hoffman, Postel-Vinay, and Rosenthal, 'Entry, Information, and Financial Development'; Hoffman, Postel-Vinay, and Rosenthal, *Dark Matter Credit*.

[32] Following Heidi Deneweth, Oscar Gelderblom, and Joost Jonker, 'Microfinance and the Decline of Poverty: Evidence from the Nineteenth-Century Netherlands', in: *Journal of Economic Development* 39:1 (2014), 79–110 we recognize that lack of privacy and expectation of reciprocity may have been a concern to some.

life through the new use of technologies, such as newspaper advertisements, to bring demand and supply together.[33] During the nineteenth and twentieth centuries, moreover, economic development also created new opportunities for non-bank credit such as salary loans and different forms of consumer credit.[34]

3 Credit in Other Parts of the World

There is a substantial literature on banks beyond Europe and the United States.[35] The revisionist literature questioning the supposed straightforward triumph of banks is also present there. Case studies show that the shape of the banking system depended on local circumstances. Whereas in nineteenth-century China the appearance of banks depended on intermediation needs, banks in nineteenth- and twentieth-century Brazil and

[33] Christiaan van Bochove and Ewout Hasken, 'The Modernization of Credit Markets: How Private Lenders Disappeared from the Dutch Mortgage Market, 1860–2000' (working paper, 2024). Diane Clements, 'The "Consequence of an Advertisement": Intermediation in the Eighteenth-Century Credit Market', in: *Historical Research* 97:277 (2024), 369–384 discusses how intermediaries used newspapers to bring together demand and supply and generate follow-up business.

[34] Lendol Calder, *Financing the American Dream: A Cultural History of Consumer Credit* (Princeton, 1999); Easterly, 'Your Job Is Your Credit' (dissertation); Easterly, 'Your Job is Your Credit' (article); Sean O'Connell, *Credit and Community: Working-Class Debt in the UK Since 1880* (Oxford, 2009).

[35] What follows is an abbreviated list of some of the major works on banking in the regions; there are far more works on individual banks, banking, and specific case studies in Latin America, Asia, and Africa. Leonor Ludlow and Carlos Marichal (eds.), *Banca y Poder en Mexico (1800–1925)* (México, 1986); Juichi Soyeda, *A History of Banking in Japan* (London, 1994); Andrés M. Regalsky, 'Banca y capitalismo en la Argentina, 1850–1930: Un ensayo crítico', in: *Ciclos* 9:18 (1999), 33–54; Marcelo Rougier (ed.), *La Banca de desarrollo en América Latina: Luces y sombras en la industrialización de la región* (Mexico, 2000); Gareth Austin and Chibuike Ugochukwu Uche, 'Collusion and Competition in Colonial Economies: Banking in British West Africa, 1916–1960', in: *Business History Review* 81:1 (2007), 1–26; Hubert Bonin, Nuno Valério, and Kazuhiko Yago (eds.), *Asian Imperial Banking History* (London, 2015); Carlos Marichal, *El Nacimiento de la Banca en América Latina: Finanzas y politica en el siglo XIX* (México, 2021); Samuel Mutarindwa, Dorothea Schäfer, and Andreas Stephan, 'Differences in African Banking Systems: Causes and Consequences', in: *Journal of Institutional Economics* 17:4 (2021), 561–581.

Mexico were shaped by the costs of information and contract enforcement.[36] In terms of economic growth, the role of banks is debatable. The formation of banks in Brazil and Mexico responded largely to the export and trade market, and so lacked a solid domestic base. In Japan, during the first half of the twentieth century, firms relied much more on capital markets than on banks to obtain funding.[37] While banks were definitely good at handling the credit and payments associated with international trade, they often provided few services to small businesses and ordinary households as this was not their primary goal.[38]

Development economists, working on more recent periods, observe contemporary credit markets and provide two major insights. On the one hand, they point out that many people in these markets have no access at all to credit provided by banks. Muhammad Yunus observed firsthand in Bangladesh that establishing the creditworthiness of loan applicants and enforcing loan payments was difficult and costly for banks. Since information about loan applicants was easier to access locally and among the local communities in which they lived, Yunus devised a mechanism by which to assess their creditworthiness in a credit market that responded to their needs. Yunus developed a group-lending mechanism that broadened access to credit to a host of borrowers that were otherwise invisible to the banking system. Yunus established Grameen Bank, was dubbed "Banker to the Poor," and won the Nobel Peace Prize.[39] His example was followed by many other initiatives and the microcredit/microfinance

[36] Stephen Haber, 'Industrial Concentration and the Capital Markets: A Comparative Study of Brazil, Mexico and the United States, 1830–1930', in: *The Journal of Economic History* 51:3 (1991), 559–580; Noel Maurer and Stephen Haber, 'Related Lending and Economic Performance: Evidence from Mexico', in: *The Journal of Economic History* 67:3 (2007), 551–581; Craig Wilson and Fan Yang, 'Shanxi Piaohao and Shanghai Qianzhuang: A Comparison of the Two Main Banking Systems of Nineteenth-Century China', in: *Business History* 58:3 (2016), 433–452.

[37] Stephen Haber (ed.), *How Latin America Fell Behind: Essays on the Economic Histories of Brazil and Mexico, 1800–1914* (Stanford, 1997); Yoshiro Miwa and J. Mark Ramseyer, 'Banks and Economic Growth: Implications from Japanese History', in: *The Journal of Law and Economics* 45:1 (2002), 127–164.

[38] Leigh Gardner, 'Financial History of Sub-Saharan Africa', in: *Oxford Research Encyclopedia of Economics and Finance* (2020).

[39] Muhammad Yunus, *Banker to the Poor: Micro-Lending and the Battle Against World Poverty* (New York, 1997).

sector is now active worldwide, although not without some concerns that banking to the poor opens the poor up to new forms of financial abuse.[40]

Hernando de Soto noticed another set of obstacles that complicated the widespread development of mortgage banking in developing economies. If property owners could not document their property rights—they could not collateralize their property.[41] Collins et al. observed how low and irregular wages coupled with small loan sizes made transaction costs prohibitively high for banks; not to mention that the costs incurred by borrowers for traveling to the nearest bank could be exorbitant.[42] Although studies like these emphasize the importance of non-bank credit suppliers, which are discussed in more detail below, it is also clear that new technologies such as mobile phones and the internet are increasingly successful in lowering the threshold to accessing financial institutions.[43]

Contemporary observers of credit markets also make clear that financial landscapes or ecosystems consist of much more than banks. Here Bouman and Hospes develop the term of "financial curb markets"—which are similar to non-bank credit markets.[44] Bouman emphasized the complementarity of banks and non-banks and focused on their relative

[40] Beatriz Armendáriz and Marc Labie (eds.), *The Handbook of Microfinance* (New Jersey, 2011); Jean-Pierre Gueyie, Ronny Manos, and Jacob Yaron (eds.), *Microfinance in Developing Countries: Issues, Policies and Performance Evaluation* (Basingstoke, 2013); Roy Mersland and R. Øystein Strøm (eds.), *Microfinance Institutions: Financial and Social Performance* (Basingstoke, 2014). On the more critical perspective, see: Joakim Sandberg, 'Mega-interest on Microcredit: Are Lenders Exploiting the Poor?', in: *Journal of Applied Philosophy* 29:3 (2012), 169–185; Marek Hudon and Joakim Sandberg, 'The Ethical Crisis in Microfinance: Issues, Findings, and Implications', in: *Business Ethics Quarterly* 23:4 (2013), 561–589; Abhijit Banerjee et al., 'The Miracle of Microfinance? Evidence from a Randomized Evaluation', in: *American Economic Journal: Applied Economics* 7:1 (2015), 22–53.

[41] Hernando De Soto, *The Mystery of Capital: Why Capitalism Triumphs in the West and Fails Everywhere Else* (New York, 2000).

[42] Daryl Collins et al., *Portfolios of the Poor: How the World's Poor Live on $2 a Day* (Princeton, 2009).

[43] Asli Demirgüç-Kunt et al., *The Global Findex Database 2017: Measuring Financial Inclusion and the Fintech Revolution* (Washington D.C., 2018).

[44] F.J.A. Bouman and Otto Hospes, 'Financial Landscapes Reconstructed', in: F.J.A. Bouman and Otto Hospes (eds.), *Financial Landscapes Reconstructed: The Fine Art of Mapping Development* (Boulder, 1994), 3–16. Prabhu Ghate, *Informal Finance: Some Findings From Asia* (Oxford, 1992), 7–10 speaks of a "financial continuum".

strengths: funding large, long-term, and distant projects for banks and funding small, short-term, and local projects for non-banks.[45] This view on credit markets rehabilitated the village moneylender, who was often vilified and looked askance at by authorities that assumed their lending practices were abusive.[46] Research, such as that by Waters on modern Mongolia, demonstrated that moneylenders are an important part of the financial system precisely because they operate where banks do not and cannot.[47] This resonates with work on the Ottoman Empire during the nineteenth and early twentieth centuries where moneylenders, rather than being the usurious thieves of novels, were one of the sources of available credit.[48] The nature of money lending makes it hard to comprehensively identify and analyze this institution because they often operated in the shadows, provided little recorded signs of their existence, combined their credit operations with other types of work, and therefore left few records.[49]

[45] Frits J.A. Bouman, 'Informal Rural Finance: An Aladdin's Lamp of Information', in: *Sociologia Ruralis* 30:2 (1990), 155–173. Also see Ghate, *Informal Finance*, 16–18, 125–135.

[46] Gareth Austin and Kaoru Sugihara, 'Local Suppliers of Credit in the Third World, 1750–1960: Introduction', in: Gareth Austin and Kaoru Sugihara (eds.), *Local Suppliers of Credit in the Third World, 1750–1960* (Basingstoke, 1993), 1–25; H. William Warner, 'The Kabuliwalas: Afghan Moneylending and the Credit Cosmopolis of British India, c. 1880–1947', in: *The Indian Economic and Social History Review* 57:2 (2020), 171–198.

[47] Hedwig Amelia Waters, 'The Financialization of Help: Moneylenders as Economic Translators in the Debt-Based Economy', in: *Central Asian Survey* 37:3 (2018), 403–418.

[48] Christopher Clay, 'The Origins of Modern Banking in the Levant: The Branch Network of the Imperial Ottoman Bank, 1890–1914', in: *International Journal of Middle East Studies* 26:4 (1994), 589–614; Mehtap Özdeğer and Emine Zeytinli, 'Ottoman Credit System and Usurers in Agriculture in the Nineteenth Century: Practices of Usury Contracts (Selem)', in: *Journal of Balkan and Near Eastern Studies* 21:5 (2019), 594–612.

[49] A.G. Chandavarkar, 'Money and Credit (1858–1947)', in: Dharma Kumar (ed.), *The Cambridge Economic History of India* 2 (Cambridge, 1983), 762–803 (who, on page 796 of his chapter on money and credit in India during the period 1858–1947, did still characterize the non-bank credit market as 'a residual sector' though); Ghate, *Informal Finance*, 3.

There is a significant literature produced by (economic) historians working on more distant periods that attests to the long history of non-bank credit. Gareth Austin and Kaoru Sugihara's 1993 trailblazing edited volume *Local Suppliers of Credit in the Third World, 1750–1960* questioned the superiority of banks and inspired many scholars studying credit markets in Africa, Asia, and South America to think outside the banking box. Their work showed that local arrangements could be more advantageous than those provided by (European) banks.[50] These studies revealed active non-bank credit markets. The nineteenth-century Japanese silk industry, Australasian farmers before World War II, Argentine industrialists, or Brazilian miners—all acquired credit from agents who knew them and knew their markets more intimately than banks could.[51]

Non-standard banks, non-bank intermediaries, and institutional investors also existed throughout the world. This included colonial institutions like convents that lent out the dowries of incoming nuns and other

50 Gareth Austin and Kaoru Sugihara (eds.), *Local Suppliers of Credit in the Third World, 1750–1960* (Basingstoke, 1993). For case studies, see Amos Nadan, 'The Competitive Advantage of Moneylenders over Banks in Rural Palestine', in: *Journal of the Economic and Social History of the Orient* 48:1 (2005), 1–39 on Palestine and Susan Wolcott, 'An Examination of the Supply of Financial Credit to Entrepreneurs in Colonial India', in: David S. Landes, Joel Mokyr, and William J. Baumol (eds.), *The Invention of Enterprise: Entrepreneurship: From Ancient Mesopotamia to Modern Times* (Princeton, 2010), 443–468 on India.

51 Simon Ville and Grant Fleming, 'Financial Intermediaries and the Design of Loan Contracts within the Australasian Pastoral Sector before the Second World War', in: *Financial History Review* 7:2 (2000), 201–218; Yoshiro Miwa and J. Mark Ramseyer, 'Japanese industrial finance at the close of the nineteenth century: Trade credit and financial intermediation', in: *Explorations in Economic History* 43 (2006), 94–118; Gail D. Triner, 'Property Rights, Family, and Business Partnership in Nineteenth- and Twentieth-Century Brazil: The Case of the St. John d'el Rey Mining Company, 1834–1960', in: *Enterprise & Society* 8:1 (2007), 35–67; Yovanna Pineda, 'Financing Manufacturing Innovation in Argentina, 1890–1930', in: *Business History Review* 83:3 (2009), 539–562.

accumulated funds,[52] confraternities that lent out endowments,[53] municipal pawn shops,[54] and rural credit cooperatives.[55] Many other parts of the world had institutions that were indigenous. Some were based on occupational affiliation, such as in the Ottoman Empire where guilds and Ahi unions used their funds to lend to their craftsmen members and where the so-called Homeland Coffers did the same for their rural members.[56] Some originated in religious institutions, such as the Buddhist convents in Japan and the *waqfs* in the Muslim world, both of which lent out the funds that they had accumulated in similar ways to the Catholic convents and churches.[57] Still others were rooted in providing a social

[52] Kathryn Burns, 'Nuns, Kurakas, and Credit: The Spiritual Economy of Seventeenth-Century', in: *Colonial Latin American Review* 6:2 (1997), 185–203; Kathryn Burns, *Colonial Habits: Convents and the Spiritual Economy of Cuzco, Peru* (Durham, 1999); Regina Grafe, 'An Empire of Debts? Spain and Its Colonial Realm', in: Nicolas Barreyre and Nicolas Delalande (eds.), *A World of Public Debts: A Political History* (Cham, 2020), 5–35.

[53] Juan O. Mesquida, 'Pious Funds across the Pacific (1668–1823): Charitable Bequests or Credit Source?', in: *The Americas* 75:4 (2018), 661–697; Juan O. Mesquida, 'Contested Philanthropy in Spanish Manila: The Santa Casa de la Misericordia (1594–1869)', in: Isabel dos Guimarães Sá and Lisbeth Rodrigues (eds.), *The Confraternities of Misericórdia and the Portuguese Diasporas in the Early Modern Period* (Leiden, 2023), 108–133.

[54] Marie Eileen Francois, *A Culture of Everyday Credit: Housekeeping, Pawnbroking, and Governance in Mexico City, 1750–1920* (Lincoln, 2006).

[55] Maanik Nath, 'Do Institutional Transplants Succeed? Regulating Raiffeisen Cooperatives in South India, 1930–1960', in: *Business History Review* 95:1 (2021), 59–85.

[56] Sertaç Dokuzlu, 'The Agricultural Credit System in the Ottoman Empire between 1863 and 1888', in: *Rural History* 28:2 (2017), 177–188; Konstantinos Giakoumis, 'The Voskopoja Guild of Tailors' Credit Lending Operations and Risk Management (1716–27)', in: *Turkish Historical Review* 9:3 (2018), 242–277.

[57] Şevket Pamuk, *The Ottoman Empire and European Capitalism, 1820–1913: Trade, Investment and Production* (Cambridge, 1987); Murat Çizakça, 'Cash waqfs of Bursa, 1555–1823', in: *Journal of the Economic and Social History of the Orient* 38:3 (1995), 313–354; Gürer Karagedikli and Ali Coşkun Tunçer, 'Microcredit in the Ottoman Empire: A Review of Cash Waqfs in Transition to Modern Banking', in: Marcella Lorenzini, Cinzia Lorandini, and D'Maris Coffman (eds.), *Financing in Europe: Evolution, Coexistence and Complementarity of Lending Practices from the Middle Ages to Modern Times* (Cham, 2018), 237–266; Timur Kuran and Jared Rubin, 'The Financial Power of the Powerless: Socio-Economic Status and Interest Rates under Weak Rule of Law', in: *The Economic Journal* 128:609 (2018), 758–796; Matthew Mitchell, 'Borrowing from the Buddha: Buddhist Temples as Financial Centers in Premodern East Asia', in: *Education About Asia* 24:2 (2019), 51–54.

function, such as the orphan chambers that lent out orphans' inheritances.[58] The centuries-old Japanese *mujin-ko* and *tanomoshi-ko* rotating credit and savings associations were more explicitly founded with an eye on mobilizing credit; and some of them eventually developed into banks.[59]

There are numerous similarities between intermediaries across the world too. Shopkeepers operated as lenders in credit markets stretching from colonial Dar es Salaam to the pampas of Argentina. They have always purchased on credit from wholesalers and sold on credit to their own customers.[60] The practice was not restricted to shopkeepers, however, and has also been documented for landowners in eighteenth-century Santafé de Bogotá.[61]

There is an increasing amount of research as well that shows that as the notarial institution was exported throughout the world, notaries became intermediaries in credit markets. As in the French case, notaries performed a significant civil and legal role in Latin America. The information that these notaries gathered in Argentina, Brazil, Mexico, and Peru allowed them, like their peers in France, to bring together demand for loans and supply of credit. This sort of credit, facilitated by notarial intermediation, was a significant form of non-bank credit in the colonial and independent economies of Latin America.[62] In other parts of the world, other

[58] Munther Al-Sabbagh, 'Before Banks: Credit, Society, and Law in Sixteenth-Century Palestine and Syria' (unpublished dissertation, Santa Barbara, 2018), 269–317. Al-Sabbagh also studies other credit arrangements used before the rise of banks, including the *waqf*, but does so with a distinctly legal perspective.

[59] Robert Dekle and Koichi Hamada, 'On the Development of Rotating Credit Associations in Japan', in: *Economic Development and Cultural Change* 49:1 (2000), 77–90.

[60] Andrea Lluch, 'The Art of Lending in the Pampas: Commercial Credit and Financial Intermediation in Argentina, 1900–1930', in: Bernardo Bátiz-Lazo and Leonidas Efthymiou (eds.), *The Book of Payments: Historical and Contemporary Views on the Cashless Society* (London, 2016), 55–64; Benjamin Brühwiler, 'Interweaving threads of credit and debt: Trading (through) textiles in colonial Dar es Salaam', in: *Business History* 60:4 (2018), 474–491.

[61] Oscar M. Granados and James V. Torres, 'Credit Networks and Business Dynamics in a Viceregal Capital: Santafé de Bogotá in the Age of Charles III', in: *Financial History Review* 30:3 (2023), 330–354. This article uses an exceptional source (i.e., an encompassing overview of notarized loans), something we hardly ever possess.

[62] Joseph James Ryan Jr., 'Credit Where Credit Is Due: Lending and Borrowing in Rio de Janeiro, 1802–1900' (unpublished dissertation, Los Angeles, 2007); Juliette Levy, *The*

groups—such as local notables in Ottoman Haifa during the late nineteenth and early twentieth centuries—also took up such an intermediary function.[63]

4 Taking Stock of Credit Markets

The literature on credit markets across the world is broad and deep, and much of the focus has been on banks. Banks are easy to identify and compare across time and place. Banks are relatively similar in function and appearance (including their name), they attract the attention of governments that charter and regulate them, and have their corporate histories written by historians. And they do deserve much of the attention they get.

However, banks are not the *sine qua non* of economic development. The literature's initial focus on an ideal-type bank has also been replaced by a more encompassing approach. As a consequence, the literature no longer primarily emphasizes economic growth and the productive loan purposes of large merchants and manufacturers. There now exists a more inclusive understanding of credit markets that addresses ordinary people, borrowing for consumption purposes, and subsistence borrowing. This broader perspective introduced a keener understanding of gender,[64]

Making of a Market: Credit, Henequen, and Notaries in Yucatán, 1850–1900 (University Park, 2012); Martín Wasserman, *Las obligaciones fundamentales: Crédito y consolidación económica durante el surgimiento de Buenos Aires* (Buenos Aires, 2018); Clemente Gentil Penna, 'Economias urbanas: Capital, créditos e escravidão na cidade do Rio de Janeiro, c.1820–1860' (unpublished dissertation, Rio de Janeiro, 2019); Luis Felipe Zegarra, 'Information Asymmetries and Agricultural Credit Evidence from the Pre-banking Era in Lima, 1825–1865', in: *Agricultural Finance Review* 79:2 (2019), 217–233.

[63] Stefania Ecchia, 'Informal Rural Credit Markets and Interlinked Transactions in the District of late Ottoman Haifa, 1890–1915', in: *Financial History Review* 21:1 (2014), 5–24. The *kātib* in the Western Indian Ocean seems to have functioned more exclusively as a scribe. See Fahad Ahmad Bishara, *A Sea of Debt: Law and Economic Life in the Western Indian Ocean, 1780–1950* (Cambridge, 2017), 58–80.

[64] Beverly Lemire, Ruth Pearson, and Gail Campbell (eds.), *Women and Credit: Researching the Past, Refiguring the Future* (Oxford, 2002); Dermineur, *Women and Credit*; Ishita Chakavarty, 'Owners, Creditors and Traders: Women in Late Colonial Calcutta', in: *The Indian Economic and Social History Review* 56:4 (2019), 1–30.

ethnicity,[65] age, and marital status[66] in the mechanics of credit markets. Instead of focusing on the institution and its label, the literature started to focus on function. This functional approach toward financial markets was exemplified by the early work of Merton and Bodie in 1995,[67] and in business history, where the focus on the Chandlerian corporation was enhanced by a realization that businesses were flexible and their structure depended on the historical context.[68]

The universal challenge of mobilizing credit was solved through an array of channels, some even very sophisticated ones, that are fairly similar in their essence across the globe. Many alternatives to banks existed before banks and coexisted with banks, and these other forms of credit could be innovative, substantial, resilient, and—depending on the historical context—superior to or an alternative to banks. In some instances the two—bank and non-bank—were interdependent, for instance when a non-bank loan was used to maintain or gain access to bank credit. Non-bank credit is part of financial history, which is particularly relevant as contemporary assessments of banks start to question their relevance. The 2007–2008 banking crisis and subsequent economic recession provoked a sea change in the reputation and position of banks and bankers. The

[65] Lila Ammons, 'The Evolution of Black-Owned banks in the United States Between the 1880s and 1990', in: *Journal of Black Studies* 26:4 (1996), 467–489; Mehrsa Baradaran, *How the Other Half Banks: Exclusion, Exploitation, and the Threat to Democracy* (Cambridge [MA], 2015); Mehrsa Baradaran, *The Color of Money: Black Banks and the Racial Wealth Gap* (Cambridge [MA], 2017); Robert E. Wright, *Financial Exclusion: How Competition Can Fix a Broken System* (Great Barrington, 2019).

[66] Van Bochove and Kole, 'Uncovering Private Credit Markets'; Christiaan van Bochove and Jaco Zuijderduijn, 'Years of Plenty, Years of Want? An Introduction to Finance and the Family Life Cycle', in: *The History of the Family. An international Quarterly* 27:2 (2022), 201–220.

[67] Robert C. Merton and Zvi Bodie, 'A Conceptual Framework for Analyzing the Financial Environment', in: Dwight B. Crane et al. (eds.), *The Global Financial System: A Functional Perspective* (Boston, 1995), 3–31.

[68] Naomi R. Lamoreaux, Daniel M.G. Raff, and Peter Temin, 'Beyond Markets and Hierarchies: Toward a New Synthesis of American Business History', in: *The American Historical Review* 108:2 (2003), 404–433.

worth of banks[69] and bankers[70] came under increased scrutiny, and in developed economies, banks increasingly withdrew from the lower end of the socio-economic spectrum, leaving ordinary customers to the fringe banking sector.[71] Fintechs, which facilitate peer-to-peer credit, and venture capital also started to eat into the market share of banks.[72]

The idea that credit markets only flourish if and when banks are present is outdated, as is the idea that credit markets develop unidirectionally into banks. The existence and continued importance of non-bank credit not

[69] Carmen M. Reinhart and Kenneth S. Rogoff, *This Time is Different: Eight Centuries of Financial Folly* (Princeton, 2009); William Quinn and John D. Turner, *Boom and Bust: A Global History of Financial Bubbles* (Cambridge, 2020); Robert Z. Aliber, Charles P. Kindleberger, and Robert N. McCauley, *Manias, Panics, and Crashes: A History of Financial Crises* (Cham, 2023).

[70] Joris Luyendijk, *Swimming with Sharks: My Journey into the World of the Bankers* (London, 2015).

[71] Caskey, *Fringe Banking*; Baradaran, *How the Other Half Banks*; Lisa Servon, *The Unbanking of America: How the New Middle Class Survives* (Boston, 2017); Wright, *Financial Exclusion*.

[72] Hubert de Vauplane, 'Les nouveaux acteurs de la finance', in: *Revue d'économie financière* 118 (2015), 27–36; Joern H. Block et al., 'New Players in Entrepreneurial Finance and Why They are There', in: *Small Business Economics* 50:2 (2018), 239–250; Raymond Atje, Ira Setiati, and Ilma Fadhil, 'Disruptive Technology in Indonesia's Banking Sector', in: *CSIS Working Paper Series* (2020); Ryan C. Berg, Juliana Rubio, and Nathaniel Laske, 'Catalysts of Change: How Entrepreneurs Are Transforming Latin America' (2024) (https://www.csis.org/analysis/catalysts-change-how-entrepreneurs-are-transforming-latin-america, consulted on May 31, 2024).

only made the rise of banks slow and partial[73] but economic development, so closely linked to banks, also facilitated the rise of new forms of non-bank credit. Banks evolved in a more diverse financial landscape and only prevailed when and where the historical context allowed them to add more value than other arrangements. In order to come to terms with credit markets where non-bank credit preexists and coexists with banks, we need to think differently about these credit markets and the interactions in them. We need more explicit and systematic vantage points to enable scholars from different disciplines and with different research interests to speak to each other. The following Section tries to articulate a path toward this.

5 Beyond Binaries

A substantial part of the literature on credit markets is dominated by a binary that separates credit markets into formal and informal categories. In its simplest form this binary defines formal loans as those provided by modern and regulated financial institutions—banks—and informal loans as provided through a range of options stretching from social networks to loan sharks. Often the binary also defines formal loans as those that are recorded in writing and enforced externally through courts, where

[73] Austin and Sugihara, 'Local Suppliers of Credit'; Gareth Austin, 'Indigenous Credit Institutions in West Africa, c.1750–c.1960', in: Gareth Austin and Kaoru Sugihara (eds.), *Local Suppliers of Credit in the Third World, 1750–1960* (Basingstoke, 1993), 93–159; Margot C. Finn, *The Character of Credit: Personal Debt in English Culture, 1740–1914* (Cambridge, 2003); Collins et al., *Portfolios of the Poor*; R. Daniel Wadhwani, 'Small-Scale Credit Institutions: Historical Perspectives on Diversity in Financial Intermediation', in: Youssef Cassis, Catherine Schenk, and Richard Grossman (eds.), *The Oxford Handbook of Banking and Financial History* (Oxford, 2016); D'Maris Coffman, Cinzia Lorandini, and Marcella Lorenzini, 'Introduction', in: Marcella Lorenzini, Cinzia Lorandini, and D'Maris Coffman (eds.), *Financing in Europe: Evolution, Coexistence and Complementarity of Lending Practices from the Middle Ages to Modern Times* (Cham, 2018), 1–18; Martin Fotta, *From Itinerant Trade to Moneylending in the Era of Financial Inclusion: Households, Debts and Masculinity among Calon Gypsies of Northeast Brazil* (Cham, 2018); Oscar Gelderblom et al., 'Exploring Modern Bank Penetration: Evidence from Early Twentieth-Century Netherlands', in: *The Economic History Review* 76:3 (2023), 892–916; Van Bochove and Hasken, 'The Modernization of Credit Markets'.

the informal loans are recorded verbally and enforced internally through social sanctions.[74]

The binary starts to break down on closer analysis. Verbal contracts were a well-established part of formal (credit) markets, but in medieval and early modern Europe and in nineteenth-century Africa, verbal contracts could be formalized by the presence of witnesses, and even without witnesses, contracting parties could establish their existence through sacred oaths.[75] Much of the non-bank credit also involved written contracts that were highly formal, embedded in the legal system, and enforceable in court. These contracts were recorded by civil servants (aldermen, whose contracts were also open to public consultation) or legal scriveners (notaries) and they were often also recorded between the two contracting parties. The involvement of official note-takers made the terms of contracts harder to contest because contracts were authentic, but this did not stop many loans from being recorded by the contracting parties themselves.[76]

[74] Chandavarkar, 'Money and Credit'; Austin and Sugihara, 'Local Suppliers of Credit'; Dale W. Adams, 'Using Contracts to Analyze Informal Finance', in: F.J.A. Bouman and Otto Hospes (eds.), *Financial Landscapes Reconstructed: The Fine Art of Mapping Development* (Boulder, 1994), 179–192; Jean-Laurent Rosenthal and R. Bin Wong, *Before and Beyond Divergence: The Politics of Economic Change in China and Europe* (Cambridge [MA], 2011); Coffman, Lorandini, and Lorenzini, 'Introduction'; D'Maris Coffman, 'Towards the Institutionalisation of Credit', in: Marcella Lorenzini, Cinzia Lorandini, and D'Maris Coffman (eds.), *Financing in Europe: Evolution, Coexistence and Complementarity of Lending Practices from the Middle Ages to Modern Times* (Cham, 2018), 345–351; Nicolussi-Köhler, 'Introduction'.

[75] Ghislaine Lydon, *On Trans-Saharan Trails: Islamic Law, Trade Networks and Cross-Cultural Exchange in Nineteenth-Century Western Africa* (Cambridge, 2009); Oscar Gelderblom, *Cities of Commerce: The Institutional Foundations of International Trade in the Low Countries, 1250–1650* (Princeton, 2013); Craig Muldrew, 'The Social Acceptance of Paper Credit as Currency in Eighteenth-Century England: A Case Study of Glastonbury c. 1720–1742', in: Marcella Lorenzini, Cinzia Lorandini, and D'Maris Coffman (eds.), *Financing in Europe: Evolution, Coexistence and Complementarity of Lending Practices from the Middle Ages to Modern Times* (Cham, 2018), 133–159; Hannah Robb, 'Contract and Trust in Fifteenth-Century Church Courts', in: Stephan Nicolussi-Köhler (ed.), *Change and Transformation of Premodern Credit Markets: The Importance of Small-Scale Credits* (Heidelberg, 2021), 275–292.

[76] Francois, *A Culture of Everyday Credit*; Juliette Levy, *The Making of a Market: Credit, Henequen, and Notaries in Yucatán, 1850–1900* (University Park, 2012); Van Bochove and Kole, 'Uncovering Private Credit Markets'; Wasserman, *Las obligaciones fundamentales*; Penna, 'Economias urbanas'; Lemercier and Trivellato, '1751 and Thereabout'.

The binary is further challenged by the fact that lenders and borrowers did not find their counterparties, record loans, or enforce their repayment in only one way. They could change recording practices and terms of the loans over the lifetime of a loan as the contracting parties saw fit. Borrowers could more strongly secure loans, verbal contracts could be recorded in writing, and loans recorded in writing by the contracting parties could be notarized. A well-known example is that of shop credit, where advances were recorded verbally or in ledgers and recorded in contracts only once they surpassed a certain threshold.[77] Lenders could also insist on writing things up or having their contracts converted into ones written by official note-takers when encountering or anticipating problems with the borrower.[78] The cause could also be external, such as when a regime change made contracting parties choose to record their contracts with the new government and under new laws.[79] All of this suggests that credit markets were flexible and responsive to specific needs and that the formal-informal binary is imprecise and conflates how loans were realized, recorded, and enforced. There is too much that undermines this simple dichotomy to continue using these terms and it confuses more than it helps understand or compare vastly different credit markets.[80]

We should, however, not throw the baby out with the bathwater. The work of Greif, focusing on the fundamental problem of exchange, emphasized that for lenders to be willing to enter credit markets there had to exist ways for borrowers to credibly secure and commit to repaying their loans.[81] Hoffman, Postel-Vinay, and Rosenthal emphasized that lenders and borrowers had to solve information asymmetries to find each other for any contracting to take place to begin with.[82] Their work generates the

[77] Willems, *Leven op de pof*; Lluch, 'The Art of Lending'.

[78] Van Bochove and Kole, 'Uncovering Private Credit Markets'; Maanik Nath, 'Credit Risk in Colonial India', in: *The Economic History Review* 75:2 (2022), 396–420, there 416.

[79] Bishara, *A Sea of Debt*, 125–149, 239–242.

[80] A point also made by Bouman and Hospes, 'Financial Landscapes Reconstructed', 6.

[81] Avner Greif, 'The Fundamental Problem of Exchange: A Research Agenda in Historical Institutional Analysis', in: *European Review of Economic History* 4:3 (2000), 251–284.

[82] Hoffman, Postel-Vinay, and Rosenthal, *Dark Matter Credit*, 229–235 outlines their research agenda and questions to assess (intermediation in) non-bank credit markets.

following interrelated questions that should inform any inquiry into and comparison of credit markets: How do the demand for and supply of loanable funds meet? Whose funds change hands exactly? In what form are the loans recorded? And what mechanisms secure and enforce their repayment? All of these questions impact transaction costs which determine whether a loan will materialize or not.[83] It is therefore worth exploring each question in more detail.

Let us start with how demand and supply meet and whose funds change hands. Instead of placing individual actors center stage, we argue that the focus should be on the mechanisms through which a counterparty is found. Over three decades ago, abstracting from fieldwork observations on non-bank credit markets in Asia, Ghate provided a classification of credit markets in this more functional way.[84] In his framework, credit is provided by individual and institutional entities on an intermittent or regular basis. The intermittent lenders are lending their own surplus funds to those in their network of family, friends, neighbors, coworkers, coreligionists, and customers. Regular lenders engage more frequently in this kind of peer-to-peer lending, be it in the form of "tied" credit (which is inextricably linked to other transactions, such as those by merchants or shopkeepers) or "untied" credit (which is provided by specialist moneylenders).

Ghate added two further aspects that are important to our purpose. First, the distinction between lending one's own money (direct lending) and lending other people's money (on-lending). The latter is quite common in trade credit, where wholesalers sell supplies on credit to shopkeepers who simultaneously provide shop credit to their consumer clients. This is the very essence of banks as well: borrowing funds from depositors and investors and on-lending these funds to businesses and households on different terms. Second, the brief observation that intermediaries may link lenders and borrowers through brokered loans.[85] Although purists would rightly argue that on-lending actually consists of two separate direct

While we fully endorse them, we want to address the whole ecosystem of non-bank credit, including direct lending and other forms of intermediation besides match-making.

[83] Douglass C. North, *Institutions, Institutional Change and Economic Performance* (Cambridge, 1990).

[84] Ghate, *Informal Finance*, 23–42.

[85] Ghate, *Informal Finance*, 26 n.2.

lending transactions, we believe that the on-lending format is helpful to recognize bank-like actors active in the non-bank credit market.

Distinguishing transactions based on how they are completed is key: are the loans made possible through networks, with the help of brokers, or via on-lenders? Instead of using the generic term of *intermediaries* to denote the latter two actors, we prefer calling them *match-makers* or *market-makers*. Match-makers are intermediaries who match lenders and borrowers and do not trade on their own account. They are best exemplified in Hoffman, Postel-Vinay, and Rosenthal's work that pointed to the clustering of information in the hands of notaries who used it to benefit their clients. Market-makers structure and organize credit transactions like banks, accepting deposits or borrowing on their own account and using these funds to provide loans at their own risk.[86] Match-makers and market-makers broaden access to credit by helping people borrow and lend beyond the confines of their respective networks.

Let us now look at the way in which loans are recorded and the social and/or financial mechanisms through which they are secured and enforced.[87] We have already discussed that loans could be recorded verbally and in writing. Although we need to be cautious, there is sufficient evidence that many people relied on social means instead of the legal system to secure and enforce loans. The existence of social means of securing and enforcing loans, including loss of reputation and individual or collective sanctions, meant that many borrowers honored loan agreements regardless of whether the legal system was effective or not.[88] Societies could rely on existing groups for this, such as the castes in

[86] The term market–maker usually refers to stock exchanges, where these intermediaries buy and sell securities on their own account and at their own risk, but do not typically hold (a net position in) these securities for long periods of time.

[87] The case of notarized credit, discussed in more detail in Sects. 2 and 3, also shows how closely these issues could be related to those of how demand and supply of funds meet and whose funds change hands. The French notaries, after all, not only linked lenders and borrowers as match-makers but also recorded the subsequent contracts in writing and made sure these contracts were secure and enforceable.

[88] Avner Greif, 'Reputation and Coalitions in Medieval Trade: The Evidence on the Maghribi Traders', in: *The Journal of Economic History* 49:4 (1989), 857–882; Avner Greif, 'Contract Enforceability and Economic Institutions in Early Trade: The Maghribi Traders' Coalition', in: *The American Economic Review* 83:3 (1993), 525–548; Rosenthal and Bin Wong, *Before and Beyond Divergence*.

India[89] or the clans in China[90] or create new groups altogether. Rotating credit and savings associations (ROSCAs) are perhaps the best example of this and can be found the world over.[91] Other ways of compelling borrowers to repay, such as badgering, threatening to hurt, and actually hurting wayward borrowers were alternatives to the social consequences, which were even effective in circles where social reputation mattered less.[92]

Even though systematic data on contractual forms and contracting parties are lacking too, there is evidence that recording, securing, and enforcing loans depended on the social distance between contracting parties. Lorandini and Odella showed for eighteenth-century Italy, for example, that the propensity to notarize loans increased with social distance.[93] The way in which lenders and borrowers in the Netherlands dealt with the stamp tax levied on written loan contracts since the 1620s reveals something quite similar. Although all contracts were admissible in

[89] Wolcott, 'An Examination of the Supply'; Malavika Nair, 'Caste as Self-Regulatory Club: Evidence from a Private Banking System in Nineteenth Century India', in: *Journal of Institutional Economics* 12:3 (2016), 677–698.

[90] Zhiwu Chen, Chicheng Ma, and Andrew J. Sinclair, 'Banking on the Confucian Clan: Why China developed Financial Markets so Late', in: *The Economic Journal* 132:644 (2022), 1378–1413.

[91] ROSCAs also pooled sums of money for people who would otherwise not be able to obtain large sums. See Clifford Geertz, 'The Rotating Credit Association: A "Middle Rung" in Development', in: *Economic Development and Cultural Change* 10:3 (1962), 241–263; Shirley Ardener, 'The Comparative Study of Rotating Credit Associations', in: *The Journal of the Royal Anthropological Institute of Great Britain and Ireland* 94:2 (1964), 201–229; F.J.A. Bouman, 'Indigenous Savings and Credit Societies in The Third World: A Message', in: *Savings and Development* 1:4 (1977), 181–219; Timothy Besley, Stephen Coate, and Glenn Loury, 'The Economics of Rotating Savings and Credit Associations', in: *The American Economic Review* 83:4 (1993), 792–810; F.J.A. Bouman, 'Rotating and Accumulating Savings and Credit Associations: A Development Perspective', in: *World Development* 23:3 (1995); Dekle and Hamada, 'On the Development'; Grietjie Verhoef, 'Stokvels and Economic Empowerment: The Case of African Women in South Africa, c.1930–1998', in: Beverly Lemire, Ruth Pearson, and Gail Campbell (eds.), *Women and Credit: Researching the Past, Refiguring the Future* (Oxford, 2002), 91–113.

[92] Easterly, 'Your Job Is Your Credit' (dissertation); Easterly, 'Your Job is Your Credit' (article); Olatunji Ojo, 'Financial Blues: The Institutional Adaptation of the Yoruba Credit System, 1851–1900', in: *The International Journal of African Historical Studies* 51:1 (2018), 17–36; Warner, 'The Kabuliwalas'.

[93] Cinzia Lorandini and Francesca Odella, 'Private Lending in an Alpine Region during the Eighteenth Century: A Family of Merchant-Bankers and Their Credit Network', in: *Enterprise & Society* 24:3 (2023), 838–865.

the Dutch courts, the users of unstamped contracts received a fine for evading taxation. Lenders not willing or expecting to pursue borrowers in court, however, could save on transaction costs and use unstamped contracts, something that was also common practice. Kin or other social relationships could explain this, but the reliance on collateral in large and unstamped loan contracts also suggests there existed an upper limit to those.[94] This resonates with Rosenthal and Bin Wong's observation that loan values could exceed the social costs imposed on defaulting borrowers, requiring even those connected through kin or social ties to rely on outside resolution instruments.[95] (Conversely, one could argue that such outside resolution instruments strengthened what networks could accomplish and label such lending as network+ credit.)

One of these instruments was collateral. Besides real estate, assets ranging from daily utensils to trade goods and from securities to human pawns served as collateral for loans.[96] As long as the asset was worth more than the loan itself, collateral was a common way of incentivizing repayment and compensating lenders in case of default. While much of this could happen without resorting to government help, this did not mean that the government remained on the sidelines. Besides establishing municipal pawn shops (see Sect. 2) and by recording and settling third-party claims on wages,[97] governments also facilitated credit markets in other ways. As the case of store credit provided by the Mexican neighborhood grocery stores (*pulperías*) suggests, government oversight

[94] Van Bochove and Kole, 'Uncovering Private Credit Markets'.

[95] Rosenthal and Bin Wong, *Before and Beyond Divergence*.

[96] On human pawns, see: Sharon Ann Murphy, 'Securing Human Property: Slavery, Life Insurance, and Industrialization in the Upper South', in: *Journal of the Early Republic* 25:4 (2005), 615–652; Paul E. Lovejoy, 'Pawnship, Debt, and "Freedom" in Atlantic Africa During the Era of the Slave Trade: A Reassessment', in: *The Journal of African History* 55:1 (2014), 55–78; John J. Clegg, 'Credit Market Discipline and Capitalist Slavery in Antebellum South Carolina', in: *Social Science History* 42:2 (2018), 343–376; Caitlin Rosenthal, *Accounting for Slavery: Masters and Management* (Cambridge [MA], 2018); Sharon Ann Murphy, *Banking on Slavery: Financing Southern Expansion in the Antebellum United States* (Chicago, 2023). Bishara, *A Sea of Debt*, 63–66 provides another interesting example of how loans could be secured: by involving future generations to guarantee loans.

[97] Christiaan van Bochove, 'Seafarers and Shopkeepers: Credit in Eighteenth-Century Amsterdam', in: *Eighteenth-Century Studies* 48:1 (2014), 67–88; Verwaaij and Van Bochove, 'Credit without banks' document how this allowed innkeepers and shopkeepers to provide credit to seafarers.

and regulation (e.g., of maximum loan sizes, pawn types, and liquidation procedures) could become stronger as collateralized lending and the attendant risk to property ownership became more important.[98] A similar point can be made for that other widely used way of securing and enforcing loans: cosigning or, as in the case of bills of exchange, endorsing. While most transactions were concluded without difficulties, bills of exchange seem to have relied on the government a bit more directly (in terms of laws) and indirectly (via notarized protests).[99] This also applied to mortgage credit, where mortgage law had to be stable and predictable and not prejudice borrowers too much.[100] The government also had to establish rules and institutions, such as (bankruptcy) courts, to deal with conflicts and insolvencies.[101]

[98] Francois, *A Culture of Everyday Credit*.

[99] Veronica Aoki Santarosa, 'Financing Long-Distance Trade: The Joint Liability Rule and Bills of Exchange in Eighteenth-Century France', in: *The Journal of Economic History* 75:3 (2015), 690–719; De Vicq and Van Bochove, 'Historical Diversity'; Gary Gorton, 'Inland Bills of Exchange: Private Money Production without Banks', in: *Explorations in Economic History* 92:101547 (2024), 1–26.

[100] Van Bochove, Deneweth, and Zuijderduijn, 'Real Estate and Mortgage Finance'; Latika Chaudhary and Anand V. Swamy, 'Protecting the Borrower: An Experiment in colonial India', in: *Explorations in Economic History* 65 (2017), 36–54; Latika Chaudhary and Anand V. Swamy, 'A Policy of Credit Disruption: The Punjab Land Alienation Act of 1900', in: *The Economic History Review* 73:1 (2020), 134–158.

[101] Julian Hoppit, *Risk and Failure in English Business 1700–1800* (Cambridge, 1987); Muldrew, *The Economy of Obligation*; Isabella Cecchini, 'When Things Go Wrong: Credit, Defaults and Institutions in Early Modern Venice', in: Marcella Lorenzini, Cinzia Lorandini, and D'Maris Coffman (eds.), *Financing in Europe: Evolution, Coexistence and Complementarity of Lending Practices from the Middle Ages to Modern Times* (Cham, 2018), 45–72. The effectiveness of courts depended on the speed and costs with which they could settle disputes. When these costs were high and the odds of default were high as well—like in regions with strong weather fluctuations where farmers had a high probability of default—some forms of credit (such as mortgage loans) were much less likely to be provided. See Nath, 'Credit risk'. Also, the effectiveness of some forms of conflict resolution provided by the government, such as debtors' prison, actually depended strongly on outside variables like the presence of local kinship networks that could mobilize funds. See Sarah Balakrishnan, 'Of Debt and Bondage: From Slavery to Prisons in the Gold Coast, c.1807–1957', in: *The Journal of African History* 61:1 (2020), 3–21; Alexander Wakelam, *Credit and Debt in Eighteenth-Century England: An Economic History of Debtors' Prisons* (London, 2021); Sarah Balakrishnan, 'The Jailhouse Divergence: Why Debtors' Prisons Disappeared in Nineteenth Century Europe and Flourished in West Africa', in: *Punishment & Society* 24:5 (2022), 807–823.

6 The Credit Continuum in Ten Chapters: An Overview of This Volume

There are many ways in which the main questions we ask about non-bank credit come to determine how credit markets form in different parts of the world, and at different times. To recap, these questions are: (1) How do borrowers and lenders meet?, (2) whose money is involved?, (3) how are the loans recorded?, and (4) how are the loans secured and enforced?

The financial relationships that undergird the answers to these questions are embedded on the one hand in incentives that are quite general, and on the other hand in structures that can be very local and specific. The ten chapters in this volume each illustrate widely different examples on this continuum. Each chapter takes the reader to a different part of the world and a different time, and each chapter also takes the reader to a set of similar circumstances, where institutions and/or individuals will borrow or lend, where loans will carry some type of security, which may be recorded verbally or on pieces of paper.

The ten cases in this volume are ordered according to the mechanisms that make borrower and lender meet or whose funds are lent. We begin with the match-makers that started our research endeavor: the notaries. Philip Hoffman, Gilles Postel-Vinay, and Jean-Laurent Rosenthal look at notaries' continued role as match-makers in credit markets in nineteenth- and twentieth-century France, the transformation of the markets in which they operated, and the transformation of the notarial role itself. Martín Wasserman takes us to Buenos Aires in the seventeenth and eighteenth centuries, where notaries were crucial to the financial development and transformation of the port on the Rio de la Plata into a city at the crossroads of South America much as they were in France and elsewhere.

Christie Swanepoel then analyzes to what extent credit intermediated by notaries coexisted with peer-to-peer lending within networks at the Cape Colony during the eighteenth century. She encounters a range of lenders, including institutional ones (see below), who helped fund production, trade, and consumption. Clemente Penna zooms in on the peer-to-peer credit market of nineteenth-century Rio de Janeiro. He looks at the *letras da terra*, debt instruments that circulated widely, and shows that the peer-to-peer credit that they helped raise, contributed to the rapid growth of the town's economy and population. Elise Dermineur studies Sweden in the nineteenth and twentieth centuries, a context where notaries were explicitly absent and credit markets relied on peer-to-peer loans. She discusses the gradual rise of banks, but also encounters a wide variety of credit provided by occasional and semi-professional lenders.

Matteo Pompermaier explicitly focuses on such semi-professional lenders: the innkeepers and wine sellers (*bastioneri*) in early modern Venice. While their core business was something else, they were key providers of small loans to ordinary people. Howard Jones looks at a quite similar type of lender: a shopkeeper-cum-moneylender in twentieth- and twenty-first-century Rajasthan. He brings us into the modern era and his observations, some of which made firsthand, provide depth to the landscape of bank and non-bank lenders.

Cyril Milhaud turns the perspective to institutional lenders by detailing the efficiency of the Theresian Carmelite order in providing credit to all kinds of borrowers in eighteenth-century Spain. He also demonstrates how governmental reforms brought this lending to an abrupt standstill. Matthew Mitchell reveals the sophisticated credit network of another type of religious institution: the Buddhist temples of early modern Japan. These temples lent out their own funds, intermediated between lenders and borrowers, and organized financial confraternities. Konstantinos Giakoumis introduces the guilds of the Ottoman Empire as a type of non-religious institutional lender. He shows how these guilds provided credit to their members between the seventeenth and nineteenth centuries, much like modern credit cooperatives would.

This catalog of cases could also have been organized around the questions of how loans were recorded, secured, and enforced. Most of the contributions either discuss loans recorded in writing—such as the contracts studied by Penna and Mitchell—or evidence of loans (including verbal ones) recorded in writing after the fact. Dermineur and Swanepoel find evidence of loans in probate inventories, Wasserman in testaments, and Hoffman, Postel-Vinay, and Rosenthal as well as Penna in the ledgers of notaries. Jones, Milhaud, and Giakoumis find loans in the records of lenders and governments, whereas Pompermaier discusses loan evidence in the form of pawn tickets.

These records also help us understand how the loans were secured and enforced. Although we do not observe social sanctions per se in the cases presented here, the existence of collateral—such as in the pawn credit discussed by Pompermaier and Jones and the reliance on enslaved people in the case studies by Penna, Swanepoel, and Wasserman—indicates a broad and general concept of securitized enforcement mechanisms. The case discussed by Penna also clearly shows that even when loans were not secured with explicit liens, lenders had recourse to borrowers' assets. The local government made sure there were consequences for not repaying a loan by providing a warehouse and personnel for impounded items.

In most chapters, governments and courts played a role in (creating the infrastructures) enforcing loans. We see it in how it regulated the *letras da terra* and provided a warehouse for impounded items in Rio de Janeiro as discussed by Penna, but also in how Pompermaier shows the Venetian government ensured that local pawn credit worked smoothly.

We did not discuss metrics such as volume or price—because as our historiographical overview demonstrated, credit markets consist of niches in their own right, making a numerical comparison less relevant to our purpose. Calculating interest rates, or annualized percentage rates (APRs), across the chapters would have been like comparing apples and oranges across time. Non-bank credit can often provide small, short-term, and risky loans and consequently charge high APRs. This makes it pointless to compare them to the much larger, longer term, and less risky loans of banks that may not even have existed at the same time, and that result in much lower APRs. Those who borrow from banks, moreover, also incur hidden costs—such as opportunity and travel costs to obtain and repay loans—that are often incorporated in the rates of the loans of moneylenders and other non-bank lenders.[102]

What matters to us here is to explore how different societies succeeded in meeting the demand for credit and to provide vantage points for allowing meaningful comparisons between different times and places. Our goal is to understand and study non-bank credit markets as such—not as an informal version or an alternative to banks. The ten chapters in this volume illustrate a set of variables that can be generalized beyond one economy, beyond one social context, and beyond one historical era or regional definition, and allow meaningful comparison between different information and contractual infrastructures. The preexisting connections, match-making, and market-making, the form of the records, and the cost of securing and enforcing all serve to distinguish each case, and reinforce that there are some vectors along which we can compare across

102 Ghate, *Informal Finance*, 14–16, 139–152; Collins et al., *Portfolios of the Poor*; Van Bochove and Van Velzen, 'Loans to Salaried Employees'; Özdeğer and Zeytinli, 'Ottoman Credit System'; Nath, 'Credit risk'; Luis Felipe Zegarra, 'Borrower income and loan rates in the credit market of Lima', in: *Economic History of Developing Regions* 37:2 (2022), 147–169.

time and place, even among widely disparate cases as the ones presented here. Yet, every angle of analysis refracts like a prism and shows us more ways in which the cases can be compared—and each exercise in comparison reveals more about each case, and reinforces the fact that non-bank credit has existed for much longer than banks, was a significant source of credit, and is an underexploited subject of exploration. This leaves us with the profound conviction that when it comes to non-bank credit, the whole is greater than the sum of its parts. If nothing else, we hope this volume provokes more comparisons and discoveries of non-bank credit markets and their intermediaries.

Archival Sources and Literature

Adams, Dale W., 'Using Contracts to Analyze Informal Finance', in: F.J.A. Bouman and Otto Hospes (eds.), *Financial Landscapes Reconstructed: The Fine Art of Mapping Development* (Boulder, 1994), 179–192.

Aliber, Robert Z., Charles P. Kindleberger, and Robert N. McCauley, *Manias, Panics, and Crashes: A History of Financial Crises* (Cham, 2023).

Allen, Robert C., *The British Industrial Revolution in Global Perspective* (Cambridge, 2009).

Al-Sabbagh, Munther, 'Before Banks: Credit, Society, and Law in Sixteenth-Century Palestine and Syria' (unpublished dissertation, Santa Barbara, 2018).

Ammons, Lila, 'The evolution of Black-Owned banks in the United States between the 1880s and 1990', in: *Journal of Black Studies* 26:4 (1996), 467–489.

Ardener, Shirley, 'The Comparative Study of Rotating Credit Associations', in: *The Journal of the Royal Anthropological Institute of Great Britain and Ireland* 94:2 (1964), 201–229.

Armendáriz, Beatriz, and Marc Labie (eds.), *The Handbook of Microfinance* (New Jersey, 2011).

Atje, Raymond, Ira Setiati, and Ilma Fadhil, 'Disruptive Technology in Indonesia's Banking Sector', in: *CSIS Working Paper Series* (2020).

Austin, Gareth, 'Indigenous Credit Institutions in West Africa, c.1750–c.1960', in: Gareth Austin and Kaoru Sugihara (eds.), *Local Suppliers of Credit in the Third World, 1750–1960* (Basingstoke, 1993), 93–159.

Austin, Gareth, and Kaoru Sugihara, 'Local Suppliers of Credit in the Third World, 1750–1960: Introduction', in: Gareth Austin and Kaoru Sugihara (eds.), *Local Suppliers of Credit in the Third World, 1750–1960* (Basingstoke, 1993), 1–25.

Austin, Gareth, and Kaoru Sugihara (eds.), *Local Suppliers of Credit in the Third World, 1750–1960* (Basingstoke, 1993).

Austin, Gareth, and Chibuike Ugochukwu Uche, 'Collusion and Competition in Colonial Economies: Banking in British West Africa, 1916–1960', in: *Business History Review* 81:1 (2007), 1–26.

Balakrishnan, Sarah, 'Of Debt and Bondage: From Slavery to Prisons in the Gold Coast, c.1807–1957', in: *The Journal of African History* 61:1 (2020), 3–21.

Balakrishnan, Sarah, 'The jailhouse divergence: Why debtors' prisons disappeared in 19th century Europe and flourished in West Africa', in: *Punishment & Society* 24:5 (2022), 807–823.

Banerjee, Abhijit V., Timothy Besley, and Timothy W. Guinnane, 'Thy Neighbor's Keeper: The Design of a Credit Cooperative with Theory and a Test', in: *The Quarterly Journal of Economics* 109:2 (1994), 491–515.

Banerjee, Abhijit, et al., 'The Miracle of Microfinance? Evidence from a Randomized Evaluation', in: *American Economic Journal: Applied Economics* 7:1 (2015), 22–53.

Baradaran, Mehrsa, *How the Other Half Banks: Exclusion, Exploitation, and the Threat to Democracy* (Cambridge [MA], 2015).

Baradaran, Mehrsa, *The Color of Money: Black Banks and the Racial Wealth Gap (Cambridge* [MA], 2017).

Bavel, Bas J.P. van, and Jan Luiten van Zanden, 'The Jump-Start of the Holland Economy during the Late-Medieval Crisis, c.1350–c.1500', in: *The Economic History Review* 57:3 (2004), 503–532.

Berg, Ryan C., Juliana Rubio, and Nathaniel Laske, 'Catalysts of Change: How Entrepreneurs Are Transforming Latin America' (2024) (https://www.csis.org/analysis/catalysts-change-how-entrepreneurs-are-transforming-latin-america, consulted on May 31, 2024).

Berger, Allen N., and Gregory F. Udell, 'A More Complete Conceptual Framework for SME Finance', in: *Journal of Banking & Finance* 30:11 (2006), 2945–2966.

Besley, Timothy, Stephen Coate, and Glenn Loury, 'The Economics of Rotating Savings and Credit Associations', in: *The American Economic Review* 83:4 (1993), 792–810.

Bishara, Fahad Ahmad, *A Sea of Debt: Law and Economic Life in the Western Indian Ocean, 1780–1950* (Cambridge, 2017).

Block, Joern H., et al., 'New Players in Entrepreneurial Finance and Why They are There', in: *Small Business Economics* 50:2 (2018), 239–250.

Bochove, Christiaan van, 'Seafarers and Shopkeepers: Credit in Eighteenth-Century Amsterdam', in: *Eighteenth-Century Studies* 48:1 (2014), 67–88

Bochove, Christiaan van, Christopher L. Colvin, and Oscar Gelderblom, 'Detecting the Function of Finance through History: An Essay in Celebration of the Work of Joost Jonker', in: *The Low Countries Journal of Social and Economic History* 18:3 (2021), 125–166.

Bochove, Christiaan van, Heidi Deneweth, and Jaco Zuijderduijn, 'Real estate and mortgage finance in England and the Low Countries, 1300–1800', in: *Continuity and Change* 30:1 (2015), 9–38.

Bochove, Christiaan van, and Ewout Hasken, 'The Modernization of Credit Markets: How Private Lenders Disappeared from the Dutch Mortgage Market, 1860–2000 (working paper, 2024).

Bochove, Christiaan van, and Heleen Kole, 'Uncovering Private Credit Markets: Amsterdam, 1660–1809', in: *The Low Countries Journal of Social and Economic History* 11:3 (2014), 39–72.

Bochove, Christiaan van, and Ton van Velzen, 'Loans to Salaried Employees: The Case of the Dutch East India Company, 1602–1794', in: *European Review of Economic History* 18:1 (2014), 19–38.

Bochove, Christiaan van, and Jaco Zuijderduijn, 'Years of Plenty, Years of Want? An Introduction to Finance and the Family Life Cycle', in: *The History of the Family. An international Quarterly* 27:2 (2022), 201–220.

Bonin, Hubert, Nuno Valério, and Kazuhiko Yago (eds.), *Asian Imperial Banking History* (London, 2015).

Bordo, Michael D., Angela Redish, and Hugh Rockoff, 'Why didn't Canada have a banking crisis in 2008 (or in 1930, or 1907, or…)?', in: *The Economic History Review* 68:1 (2015), 218–243.

Bouman, F.J.A., 'Indigenous Savings and Credit Societies in The Third World: A message', in: *Savings and Development* 1:4 (1977), 181–219.

Bouman, Frits J.A., 'Informal Rural Finance: An Aladdin's Lamp of Information', in: *Sociologia Ruralis* 30:2 (1990), 155–173.

Bouman, F.J.A., 'Rotating and Accumulating Savings and Credit Associations: A Development Perspective', in: *World Development* 23:3 (1995), 371–384.

Bouman, F.J.A., and Otto Hospes, 'Financial Landscapes Reconstructed', in: F.J.A. Bouman and Otto Hospes (eds.), *Financial Landscapes Reconstructed: The Fine Art of Mapping Development* (Boulder, 1994), 3–16.

Broadberry, Stephen, et al., *British Economic Growth 1270–1870* (Cambridge, 2015).

Broberg, Oskar, and Anders Ögren, 'Names, Shares and Mortgages: The Formalisation of Swedish Commercial Bank Lending, 1870–1938', in: *Financial History Review* 26:1 (2019), 81–108.

Brühwiler, Benjamin, 'Interweaving Threads of Credit and Debt: Trading (through) Textiles in Colonial Dar es Salaam', in: *Business History* 60:4 (2018), 474–491.

Buist, Marten G., *At Spes Non Fracta: Hope & Co. 1770–1815* (The Hague, 1974).

Bünz, Enno, 'Kredit bei den Heiligen: Die Dorfkirche als Geldinstitut in Spätmittelalter und Frühneuzeit', in: Kurt Andermann and Gerhard Fouquet (eds.),

Zins und Gült: Strukturen des Ländlichen Kreditwesens in Spätmittelalter und Frühneuzeit (Epfendorf, 2016), 41–67.

Burns, Kathryn, 'Nuns, Kurakas, and Credit: The Spiritual Economy of Seventeenth-Century', in: *Colonial Latin American Review* 6:2 (1997), 185–203.

Burns, Kathryn, *Colonial Habits: Convents and the Spiritual Economy of Cuzco, Peru* (Durham, 1999).

Calder, Lendol, *Financing the American Dream: A Cultural History of Consumer Credit* (Princeton, 1999).

Cameron, Rondo, *Banking in the Early Stages of Industrialization: A Study in Comparative Economic History* (Oxford, 1967).

Carbonell-Esteller, Montserrat, 'Montes de piedad and Savings Banks as Microfinance Institutions on the Periphery of the Financial System of Mid-Nineteenth-Century Barcelona', in: *Business History* 54:3 (2012), 363–380.

Carboni, Mauro, and Massimo Fornasari, 'The 'Untimely' Demise of a Successful Institution: The Italian Monti di pietà in the Nineteenth Century', in: *Financial History Review* 26:2 (2019), 147–170.

Caskey, John P., *Fringe Banking: Check-Cashing Outlets, Pawnshops, and the Poor* (New York, 1994).

Cassis, Youssef, Richard S. Grossman, and Catherine R. Schenk (eds.), *The Oxford Handbook of Banking and Financial History* (Oxford, 2016).

Cecchini, Isabella, 'When Things Go Wrong: Credit, Defaults and Institutions in Early Modern Venice', in: Marcella Lorenzini, Cinzia Lorandini, and D'Maris Coffman (eds.), *Financing in Europe: Evolution, Coexistence and Complementarity of Lending Practices from the Middle Ages to Modern Times* (Cham, 2018), 45–72.

Chakravarty, Ishita, 'Owners, Creditors and Traders: Women in Late Colonial Calcutta', in: *The Indian Economic and Social History Review* 56:4 (2019), 1–30.

Chandavarkar, A.G., 'Money and credit (1858–1947)', in: Dharma Kumar (ed.), *The Cambridge Economic History of India* 2 (Cambridge, 1983), 762–803.

Chaudhary, Latika, and Anand V. Swamy, 'Protecting the Borrower: An Experiment in Colonial India', in: *Explorations in Economic History* 65 (2017), 36–54.

Chaudhary, Latika, and Anand V. Swamy, 'A Policy of Credit Disruption: The Punjab Land Alienation Act of 1900', in: *The Economic History Review* 73:1 (2020), 134–158.

Chen, Zhiwu, Chicheng Ma, and Andrew J. Sinclair, 'Banking on the Confucian Clan: Why China Developed Financial Markets so Late', in: *The Economic Journal* 132:644 (2022), 1378–1413.

Çizakça, Murat, 'Cash waqfs of Bursa, 1555–1823', in: *Journal of the Economic and Social History of the Orient* 38:3 (1995), 313–354.

Clay, Christopher, 'The Origins of Modern Banking in the Levant: The Branch Network of the Imperial Ottoman Bank, 1890–1914', in: *International Journal of Middle East Studies* 26:4 (1994), 589–614.

Clegg, John J., 'Credit Market Discipline and Capitalist Slavery in Antebellum South Carolina', in: *Social Science History* 42:2 (2018), 343–376.

Clements, Diane, 'The "Consequence of an Advertisement": Intermediation in the Eighteenth-Century Credit Market', in: *Historical Research* 97:277 (2024), 369–384.

Clemens, Gabriele B. (ed.), *Schuldenlast und Schuldenwert: Kreditnetzwerke in der europäischen Geschichte (1300–1900)* (Trier, 2008).

Clemens Gabriele B., and Daniel Reupke, 'Challenging the Institutional Revolution of Credit Markets in the Nineteenth Century', in: Marcella Lorenzini, Cinzia Lorandini, and D'Maris Coffman (eds.), *Financing in Europe: Evolution, Coexistence and Complementarity of Lending Practices from the Middle Ages to Modern Times* (Cham, 2018), 267–288.

Coffman, D'Maris, 'Towards the Institutionalisation of Credit', in: Marcella Lorenzini, Cinzia Lorandini, and D'Maris Coffman (eds.), *Financing in Europe: Evolution, Coexistence and Complementarity of Lending Practices from the Middle Ages to Modern Times* (Cham, 2018), 345–351.

Coffman, D'Maris, Cinzia Lorandini, and Marcella Lorenzini, 'Introduction', in: Marcella Lorenzini, Cinzia Lorandini, and D'Maris Coffman (eds.), *Financing in Europe: Evolution, Coexistence and Complementarity of Lending Practices from the Middle Ages to Modern Times* (Cham, 2018), 1–18.

Collins, Daryl, Jonathan Morduch, Stuart Rutherford, and Orlanda Ruthven, *Portfolios of the Poor: How the World's Poor Live on $2 a Day* (Princeton, 2009).

Collins, Michael, *Money and Banking in the UK: A History* (London, 1988).

Colvin, Christopher L., 'Organizational Determinants of Bank Resilience. Explaining the Performance of SME Banks in the Dutch Financial Crisis of the 1920s', in: *Business History Review* 92:4 (2018), 661–690.

Dekle, Robert, and Koichi Hamada, 'On the Development of Rotating Credit Associations in Japan', in: *Economic Development and Cultural Change* 49:1 (2000), 77–90.

Demirgüç-Kunt, Asli, Erik Feyen, and Ross Levine, 'The Evolving Importance of Banks and Securities Markets', in: *The World Bank Economic Review* 27:3 (2013), 476–490.

Demirgüç-Kunt, Asli, et al., *The Global Findex Database 2017: Measuring Financial Inclusion and the Fintech Revolution* (Washington D.C., 2018).

Deneweth, Heidi, Oscar Gelderblom, and Joost Jonker, 'Microfinance and the Decline of Poverty: Evidence from the Nineteenth-Century Netherlands', in: *Journal of Economic Development* 39:1 (2014), 79–110.

Dermineur, Elise M. (ed.), *Women and Credit in Pre-Industrial Europe* (Turnhout, 2018).

De Soto, Hernando, *The Mystery of Capital: Why Capitalism Triumphs in the West and Fails Everywhere Else* (New York, 2000).

De Vicq, Amaury, 'Caught Between Outreach and Sustainability: The Rise and Decline of Dutch Credit Unions', in: *Business History* 66:6 (2022), 1524–1551.

De Vicq, Amaury, and Christiaan van Bochove, 'Historical Diversity in Credit Intermediation: Cosignatory Lending Institutions in Europe and North America, 1700s–1960s', in: *Social Science History* 47:1 (2023), 95–119.

De Vicq, Amaury, and Christiaan van Bochove, 'Lending a Hand: Help Banks in the Netherlands, 1848–1898', in: *European Review of Economic History* 28:2 (2024), 163–192.

Dokuzlu, Sertaç, 'The Agricultural Credit System in the Ottoman Empire between 1863 and 1888', in: *Rural History* 28:2 (2017), 177–188.

Easterly, Michael Edward, 'Your Job Is Your Credit: Creating a Market for Loans to Salaried Employees in New York City, 1885–1920' (unpublished dissertation, Los Angeles, 2008).

Easterly, Michael, 'Your Job is Your Credit: Creating a Market for Loans to Salaried Employees in New York City, 1885–1920', in: *Enterprise & Society* 10:4 (2009), 651–660.

Ecchia, Stefania, 'Informal Rural Credit Markets and Interlinked Transactions in the District of late Ottoman Haifa, 1890–1915', in: *Financial History Review* 21:1 (2014), 5–24.

Finn, Margot C., *The Character of Credit. Personal Debt in English Culture, 1740–1914* (Cambridge, 2003).

Fohlin, Caroline, 'Universal Banking in Pre-World War I Germany: Model or Myth?', in: *Explorations in Economic History* 36:4 (1999), 305–343.

Fohlin, Caroline, *Finance capitalism and Germany's Rise to Industrial Power* (Cambridge, 2007).

Fontaine, Laurence, *History of Pedlars in Europe* (Durham, 1996).

Fontaine, Laurence, *The Moral Economy: Poverty, Credit, and Trust in Early Modern Europe* (Cambridge, 2014).

Fotta, Martin, *From Itinerant Trade to Moneylending in the Era of Financial Inclusion: Households, Debts and Masculinity among Calon Gypsies of Northeast Brazil* (Cham, 2018).

Francois, Marie Eileen, *A Culture of Everyday Credit: Housekeeping, Pawnbroking, and Governance in Mexico City, 1750–1920* (Lincoln, 2006).

Gardner, Leigh, 'Financial History of Sub-Saharan Africa', in: *Oxford Research Encyclopedia of Economics and Finance* (2020).

Geertz, Clifford, 'The Rotating Credit Association: A "Middle Rung" in Development', in: *Economic Development and Cultural Change* 10:3 (1962), 241–263.
Gelderblom, Oscar, *Cities of Commerce: The Institutional Foundations of International Trade in the Low Countries, 1250–1650* (Princeton, 2013).
Gelderblom, Oscar, Mark Hup, and Joost Jonker, 'Public Functions, Private Markets: Credit Registration by Aldermen and Notaries in the Low Countries, 1500–1800', in: Marcella Lorenzini, Cinzia Lorandini, and D'Maris Coffman (eds.), *Financing in Europe: Evolution, Coexistence and Complementarity of Lending Practices from the Middle Ages to Modern Times* (Cham, 2018), 161–192.
Gelderblom, Oscar, and Joost Jonker, 'With a View to Hold: The Emergence of Institutional Investors on the Amsterdam Securities Market during the Seventeenth and Eighteenth Centuries', in: Jeremy Atack and Larry Neal (eds.), *The Origins and Development of Financial Markets and Institutions: From the Seventeenth Century to the Present* (Cambridge, 2009), 71–98.
Gelderblom, Oscar, Joost Jonker, Ruben Peeters, and Amaury de Vicq, 'Exploring Modern Bank Penetration: Evidence from Early Twentieth-Century Netherlands', in: *The Economic History Review* 76:3 (2023), 892–916.
Gerschenkron, Alexander, *Economic Backwardness in Historical Perspective: A Book of Essays* (Cambridge [MA], 1962).
Ghatak, Maitreesh, and Timothy W. Guinnane, 'The Economics of Lending with Joint Liability: Theory and Practice', in: *Journal of Development Economics* 60:1 (1999), 195–228.
Ghate, Prabhu, *Informal Finance: Some Findings From Asia* (Oxford, 1992).
Giakoumis, Konstantinos, 'The Voskopoja Guild of Tailors' Credit Lending Operations and Risk Management (1716–27)', in: *Turkish Historical Review* 9:3 (2018), 242–277.
Gilomen, Hans-Jörg, 'Klöster und Spitäler als Kreditgeber der ländlichen Gesellschaft: Hilfe oder Ausbeutung', in: Kurt Andermann and Gerhard Fouquet (eds.), *Zins und Gült: Strukturen des Ländlichen Kreditwesens in Spätmittelalter und Frühneuzeit* (Epfendorf, 2016), 69–92.
Giuffrida, Antonino, Roberto Rossi and Gaetano Sabatini, *Informal Credit in the Mediterranean Area (XVI-XIX Centuries)* (Palermo, 2016).
Goldsmith, Raymond W., *Financial Structure and Development* (New Haven, 1969).
Gorton, Gary, 'Inland Bills of Exchange: Private Money Production without Banks', in: *Explorations in Economic History* 92:101547 (2024), 1–26.
Graeber, David, *Debt: The First 5,000 Years* (New York, 2011).

Granados, Oscar M., and James V. Torres, 'Credit Networks and Business Dynamics in a Viceregal Capital: Santafé de Bogotá in the age of Charles III', in: *Financial History Review* 30:3 (2023), 330–354.

Grafe, Regina, 'An Empire of Debts? Spain and Its Colonial Realm', in: Nicolas Barreyre and Nicolas Delalande (eds.), *A World of Public Debts: A Political History* (Cham, 2020), 5–35.

Greif, Avner, 'Reputation and Coalitions in Medieval Trade: The Evidence on the Maghribi Traders', in: *The Journal of Economic History* 49:4 (1989), 857–882.

Greif, Avner, 'Contract Enforceability and Economic Institutions in Early Trade: The Maghribi Traders' Coalition', in: *The American Economic Review* 83:3 (1993), 525–548.

Greif, Avner, 'The Fundamental Problem of Exchange: A Research Agenda in Historical Institutional Analysis', in: *European Review of Economic History* 4:3 (2000), 251–284.

Grossman, Richard S., *Unsettled Account: The Evolution of Banking in the Industrialized World since 1800* (Princeton, 2010).

Gueyie, Jean-Pierre, Ronny Manos, and Jacob Yaron (eds.), *Microfinance in Developing Countries: Issues, Policies and Performance Evaluation* (Basingstoke, 2013).

Guinnane, Timothy W., 'Cooperatives as Information Machines: German Rural Credit Cooperatives, 1883–1914', in: *The Journal of Economic History* 61:2 (2001), 366–389.

Haber, Stephen, 'Industrial Concentration and the Capital Markets: A Comparative Study of Brazil, Mexico and the United States, 1830–1930', in: *The Journal of Economic History* 51:3 (1991), 559–580.

Haber, Stephen (ed.), *How Latin America Fell Behind: Essays on the Economic Histories of Brazil and Mexico, 1800–1914* (Stanford, 1997).

Heblich, Stephan, and Alex Trew, 'Banking and Industrialization', in: *Journal of the European Economic Association* 17:6 (2019), 1753–1796.

Hoffman, Philip T., Gilles Postel-Vinay, and Jean-Laurent Rosenthal, *Priceless Markets: The Political Economy of Credit in Paris, 1660–1870* (Chicago, 2000).

Hoffman, Philip T., Gilles Postel-Vinay, and Jean-Laurant Rosenthal, 'Entry, Information, and Financial Development: A Century of Competition between French Banks and Notaries', in: *Explorations in Economic History* 55 (2015), 39–57.

Hoffman, Philip T., Gilles Postel-Vinay, and Jean-Laurent Rosenthal, *Dark Matter Credit: The Development of Peer-to-Peer Lending and Banking in France* (Princeton, 2019).

Hoppit, Julian, *Risk and Failure in English Business 1700–1800* (Cambridge, 1987).

Hudon, Marek, and Joakim Sandberg, 'The Ethical Crisis in Microfinance: Issues, Findings, and Implications', in: *Business Ethics Quarterly* 23:4 (2013), 561–589.

Jonker, J.P.B., *MeesPierson. Schakel tussen verleden en toekomst. 275 jaar traditie en vernieuwing in het Nederlands bankwezen* (Amsterdam, 1997).

Jonker, Joost, 'Competing in Tandem: Securities Markets and Commercial Banking Patterns in Europe during the Nineteenth Century', in: Douglas J. Forsyth and Daniel Verdier (eds.), *The Origins of National Financial Systems: Alexander Gerschenkron reconsidered* (London, 2003), 64–86.

Jonker, Joost, and Keetie Sluyterman, *At Home on the World Markets: Dutch International Trading Companies from the 16th Century until the Present* (The Hague, 2000).

Karagedikli, Gürer, and Ali Coşkun Tunçer, 'Microcredit in the Ottoman Empire: A Review of Cash Waqfs in Transition to Modern Banking', in: Marcella Lorenzini, Cinzia Lorandini, and D'Maris Coffman (eds.), *Financing in Europe: Evolution, Coexistence and Complementarity of Lending Practices from the Middle Ages to Modern Times* (Cham, 2018), 237–266.

King, Robert C., and Ross Levine, 'Finance and Growth: Schumpeter Might be Right', in: *The Quarterly Journal of Economics* 108:3 (1993), 717–737.

Kuran, Timur, and Jared Rubin, 'The Financial Power of the Powerless: Socio-Economic Status and Interest Rates under Weak Rule of Law', in: *The Economic Journal* 128:609 (2018), 758–796.

Lamoreaux, Naomi, *Insider Lending: Banks, Personal Connections and Economic Development in Industrial New England* (Cambridge, 1996).

Lamoreaux, Naomi R., Daniel M.G. Raff, and Peter Temin, 'Beyond Markets and Hierarchies: Toward a New Synthesis of American Business History', in: *The American Historical Review* 108:2 (2003), 404–433.

Lauer, Josh, *Creditworthy: A History of Consumer Surveillance and Financial Identity in America* (New York, 2017).

Lemercier, Claire, and Francesca Trivellato, '1751 and Thereabout: A Quantitative and Comparative Approach to Notarial Records', in: *Social Science History* 46:3 (2022), 555–583.

Lemire, Beverly, Ruth Pearson, and Gail Campbell (eds.), *Women and Credit: Researching the Past, Refiguring the Future* (Oxford, 2002).

Levine, Ross, 'Financial Development and Economic Growth: Views and Agenda', in: *Journal of Economic Literature* 35:2 (1997), 688–726.

Levine, Ross, 'Finance and Growth: Theory and Evidence', in: Philippe Aghion and Steven N. Durlauf (eds.), *Handbook of Economic Growth* 1A (Amsterdam, 2005), 865–934.

Levine, Ross, and Sara Zervos, 'Stock Markets, Banks, and Economic Growth', in: *The American Economic Review* 88:3 (1998), 537–558.

Levy, Juliette, *The Making of a Market: Credit, Henequen, and Notaries in Yucatán, 1850–1900* (University Park, 2012).

Lindgren, Håkan, 'The Modernization of Swedish Credit Markets, 1840–1905: Evidence from Probate Records', in: *The Journal of Economic History* 62:3 (2002), 810–832.

Lindgren, Håkan, 'Parish Banking in Informal Credit Markets: The Business of Private Lending in Early Nineteenth-Century Sweden', in: *Financial History Review* 24:S1 (2017), 83–102.

Lorandini, Cinzia, and Francesca Odella, 'Private Lending in an Alpine Region during the Eighteenth Century: A Family of Merchant-Bankers and Their Credit Network', in: *Enterprise & Society* 24:3 (2023), 838–865.

Lorenzini, Marcella, 'The Credit Market and Notaries in Verona in the Second Half of the Seventeenth Century', in: *The Journal of European Economic History* 44:1 (2015), 123–148.

Lorenzini, Marcella, Cinzia Lorandini, and D'Maris Coffman (eds.), *Financing in Europe: Evolution, Coexistence and Complementarity of Lending Practices from the Middle Ages to Modern Times* (Cham, 2018).

Lovejoy, Paul E., 'Pawnship, Debt, and "Freedom" in Atlantic Africa during the Era of the Slave Trade: A Reassessment', in: *The Journal of African History* 55:1 (2014), 55–78.

Lluch, Andrea, 'The Art of Lending in the Pampas: Commercial Credit and Financial Intermediation in Argentina, 1900–1930', in: Bernardo Bátiz-Lazo and Leonidas Efthymiou (eds.), *The Book of Payments: Historical and Contemporary Views on the Cashless Society* (London, 2016), 55–64.

Ludlow, Leonor, and Carlos Marichal (eds.), *Banca y Poder en Mexico (1800–1925)* (México, 1986).

Luyendijk, Joris, *Swimming with Sharks: My Journey into the World of the Bankers* (London, 2015).

Lydon, Ghislaine, *On Trans-Saharan Trails: Islamic Law, Trade Networks and Cross-Cultural Exchange in Nineteenth-Century Western Africa* (Cambridge, 2009).

Maassen, H.A.J., *Tussen commercieel en sociaal krediet: De ontwikkeling van de Bank van Lening in Nederland van Lombard tot Gemeentelijke Kredietbank 1260–1940* (Hilversum, 1994).

Marichal, Carlos, *El Nacimiento de la Banca en América Latina: Finanzas y politica en el siglo XIX* (México, 2021).

Maurer, Noel, and Stephen Haber, 'Related Lending and Economic Performance: Evidence from Mexico', in: *The Journal of Economic History* 67:3 (2007), 551–581.

McLaughlin, Eoin, and Rowena Pecchenino, 'Fringe Banking and Financialization: Pawnbroking in Pre-Famine and Famine Ireland', in: *The Economic History Review* 75:3 (2022), 903–931.

Mersland, Roy, and R. Øystein Strøm (eds.), *Microfinance Institutions: Financial and Social Performance* (Basingstoke, 2014).

Merton, Robert C., and Zvi Bodie, 'A Conceptual Framework for Analyzing the Financial Environment', in: Dwight B. Crane et al. (eds.), *The Global Financial System: A Functional Perspective* (Boston, 1995), 3–31.

Mesquida, Juan O., 'Pious Funds across the Pacific (1668–1823): Charitable Bequests or Credit Source?', in: *The Americas* 75:4 (2018), 661–697.

Mesquida, Juan O., 'Contested Philanthropy in Spanish Manila: The Santa Casa de la Misericordia (1594–1869)', in: Isabel dos Guimarães Sá and Lisbeth Rodrigues (eds.), *The Confraternities of Misericórdia and the Portuguese Diasporas in the Early Modern Period* (Leiden, 2023), 108–133.

Milhaud, Cyril, 'Interregional Flows of Capital and Information in Spain: A Case Study of the Theresian Carmelite Order', in: *Revista de Historia Económica* 37:1 (2019), 81–110.

Mitchell, Matthew, 'Borrowing from the Buddha: Buddhist Temples as Financial Centers in Premodern East Asia', in: *Education About Asia* 24:2 (2019), 51–54.

Miwa, Yoshiro, and J. Mark Ramseyer, 'Banks and Economic Growth: Implications from Japanese History', in: *The Journal of Law and Economics* 45:1 (2002), 127–164.

Miwa, Yoshiro, and J. Mark Ramseyer, 'Japanese Industrial Finance at the Close of the 19th Century: Trade Credit and Financial Intermediation', in: *Explorations in Economic History* 43 (2006), 94–118.

Mokyr, Joel, *The Lever of Riches: Technological Creativity and Economic Progress* (Oxford, 1990).

Muldrew, Craig, *The Economy of Obligation: The Culture of Credit and Social Relations in Early Modern England* (Basingstoke, 1998).

Muldrew, Craig, 'The Social Acceptance of Paper Credit as Currency in Eighteenth-Century England: A Case Study of Glastonbury c. 1720–1742', in: Marcella Lorenzini, Cinzia Lorandini, and D'Maris Coffman (eds.), *Financing in Europe: Evolution, Coexistence and Complementarity of Lending Practices from the Middle Ages to Modern Times* (Cham, 2018), 133–159.

Murphy, Sharon Ann, 'Securing Human Property: Slavery, Life Insurance, and Industrialization in the Upper South', in: *Journal of the Early Republic* 25:4 (2005), 615–652.

Murphy, Sharon Ann, *Banking on Slavery: Financing Southern Expansion in the Antebellum United States* (Chicago, 2023).

Mutarindwa, Samuel, Dorothea Schäfer, and Andreas Stephan, 'Differences in African Banking Systems: Causes and Consequences', in: *Journal of Institutional Economics* 17:4 (2021), 561–581.

Mutch, Alistair, 'The Business of Religion: Lending and the Church of Scotland in the Eighteenth Century', in: *Journal of Scottish Historical Studies* 37:2 (2017), 136–154.

Nadan, Amos, 'The Competitive Advantage of Moneylenders over Banks in Rural Palestine', in: *Journal of the Economic and Social History of the Orient* 48:1 (2005), 1–39.

Nair, Malavika, 'Caste as Self-Regulatory Club: Evidence from a Private Banking System in Nineteenth Century India', in: *Journal of Institutional Economics* 12:3 (2016), 677–698.

Nath, Maanik, 'Do Institutional Transplants Succeed? Regulating Raiffeisen Cooperatives in South India, 1930–1960', in: *Business History Review* 95:1 (2021), 59–85.

Nath, Maanik, 'Credit Risk in Colonial India', in: *The Economic History Review* 75:2 (2022), 396–420.

Newton, Lucy, 'Trust and Virtue in English Banking: The Assessment of Borrowers by Bank Managements at the Turn of the Nineteenth', in: *Financial History Review* 7:2 (2000), 177–199.

Nicolussi-Köhler, Stephan, 'Introduction', in: Stephan Nicolussi-Köhler (ed.), *Change and Transformation of Premodern Credit Markets: The Importance of Small-Scale Credits* (Heidelberg, 2021), 1–21.

Nicolussi-Köhler, Stephan (ed.), *Change and Transformation of Premodern Credit Markets: The Importance of Small-Scale Credits* (Heidelberg, 2021).

North, Douglass C., *Institutions, Institutional Change and Economic Performance* (Cambridge, 1990).

O'Connell, Sean, *Credit and Community: Working-Class Debt in the UK Since 1880* (Oxford, 2009).

Ogilvie, Sheilagh, Markus Küpker, and Janine Maegraith, 'Household Debt in Early Modern Germany: Evidence from Personal Inventories', in: *The Journal of Economic History* 72:1 (2012), 134–167.

Ojo, Olatunji, 'Financial Blues: The Institutional Adaptation of the Yoruba Credit System, 1851–1900', in: *The International Journal of African Historical Studies* 51:1 (2018), 17–36.

Olegario, Rowena, 'Credit Reporting Agencies: A Historical Perspective', in: Margaret J. Miller (ed.), *Credit Reporting Systems and the International Economy* (Cambridge [MA], 2003), 115–159.

Olegario, Rowena, *A Culture of Credit: Embedding Trust and Transparency in American Business* (Cambridge [MA], 2006).

Özdeğer, Mehtap, and Emine Zeytinli, 'Ottoman Credit System and Usurers in Agriculture in the Nineteenth Century: Practices of Usury Contracts (Selem)', in: *Journal of Balkan and Near Eastern Studies* 21:5 (2019), 594–612.

Pamuk, Şevket, *The Ottoman Empire and European Capitalism, 1820–1913: Trade, Investment and Production* (Cambridge, 1987).

Pastureau, Guillaume, and Bertrand Blancheton, 'The Success of the Bordeaux Mont-de-Piété, 1801–1913', in: *Financial History Review* 21:3 (2014), 281–299.

Penna, Clemente Gentil, 'Economias urbanas: Capital, créditos e escravidão na cidade do Rio de Janeiro, c.1820–1860' (unpublished dissertation, Rio de Janeiro, 2019).

Perlinge, Anders, 'International Mercantile Networks and Financial Intermediation in Nineteenth Century Scania (Sweden): Foreign Private Capital Imports and Informal Credit Market Imbalances', in: *Business History* 63:6 (2021), 1030–1047.

Pineda, Yovanna, 'Financing Manufacturing Innovation in Argentina, 1890–1930', in: *Business History Review* 83:3 (2009), 539–562.

Pomeranz, Kenneth, *The Great Divergence: China, Europe, and the Making of the Modern World Economy* (Princeton, 2000).

Pressnell, L.S., *Country Banking in the Industrial Revolution* (Oxford, 1956).

Quinn, William, and John D. Turner, *Boom and Bust: A Global History of Financial Bubbles* (Cambridge, 2020).

Regalsky, Andrés M., 'Banca y capitalismo en la Argentina, 1850–1930: Un ensayo crítico', in: *Ciclos* 9:18 (1999), 33–54.

Reinhart, Carmen M., and Kenneth S. Rogoff, *This Time is Different: Eight Centuries of Financial Folly* (Princeton, 2009).

Robb, Hannah, 'Contract and Trust in Fifteenth-Century Church Courts', in: Stephan Nicolussi-Köhler (ed.), *Change and Transformation of Premodern Credit Markets: The Importance of Small-Scale Credits* (Heidelberg, 2021), 275–292.

Rosenthal, Caitlin, *Accounting for Slavery: Masters and Management* (Cambridge [MA], 2018).

Rosenthal, Jean-Laurent, and R. Bin Wong, *Before and Beyond Divergence: The Politics of Economic Change in China and Europe* (Cambridge [MA], 2011).

Rougier, Marcelo (ed.), *La Banca de desarrollo en América Latina: Luces y sombras en la industrialización de la región* (Mexico, 2000).

Rousseau, Peter L., and Richard Sylla, 'Financial Systems, Economic Growth, and Globalization', in: Michael D. Bordo, Alan M. Taylor, and Jeffrey G. Williamson (eds.), *Globalization in Historical Perspective* (Chicago, 2003), 373–415.

Rudolph, Julia, 'A Broker's Advice: Credit Networks and Mortgage Risk in the Eighteenth-Century Empire', in: Michael Lobban and Ian Williams (eds.), *Networks and Connections in Legal History* (Cambridge, 2020), 185–209.

Ryan Jr., Joseph James, 'Credit Where Credit Is Due: Lending and Borrowing in Rio de Janeiro, 1802–1900' (unpublished dissertation, Los Angeles, 2007).

Sandberg, Joakim, 'Mega-interest on Microcredit: Are Lenders Exploiting the Poor?', in: *Journal of Applied Philosophy* 29:3 (2012), 169–185.

Santarosa, Veronica Aoki, 'Financing Long-Distance Trade: The Joint Liability Rule and Bills of Exchange in Eighteenth-Century France', in: *The Journal of Economic History* 75:3 (2015), 690–719.

Schlumbohm, Jürgen (ed.), *Soziale Praxis des Kredits 16.–20. Jahrhundert* (Hannover, 2007).

Schnitzeler, J.W., 'In Loco Parentis: Holland's Orphan Chambers in a European Context', in: *The History of the Family* 27:2 (2022), 243–267.

Schumpeter, Joseph, *The Theory of Economic Development: An Inquiry into Profit, Capital, Credit, Interest and the Business Cycle* (Abingdon, 2021).

Servon, Lisa, *The Unbanking of America: How the New Middle Class Survives* (Boston, 2017).

Slavíčková, Pavla (ed.), *A History of the Credit Market in Central Europe: The Middle Ages and Early Modern Period* (Abingdon, 2021).

Soetaert, Paul, *De Bergen van Barmhartigheid in de Spaanse, de Oostenrijkse en de Franse Nederlanden (1618–1795)* (s.l., 1986).

Soyeda, Juichi, *A History of Banking in Japan* (London, 1994).

Sylla, Richard, 'Financial Systems and Economic Modernization', in: *The Journal of Economic History* 62:2 (2002), 277–292.

Tebbutt, Melanie, *Making Ends Meet: Pawnbroking & Working-Class Credit* (Leicester, 1983).

Triner, Gail D., 'Property Rights, Family, and Business Partnership in Nineteenth- and Twentieth-Century Brazil: The Case of the St. John d'el Rey Mining Company, 1834–1960', in: *Enterprise & Society* 8:1 (2007), 35–67.

Ugolini, Stefano, 'The Coevolution of Banks and Corporate Securities Markets: The Financing of Belgium's Industrial Take-Off in the 1830s', in: *Business History* 63:6 (2021), 892–913.

Vauplane, Hubert de, 'Les nouveaux acteurs de la finance', in: *Revue d'économie financière* 118 (2015), 27–36.

Verhoef, Grietjie, 'Stokvels and Economic Empowerment: The Case of African Women in South Africa, c.1930–1998', in: Beverly Lemire, Ruth Pearson, and Gail Campbell (eds.), *Women and Credit: Researching the Past, Refiguring the Future* (Oxford, 2002), 91–113.

Verwaaij, Daan, and Christiaan van Bochove, 'Credit without Banks: The Amsterdam Water Bailiff's Ledger of 1856', in: *Financial History Review* 26:2 (2019), 171–195.

Ville, Simon, and Grant Fleming, 'Financial Intermediaries and the Design of Loan Contracts within the Australasian Pastoral Sector Before the Second World War', in: *Financial History Review* 7:2 (2000), 201–218.

Vries, Joh. de, Wim Vroom, and Ton de Graaf (eds.), *Worldwide Banking: ABN AMRO Bank 1824–1999* (Amsterdam 1999).

Wadhwani, R. Daniel, 'Small-scale Credit Institutions: Historical Perspectives on Diversity in Financial Intermediation', in: Youssef Cassis, Catherine Schenk,

and Richard Grossman (eds.), *The Oxford Handbook of Banking and Financial History* (Oxford, 2016).
Wakelam, Alexander, *Credit and Debt in Eighteenth-Century England: An Economic History of Debtors' Prisons* (London, 2021).
Warner, H. William, 'The Kabuliwalas: Afghan Moneylending and the Credit Cosmopolis of British India, c. 1880–1947', in: *The Indian Economic and Social History Review* 57:2 (2020), 171–198.
Wasserman, Martín, *Las obligaciones fundamentales: Crédito y consolidación económica durante el surgimiento de Buenos Aires* (Buenos Aires, 2018).
Waters, Hedwig Amelia, 'The Financialization of Help: Moneylenders as Economic Translators in the Debt-Based Economy', in: *Central Asian Survey* 37:3 (2018), 403–418.
Willems, Bart, *Leven op de pof: Krediet bij de Antwerpse middenstand in de achttiende eeuw* (Amsterdam, 2009).
Wilson, Craig, and Fan Yang, 'Shanxi Piaohao and Shanghai Qianzhuang: A Comparison of the Two Main Banking Systems of Nineteenth-Century China', in: *Business History* 58:3 (2016), 433–452.
Wolcott, Susan, 'An Examination of the Supply of Financial Credit to Entrepreneurs in Colonial India', in: David S. Landes, Joel Mokyr, and William J. Baumol (eds.), *The invention of enterprise: entrepreneurship: From ancient Mesopotamia to modern times* (Princeton, 2010), 443–468.
Wright, Robert E., *Financial Exclusion: How Competition Can Fix a Broken System* (Great Barrington, 2019).
Yunus, Muhammad, *Banker to the Poor: Micro-Lending and the Battle Against World Poverty* (New York, 1997).
Zanden, Jan Luiten van, and Bas van Leeuwen, 'Persistent But Not Consistent: The Growth of National Income in Holland 1347–1807', in: *Explorations in Economic History* 49:2 (2012), 119–130.
Zegarra, Luis Felipe, 'Information Asymmetries and Agricultural Credit Evidence from the Pre-Banking Era in Lima, 1825–1865', in: *Agricultural Finance Review* 79:2 (2019), 217–233.
Zegarra, Luis Felipe, 'Borrower Income and Loan Rates in the Credit Market of Lima', in: *Economic History of Developing Regions* 37:2 (2022), 147–169.
Zwarts, Harm, 'Institutional Investors in the Countryside of the Dutch Republic: An Analysis of the Investment Portfolios of Reformed Deaconries in the Countryside of the Dutch Republic, c.1750–1800' (unpublished thesis, Utrecht University, 2015).

The Decline of a Great Financial Intermediary: Notaries in France, 1851–1934

Philip Hoffman, Gilles Postel-Vinay, and Jean-Laurent Rosenthal

1 Introduction

This chapter continues our decades' long effort to understand traditional credit markets and their intermediaries.[1] Traditional intermediaries are ubiquitous across early modern Europe and persist long after the arrival of banks as important player in the financial markets. Notaries are also

[1] Philip T. Hoffman, Gilles Postel-Vinay, and Jean-Laurent Rosenthal, *Priceless Markets: The Political Economy of Credit in Paris, 1660–1870* (Chicago, 2000); Philip T. Hoffman, Gilles Postel-Vinay, and Jean-Laurent Rosenthal, *Dark Matter Credit: The Development of Peer-to-Peer Lending and Banking in France* (Princeton, 2019).

P. Hoffman (✉) · J.-L. Rosenthal
California Institute of Technology, Pasadena, CA, USA
e-mail: pth@hss.caltech.edu

J.-L. Rosenthal
e-mail: rosentha@caltech.edu

G. Postel-Vinay
Paris School of Economics, Paris, France
e-mail: gilles.postel-vinay@psemail.eu

C. van Bochove and J. Levy (eds.), *Beyond Banks*, Palgrave Studies in the History of Finance,
https://doi.org/10.1007/978-3-031-75819-5_2

ubiquitous across the western world. Nevertheless, as this volume's chapters demonstrate, the specific roles and institutions governing financial markets vary from country to country and at times even across markets within countries.

In France, long before banks spread, notaries were the financial intermediaries who made it possible for large numbers of borrowers to take out loans. As early as 1740, nearly a third of French families benefitted from credit arranged by these semi-public, semi-private scriveners, who besides arranging peer-to-peer loans also provided services assured in other economies by lawyers, city-officials, financial advisers, recorders of deeds, and real estate brokers. If measured relative to GDP by 1840, French notaries were mobilizing as much credit for mortgages as the United States banking system did in the 1950s. The lending facilitated transfers of property within families, and in the broader economy it financed infrastructure, industry, and especially agriculture and urban real estate, sectors that banks avoided because of the liquidity risks involved with making long-term loans.

Notaries are among the numerous intermediaries across the world who arranged loans for places without banks and for kinds of loans banks would not provide. While the financial histories of most countries have told us a lot about banks and bankers, we know less about these other intermediaries. Some essential questions about them need to be answered if we are to make headway in understanding the role of reputation and trust in creating the basis for the peer-to-peer lending networks that were ubiquitous in France and elsewhere. One model, which takes the embeddedness of reputation literally, would suggest that these peer-to-peer markets are purely local: they in effect function as islands, with intermediaries operating in a neighborhood limited by where they were born. But reputation models do not require such hermetically sealed markets, and as we have shown, it is the interconnections among credit markets that were in fact essential to their effectiveness. But what about the notaries themselves? Did they conform to behaviors consistent with locally created and maintained reputations or were they part of a more regional or national market?

Economists and economic historians have often taken reputational models as out-of-time abstractions that help justify informal arrangements of one kind of another, and modernization has been seen as breaking down these arrangements. Yet we have shown that in French credit markets at least, the apogee of the notarial system lagged behind the rise of banks by several decades.[2] Beyond changes brought on by modernization and the changes in the demand for different kinds of credit and capital, one can also ask how changes in communication and transportation (in particular railroads) affected notaries' geographical origins and their training.

By the 1850s the notaries' business was in decline, and the government continued a policy (begun during the French Revolution) to reduce their numbers in an effort to shore up rural notaries' income. But just how did their partial demise play out across France? What can it tell us about the inevitable demise of them as financial intermediaries as economies and politics change? Did the notaries adapt their training? Did sons stop following their fathers into a waning profession? How did the government react?

As a profession, notaries were regulated, with the government assuring that each locality had enough of them to assure Cournot-like competition. The Cournot competition model is one where different firms face a common set of clients, and rather than compete on price (the Bertrand model), they choose how much output to produce. The model has a stark prediction: cutting the number of firms/notaries boosts each remaining notary's income. But officials also worried that some areas were endowed with too many notaries, so they suppressed notarial businesses (*études*) when the owners died or retired. The officials then made the remaining local notaries indemnify the notary who retired or his heirs. What happened to the price incoming notaries paid for the offices they assumed? The price, after all, measures the present value of future stream of profits. Did it stagnate or fall? How did the notaries' lending business react throughout the decline? Did lending fall faster than business as a whole? How much variation was there in notarial credit, across France and over time?

Those are all questions that we can answer thanks to records preserved by the court system and the Ministry of Justice, which regulated

[2] Philip T. Hoffman, Gilles Postel-Vinay, and Jean-Laurent Rosenthal, 'Entry, Information, and Financial Development: A Century of Competition Between French Banks and Notaries', in: *Explorations in Economic History* 55:1 (2015), 39–57; Hoffman, Postel-Vinay, and Rosenthal, *Dark Matter Credit*.

notarial practice.[3] The records described the careers, training, background, revenues, business activity, and *étude* prices for everyone who entered or left the notarial profession or moved to a different location. The archives also shed light on the notaries' political opinions and on their weaknesses, from fraud to flirtations with banking despite increasingly rigorous prohibitions against it, beginning in the eighteenth century and continuing through the nineteenth and twentieth centuries.[4] We sampled those records by selecting adjacent years approximately every two decades: specifically in 1851–1852, 1872–1873, 1891–1892, 1911–1912, 1927–1928, and 1932–1933.[5]

We begin with the long decline of the notarial business and focus in particular on their lending. We then see how the notaries adjusted their careers and training as their activity shrank and examine how regulation of the notaries adapted. The drift downward was generally slow, but some of the changes were large, such as the prices paid for *études*, or rapid, such as the resurgence of lending in the 1930s. We examine these brusque movements in detail and ask if they are tied to notarial lending and if notaries were more likely to get into trouble after economic crises. The conclusion raises some broader issues involved in regulating financial intermediaries.

2 The Decline of the Notarial Business

Notaries, then and now, are a medallion business. Like taxi cabs in New York, you can only become a notary by purchasing an office from a current notary (or replacing one who is dismissed by the authorities).

[3] For regulation of notaries in the nineteenth century, see Adeline Daumard, *Les fortunes françaises au XIXe siècle* (Paris, 1973). For the development of notaries before then, see Marie-Françoise Limon, *Les notaires au Châtelet sous le règne de Louis XIV* (Toulouse, 1992) and Robert Descimon, 'Les auxiliaires de justice du Châtelet de Paris: aperçus sur l'économie du monde des offices ministériels (XVIe-XVIIIe siècle)', in: Claire Dolan (ed.) *Entre justice et justiciables: les auxiliaires de la justice du moyen âge au XXe siècle* (Laval, 2005), 301–326.

[4] Hoffman, Postel-Vinay, and Rosenthal, *Priceless Markets*; Philip T. Hoffman, Gilles Postel-Vinay, and Jean-Laurent Rosenthal, 'No Exit: Notarial Bankruptcies and the Evolution of Financial Intermediation in Nineteenth Century Paris', in: Stanley L. Engerman et al. (eds.), *Finance, Intermediaries, and Economic Development* (New York, 2003), 75-108; Hoffman, Postel-Vinay and Rosenthal, *Dark Matter Credit*.

[5] We added the years in the late 1920s and early 1930s to chart the rapid changes of the Great Depression. For a detailed description of our sample, which was stratified to better estimate the notaries activity in large and small markets, see the appendix.

Each position comes with a fixed town or city for the *étude's* location and a surrounding territory within which the notary can draw up acts for clients. On the eve of the French Revolution notaries were ubiquitous, in particular in the south of France, where Roman Law left a deeper imprint than in northern France. Revolutionaries attempted to transform the notaries and all other public officials into administrative agents, because venality (i.e. the market for public positions) was one of their bugaboos. Although the reform largely succeeded, over time the medallion system was reintroduced for notaries, auctioneers, and stockbrokers, even if the state did take a far more active role in regulating the profession.[6] Moreover, growing literacy and a succession of reforms further reduced the need and demand for their services.

To track the broad evolution of the profession, we relied on the *Compte général de l'administration de la justice civile et commerciale en France* published by the *Ministère de la Justice*. That publication records the number of notaries by *arrondissement* (district) in 1831 and then starting in 1835 it reports both the total number of active notaries and the total number of acts or contracts drawn up by notaries each year.[7] In 1835 there were more than ten thousand active notaries, and they drew up three million acts when the French population was about 34 million. A hundred years later, slightly more than seven thousand notaries drew up the same number of contracts and the French population than was just about 41 million—over the course of 100 years, the average population each notary served had roughly doubled.

The decline in the number of notaries is displayed in Fig. 1. It shows that at the national level the decline in the number of notaries is a long-run and relatively regular process. As Fig. 1 also shows, the number of acts by contrast is volatile with very large drops during both the short-lived Second Republic (1848–1851) and the tumultuous Franco-Prussian war and Paris Commune uprising (1870–1871). The national series of contracts then reached two lows, one just before World War I at 2.7 million per year and another in 1935 at 2.5 million per year. The series has a peak in 1919 as families and businesses dealt with a backlog of contracting and legal issues that had been postponed during the war. Figure 2 scales the number of acts by the number of notaries and the

[6] Daumard, *Les fortunes françaises*.

[7] We will use acts and contracts as synonyms.

number of adults (potential users of the notary's services). Before World War I, the number of contracts per notary is almost constant over time at about 350. There is a massive jump in the 1920s followed by a decline, and when our series ends notaries were again drawing up an act per day on average. Because the French adult population grew slowly the number of contracts per 1,000, adults declined by half between 1830 and 1913.

The drop in the number of acts was widespread and cushioned only in places with very rapid economic growth. We collected the number of contracts and notaries for each of France's twenty appellate court districts (*cours d'appel*). Yet even in Douai, the court that covers the most industrial departments (Nord and Pas-de-Calais), witnessed a 10% reduction in the number of notaries from 1831 to 1935 even though the number of acts was relatively stable. The Paris appellate district also lost 15% of its notaries, despite being the one region where the number of acts grew substantially over the century (40% in the mid-1920s and early 1930s). Southern districts (Aix, Nîmes, Montpellier, Agen, Toulouse) all suffered sharp declines (between 40 and 50%) in the number of notaries. These dramatic purges of notaries pale beside the collapse in the number of contracts they recorded. In the Agen district the number of acts in 1912 was 41% of what it had been in 1840, and the post-World War I bounce

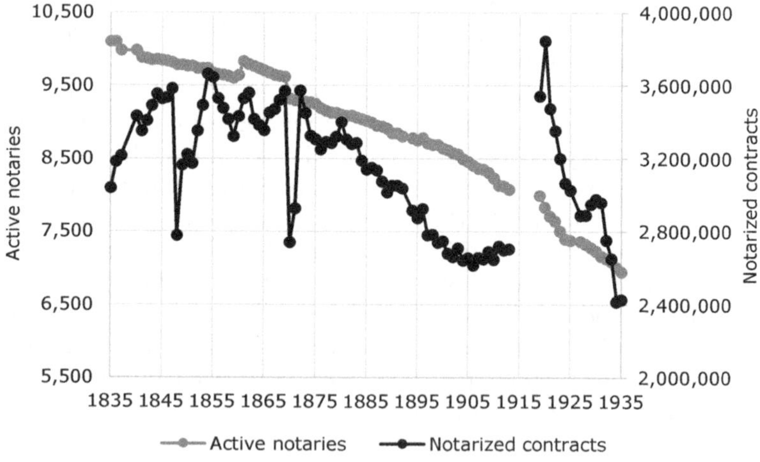

Fig. 1 Number of active notaries and notarized contracts in France, 1835–1935 (*Source* See text)

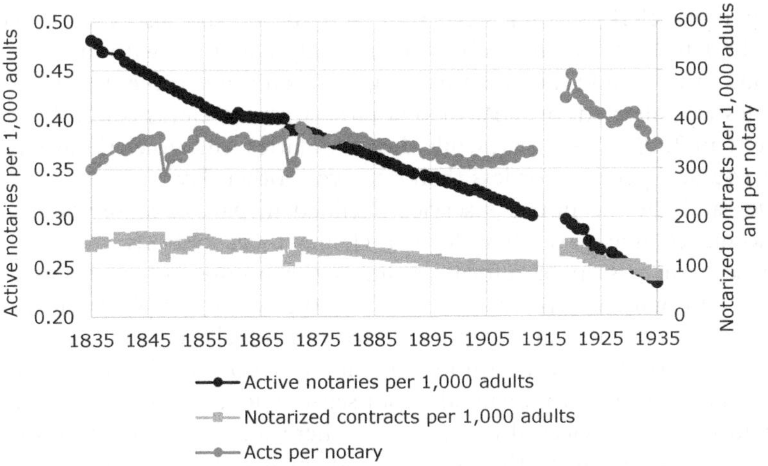

Fig. 2 Contracts and active notaries per person, 1835–1935 (*Source* See text)

was short lived. By the 1930s notaries in the Agen district were drawing up only 30% of the number of contracts they had managed a century before.

The number of notaries was slipping because the government closed notarial businesses when notaries retired or failed. In doing so, the government had to balance two imperatives imposed by the medallion structure of the industry: one was that the web of notaries would not be too sparse in any area, and the other was that the value of the office be sufficient to attract bidders for the positions that were being released. The first imperative was driven by the need to provide everyone access to notarial services that were in many cases legally required (e.g. all deeds impacting real estate ownership needed to be recorded by a notary—like e.g. mortgages). The second was a direct consequence of the fact that the notarial offices were a financial asset. When the position's price fell too much because of limited business the local district attorney arranged to have the other notaries buy out the retiree (or indemnify his heirs) and then take possession of his archives.

The number of acts dropped because the demand for notarial services shrank. One might assume that the closures would have restricted the supply of notaries' services, but there is no evidence that there were serious supply constraints. Notaries could expand their businesses by hiring more clerks if they were busy and they could also cut business back by letting clerks go or by working only part-time without a clerk, although they would then be prime candidates for government closure. In the files we collected, busy Parisian notaries with ten clerks could draw up more than 2,000 acts a year, while the 53 notaries with no clerks averaged only 142 acts per year, or less than one every other day.

Demand for the notary's service declined in part because social and economic change gave their former clients more options and in part because a succession of reforms reduced the number of contracts that had to be notarized. As we discussed in earlier work the plurisecular rise of literacy meant that it was possible for individuals to bind themselves to a variety of contracts without the aid of a notary. The move of an ever-larger number of individuals from self-employed to salaried workers in industry and services also meant that there were fewer contracts over assets like land or capital that peasants and small-scale entrepreneurs once utilized.

Similarly, over the course of the nineteenth century recourse to marriage contracts and probates fell as individuals opted for the standard French matrimonial regime and as filings with the estate tax administration provided a substitute way to deal with bequests. These two changes were driven by legal and fiscal reforms initiated under the Revolution and continued under Napoleon, and subsequent legal reforms in the nineteenth century had a similar effect. The rise of indefinitely-lived corporations that were much larger than the Old Regime businesses reduced the frequency of business contracting. Some of these corporations, like insurance companies bought real estate to back their policies and withdrew it from the land sales market and, as a result, removed them from the sphere where notaries would intermediate the contracting. Finally, a growing variety of assets issued by public and private entities (including the national debt) could be held and traded with no recourse to a notary.

One thing the Revolution did not touch was notaries' stranglehold on mortgages. If someone wanted to pledge a real asset as collateral for a loan and have that pledge registered with the *hypothèques* (the government mortgage recorder), a notary had to be involved. No subsequent political regime has touched this third rail of finance. Yet change in the mortgage market did come and it reduced notaries' income. In credit markets, which we have studied extensively, notaries earned fees both as strictly legal intermediaries (draft debt contracts, registering liens) and as mortgage brokers. Over the course of the nineteenth century increasing literacy meant that small, short-term, unsecured loans were more and more likely to be drawn up privately, a trend that had started before 1789. At the other end of the spectrum, large and long-term loans became the business of mortgage banks. A government-backed mortgage bank, the *Crédit Foncier de France* (CFF), siphoned off borrowers in Paris and big cities. It had a monopoly on the issue of government-backed securities and an implicit government guarantee for the mortgage bonds it sold, and it could lend money for longer terms than the mortgages brokered by notaries—50 years, for instance, instead of five. By 1899, the CFF held some 24% of French mortgages. Although CFF loans were notarized, actual recourse to the notary was infrequent because the loans were self-amortizing and very long term. At the end of the nineteenth century the CFF had open branches in most departments and thus short-circuited the brokerage side of the notaries' business. But that was not the end of notaries' credit woes. After World War I, the government began providing subsidized mortgages, which cut deeper into the notaries' lending business. As for investors, the government was offering them the chance to put money into secure government debt, and banks with branches were soon opening the door to placements in other assets. The investors' demand for diversification drained away more of the notaries business.

The effect of these changes on the notaries' profits was complex. We measure their earnings by the real price they paid for the offices, which should capture expected profits, and we distinguish notaries by the approximate size of the market they served.[8] Paris was in a class by itself. Below Paris were the notaries in the 26 or so other cities with an appellate court. They enjoyed big markets because they could deal with clients throughout the entire appellate district, which, in the case of the appellate court in the city of Rennes, for instance, could stretch across five of France's county-like departments. Below these appellate court notaries were their colleagues in the roughly 400 or so cities that had the major courts (*tribunaux de première instance*) in each department. They handled clients in one of the four or so *arrondissements* that typically made up each department. Still lower in the hierarchy were notaries in 2,500 towns with only a justice of the peace (*juge de paix*). Their range

[8] Real prices are computed using a CPI from Thomas Piketty and Gabriel Zucman, 'Capital is Back: Wealth-Income Ratios in Rich Countries 1700–2010', in: *The Quarterly Journal of Economics* 129:3 (2014), 1255–1310 and set at 100 in 1912.

was limited to the surrounding *canton*, typically a handful of villages clustered about the major local town or city (*chef-lieu*). At the bottom of the hierarchy were notaries in villages with no court at all.

If we arrange notaries by their level in this hierarchy of markets and aggregate prices by decade, then the mean real price of notarial businesses falls between 63 and 73% in the years from the 1850s to the 1920s, although in most markets it had risen up until the 1910s just before the 1920s collapse. The median price follows a similar pattern of rising through the 1910s and then falling, although the median fell much less between the 1850s and the 1920s than the mean in the smallest markets (Table 1). Both median and mean prices then revived at least partially in the 1930s, as notaries were able to draw on their superior information about creditworthiness to select low-risk borrowers and lend to them at a time when banks were cutting off credit. We return to that revival below, when we also analyze the other short-term fluctuations in *étude* prices and in notarial credit. Overall, though, due both to the elimination of the smallest *études* and to increasing wealth, the median notary in any market watched the real price of his *étude* appreciate between the 1850s and the 1910s. His expected profits presumably did the same.

Table 1 Mean and median real price for notarial businesses (étude) by decade and market size, 1850s–1930s

Market size	*1850s*	*1870s*	*1890s*	*1910s*	*1920s*	*1930s*
Panel A: Mean real price (1912 francs)						
Paris	537,429	498,621	580,959	589,200	144,979	331,150
Appellate court	188,268	232,286	368,518	349,448	-	320,270
Arrondissement	120,492	142,119	200,741	144,101	42,062	184,191
Canton	99,248	69,059	71,747	84,835	37,174	74,254
Village	82,804	65,748	51,246	145,293	28,366	56,473
Panel B: Median real prices (1912 francs)						
Paris	512,089	488,540	657,694	594,875	146,873	303,920
Appellate court	188,268	251,340	368,518	326,370	-	232,924
Arrondissement	131,788	83,780	153,276	148,350	38,662	120,555
Canton	51,209	40,610	55,737	74,175	24,653	43,562
Village	26,358	31,473	26,754	49,450	21,089	36,470

Source Our sample. See appendix for details
Note For the categories of market size, see the text

It behooves us to be cautious in our description of the trends, because the number of observations for the largest markets (Paris and the appellate districts) is small (see Table 6 in the appendix). The prices in the 1920s for all markets were likely depressed for another unusual reasons: a freeze on rents since 1914 that cast a pall over real estate transactions, and price inflation that cut the real price sharply.[9]

For Paris at least, we can go much further back, to the seventeenth century.[10] In the eighteenth century, the price of *études* in Paris (measured in livres of constant value in silver) grew slowly and then accelerated from the 1760s to the 1780s. Prices (measured in francs of the same silver value as the livre) collapsed during the French Revolution. Yet by 1825, the value of *études* had recovered: a notary's business was worth about as much as it had been in the eighteenth century. For Paris we have a longer time series because we can link data from our sample with transactions collected for our work in *Priceless Markets*.[11] This expanded data set is displayed in Fig. 3. Compared with the decades prior to the Revolution, *étude* prices were low in Paris under Napoleon, but they then swiftly recovered, to reach a plateau of a half a million 1912 francs that endured through the Second Empire (1852–1870). Thereafter, real prices rose, fell back to the secular plateau, and then plummeted during and after World War I before a limited recovery in the 1930s.

The other striking pattern in the graph is the very wide range of prices at any time, with some *études* selling for almost three times the price of others. That is clear evidence that a notary's clientele and particular practices were of great value and could be transmitted with his medallion. Those practices and the attachment of clients were the reputational part of the notarial profession. That they were so important in Paris, the most modern and capitalist part of the country, is yet another sign that the modern economy relies heavily on such informal and personal arrangements.

Another way to analyze the long-run pattern of *étude* prices is to divide the sales price by the population and the number of notaries in each market. Doing so compensates more accurately for the size of the

[9] The French Government imposed emergency war-time rent controls in 1914, these measure persisted through the interwar period.

[10] Descimon, 'Les auxiliaires de justice'; Hoffman, Postel-Vinay and Rosenthal, *Priceless Markets*; Limon, *Les notaires*.

[11] Hoffman, Postel-Vinay, and Rosenthal, *Priceless Markets*.

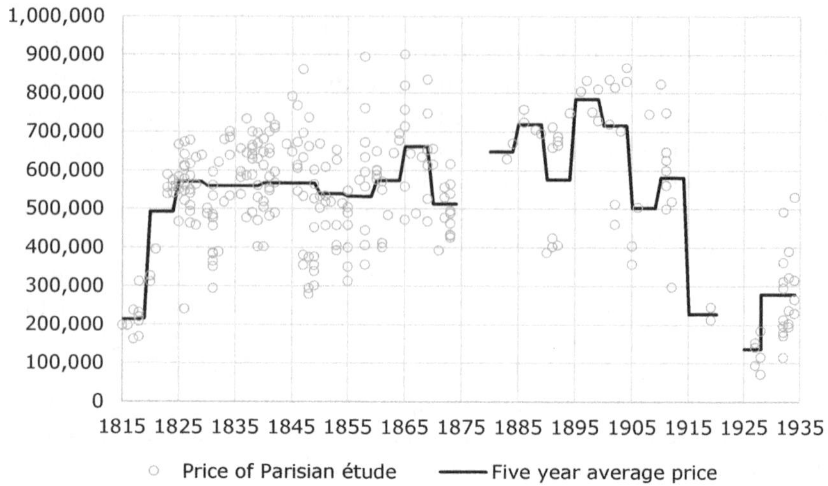

Fig. 3 Real prices of Parisian études, 1815–1935 (*Source* See text; *Note* Real prices calculated using a CPI from Piketty and Zucman, 'Capital is back' with the value of the CPI set at 100 in 1912. The dots are transactions while the line is the average price by five-year period (the line is interrupted in 1875–1879 and 1920–1924 because we have no transaction prices for these two periods)

markets and for the expected competition from other notaries. Like the prices themselves, this index collapses in the 1920s and then stages a partial recovery in the 1930s (Table 2). But the prelude to the 1910s is complex. Between the 1850s and 1910s the index rose in the smallest markets but declined in the largest ones. The likely explanation is that the big markets bore the brunt of the reduced property sales and loss of business to investors shifting to alternative assets.

3 Constants for the Notaries

Despite reduced demand for their services and fluctuations in their profits, some things remained by and large the same for notaries across the nineteenth and early twentieth centuries: the administrative procedures for vetting them, their training and the limited tendency of notarial businesses being passed along within families. The vetting procedure assured that notaries had the required knowledge of the law and of the legal duties imposed on notaries, but this technical competence did not guarantee that

Table 2 Real price of notarial businesses divided by population and number of notaries in canton: means by market size and decade, 1850s–1930s

Market size	*1850s*	*1870s*	*1890s*	*1910s*	*1920s*	*1930s*
Paris	0.005	0.0017	0.0020	0.0014	0.0004	0.001
Appellate court	0.275	0.225	0.287	0.258	-	0.253
Arrondissement	1.198	0.707	1.122	2.212	0.460	2.006
Canton	2.552	1.789	2.606	2.813	1.102	2.352
Village	1.551	1.298	1.095	2.239	0.629	1.456

Source As in Table 1
Note Prices as in Table 1

they would thrive—that required more. To succeed, a notary had to drum up business. For instance, he might arrange a large number of loans by harnessing his knowledge of investors, of credit risks, and of investment opportunities. At the very least, success demanded energy plus profiting from the experience all notaries gained when they served as clerks in what amounted to an apprenticeship before they became notaries themselves.

It is worth keeping in mind here that although notaries were regulated, their *études* were medallion businesses—private firms that were bought and sold subject to governmental approval. That inheritance of Old Regime venality had survived both the French Revolution and the Napoleonic Empire for fiscal reasons and administrative convenience. It is worth remembering too that notaries themselves had a hand in their own regulation—an example of regulatory capture that was facilitated by their training the clerks who might someday become notaries themselves.

When a notary decided to sell his business, the buyer was subject to a screening process that involved both the local corporation of notaries and the Ministry of Justice. The Ministry and the courts checked that would-be notaries had the requisite training, that they had served as clerks in notarial businesses for the required amount of time (six years, including one as a number one clerk, with a law degree or notarial studies diploma serving as a substitute for two years as a clerk), that they had enough personal assets and good-enough reputation to serve as a notary, and that their political opinions would not lead them to oppose the institutions of the existing regime. Representatives of local notaries helped in the process: they vouched for the time would-be notaries had spent as clerks, and they examined the candidates to ensure they knew the law and relevant government regulations of the notarial business.

Beyond all this verification of training, the Ministry of Justice would also reduce the price that a candidate offered when buying an *étude* if it was too high and would saddle the incoming notary with too much personal debt or induce him to engage in the risky and profitable forbidden business of banking. More rarely the Ministry increased the price if the candidate and the outgoing notary were suspected of hidden side-payments to escape taxes on the transaction. To check if the price was too high or too low, the Ministry calculated an estimated value for the *étude* by analyzing costs and revenue over the past five years. The *dossiers* the Ministry constructed for this calculation and for the rest of the vetting covered all the transfers or suppressions of *études*. The archived dossiers gave us the information we have about the notaries and about their businesses (see appendix for details).

The amount of time notaries spent in training as clerks rose slightly in most markets after 1850, subsided in most in 1920 and then recovered. But the general pattern was of little change: candidates spent an average of eight to twenty years as clerks before becoming notaries, with the longer times probably necessary for clerks to save up enough money to acquire an *étude* (Table 3). Median training times were similar. A growing number of notaries also had a law degree (only 12% in the 1850s versus 31% in the 1920s and 24% in the 1930s). The degree was particularly common in Paris and in the markets with an appellate court (52% in the 1920s and 41% in the 1930s). Rural notaries were much less likely to get a law degree, but after World War I over a third had a degree or attended a notarial school.

The average distance these new notaries traveled from their birthplace to their clerkships and to the location of the *étude* they finally purchased rose over time as railroads and then automobiles cut transportation costs. The only exception was Paris, where distances shrank (Table 4). There, over half the new notaries were natives who had trained only in Paris, for all our cross-sections except the 1870s and 1890s. 99% of the notaries who acquired an *étude* in Paris had trained there, and 61% of the notaries in cities with appellate courts had served clerkships in such cities. That sort of clerkship seemed to be a prerequisite for notarial business at the top of the court hierarchy, probably because of the sort of learning and professional connections common in the biggest markets.

Amidst all the sales of *études*, there was little change in the fraction of notaries who inherited the business from their fathers. It ranged from a high of 12% in the 1850s to a low of 4% in the 1890 but showed no

Table 3 Mean and median training times for new notaries by decade, 1850s–1930s

Market size	*1850s*	*1870s*	*1890s*	*1910s*	*1920s*	*1930s*
Panel A: Mean training times (years)						
Paris	9	11	11	11	9	15
Appellate court	9	10	20	9	-	11
Arrondissement	9	13	9	8	9	9
Canton	8	8	10	10	9	12
Village	8	10	9	10	8	9
Panel B: Median training times (years)						
Paris	9	11	10	12	9	13
Appellate court	9	10	20	9	-	11
Arrondissement	8	9	9	7	9	9
Canton	8	7	9	10	8	11
Village	7	9	8	9	7	9

Source As in Table 1

Table 4 Distance traveled (kilometers) from birth through training to purchase of étude: mean by market size and decade

Market size	*1850s*	*1870s*	*1890s*	*1910s*	*1920s*	*1930s*
Paris	18	64	127	0	0	26
Appellate court	0	515	481	171	-	280
Arrondissement	98	166	198	408	302	378
Canton	191	217	343	306	319	438
Village	85	249	235	309	351	323

Source As in Table 1
Note The distance in each cell is the mean of the sum of the lengths of the paths that connect a notary's birth place to the site of his first clerkship, then connects that site to the next clerkship, and so on until the path reaches the *étude* he buys

trend. Transfers to other family members were even rarer, between 3 and 7%. Some notarial dynasties did exist, like the Tricou family in Lyon with five generations of notaries if you count the son in law who inherited the *étude* in 1961, but these were an exception.[12]

[12] Jean Hours, 'Jean Tricou', in: *Revue du Lyonnais* 1 (1977), 25–33; Jean Lafaurie, 'Jean Tricou 1890–1977', in: *Revue numismatique* 18 (1976), 7–10.

Although family transfers of *études* were uncommon in general, they did crop up for the *études* at the top of the notarial hierarchy: between 14 and 30% if we consider Paris and cities with either an appellate court or one of the major *arrondissement* courts. The reason was likely the higher prices paid for these *études* (Table 1) and the larger portfolio of personal assets needed to operate them. Incoming notaries borrowed to buy *études*, but they had to have a down payment and enough other personal assets to operate the *étude* and assure the Ministry of Justice that they would not teeter into bankruptcy. A more expensive *étude* would require a bigger down payment and more personal assets, and a clerk would have to save longer to come up with the money. A notarial family could furnish the money, and they would be willing to (if the *étude* was prospering) since they had inside information about what the young notary's business prospects would be.

The reasons that prompted notaries to sell their *études* changed over time, but not greatly. Death brought on between 12 and 20% of the sales and retirement between 39 and 58% (Table 5). Trade-ups rose in the twentieth century as a small but growing number of notaries sold one *étude* to buy a bigger one. Suppressions also increased as the Ministry of Justice whittled away at the oversupply of rural notaries particularly in the south of France. And ill health accounted for a rising fraction of the transactions too (between 7 and 10% in the nineteenth century and between 17 and 22% in the twentieth). Here one might imagine that notaries were obliged to work longer because World War I had decimated the pool of candidates to buy their *études*, but health was growing more common as a motive before the war, and prices could have adjusted to attract more candidates. As we do not know the ages of the outgoing notaries, we cannot simply check that they were older. We do know tenure length in most cases. For *études* in category 1 and 2, the 1920's outgoing notaries in fact had among the shortest tenures (this is true whether we remove the notaries who got into trouble or not). In more rural areas notaries traditionally had shorter tenures (they left at least four years earlier than their urban colleagues) and the 1920s saw a big jump so that they left after average tenures of 26 years in the 1920s and 23 years in the 1930s. But if we estimate their ages by adding the average time notaries operated *études* to their average age when they began, then notaries were leaving at about age 60 both in the nineteenth and early twentieth century, and those who retired for health reasons were no younger.

Table 5 Reasons études are transferred by decade, 1850s–1930s (%)

Reason notary leaves	*1850s*	*1870s*	*1890s*	*1910s*	*1920s*	*1930s*
Death	17.0	19.7	21.7	12.1	17.6	14.5
Retirement	55.3	57.8	49.6	38.8	41.7	33.6
Ill health	8.5	10.4	7.0	17.2	16.7	21.7
Trade up to bigger *étude*	0.0	4.0	4.3	10.3	9.3	11.2
Problem with *étude*	19.1	8.1	13.9	7.8	5.6	14.5
Suppression of *étude*	0.0	0.0	3.5	13.8	9.3	4.6

Source As in Table 1
Note The table does not include cases in which there was no transfer or suppression of the *étude*, as when a holder becomes an honorary notary. Problems occurred when notaries went bankrupt, owed clients money, failed to keep adequate records or properly perform services for clients, or violated rules against engaging in banking

One might wonder who cared why or when notaries retired. Obviously, the incoming notary who was going to buy the office wanted to avoid buying a lemon. Clients also wanted to avoid offices that faced difficulties because transactions might be held up when a notary failed. Finally, the government's efforts at protecting the profession as a whole meant that it had an interest in smooth transmission. In the absence of public scandal, outgoing notaries made every effort to reassure current and future clients that all was well with the *étude*.

This concern may have been necessary at a time when the notaries' fortunes were no longer as big as in the past. Real median *étude* prices had peaked in large markets in the 1890s and dropped more as we know in the 1920s, in part because of the inflation after World War I. Inflation must have eroded some of the other personal assets notaries held. If all of this was common knowledge, people might have worried about the financial viability of the *étude*, all the more so if the outgoing notary lived in straightened circumstances and could not devote himself to the leisurely retirement his more prosperous colleagues could afford. Clients might desert the notary, and his *étude* would be worth less. But if he retired for his health, there would be no cause for alarm. Illness would dictate modest living, and a younger successor would have more energy to make the *étude* prosper.

There were also sales because of problems facing the outgoing notary. These sales rose during economic crises, such as the 1930s, because clients would delay paying the notaries' bills; or the notaries was more likely to be caught engaging in risky speculation, in the forbidden practice of banking, or simply withhold money due to their clients. The spendthrift notary Brunie owed money to his clients in 1911, and his colleague Rigal engaged a strawman to flip real estate.[13] The risky behavior could happen at all times but it would be more likely to be revealed when an economic crisis impacted the finances of the notaries or their clients.

As in the cases of Rigal and Brunie, the Ministry of Justice handled these affairs quietly. The reason was in part regulatory capture by the local notaries, and the fear of possible damage to creditors. In the case of Brunie, the *Procureur Général* in the Bordeaux Appeals Court explained why: "A notary who engaged in such behavior would certainly deserve to be relieved of his duties and even to be indicted if we did not keep in mind that criminal charges would harm his creditors, who were the victims of his public office." It was better therefore to force him to resign.[14] Similar arguments had been made since the eighteenth century.

Notaries as legal intermediaries changed rather little between 1850 and 1935. They became more likely to get a professional education, and they traveled a bit further to train. The industry and its regulatory practices remained firmly anchored in the local, with the key organization aimed at policing notaries being the arrondissement's chamber of notaries. But even in the 1850 and even more so in the 1890s, there was a broad market for notarial position, for outside Paris many notaries came from outside the jurisdiction where they bought a position. They were also unlikely to have worked for a long period of time in the office they purchased. The implication is that the value of *études* came not from the formal roles that notaries played but from clients' attachment to a particular office. Evidence for this attachment is plentiful. First, offices in the same location do not all have the same prices. Second the narratives provide abundant evidence of the specific characteristics of notaries' clienteles that emphasize the particular role of the outgoing notary in building or destroying that clientele. Even in the problematic offices, the narratives focus on the specific decision that notaries made to attract clients who sought to complete dubious transactions. That is striking evidence of a market for clienteles.

[13] Archives Nationales (=AN), Archives du ministère de la Justice: notaires (entry number BB10) (=Notaires), inv.nr. 2586-24 (Dordogne, dossiers Lagarde and Goujon).

[14] AN, Notaires, inv.nr. 2586 (Dordogne, dossier Lagarde, 28 January 1911).

4 What Changed for the Notaries

Despite the constants for notaries over the course of the nineteenth and early twentieth centuries, some things changed rapidly. Prices in the 1920s and 1930s are the clearest example (Table 1). As we know, real prices dropped in the 1920s, in part because of a freeze on rents that cast a pall over real estate transactions, and in part because of price inflation. They then recovered partially in most markets in the 1930s.

There are signs that the recovery in the 1930s was brought on by resurgence in notarial lending. The fraction of notarial acts devoted to borrowing had been slipping since the 1850s (Fig. 4) for reasons we have explained: competition from the CFF and government-subsidized mortgages, the ability of branch banks to offer alternative investments to potential lenders, legislation in 1843 and 1890 that barred notaries from entering banking themselves, and, last but not least, real estate that was withdrawn from markets when it became infrastructure or was purchased by insurance companies. In the 1930s, the fraction of credit acts climbed back up to the level of the 1910s. The capitalized value that the Ministry of Justice assigned to notaries' income from their credit dealings jumped even higher in the 1930s, beyond even the level of the 1870s and 1890s (Fig. 5), although the renaissance of lending was not shared by all *études*.

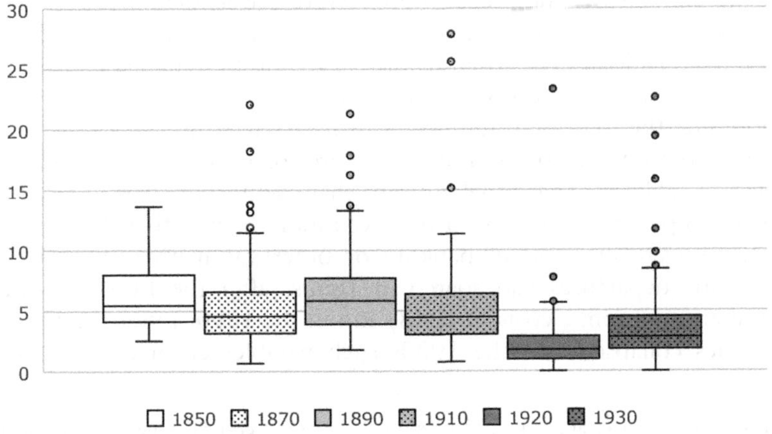

Fig. 4 % of notarial contracts devoted to borrowing, 1850s–1930s (*Source* Our sample)

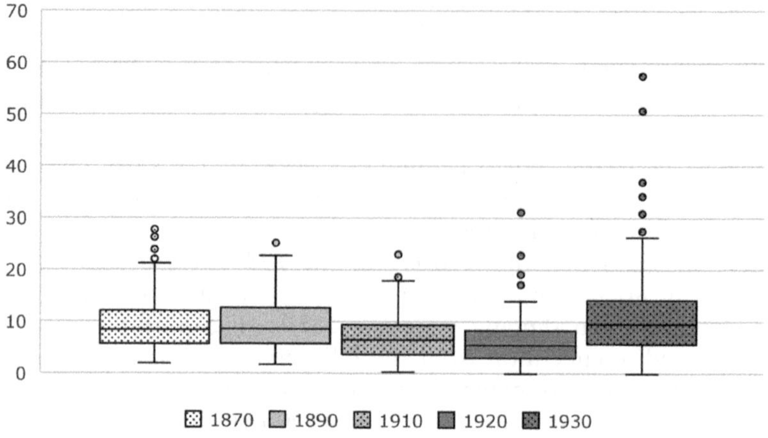

Fig. 5 Capitalized value of credit contracts as a % of capitalized value of all acts, 1870s–1930s (*Source* Our sample)

We suspect that notaries were using their information about borrowers to siphon off the best credit risks in the 1930s, when banks cut back on lending.[15] The sources are unfortunately silent about the borrowers in the 1930s and about the lenders too. Had the borrowers been cut off from the bank credit they relied upon? Were the lenders investors who trusted in the notaries' information? Or ones willing to shoulder the risks of an individual loan even when it was backed up by valuable real estate? Without the loan contracts we cannot tell.

Alongside the increased number of loans arranged in the 1930s came a jump in the fraction of notaries who were forced to resign because of problems (Table 5). That usually meant that clients were having troubles and slow to pay what they owed or—even more likely—that the notaries themselves were engaged in banking or other speculative investments. Problematic departures had soared in 1850s (after the European-wide political and economic crisis of 1848) and in the 1890s (after rural property values collapsed). In the 1930s such troubles erupted again. The

[15] Patrice Baubeau et al., 'Flight-to-safety and the credit crunch: a new history of the banking crises in France during the Great Depression', in: *The Economic History Review* 74:1 (2020), 223-250; Eric Monnet, Angelo Riva, and Stefano Ungaro, 'The Real Effects of Bank Runs. Evidence from the French Great Depression (1930–1931)', (CEPR working paper, 2021).

cause, once again, was speculation by notaries or their making loans with money on deposit, although this time the notaries' lending was a swan song.

In Dordogne, the borrowers fell behind in paying their loans.[16] In Paris and its suburbs, real estate speculation was the problem,[17] and one notary made a loan to Alexandre Stavisky, the financier whose collapse triggered a political scandal.[18] To reassure the public, the government in 1934 created deposit insurance financed by fees levied on all the notaries in each appellate court district. The insurance guarantees the money notaries held, though it did not cover losses due to a notary making forbidden bank loans.[19] The temptation of moral hazard was no doubt too great to cover those risks.

5 Conclusion

In our work on peer-to-peer lending markets in France, we emphasized that the chronology of medium and long-term credit did not fit the modernization narrative or the idea that the French economy experienced a post-1850 growth spurt driven by financial innovation. We showed that in Paris these markets stretched back to the seventeenth century and that they underwent spectacular transformation in the nineteenth century. The rise of the CFF coincided with this transformation, but it was a mortgage bank whose principal business was the reconstruction of Paris, not French industrialization. Later when we looked at the rest of the country, we found that peer-to-peer markets endured well into the twentieth century. It was as if modern financial capitalism had simply been added on top of more traditional means of securing capital. In that sense the opposition between old and new financial ways has been seriously overstated.

In this paper we return to the intermediaries themselves and ask what can we say about the notaries in general? We know that their business depended on their reputation, but it is worth emphasizing their dealings were not contained in the sort of islands that figure in simple models of repeat dealings among two individuals. They passed clients on to one

[16] AN, Notaires, inv.nr. 3279 (notary Courty).

[17] AN, Notaires, inv.nr. 3345 (notary Billiard).

[18] AN, Notaires, inv.nr. 3294 (notary Robineau).

[19] AN, Notaires, inv.nr. 3345 (notary Moreau).

another within a region limited by transportation costs.[20] In the city of Paris, the referrals stretched across the entire city.[21] These were local networks, but they were hardly islands. Their training did not fit into any closed-off space either; it too was not an island. The lesson here is that scholars who emphasize reputation should abandon the notion that it is an endowment or based on exclusive dealings because in fact it is capital that can be accumulated, lost, and even sold, and markets where reputation matters can be structurally interconnected, as it was with the notaries.

A second lesson is that this traditional economy was profoundly sensitive to political and economic crises. The short-lived Second Republic, the Franco-Prussian War, and the Paris Commune all cut the number of acts notaries passed. The sharp declines occur everywhere in France suggesting that by the 1840s at least the country was more integrated than scholars might think. Even before the nineteenth century, the notaries' business was shaken—or sometimes strengthened—by political and economic upheavals. The fiscal crisis of the Law Affair back in the early eighteenth century drove them to register hundreds of loan repayments, and that in turn gave them added information about creditworthiness that propelled them into arranging loans. And over 200 years later, the crisis of the 1930s drew them back into lending when banks shut off the credit spigot. The notaries and the networks they operated in were never islands isolated from politics or the rest of the economy.

Their return to lending in the 1930s teaches a third lesson as well, for some of them, we know, were not just arranging peer-to-peer loans: they were engaging in banking. They were funding medium-term credit with short-term deposits, a practice repeatedly forbidden since the eighteenth century but clearly too profitable to resist. And borrowers were still turning to notaries, despite the spread of branch banking, the rise of the government-backed CFF, and the existence of the Banque de France, which could help banks deal with liquidity problems. Clearly, financial institutions still had trouble meeting the demand for loans secured by real estate, and so did the notaries' own peer-to-peer lending, despite all their referrals. There were arbitrage opportunities, which notaries tried to seize, but they were obviously risky. Would letting competitors issue mortgage

[20] Hoffman, Postel-Vinay, and Rosenthal, *Dark Matter Credit*.

[21] Hoffman, Postel-Vinay, and Rosenthal, *Priceless Markets*.

bonds and compete with the CFF market have helped? Or would that have risked an even greater melt down and put the state's credit at risk?

Appendix

In addition to statistics collected from the *Compte général de l'administration de la justice civile et commerciale en France*, we gathered data from the dossiers the Ministry of Justice (*Ministère de la Justice*) assembled for each incoming and outgoing notary and for notaries who ran into trouble. As we explain in the text, the dossiers (in the series BB10 at the Archives Nationales in Paris) furnish valuable information (which is increasingly detailed over time) concerning the notaries' training and origins, the prices and revenues of their *études*, and the problems notaries caused.

The records are filed by year and department, and this fact guided our sampling procedure. We selected nine French departments to reflect the greater density of *études* in southern France, the larger amount of business for urban notaries and the greater range over which notaries could operate if they were in towns with important courts (the department names here are those used in the years of our sample): Côtes-du-Nord, Dordogne, Gard, Seine, Seine-Inférieure, Seine-et-Marne, Seine-et-Oise, Somme, and Tarn.

For each of these departments, we sampled records at approximately 20-year intervals from the 1850s to the 1930s so that we could trace the notaries' rise and fall. Specifically, we read the records from 1851–1852, 1872–1873, 1891–1892, 1911–1912, 1927–1928 and 1932–1933. We read more records for the late 1920s and early 1930s to understand the impact of the 1930s depression. From the files we collected information about the entering notary (place of birth, places of training, legal education, military service, and family connection to outgoing notary). We also gathered information on the *étude* that was being transferred, and in particular on markets of its activity (total contracts, tax payments, and fees collected by the notary, and—when available—total debt contracts, and taxes and fees on those contracts). We also noted information on notaries' costs—in particular the cost of clerks—and on the transaction (price, how much was financed, for how long and at what interest rate). Finally, we collected information on the outgoing notary, in particular, the reason for the sale (Table 6).

Table 6 The sample by type of residence

Type of residence	*1850*	*1870*	*1890*	*1910*	*1920*	*1930*
Paris	3	13	9	7	6	21
Appellate court	1	3	2	3	-	3
Arrondissement	4	21	12	18	15	19
Canton	22	71	45	39	44	67
Village	18	65	45	43	43	41

Source See text

Archival Sources and Literature

Archives Nationales, Archives du ministère de la Justice: notaires (entry number BB10).

Baubeau, Patrice et al., 'Flight-to-Safety and the Credit Crunch: A New History of the Banking Crises in France During the Great Depression', in: *The Economic History Review* 74:1 (2020), 223–250.

Daumard, Adeline, *Les fortunes françaises au XIXe siècle* (Paris, 1973).

Descimon, Robert, 'Les auxiliaires de justice du Châtelet de Paris: aperçus sur l'économie du monde des offices ministériels (XVIe-XVIIIe siècle)', in: Claire Dolan (ed.) *Entre justice et justiciables: les auxiliaires de la justice du moyen âge au XXe siècle* (Laval, 2005), 301–326.

Hoffman, Philip T., Gilles Postel-Vinay, and Jean-Laurent Rosenthal, *Priceless Markets: The Political Economy of Credit in Paris, 1660–1870* (Chicago, 2000).

Hoffman, Philip T., Gilles Postel-Vinay, and Jean-Laurent Rosenthal, 'No Exit: Notarial Bankruptcies and the Evolution of Financial Intermediation in Nineteenth Century Paris', in: Stanley L. Engerman et al. (eds.), *Finance, Intermediaries, and Economic Development* (New York, 2003), 75–108.

Hoffman, Philip T., Gilles Postel-Vinay, and Jean-Laurent Rosenthal, 'Entry, Information, and Financial Development: A Century of Competition Between French Banks and Notaries', in: *Explorations in Economic History* 55:1 (2015), 39–57.

Hoffman, Philip T., Gilles Postel-Vinay, and Jean-Laurent Rosenthal, *Dark Matter Credit: The Development of Peer-to-Peer Lending and Banking in France* (Princeton, 2019).

Hours, Henri, 'Jean Tricou', in: *Revue du Lyonnais* 1 (1977), 25–33.

Lafaurie, Jean, 'Jean Tricou 1890-1977', in: *Revue numismatique* 18 (1976), 7–10.

Limon, Marie-Françoise, *Les notaires au Châtelet sous le règne de Louis XIV* (Toulouse, 1992).

Ministère de la Justice, *Compte général de l'administration de la justice civile et commerciale en France* (Paris, 1831–1935).

Monnet, Eric, Angelo Riva, and Stefano Ungaro, 'The Real Effects of Bank Runs. Evidence from the French Great Depression (1930–1931)', (CEPR working paper, 2021).

Piketty, Thomas and Gabriel Zucman, 'Capital is Back: Wealth-Income Ratios in Rich Countries 1700–2010', in: *The Quarterly Journal of Economics* 129:3 (2014), 1255–1310.

Financial Intermediation in Colonial Seventeenth- and Eighteenth-Century Buenos Aires: Credit, Trust, and Asymmetric Information

Martín Wasserman

1 Introduction

Much as they did in many European cities and economies, notaries were important financial intermediaries in Latin America before the creation of banks.[1] This chapter will introduce the reader to notaries in Buenos Aires throughout the seventeenth and eighteenth centuries, a period during which this small colonial port village at the edge of the Spanish empire developed into one of the most important thoroughfares in Latin America. The case of early Buenos Aires and its development

[1] Philip T. Hoffman, Gilles Postel-Vinay and Jean-Laurent Rosenthal, *Priceless Markets: The Political Economy of Credit in Paris. 1660–1870* (Chicago, 2000); Kathrin Burns, *Into the Archive: Writing and Power in Colonial Peru* (Durham, 2010); Tamar Herzog, *Mediación, archivos y ejercicio. Los escribanos de Quito (siglo XVII)* (Frankfurt am Main, 1996).

M. Wasserman (✉)
Universidad de Buenos Aires, Buenos Aires, Argentina

CONICET, Buenos Aires, Argentina

C. van Bochove and J. Levy (eds.), *Beyond Banks*, Palgrave Studies in the History of Finance,
https://doi.org/10.1007/978-3-031-75819-5_3

over two centuries gives us a perspective over the singular way notarial intermediation took place in colonial Spanish America.

Soon after the establishment of Buenos Aires in 1580, the Spanish Crown imposed restrictions on the commercial activities of this city. In 1594 the Peruvian traders of Lima objected forcefully to trade going through the rival port of Buenos Aires, so the King forbade the trade of slaves and merchandise through the Río de la Plata unless they were transported on ships dispatched from Seville by the *Casa de Contratación*. A few years later, 1602 the Spanish king granted a permit to Buenos Aires residents to export limited quantities of flour, beef jerky and tallow to Brazil and Guinea and to import a few things for local consumption on their own vessels—except silver exports and imports of slaves, which remained prohibited, as well as the re-export of imports to regional markets. In 1623, new constraints further restricted trade from Buenos Aires, limiting it to a few registered vessels and some special licenses to import a few slaves. Meanwhile, Buenos Aires' contact with regional markets was also limited by the establishment of a customs office in Córdoba (700 kilometers inland from Buenos Aires) in 1623 (transferred to Jujuy in 1695, which is 900 kilometers further north and 600 kilometers closer to Potosí). Toward 1674 a permit was granted so that every two years two 100-ton vessels could arrive in Buenos Aires, with fruits and clothes worth 100,000 *pesos* destined only for consumption in the provinces of Río de la Plata, Paraguay, and Tucumán, enabling their return with 200,000 *pesos* in silver and, the rest, in hides and fruits.[2]

The mercantile rivalries between merchants of Lima and those of Buenos Aires seemed to put the latter at a disadvantage. However, the proximity of the Portuguese territories (which were trying to expand the limits of Brazil over the River Plate territory controlled by Spain) and the constant threat of rival powers (such as England, France and the Netherlands seeking access to Spanish-American silver across the Río de la Plata) forced the Spanish crown to tacitly allow the development of trade in

[2] Raúl Molina, *Las primeras experiencias comerciales del Plata* (Buenos Aires, 1966); Rodolfo E. González Lebrero, *La pequeña aldea: Sociedad y economía en Buenos Aires (1580–1640)* (Buenos Aires, 2002), 50 and 157–158; Alice Canabrava, *O comércio português no Rio da Prata, 1580–1640* (San Pablo, 1944).

Buenos Aires in order to bolster it as a defensive bastion, despite laws that would suggest the opposite.[3]

Toward 1760, Buenos Aires began to consolidate itself as a receiving and redistributing center of fiscal resources coming primarily from the mines of Potosí (in Peru), funds that were meant to sustain a growing and complex defensive and military system. A culminating point in this process was in 1777, when the largest expedition sent from the Peninsula to its American dominions reached the Río de la Plata: more than ten thousand men led by Pedro de Cevallos arrived that year at Río de la Plata estuary to evict the Portuguese population from Colonia del Sacramento. In accordance with this, a Major Accounting Office was established in Buenos Aires around 1767, transformed into a Court of Accounts in 1780. The city became the head of a new viceroyalty in 1777 and the following year the Superintendency of Royal Finance was established, a prelude to the Royal Ordinance of Intendants promulgated in 1782, the first step in the spatial reorganization of the viceregal treasury.[4]

In this context, both the free internment decree of 1777 and the promulgation of the Royal Free Trade Decree of 1778 implied an expansion of the monopoly framework and an acceleration of port trade. From 1778 onward the Río de la Plata port complex was consolidated, and the rapidly expanding port trade increased the volume of the Buenos Aires market, and its population, among which was an ever-larger proportion of part-time residents and itinerant travelers, like carters, boatmen, or muleteers, all of whom would participate in the market and contribute to the persistence of informational asymmetries in it.[5]

[3] Roberto Levillier, *La Audiencia de Charcas. Correspondencia de presidentes y oidores, documentos del Archivo de Indias* III (Madrid, 1918–1922), 23.

[4] Ricardo Rees Jones, *El Superintendente Manuel Ignacio Fernández (1778–1783): Las reformas borbónicas en el Virreinato de Buenos Aires* (Buenos Aires, 1992), 203.

[5] Raúl Fradkin, 'Población y sociedad', in: Jorge Gelman (ed.), *Argentina. Crisis imperial e independencia* (Madrid, 2010), 193–242, there 195 and 199; Zacarías Moutoukias, 'El crecimiento en una economía colonial de Antiguo Régimen: reformismo y sector externo en el Río de la Plata (1760-1796)', in: *Arquivos do Centro Cultural Calouste Gulbenkian* 34 (1995), 771–813, there 771. On the itinerant population of Buenos Aires, see María Claudia Errecart, 'Comercio y comunicación en el Río de la Plata. La articulación de los mercados regionales en el período virreinal rioplatense. Los caminos, los transportes y los transportistas', in: *El Taller de la Historia* 11:11 (2019), 230–268, there 257. On the Río de la Plata port complex, see Fernando Alberto Jumar, *Le commerce atlantique au Río de la Plata, 1680–1778* (La Plata, 2000).

In the following sections I will explain how population size and movements generated financial needs and opportunities in Buenos Aires, and following that I will analyze how notaries matched demand and supply of credit in the area—and what institutional and legal structures provided them with the context in which to do this.

2 Demographics and Debt

Throughout the seventeenth and eighteenth centuries, in the absence of a locally established banking system, the need for credit in Buenos Aires led to a variety of instruments that reflected not only the different needs for credit, but also corresponded to a variety of legal constraints and circumstances. Among the written forms of contracts and credit agreements, Buenos Aires borrowers signed public deeds, certificates, vouchers, receipts, letters, drafts, account books, reports, and informal acknowledgments of debt that were formalized by being put on paper—a sundry list of texts that did not follow a specific form but conveyed an obligation and might eventually need to be recognized as legal before a competent authority. The *Cabildo* (town hall), composed by notable *vecinos* (neighbors) of the city, functioned as the local court of first instance, while the appeals had to be settled at the *Real Audiencia* (the court of last resort). Buenos Aires had its own town hall since its foundation, but the *Real Audiencia* was established in Charcas, some 1800 kilometers away from the Buenos Aires port, until the year of 1785 (when the Real Audiencia was established in Buenos Aires, after a short-lived attempt to install it in 1663).

There was an initial distinction between *public instruments* (certified by public authorities) and *private instruments* (that lacked that public certification). The difference was not only in regard to their preparation but also in regard to the different value the document had in court.[6] The variety of documents allow us to know the broad universe of instruments employed to assure financial obligations in early colonial Argentina.

[6] Juan de Hevia y Bolaños,*Primera y Segunda parte de la Curia Filipica*(Madrid, 1652), 59.

The analysis of a sample of 422 testaments granted in Buenos Aires throughout four key periods of the seventeenth century reveals the coexistence of many forms of debt in this corner of the Spanish empire.[7] These four time periods (a decade each) refer to historical inflection points in Buenos Aires society. In the first decade, authorizations were granted by the Crown to merchants living in Buenos Aires to trade with the Portuguese in Brazil, and the Andalusia-Buenos Aires sea route was established, by means of registered ships, as the only legal commercial channel (1618–1622). The second decade under analysis corresponds to the rupture of the Iberian Union and the separation of the crowns of Castile and Portugal (1640) that unleashed a crisis in the Buenos Aires port trade, followed by an attempt to expel the Portuguese from Buenos Aires (1643). During the third period the Royal Audience of Buenos Aires was created and commercial restrictions by the Crown (1661–1663) were renewed. The fourth period overlaps with the creation of Colonia do Sacramento and the subsequent initial development of the Río de la Plata port complex (1680–1683).

The exploration of testaments during these periods (a deeper analysis of which exceeds the topic of this chapter) reveals the characteristics, dynamics, and significance of credit instruments in the emerging port of Buenos Aires. Oral agreements coexisted with private instruments such as vouchers, drafts, certificates, account books, memoirs, letters, and with very occasionally public instruments, which were mainly notarized deeds (see Appendix 1). The testaments show that most of the instruments used to record a debt in the early colonial period were private instruments. They also show that public instruments were used when the operation involved higher amounts. Large loans used to be formalized through public instruments such as notarial obligations, which could be brought before the higher courts to quickly support a creditor's appeal. Small loans were formalized through private instruments such as drafts or merchants account books, which were sufficient to register the debt even if they were

[7] See Martín Wasserman, Las obligaciones fundamentales. Crédito y consolidación económica *durante el surgimiento de Buenos Aires* (Buenos Aires, 2018). These testaments, kept in the notarial archive, belong to men (61%) and women (39%) who granted their last wills in Buenos Aires during four critical periods: 1619–1628 (59 testaments), 1635–1644 (117), 1656–1665 (107) and 1676–1685 (139). The socially privileged social groups of Spanish and American born Spaniards and Portuguese are in much greater proportion than indigenous people (*indios*), and other *mestizo groups*.

less likely to be usable in a higher court.[8] The amounts involved were, as it seems, a variable in the decision to involve a notary in the transaction or not.[9]

The systemic shortage of fractional money forced local businesses, especially grocery stores, to open current accounts with their clients, to whom they sold on credit until the accumulation of sums that allowed them to settle the debt in available denominations. The settlement usually happened in one of two ways: (1) the debt was repaid in cash, or (2) more commonly the debt was repaid through a delivery of tradable goods in the store (such as wheat, fruits, *yerba mate*, wine, tobacco, fabrics, furniture, clothes, tools) that the merchant could sell to cover the debts. This sort of consignment allowed small daily purchases at a local shop, where small debts were formalized through vouchers or an open tab of current accounts or even oral commitment. This was possible to the extent that both the customers, grocers, and storekeepers participated in the same local community and shared a social context in which the reputational sanctions in case of default were mutually understood. These sanctions ranged from being barred from the shop (and therefore barred from buying basic goods), or at worst being driven from the city. *Pulperos* (grocers) and *tenderos* (storekeepers) were in this sense, credit providers in the local marketplace. The private debts that were declared in testaments mainly correspond to this kind of small debts incurred in daily life.[10]

While small, the port of Buenos Aires was a significant point of connection between the Atlantic and the regional inland markets. Trading

[8] As Hevia y Bolaños explained, when the amount disputed in a lawsuit did not exceed 60,000 *maravedíes* (221 silver *pesos* of eight *reales* each), the first verdict was appealable before the *Cabildo* (the town hall). If the sum exceeded that limit, the verdict was appealable before the *Real Audiencia* (the court of last resort). In other words, the greater the amounts involved, the greater possibility of appeals before the higher courts. Hevia y Bolaños, *Primera*, 194.

[9] In fact, 76% of the loans declared in wills involved amounts under 221 pesos, and were mainly formalized by means of private instruments, while just 42% of the loans declared involved amounts above that sum, and were mainly formalized by means of public instruments. Statistical testing carried out shows a statistically significant difference between the two sorts of data. See Wasserman, *Las obligaciones*, p. 299.

[10] Regarding the persistence of such credit activities in the region see Andrea Lluch, 'The Art of Lending in the Pampas: Commercial Credit and Financial Intermediation in Argentina, 1900–1930', in: Bernardo Bátiz-Lazo and Leonidas Efthymiou (eds.), *The Book of Payments: Historical and Contemporary Views on the Cashless Society* (London, 2016), 55–64.

companies operated with the help of local merchants and local authorities, and Buenos Aires became a port through which cargoes of enslaved people, silver, hides, and other regional merchandise crisscrossed the Atlantic. These imports and exports were mostly illegal because of the restrictions on interregional trade imposed by the Spanish Crown (more on this in the following section)—but the personal networks managed to side-step these constraints.

The silver mines of Potosí (in the viceroyalty of Perú, in current-day Bolivia) generated enormous demands for labor and transportation—the silver was shipped by mule train north to Panama City, and via the Río de la Plata to Buenos Aires. These trading routes fostered the creation of intricate credit distribution networks among the many informal workers, traders, and porters that supported the trade. Among them were itinerant merchants who traveled between Potosí and Buenos Aires, with their carts and mules, selling merchandise, and slaves to bring the proceeds back to Buenos Aires (mainly silver, exported then to the Atlantic in payment for imports). Much of this trade was handled with credit, and in the absence of the trust that can exist between people who might know each other, these credit commitments were formalized through public instruments and the enforcement they guaranteed. The demographic dynamics of Buenos Aires, and the legal restrictions that framed trade there reinforced the necessity of a debt instrument that included enforceability through legal process.

The diverse origins of the population of Buenos Aires at the beginning of the seventeenth century contributed to the variety of debt instruments found in circulation. During its first century of existence, Buenos Aires experienced a continuous influx of seafarers, merchants from the interior or overseas, carters, soldiers, free passengers, and slaves in transit from Western Africa to other parts of the Americas. The itinerant population in Buenos Aires outnumbered the settlers for a significant part of the century.

In 1611, the settled population of Buenos Aires numbered 2,200, while more than 9,500 individuals are estimated to have passed through during the five-year period 1611–1615. By 1622 (after a smallpox epidemic in 1621), some 2,400 people had settled in Buenos Aires, and during the five-year period of 1621–1625, 8,850 passed through. In 1633 there were 3,300 settled people, and 4,300 individuals passed through Buenos Aires during the five-year period of 1631 and 1635. The interruption of sea trade caused by conflicts in December 1640 between

Spain and Portugal temporarily reduced the influx of people in the port during the first half of the 1640s. Meanwhile, an epidemic that began in 1651 was felt on population numbers until at least 1653, reducing mainly the population of enslaved people and indigenous people, that decreased by a third. The arrival of Dutch ships in the mid-1650s reversed the trend, as travelers/temporary residents returned. The settler population was recomposed by the beginning of the 1660s. Toward the end of the seventeenth century, a stable population of approximately 7,000 people lived in Buenos Aires, and visitors continued to pass through, even after ships were redirected to the eastern side of the river toward the 1680s.[11]

3 Contraband and Notaries

The constant influx of newcomers to the small town embedded information asymmetries in their relationships—since it was not always obvious how to have reliable information about them, but demographics aside, the most significant aspect of this trading port and its debt universe is that most of the interregional trade that flowed through it was actually illegal.[12]

Buenos Aires was an urban frontier characterized by a constant migratory flow, which not only gave rise to a mobile and fluid society but to an environment in which the risks derived from asymmetric information were combined with the risks inherent to the illegality of a large part of the transactions.[13] The result was the coexistence of different devices to structure financial commitments, according to different legal, social, and cultural norms and needs.

Buenos Aires was a late arrival to main colonial trade routes (the routes of the *Carrera de Indias*) which left it narrow channels for operations that were legally permitted by the Spanish crown. The growth of Buenos Aires far outran the lifting of any of these constraints, which created an environment rife with contraband. Faced with this, a royal decree in 1618 provided that in the case of seized contraband, one-third of the seized merchandise was to be granted to whomever denounced the crime.

[11] Wasserman, *Las obligaciones*, 57.

[12] Wasserman, *Las obligaciones*, 34–41.

[13] On the mobility of the population of Buenos Aires, Emir Reitano, *Los portugueses del Buenos Aires tardocolonial: Inmigración, sociedad, familia, vida cotidiana y religión* (dissertation, La Plata, 2003), 54.

Considering the possibility of debt contracts arising from illegal deals, the decree created a powerful moral hazard problem: the decree could be an incentive to accuse a lender of contraband in order to avoid repaying, and similarly, it could become a graft mechanism for lenders.[14]

The documents produced by the notary were key to a judicial claim, and trust imbued in the notarial public faith endowed the document with enforceability in the case of litigation, as well as legality in any context. Private instruments on the other hand had to be recognized by witnesses in a trial to acquire the same force.[15] Lenders on private instruments avoided the notarial fee cost, but they also assumed potentially higher execution costs in case of default or conflict. In other words, notarial deeds became necessary when lender and borrower did not share a common social context, and if the trade itself was illegal. The notarial deed made it possible to transact with strangers, because trust was embedded in the deed.

The use of private instruments or oral commitment may have been useful when parties could settle potential conflicts within organizations or institutions not legally regulated by the king's law. Public instruments, private instruments, and oral commitments not only differed in terms of the nature of their origin and the amounts involved, but also in terms of their enforceability in a civil or executive trial. Notarial deeds were used not only to safeguard debts that involved high amounts, but also when the operation was generated between borrowers and lenders whose potential conflicts would have to be settled within the framework of judicial institutions. The rules that regulated the relationship between lender and borrower (as expressed in the instrument used) were an indicator of their relationship and the context in which they unfolded.

In sum, the brokerage role of the notary in the interregional commerce of early Buenos Aires proved to be fundamental to that commerce.

[14] The notaries of Buenos Aires could for their part legalize the loan commitments arising from illegal trade by recording them as pecuniary obligations. When illegally imported slaves or merchandise were delivered on credit for regional redistribution, the borrower offered his lender a notarial deed of *obligación* (an IOU) in which only the monetary value of that illegal asset was described. In this way, the commercial transaction figured in the contract as a monetary loan, erasing the illegal object of credit. This became a very simple way to launder the transaction and to reduce moral hazard. Wasserman, *Las obligaciones*, 187–194.

[15] Hevia y Bolaños, *Primera*, 65.

Notaries provided formal cover to commitments arising from illegal transactions, and they provided contractual instruments to resolve disagreements in court.

4 Kinship, Trust, and Notaries

What kind of interpersonal relationships relied on notarial deeds to formalize their credit obligations? A possible answer can be found in the notarial *obligaciones* (IOUs) that were recorded during the seventeenth century in the Public Notary Office of the Town Hall of Buenos Aires (the only notarial registry office that functioned in the city throughout that century).[16] The analysis of a sample of the 942 debts recorded in Buenos Aires throughout that period show how they were used to secure the loans arising from transactions involved in the small-scale redistribution of merchandise and slaves from the Atlantic trade. A small majority of the amounts mobilized by these contracts exceeded 500 silver *pesos* (55.3% of the deeds), followed closely by those between 100 and 500 *pesos* (39.5% of the contracts). It is worth noting that this is roughly equivalent to the average price of a slave in Buenos Aires: 212 *pesos* at the beginning of the seventeenth century, 300–400 *pesos* in the middle of the century, and 500 *pesos* at the end of the century.[17]

Almost half (49.5%) the notarial obligation contracts had terms of six months to one year (and 31%, from one month to six months) which was an adequate amount of time for the journey between Buenos Aires and Potosí—the round trip could take between eight months and a year; or to Mendoza—which was six months round trip. 20.2% of the obligation

[16] The *obligación de pago* (payment obligation) committed the borrower to reimburse the lender within a specified period, at a specific place, in explicit specie. While the lender delivered an asset of a certain value, the borrower committed to repaying that value in specie, and thereby formalizing and legalizing a debt for a transaction that may not have been exactly legal. Ivonne Mijares Ramírez, *Escribanos y escrituras públicas en el siglo XVI: El caso de la Ciudad de México* (Mexico City, 1997), 165.

[17] Miguel Ángel Rosal, 'El comercio de esclavos en la ciudad de Buenos Aires a principios delsiglo XVII', in: *Anuario del Centro de Estudios Históricos "Prof. Carlos S. A. Segreti"* 10 (2010), 93–113; Miguel Á. Rosal, 'Modalidades del comercio de esclavos en Buenos Aires durante la tercera década del siglo XVII', in: Revista Digital Estudios Históricos 3:7 (2011), 1–17; Rolando Mellafe, *Breve historia de la esclavitud negra en América Latina* (Mexico City, 1973); Wasserman, *Las obligaciones*, 66.

contracts had mortgage collateral which in colonial Argentina was constituted by slaves, landed estates, rural machinery, and livestock. 46% of the deeds offered slaves as mortgage, making the illegal object of the loan appear in the form of collateral in the contract. Consequently, almost 80% of the IOUs used the default term for general personal mortgage, namely "present and future assets" belonging to the borrower, without the designation of a specific asset to guarantee the commitment.[18]

Only seven operations (0.7%) in the sample denote a primary kinship link between borrowers and lenders. Kinship here was defined as siblings, nephews, grandchildren, putative parents, as well as male in-laws by marriage. The information from the notarial archive is complemented by that of the parish archive. In colonial Latin America, Christian sacramental instances forged parental bonds, such as marriage and baptism that had similar or greater binding force than the laws of the king and the royal justice. The *compadrazgo* (the relationship between parent and god-parent) implied the public formalization, *in facie communitatis*, of a connection established under divine scrutiny. To the extent that the breaking of the rules belonging to that connection would provoke the wrath of God, this legitimized the social sanctions and the economic damages derived from mistrust and loss of reputation in case of non-compliance.[19]

Sacramental kinship is perhaps one of the better expressions of personal relations belonging to a close social circle, in which its members (godfathers, godmothers, godchildren, goddaughters, and witnesses) interact in a way that regulates and reinforces the mutual commitments through reputational sanctions. The construction of these close links, built and reinforced trust.[20] To what extent did the interpersonal connection overlap in both the sacramental kinship and the notarial formalization of credit obligations? In other words, how often was an interpersonal relationship regulated both by the legal order of notarial deeds, and by the

[18] Wasserman, *Las obligaciones*, 167–187.

[19] Guido Alfani, 'Reformation, "Counter-reformation" and Economic Development from the Point of View of Godparenthood: An Anomaly? (Italy and Europe, 14th–19th Centuries)', in: Francesco Ammannati (ed.), *Religione e istituzioni religiose nell'economia europea. 1000–1800* (Florence, 2012), 477–490, there 482–483.

[20] See Darío Barriera and Griselda Tarragó, 'Elogio de la incertidumbre. La construcción de la confianza: entre la previsión y el desamparo (Santa Fe, Gobernación del Río de la Plata, siglo XVIII)', in: *Revista Historia* 48:1 (2003), 183–223, there 193.

sacramental regulatory framework? The marriages and baptisms recorded in the parish books make it possible to observe the ritual kinship ties established by such notarial lenders.

Taking into account a group of lenders in the notarial contracts that lent the most often (a segment of lenders in the sample, made up of twenty-three people), their participation in the sacramental construction of parental relationships may be indicative of the relational place of the notarial obligations. Only three of these 23 lenders (13%) had a sacramentally consecrated bond with a borrower from whom they also requested a legalized commitment through notarial obligation. This is consistent, as shown in Fig. 1, with the fact that those who had an extensive social capital, expressed as a large list of sacramental relatives, tended to resort less to public instruments to secure their commitments. Figure 1 shows a list of the main lenders, including for each one the number of their debtors and the number of sacramental relatives: it seems that the smaller the social circle (expressed in the number of sacramental relatives), the bigger the use of notarial formalization of the loans.

In contrast, while only 13% of the main lenders notarized credit commitments with relatives or members of close social circles, 41.7% of notaries were related in some way to their clients.[21] The notaries were thus more involved interpersonally with the contractual parties than the lenders were with their borrowers. This suggests that the lenders tended to place their trust in the notary rather than in the borrower, which allowed the lender to resort to the notary public as a mediator for the placement of his resources on credit.

One case shows it clearly. On October 10, 1637, Antonio Nuñez, a Portuguese trader from Lisbon and temporary resident of Buenos Aires, signed an *obligación* to reimburse the sum of 405 silver *pesos* to General Juan de Tapia de Vargas (one of the most important merchants and slaveholders of the period and also one of the main lenders in the notarial office). However, that same day the public notary himself, Pablo Nuñez de Victoria, incorporated an endorsement on the document which read: "*This day General Juan de Tapia de Vargas appeared before me and, seeing this scripture read to him, he said that it was not done properly, nor does Antonio Nuñez owe him anything. And he considers this deed*

[21] Martín L.E. Wasserman, 'La mediación notarial en la interacción económica: confianza, información y conexiones en la temprana Buenos Aires', in: *Prohistoria* 24:1 (2015), 69–100.

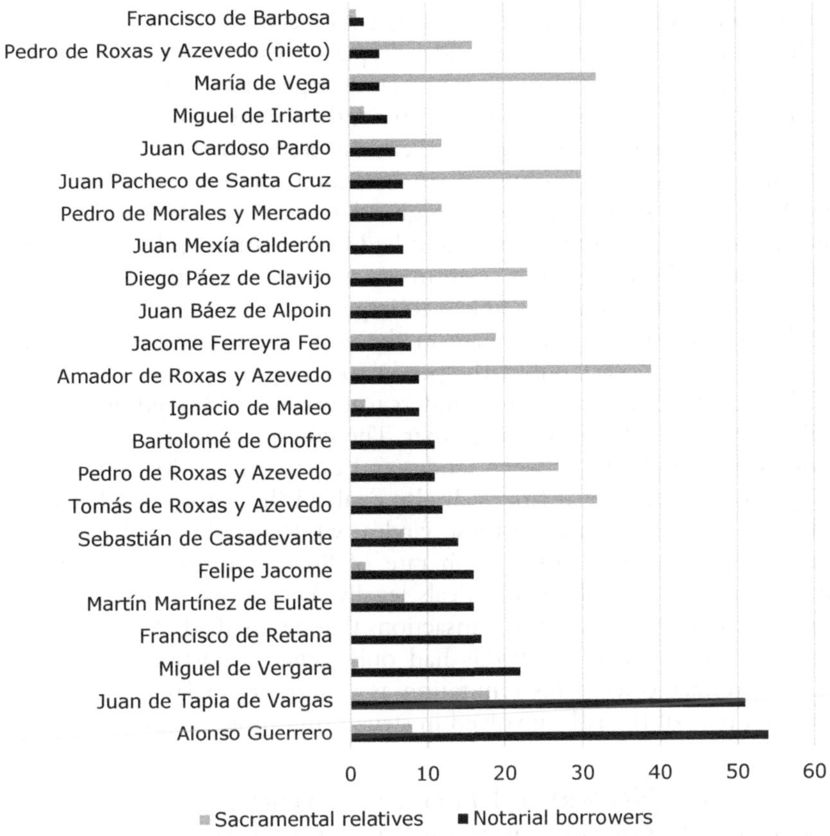

Fig. 1 Main lenders, their borrowers and their sacramental relatives (Buenos Aires, seventeenth century) (*Source* National General Archive of the Nation of Argentina (hereinafter, AGN), Sala IX (hereinafter, IX), Escribanías Antiguas (hereinafter, EA), Volume IX, X, XI, XII, XIII, XIV, XV, XXI, XXII, XXIII, XXIV, XXV, XXVI, XXVII, XXXI, XXXIII, XXXIV, XXXV, XXXVI, XXXVII, XLII, XLIII, XLIV, XLV, XLVI, XLVII; Baptisms and Marriages Book of the Parish Archive of Nuestra Señora de La Merced, Buenos Aires; Raúl Molina, *Matrimonios, Bautismos y Defunciones de la Catedral de Buenos Aires, 1601–1644. Y Legajos I y II de expedientes matrimoniales del archivo del Arzobispado de Buenos Aires* (Buenos Aires, 2002))

broken, canceled."[22] The notary canceled the deed at the request of the lender. This shows us how the lender, Tapia de Vargas, delegated to the public notary the power to carry out credit operations on his behalf in accordance with certain elementary criteria, thus granting him the administration of his resources to place them on credit to those who could present themselves requesting a loan or asking for the consignment of merchandise or slaves for sale in regional markets, as shown by other similar cases.[23] Once the commitment had been written up by the notary public, the lender would later confirm or (as happened in this case) reject the deal. In those operations linked to large-scale trade, in which lenders and borrowers did not participate in the same social circle, the lenders delegated to the notary public the power to set up the deal.

The notarial office connected lenders to borrowers who did not necessarily know each other or of each other. The notarial contract was a useful device when the bond between lender and borrower was located on the margins of primary social circles. It also enabled the connection between unknown actors, external to these circles, which would not have been uncommon in a port with a high rate of fluctuating population. The notary not only formalized the deals legally: he also exercised an active role in the construction of the transactions that he certified. As mentioned above, almost 80% of the IOUs had only general mortgage as collateral: the notary offered his reputation as a warranty of last resort, thus assuming part of the risks involved in structuring those commitments.

5 Notarial Records, Information, and the Transfer of Trust in a Growing Economy

The granting of the power to record credit transactions rested, largely on the quality of the information available to the notary. The archive of the notary's office contained an invaluable collection of information on the assets and businesses of his clients, including a partial credit history.[24] The importance of this information is revealed in early concerns about

[22] AGN, IX, EA, Volume 23, ff. 570r-571r.

[23] Wasserman, *Las obligaciones*, 257.

[24] On the challenges imposed by the asymmetric distribution of information in financial markets of the Ancien Régime, see Hoffman, Postel-Vinay, and Rosenthal, *Priceless Markets*, 114.

the access to this information and in disputes over its control. In 1619, when the Public Notary Office of the Town Hall of Buenos Aires was the only notarial registry office in the city (a situation that would only change at the beginning of the eighteenth century), there were already concerns about control over the notary's archives. That year, the *alcalde mayor* (the judicial head of the city) Sebastián de Orduña observed that "the notary has his office in a room in his house," but since the offices "of the houses of City Hall where the notary used to work" were unoccupied, he suggested that the notary move there "for the best comfort and expedience of business."[25] Nothing came of this and the notarial office and his archive remained under his personal control.[26]

Attempts to remove the notarial archive from the notary's personal orbit would become a recurring topic over time. When the notary Pablo Núñez Victoria left Buenos Aires in 1634 to perform functions on an official visit of the Royal Audience of Charcas (north of Buenos Aires in what is now Bolivia), the authorities were concerned about the notarial documentation, which had been left in the care of the notary's son, Juan Vicente de Victoria. The authorities warned that there was a risk of losing the documentation "because the house of said Pablo Nuñez caught fire, where said papers are."[27] Indeed, still on September 2, 1639, the authorities of the Buenos Aires Town Hall asked that "the boxes from the archive should be taken to the Town Hall offices and put under three keys as is customary."[28] Information mattered. Its materialization in an archive not only unleashed disputes around its control, but also showed the importance of having access to its content. The key was the notary.

Meanwhile, the demographic growth of Buenos Aires during the eighteenth century would reinforce the importance of that information and access to it. The estimated total population of Buenos Aires had reached 11,600 inhabitants in 1744, and by 1778 the city had a population of just over 26,000 stable inhabitants (to which some 11,000 inhabitants would

[25] Acuerdos del Extinguido Cabildo de Buenos Aires (hereafter, AECBA), Volume IV, Book III, 145–146, January 21, 1619.

[26] Similar cases can be seen in Amelia García Medina and Reyes Rojas García, 'El poder de la memoria y la memoria del poder', in: Antonio Jiménez Estrella and Julián José Lozano Navarro (eds.), *Actas de la XI Reunión Científica de la Fundación Española de Historia Moderna* I (Granada, 2012), 308–318; Herzog, *Mediación,* 18.

[27] AECBA, Volume IX, Book VI, 334.

[28] AECBA, Volume VIII, Book V, 431.

have to be added in the countryside).[29] In the expansion process that took shape during the eighteenth century, the years between 1766 and 1784 were crucial for Buenos Aires. In this period the city experienced not only the acceleration of the growth in its commercial economy, but it also witnessed the imperial institutional formulations that centered the economy of Buenos Aires in the Río de la Plata.

This growth also translated into a boom of institutional devices that structured the city. Gradually, by the middle of the century, Buenos Aires acquired a total of six notarial offices.[30] During those years, the three most active notaries' offices in the city were Registry 3 (run by Francisco Javier Conget), Registry 5 (run by Eufrasio Boyso and his son, Tomás Boyso), and Registry 6 (run by José García de Echaburu).[31]

Figure 2 suggests that notarial *obligaciones de pago* were correlated to the port trade (just as those public instruments did during the previous century).

Not all notarial offices participated equally, though as the three notary offices show: Registry 3 certified 26.7% of the *obligaciones* notarized by the three notaries during those years; Registry 5 certified 31.7%; and Registry 6 notarized 41.6%. This uneven performance, which favored Registry 6 by García de Echaburu, may say something more about the role of notaries.

[29] Fradkin, *Población y sociedad*, 195 and 199; Moutoukias, 'El crecimiento en una economía colonial', 771.

[30] The second notarial registry in Buenos Aires opened around 1707. The first records of Registry 3 appear in 1716, and Registers 4 and 5 began to function in 1748. Registry 6 opened in 1754. It was not until 1788 that Registry 7 opened, the year in which the notaries of Buenos Aires joined as a collegiate body through the founding of the Brotherhood of San Ginés. Martín Wasserman, 'Escribanos y escrituras en Hispanoamérica', in: Rosana Vassallo (ed.), *Introducción a la Paleografía. Herramientas para la lectura y análisis de documentos antiguos* (La Plata, 2019), 173–198.

[31] For the initial analysis, a sample is built based on the *alphabet* (or indexes), of the books of notarial protocols existing in AGN, Escribanías de Registro (henceforth ER), Protocolos de Escribanos (henceforth PE), on those years in which the protocols of the three notaries' offices are preserved: 1766, 1769, 1771, 1773, 1775, 1777, 1779, 1780 and 1781. In this way, the sample on which the present analysis is carried out is made up of the existing alphabet books in the 27 protocols signed by the three notaries' offices with the most dynamic performance. See Martín Wasserman et al., 'La conexión en el Registro. Una aproximación primaria a las características básicas de la operatoria en las Escribanías de Registro de Buenos Aires durante el siglo XVIII (1760–1780)', in: *Illes i imperis* 22:1 (2020), 199–230.

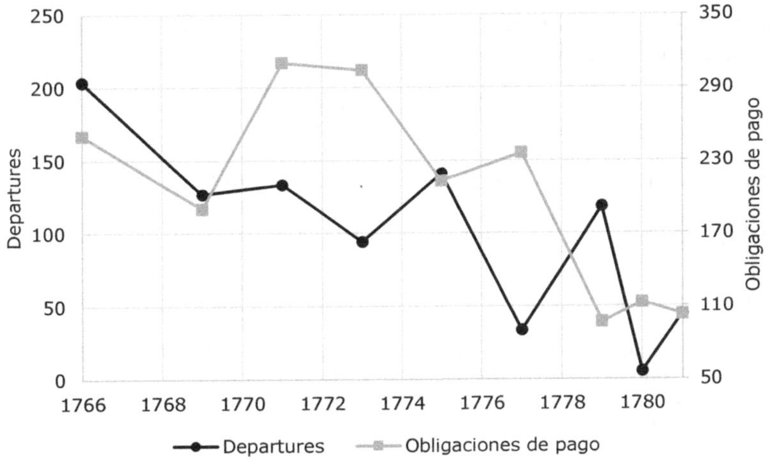

Fig. 2 Correlation between the registered nominal value of departures from the port of Buenos Aires and notarized obligaciones de pago for the following period (*Source* AGN, ER, PE, Registries 3, 5 & 6, years 1766, 1769, 1771, 1773, 1775, 1777, 1779, 1780 & 1781; Juan Carlos Garavaglia, *El comercio virreinal 1779–1784* (Buenos Aires, 1970), 73; Jumar, *Le commerce*, 671)

As in the seventeenth century, during this period the link between clients and notaries was more solid than the link between clients. This can be verified through the low frequency of contracting between the same parties compared to a higher frequency of connections between a party and a notary. While 32% of lenders and 31% of borrowers went to the same notary public on more than one occasion, only 6.76% of the interactions were more than once between the same parties. This data suggests that as in the seventeenth century, the business opportunities arose largely because the notary connected potential business partners.

In turn, the link between the notary and the lender was the most frequent, which suggests that this was the link that determined the existence of the contract (Table 1). In this sense, 32.7% of the lenders did so repeatedly and generated 79.56% of the deeds (accordingly, 67.27% of the lenders only did so once, and this majority of infrequent lenders

Table 1 Participation of frequent lenders and borrowers in IOUs. Buenos Aires, eighteenth century (selected years)

Role	*Frequent Clients****	*% Clients*	*Deeds*	*% Deeds*	*Deeds per frequent client*
Lenders (544)*	178	32.7	1,425	79.5	8
Borrowers (1,017)**	324	31.8	1,111	61.5	3.4

Source AGN, ER, PE, Registries 3, 5 & 6, years 1766, 1769, 1771, 1773, 1775, 1777, 1779, 1780 & 1781

Note (*) The total number of lenders identified is 544, out of a total of 1791 deeds. (**) The total number of borrowers identified is 1017, out of a total of 1804 deeds. (***) In this Table, the clients who appear more than once in any of the notarial offices analyzed throughout the selected years are considered frequent

mobilized the production of only 20.43% of the deeds).[32] Meanwhile, frequent borrowers accounted for 61.58% of the credit contracts.

The notary's income consisted formally of the collection of fees set at four silver *reales* per notarized sheet, an increase in certified businesses had a direct proportional impact on his profitability.[33] A notary's frequent lenders were the largest source of income from credit contracts, and the loyalty of his lenders was directly related to his profitability. Interest rates did not play a role here insofar as in Ancien Régime catholic economies interest rates were regulated within precise limits.[34] Since the end of the twelfth century, the canonical regime of usury declared the collection of interest illegitimate when it was a profit exclusively obtained from the market or finance, and not as a reward, salary compensation or price.[35] The collection of interest was only lawful by appealing to "extrinsic titles," such as loss of earnings (*lucro cesante*), consequential damage (*daños emergentes*), danger or risk involved in the operation, remuneration for

[32] Martín L.E. Wasserman, 'El escribano y la mano visible. Intermediación financiera y crédito en un contexto de información asimétrica (Buenos Aires, siglo XVIII)', in: *Revista de Historia Americana y Argentina* 56:1 (2021), 19–62.

[33] Legally, the notary could charge for deposits nor for their intermediation. Gabriel de Monterroso y Alvarado, *Practica civil, y criminal, y instrucion de escrivanos* (Valladolid, 1626 [1563]), 234v.

[34] Wasserman, *Las obligaciones*, 195.

[35] Tomás de Mercado, *Suma de tratos y contratos* (Alicante, 2002 [1570]), 47–48.

work, or loss of resulting profit (*lucro adveniente*).[36] Although from the middle of the seventeenth century various jurisconsults and canonical authors began to account for usury,[37] and in the eighteenth century they barely adjusted them, preserving the concept in its foundations.[38] For this reason alone, notaries would not use interest rates to attract clients—they had little room to adjust rates. Instead of it, they used their informational advantages.[39]

The management of information was key to the notary's ability to attract and retain customers, and some offices were better at it than others. Registry 6 belonging to the notary García de Echaburu not only had a greater number of certified borrowers as a result of a higher volume of certified deeds, but also a high proportion of frequent borrowers—that is, those who resorted to the same notary's office on more than one occasion over one year to get credit. 21.29% of its borrowers were frequent, while in Registers 5 and 3 only 19.48% and 9.02%, respectively, of its borrowers were repeaters (see Fig. 3). In other words, the registry that

36 María del Pilar Martínez López-Cano, *La génesis del crédito colonial. Ciudad de México, siglo XVI* (Mexico City, 2001), 29; Hevia y Bolaños, *Primera*, 87–88, explained that the interest charges covered by said titles would be legitimate to the extent that "it does not exceed a rate of 10% per year, according to a Recopilación law." Since the seventeenth century in Buenos Aires fees were "at the rate of 10% as is customary", as it is usual "between merchants." See AGN, IX, EA, Volume 26, ff. 262r–263v and 697v–701r.

37 Antonio Miguel Bernal, *La financiación de la Carrera de Indias. Dinero y crédito en el comercio colonial español con América* (Sevilla, 1992), 282.

38 Francisco Manuel de Herrera, *Reglas del comercio lícito, libre del contagio de la usura* (Madrid, 1735), 146–147, 152–153, explained that rates of 12% should not be considered usury, and that in commerce it was acceptable and legitimate to "carry ten percent" based on use, custom and the "Law of these Kingdoms", such as Hevia y Bolaños had already pointed it out.

39 In this sense, the assumption according to which prices represent the priority variable in the creation of incentives is, rather, a theoretical construct that is not always factually validated. As Stiglitz and Weiss have pointed out, empirical analysis of contemporary credit markets continues to suggest that the incentives provided by managing the risks derived from imperfect information take precedence over the incentives generated by the interest rate. See Joseph E. Stiglitz and Andrew Weiss, 'Credit Rationing in Markets with Imperfect Information', in: *The American Economic Review* 71:3 (1981), 393–410. On the role of notarial information in mortgage market in Mexico during the nineteenth century, see Juliette Levy, 'Notaries and Credit Markets in Nineteenth-Century Mexico', in: *Business History Review* 84:3 (2010), 459–478, there 467.

reported the greatest number of borrowers was, in turn, the one that most intensively placed credit among its own clients.

This greater volume of borrowers in García de Echaburu office expanded the reach of his connections. It also created a credit history for each of these borrowers, which provided lenders with an environment of attenuated risks. The notarial archive contained the borrower's credit history, and this information made this particular notary's connections more trustworthy. Considering the known traditional practice from the seventeenth century in Buenos Aires, where creditors asked notaries to match them with cosignatories that took merchandise on credit to sell it in regional markets, or borrowers looking for lenders, the allocation of credit between frequent borrowers suggests that this practice continued during the eighteenth century, translating trust into lender loyalty and therefore into a growing intermediation business.

In fact, the proportion of IOUs generated by frequent lenders was also higher in Registry 6 than in the other two registries: while in said notary's office that ratio was 2.87 deeds per frequent lender, in Registers 5 and 3

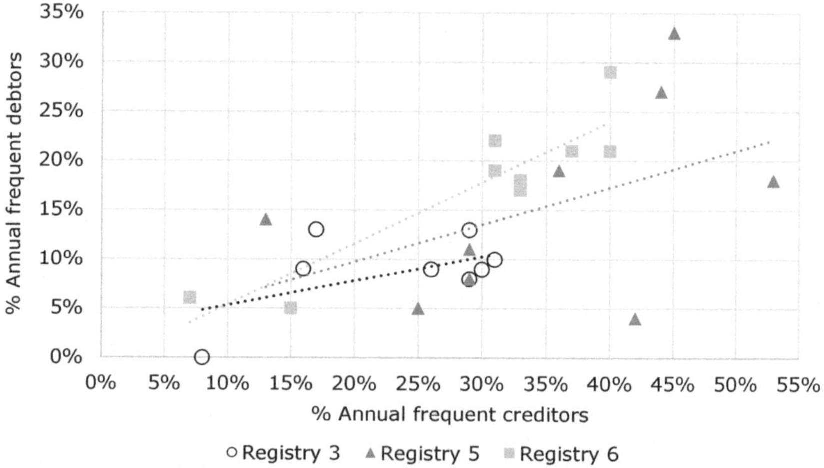

Fig. 3 Correlation between frequent creditors and debtors. Registries 3, 5 and 6 (*Source* AGN, ER, PE, Registries 3, 5 & 6, years 1766, 1769, 1771, 1773, 1775, 1777, 1779, 1780 & 1781; *Note*: Frequent lenders or borrowers are defined as those who have attended the same notary's office on more than one occasion within the same year)

it was 2.47 and 2.79 respectively. García de Echaburu's frequent lenders accounted for a good part of his profitability. This lender loyalty is more evident in the behavior of the few clients who only frequented a single notary's office: while in Registry 6, 27% of lenders were exclusive clients of García de Echaburu, this proportion drops to 17% and 16% in Registers 5 and 3 respectively (see Fig. 3).

Meanwhile, and as can be seen in Fig. 3, the notary mobilized his own clients to generate new loans between them. Register 6 shows a higher positive correlation between frequent borrowers and lenders than that of the other notaries, showing a deliberate strategy to connect frequent lenders with those borrowers for which the archive had a credit history: while Registry 3 shows a correlation coefficient of $R^2 = 0.29$ between frequent creditors and frequent debtors, Registry 5 shows a coefficient $R^2 = 0.22$. But Registry 6 shows an overwhelmingly higher correlation between frequent borrowers and frequent creditors $R^2 = 0.84$.

García de Echaburu, in charge of Registry 6, not only had the largest office, and therefore the largest number of lenders and borrowers: he was, as well, the notary that more intensively used his frequent borrowers to allocate credit from his clients. Allocating credit among its own clientele guaranteed the creditors less informational asymmetry, due to the better known borrowers. This informational mechanism of lowering risk could, in turn, feed his business. This element confirms not only the importance of the information but also the active role of the notary as an intermediary in the allocation of credit in Buenos Aires.

6 Conclusions

Notaries in early colonial Buenos Aires became intermediaries in a quickly developing economy whose growth relied on long-distance trading along the route between Buenos Aires and the silver mines 1,000 miles up the Río de la Plata. Their role in recording debt contracts was one of the ways in which the flow of credit expanded beyond close kinship circles, broadening the scope of potential business. Notaries managed privileged information, and conferred legal enforceability to the obligations that were forged beyond close kindship networks.

Notaries were insiders to the lenders close relational networks, and offered them the instruments needed to risk their capital outside of their social circle, thereby connecting lenders to borrowers who were otherwise not known to or inherently trusted by each other. The contracts that notaries wrote and signed became the legal tools that enforced debt repayment beyond close social networks, even when those financial relations were illegal. This bridge between illegal transactions and legal enforceability was built by notaries in Buenos Aires. Beyond this, like notaries elsewhere, Buenos Aires notaries used the deep well of information in their records to match lenders and borrowers, expanding credit networks beyond social networks. By the time the first bank opened in Buenos Aires in 1822, the notaries had spent the last 100 years contributing to the creation of a complex infrastructure for the financing of trade in the port city.

Appendix I

See Table 2.

Table 2 Credit declared in testaments and instruments employed. Buenos Aires, seventeenth century (selected periods)

Instrument	*Number of declarations*			*Amounts mobilized*			
	Number	*% Subtotal*	*% Total*	*Amount*	*% Subtotal*	*% Total*	*Mean Value*
Public instruments	*190*	*27.3%*	*9.4%*	*196,360.6*	*59.1%*	*27.5%*	*1,033.4*
Notarial deed	173	24.8%	8.6%	169,854.0	51.1%	23.8%	981.8
Authentic instrument	17	2.4%	0.8%	26,506.6	7.9%	3.7%	1,559.2
Private instruments	*458*	*65.9%*	*22.8%*	*111,384.2*	*33.5%*	*15.6%*	*243.2*
Accounting book	152	21.8%	7.5%	57,750.7	17.4%	8.1%	379.9
Private IOU ("Cédula Simple", "Obligación Simple", "Resguardo")	116	16.6%	5.7%	15,735.1	4.7%	2.2%	135.6
Voucher ("Vale")	64	9.2%	3.1%	7,101.9	2.1%	1.0%	110.9

(continued)

Table 2 (continued)

Instrument	*Number of declarations*			*Amounts mobilized*			
	Number	*% Subtotal*	*% Total*	*Amount*	*% Subtotal*	*% Total*	*Mean Value*
"Paper"	43	6.1%	2.1%	8,693.9	2.6%	1.2%	202.1
"Memoria"	37	5.3%	1.8%	6,233.1	1.8%	0.8%	168.4
Letter	15	2.1%	0.7%	6,014.0	1.8%	0.8%	400.9
Acquittance	10	1.4%	0.5%	5,956.1	1.7%	0.8%	595.6
Recognizance	8	1.1%	0.4%	774.4	0.2%	0.1%	96.8
Bill	7	1.0%	0.3%	2,353.0	0.7%	0.3%	336.1
Combined private instruments	6	0.8%	0.3%	772.0	0.2%	0.1%	128.6
Oral commitment	*28*	*4.0%*	*1.3%*	*9,701.6*	*2.9%*	*1.3%*	*346.4*
Oral Commitment	28	4.0%	1.3%	9,701.6	2.9%	1.3%	346.4
Other	*19*	*2.7%*	*0.9%*	*14,398*	*4.3%*	*2.0%*	*757.7*
Other	19	2.7%	0.9%	14,398.0	4.3%	2.0%	757.7
Subtotal	**695**	**100.0%**	**34.6%**	**331,844.4**	**100.0%**	**46.6%**	
Not declared instrument	*1,313*		*65.4%*	*380,316.7*		*53.4%*	*289.6*
Not declared	1,313		65.4%	380,316.7		53.4%	289.6
Total	**2,008**		**100.0%**	**712,161.1**		**100.0%**	

Source AGN, IX, EA, Volume IX, X, XI, XII, XIII, XIV, XV, XXI, XXII, XXIII, XXIV, XXV, XXVI, XXVII, XXXI, XXXIII, XXXIV, XXXV, XXXVI, XXXVII, XLII, XLIII, XLIV, XLV, XLVI, XLVII
Note The sums are expressed in silver *pesos* of eight *reales* each

Archival Sources and Literature

Acuerdos del Extinguido Cabildo de Buenos Aires, Volume IV, VIII, and IX, Book III, V, and VI.

Alfani, Guido, 'Reformation, "Counter-reformation" and Economic Development from the Point of View of Godparenthood: an Anomaly? (Italy and Europe, 14th–19th Centuries)', in: Francesco Ammannati (ed.), *Religione e istituzioni religiose nell'economia europea. 1000–1800* (Florence, 2012), 477–490.

Barriera, Darío and Griselda Tarragó, 'Elogio de la incertidumbre. La construcción de la confianza: entre la previsión y el desamparo (Santa Fe, Gobernación del Río de la Plata, siglo XVIII)', in: *Revista Historia* 48:1 (2003), 183–223.

Bernal, Antonio Miguel, *La financiación de la Carrera de Indias. Dinero y crédito en el comercio colonial español con América* (Sevilla, 1992).

Burns, Kathrin, *Into the Archive: Writing and Power in Colonial Peru* (Durham, 2010).
Canabrava, Alice, *O comércio português no Rio da Prata, 1580–1640* (San Pablo, 1944).
Errecart, María Claudia, 'Comercio y comunicación en el Río de la Plata. La articulación de los mercados regionales en el período virreinal rioplatense. Los caminos, los transportes y los transportistas', in: *El Taller de la Historia* 11:11 (2019), 230–268.
Fradkin, Raúl, 'Población y sociedad', in: Jorge Gelman (ed.), *Argentina. Crisis imperial e independencia* (Madrid, 2010), 193–242.
Garavaglia, Juan Carlos, *El comercio virreinal 1779–1784* (Buenos Aires, 1970).
García Medina, Amelia, and Reyes Rojas García, 'El poder de la memoria y la memoria del poder', in: Antonio Jiménez Estrella and Julián José Lozano Navarro (eds.), *Actas de la XI Reunión Científica de la Fundación Española de Historia Moderna* I (Granada, 2012), 308–318.
González Lebrero, Rodolfo E., *La pequeña aldea: Sociedad y economía en Buenos Aires (1580–1640)* (Buenos Aires, 2002).
Herrera, Francisco Manuel de, *Reglas del comercio lícito, libre del contagio de la usura* (Madrid, 1735).
Herzog, Tamar, *Mediación, archivos y ejercicio. Los escribanos de Quito (siglo XVII)* (Frankfurt am Main, 1996).
Hevia y Bolaños, Juan de, *Primera y Segunda parte de la Curia Filipica* (Madrid, 1652).
Hoffman, Philip T., Gilles Postel-Vinay, and Jean-Laurent Rosenthal, *Priceless Markets: The Political Economy of Credit in Paris. 1660–1870* (Chicago, 2000).
Jumar, Fernando Alberto, *Le commerce atlantique au Río de la Plata, 1680–1778* (La Plata, 2000).
Levillier, Roberto, *La Audiencia de Charcas. Correspondencia de presidentes y oidores, documentos del Archivo de Indias* III (Madrid, 1918–1922).
Levy, Juliette, 'Notaries and Credit Markets in Nineteenth-Century Mexico', in: *Business History Review* 84:3 (2010), 459–478.
Lluch, Andrea, 'The Art of Lending in the Pampas: Commercial Credit and Financial Intermediation in Argentina, 1900–1930', in: Bernardo Bátiz-Lazo and Leonidas Efthymiou (eds.), *The Book of Payments: Historical and Contemporary Views on the Cashless Society* (London, 2016), 55–64.
Martínez López-Cano, María del Pilar, *La génesis del crédito colonial. Ciudad de México, siglo XVI* (Mexico City, 2001).
Mellafe, Rolando, *Breve historia de la esclavitud negra en América Latina* (Mexico City, 1973).
Mercado, Tomás de, *Suma de tratos y contratos* (Alicante, 2002 [1570]).

Mijares Ramírez, Ivonne, *Escribanos y escrituras públicas en el siglo XVI: El caso de la Ciudad de México* (Mexico City, 1997).

Molina, Raúl, *Las primeras experiencias comerciales del Plata* (Buenos Aires, 1966).

Molina, Raúl, *Matrimonios, Bautismos y Defunciones de la Catedral de Buenos Aires, 1601–1644. Y Legajos I y II de expedientes matrimoniales del archivo del Arzobispado de Buenos Aires* (Buenos Aires, 2002).

Monterroso y Alvarado, Gabriel de, *Practica civil, y criminal, y instrucion de escrivanos* (Valladolid, 1626 [1563]).

Moutoukias, Zacarías, 'El crecimiento en una economía colonial de Antiguo Régimen: reformismo y sector externo en el Río de la Plata (1760-1796)', in: *Arquivos do Centro Cultural Calouste Gulbenkian* 34 (1995), 771–813.

National General Archive of the Nation of Argentina, Escribanías de Registro, Protocolos de Escribanos.

National General Archive of the Nation of Argentina, Sala IX, Escribanías Antiguas.

Rees Jones, Ricardo, *El Superintendente Manuel Ignacio Fernández (1778–1783): Las reformas borbónicas en el Virreinato de Buenos Aires* (Buenos Aires, 1992).

Reitano, Emir, *Los portugueses del Buenos Aires tardocolonial: Inmigración, sociedad, familia, vida cotidiana y religión* (dissertation, La Plata, 2003).

Rosal, Miguel Ángel, 'El comercio de esclavos en la ciudad de Buenos Aires a principios del siglo XVII', in: *Anuario del Centro de Estudios Históricos "Prof. Carlos S. A. Segreti"* 10 (2010), 93–113.

Rosal, Miguel Á., 'Modalidades del comercio de esclavos en Buenos Aires durante la tercera década del siglo XVII', in: *Revista Digital Estudios Históricos* 3:7 (2011), 1–17.

Stiglitz, Joseph E. and Andrew Weiss, 'Credit Rationing in Markets with Imperfect Information', in: *The American Economic Review* 71:3 (1981), 393–410.

Wasserman, Martín L.E., 'La mediación notarial en la interacción económica: confianza, información y conexiones en la temprana Buenos Aires', in: *Prohistoria* 24:1 (2015), 69–100.

Wasserman, Martín, *Las obligaciones fundamentales. Crédito y consolidación económica durante el surgimiento de Buenos Aires* (Buenos Aires, 2018).

Wasserman, Martín, 'Escribanos y escrituras en Hispanoamérica', in: Rosana Vassallo (ed.), *Introducción a la Paleografía. Herramientas para la lectura y análisis de documentos antiguos* (La Plata, 2019), 173–198.

Wasserman, Martín L.E., 'El escribano y la mano visible. Intermediación financiera y crédito en un contexto de información asimétrica (Buenos Aires, siglo XVIII)', in: *Revista de Historia Americana y Argentina* 56:1 (2021), 19–62.

Wasserman, Martín et al., 'La conexión en el Registro. Una aproximación primaria a las características básicas de la operatoria en las Escribanías de Registro de Buenos Aires durante el siglo XVIII (1760–1780)', in: *Illes i imperis* 22:1 (2020), 199–230.

A Network Analysis of Credit Transactions at the Cape Colony During the Eighteenth Century

Christie Swanepoel

1 Introduction

The Cape Colony was first settled by the Dutch East India Company (VOC, or the Company) in 1652, not with the aim to establish a new colony but rather to serve as a refreshment stop for ships between Europe and the East Indies. The demand for fresh produce on these ships quickly outstripped the Company's ability to provide for them and seven years after the arrival of the Europeans, the decision was made to create a permanent settlement. Under the first and second governors, Simon van der Stel and his son Willem Adriaan, the boundaries of the colony moved inward toward the mountainous regions in the north and later eastward. The colony continued to expand throughout the seventeenth and eighteenth centuries. One reason for the geographical expansion of the colony was the absence of any great natural barriers present in other

C. Swanepoel (✉)
Faculty of Economic and Management Science, Department of Economics, University of the Western Cape, Cape Town, South Africa
e-mail: cswanepoel@uwc.ac.za

C. van Bochove and J. Levy (eds.), *Beyond Banks*,
Palgrave Studies in the History of Finance,
https://doi.org/10.1007/978-3-031-75819-5_4

regions, like in Canada or Australia. De Kiewiet argues that the topological barriers present in Canada and Australia were absent in the Cape.[1] It neither has the extreme cold of Canada nor the extreme desert conditions of Australia, which meant that European settlers migrated as needed to find suitable soil and space. In 1795, the colony had viticulture and grain production in the south-western region, and sheep and cattle farms toward the eastern regions. There was an absence of large urban centers outside of Cape Town with some exceptions like Swellendam and Graaff Reinet, both of which were small towns used as way points for farmers toward Cape Town.

The geographical expansion coincided with an increase in the European population. At first, only seven company employees became settler farmers in Cape Town but by 1795,[2] there were about 10,000 settlers.[3] Most of these settlers were of Dutch and German descent and came to the colony by way of the Company. They were supplemented by a group of French Huguenots who arrived in 1688. Most of these settlers became farmers and sold their produce to the Company, who had monopsony power in Cape Town. Despite the buying power of the Company, recent work by Fourie and Swanepoel showed that extensive trading also took place between the settlers at the Cape and that the required credit was raised on a peer-to-peer basis. They further show that the three main institutions—the Company, the Orphan Chamber, and the church—were also active in the credit market. The "church" here refers to the Dutch Reformed Church, which had a monopoly on organized religion until the establishment of the Lutheran Church in 1780. These institutions were imported with the Dutch and their settlement and was key in connecting individuals through social links. They further contend that, despite the contemporary and historiographic views that the extensive use of credit was a source of concern and would lead to impoverishment, these credit

[1] Cornelis de Kiewiet, *A History of South Africa: Social and Economic* (Oxford, 1941), 11.

[2] The British occupied the Cape Colony in 1795 when France occupied the Dutch Republic. This was an attempt to stop France from reaching the East Indies. It was returned to Batavian control between 1803 and 1806, before becoming a fully-fledged British colony in 1806. This first British occupation is chosen as a natural end to the period of study, and it is close to the end of the century.

[3] Jeanne Cilliers and Johan Fourie, 'New Estimates of Settler Life Span and Other Demographic Trends in South Africa, 1651–1948', in: *Economic History of Developing Regions* 27:2 (2012), 61–86.

transactions were related to the notable wealth of the settlers at the colony and that it was those with wealth (or collateral) that used debt the most often.[4] As in other pre-industrial regions, these transactions allowed for investments and consumption smoothing (because there were cash shortages in the colony and the money supply was unreliable).[5]

Given the interpersonal nature of credit transactions at the Cape, there are two aspects important to identifying the structure of the credit market in this edited volume: familiarity between parties and types of sanctions. There is evidence of familiarity between parties at the Cape, mainly through marriage patterns. Two examples of this can be found in Dooling who studied the alcohol *pachters* (lease holders) and their marriage networks.[6] Mitchell also shows how important marriage was for economic success at the Cape Colony.[7] This is then supported by Fourie and Swanepoel's conclusion that much credit was raised on a peer-to-peer basis.[8] For the nineteenth century, after the period studied here, Ekama describes a similar network of personal credit transactions among slaveowners.[9]

[4] Johan Fourie and Christie Swanepoel, "'Impending Ruin' or 'Remarkable Wealth'? The Role of Private Credit Markets in a Settler Colony', in: *Journal of Southern African Studies* 44:1 (2018), 7–25.

[5] The first financial institution was the Lombard Bank which was established in 1795. Because this is at the end of the chosen end date of this study, I ignore the establishment of the bank here. See: Robert C. Merton and Zvi Bodie, 'A Conceptual Framework for Analyzing the Financial Environment', in: Dwight B. Crane et al. (eds.), *The Global Financial System: A Functional Perspective* (Boston [MA]., 1995); Thijs Schofield and Philip Lambrecht, 'Introduction', in: Thijs Schofield and Philip Lambrecht (eds.), *Credit and the Rural Economy in North-Western Europe, c. 1200–1850* (Brepols, 2009), 1–18; Craig Muldrew, *The Economy of Obligation: The Culture of Credit and Social Relations in Early Modern England* (New York, 1998); Muldrew, Craig, 'Debt, Credit and Poverty in Early Modern England', in: Ralph Brubaker, Robert M. Lawless, and Charles J. Tabb (eds.) *A Debtor World: Interdisciplinary Perspectives on Debt* (Oxford, 2012), 10–23.

[6] Wayne Dooling, 'The Making of a Colonial Elite: Property, Family and Landed Stability in the Cape Colony, c.1750–1834', in: *Journal of Southern African Studies* 31:1 (2005), 147–162; Wayne Dooling, *Slavery, Emancipation and Colonial Rule in South Africa* (Pietermaritzburg, 2005).

[7] Laura Jane Mitchell, *Belongings: Property, Family, and Identity in Colonial South Africa (An Exploration of Frontiers, 1725–c.1830)* (Columbia, 2008).

[8] Fourie and Swanepoel, "Impending Ruin".

[9] Kate Ekama, 'Bondsmen: Slave Collateral in the 19th-Century Cape Colony', in: *Journal of Southern African Studies* 47:3 (2021), 437–453.

There is little evidence on extra-legal sanctions at the Cape, but Dooling writes that the widespread use of credit that extended both vertically and horizontally in families, created a "moral community". He continues that this "moral community" enabled many to easily become insolvent but escape from this soon afterward using family capital. One reason for the limited evidence on extra-legal sanctions is the open frontier at the Cape and the ability to move somewhere to avoid penalties.[10] However, the existence of written contracts and insolvency records suggests that some legal penalties would have been implemented during this time.[11] This, with the results presented below, suggests that the Cape's credit market was a network + market, with a high reliance on familiarity between parties in a transaction, but supplemented with written contracts and extra-legal sanctions.

Early credit markets, like the Cape's, have been shown to be large and formal, to function with or without intermediaries, and be resilient over time. The main aim, like modern credit markets with banks, was to allocate resources. This means the demand and supply of credit in regions should be considered. The demand-side considerations include consumption smoothing and trading over long distances. Consumption smoothing happened especially in societies with a reliance on agriculture, where seasonality meant cash shortages in some seasons and a reliance on credit until the harvest season to repay debts.[12] Credit markets also allowed for trade over long terms and distances. In cash-scarce societies like the Low Countries, France, and Britain, Muldrew suggests that "most market transactions involved the extension of informal credit because of the lack of ready cash".[13]

The allocation of resources through credit, however, requires that asymmetric information between parties be solved.[14] Information is asymmetric when either borrower or lender has more information than the

[10] Wayne Dooling, 'The Decline of the Cape Gentry, 1838–1900', in: *Journal of African History*, 40:2 (1999), 215–242.

[11] Dooling, 'The Making of Colonial Elite'.

[12] B.A. Holderness, 'Credit in English Rural Society Before the Nineteenth Century, with Special Reference to the Period 1650–1720', in: *The Agricultural History Review* 24:2 (1976), 97–109.

[13] Muldrew, 'Debt, Credit and Poverty', 10.

[14] Philip Hoffman, Gilles Postal-Vinay, and Jean-Laurent Rosenthal, *Priceless Markets: The Political Economy of Credit in Paris, 1660–1870* (Chicago, 2000), 102–107.

other in the transaction and is usually solved through the interest rate or the use of collateral.[15] However, usury laws in pre-industrial societies complicate a solution via interest rates. Other scholars suggest that information asymmetries can be resolved in peer-to-peer lending through strong social bonds for smaller loans and through intermediaries—such as notaries in Paris—for longer, larger loans.[16] Despite some key similarities in the role of notaries, there are significant differences. While the Parisian notaries became central to the network and key to credit markets, the Dutch and Flemish alderman and notaries only registered the contracts.[17] These cases with similar roles but different outcomes, led Hoffman, Postal-Vinay, and Rosenthal to conclude that more research is required on the informational and contractual infrastructures.[18] Notaries at the Cape remain understudied, but Fourie and Swanepoel suggest that, with the strong Dutch influence, they played an official role of registering contracts rather than an intermediary role in the credit market.[19]

There are two techniques to study how credit market solved asymmetric information and allocated resources: descriptive case studies[20]

[15] J. E. Stiglitz and A. Weiss, 'Asymmetric Information in Credit Markets and Its Implications from Macro-Economics', in: *Oxford Economic Papers* 44:4 (1992), 694–724.

[16] Elise Dermineur, 'Peer-to-Peer Lending in Pre-industrial France', in: *Financial History Review* 26:3 (2019), 359–388; Hoffman, Postel-Vinay and Rosenthal, *Priceless Markets*.

[17] Hoffman et al. 'Priceless markets'; Christiaan van Bochove and Heleen Kole, 'Uncovering Private Credit Markets: Amsterdam, 1660–1809', in: *Low Countries Journal* 11:3 (2014), 39–72; Oscar Gelderblom, Joost Jonker and Mark Hup, 'Public Functions, Private Markets: Credit Registration by Aldermen and Notaries in the Low Countries, 1500–1800', in: Marcella Lorenzini, Cinzia Lorandini and D'Maris Coffman (eds.), *Financing in Europe: Evolution, Coexistence and Complementarity of Lending Practices from the Middle Ages to Modern Times* (London, 2018), 163–194.

[18] Philip Hoffman, Gilles Postal-Vinay, and Jean-Laurent Rosenthal, *Dark Matter Credit: The Development of Peer-to-Peer Lending and Banking in France* (Princeton, 2019).

[19] Fourie and Swanepoel, "Impending Ruin".

[20] Muldrew, 'Debt, Credit and Poverty'; Daniel Vickers, 'Credit and Misunderstanding on Nantucket Island, Massachusetts (1683–1763)', in: *Quaderni Storici* 46:2 (2011), 415–440; Sheilagh Ogilvie, Markus Küpker, and Janine Maegraith,, 'Household Debt in Early Modern Germany: Evidence from Personal Inventories', in: *Journal of Economic History* 72:1 (2012), 134–167; Van Bochove and Kole, 'Uncovering Private Credit Markets'; Naomi R. Lamoreaux, Daniel M.G. Raff, and Peter Temin, 'Beyond Markets and Hierarchies: Toward a New Synthesis of American Business History', in: *The American Historical Review* 108:2 (2003), 404–433; Winifred B. Rothenberg, 'The Emergence of a

or network analysis.[21] Muldrew studied the expanding use of credit in England during the early modern period and writes that "(e)very household in the country (...) was to some degree enmeshed within the increasingly complicated webs of credit and obligation".[22] He continues that networks remained vital to determine trust between households. Vickers, on the other hand, illustrated the interaction among settlers from New England and the indigenous population on Nantucket Island. Using extensive bookkeeping of transactions kept by settlers, this case study showed how the use of credit can differ if culture differs.[23] Ogilvie, Küpker, and Maegraith provided evidence that even individuals from outside a particular locality were incorporated into the local credit network through who they knew there.[24] Van Bochove and Kole noted how the Amsterdam market relied on networks to link supply and demand through loan forms.[25] Lamoreaux et al. postulated that repeated interaction between households, shops, and stores in nineteenth century East Coast USA built mutual trust and discouraged cheating and defaulting on debts, while Rothenberg showed an expanding network by reporting how the absolute number and average number of creditors and debtors per probate inventory increased over time, leading to a wider credit network in early modern rural Massachusetts.[26]

A second technique to study information and contractual infrastructures is network analysis and graph theory. As the case studies above indicate, networks have always been an important element in debt and credit relations and can play a crucial role in answering questions about asymmetric information. One reason for this is that networks allow for

Capital Market in Rural Massachusetts, 1730–1838', in: *The Journal of Economic History* 45:4 (1984), 781–808.

[21] John F. Pagett and Christopher K. Ansell, 'Robust Action and the Rise of the Medici, 1400–1434', in: *American Journal of Sociology* 98:6 (1993), 1259–1319; John F. Pagett and Paul D. McLean, 'Economic Credit in Renaissance Florence', in: *The Journal of Modern History* 83:1 (2011), 1–47; Ekama, 'Bondsmen'.

[22] Muldrew, 'Debt, Credit and Poverty', 6.

[23] Vickers, 'Credit and Misunderstanding'.

[24] Ogilvie, Küpker and Maegraith, 'Household Debt'.

[25] Van Bochove and Kole, 'Uncovering Private Credit Markets'.

[26] Lamoreaux et al. 'Beyond Markets and Hierarchies'; Rothenberg, 'The Emergence of a Capital Market'.

information to flow between individuals.[27] Pagett and Ansell use network analysis and graph theory to study the impact of position in the network or reputation effects in credit transactions.[28] Further, in this edited volume's framework, networks are identified as a key determinant of the market type.

The widespread use of credit and emersion of all classes within society in the credit market is observed in the Cape Colony as well: the occupations of those who were involved in both credit and debt transactions range from the highest to the lowest echelons of Cape society.[29] There is also evidence from inventories that individuals had large and small debts, with and without contracts.[30] The size of debts to GDP is evidence of the reliance on debts and credits to interact economically.[31] While some studies show a renewed interest in the Cape Colony, they omit the wider credit structure of the Colony's credit market and how it compares to other regions. It is the aim of this chapter to use the extensive coverage of the probate records at the Cape to investigate the wider structure of the credit market. It will illustrate the use of credit between peers as well as the institutions through the network.

The first part of the chapter will describe the data used here. This is followed by a description of the credit market at the Cape Colony and will provide more detail on the two types of transactions in the Cape Colony, peer-to-peer and intermediated transactions. It will show how the type of transactions related to individuals and institutions. The institutions that were involved in the credit market brought with them individuals that used their connections to promote their status. One such example, about whom I elaborate upon in this chapter, is Tobias Christiaan Rönnenkamp, identified through the three centrality measures in

[27] Ronald S. Burt, 'Structural Holes versus Network Closure as Social Capital', in: Nan Lin, Karen Cook, and Ronald S. Burt (eds.), *Social Capital: Theory and Research* (New York, 2001); Matthew O. Jackson, *Social and Economic Networks* (Princeton, 2008).

[28] Pagett and Ansell, 'Robust Action'; Pagett and Ansell, 'Economic Credit'.

[29] Dooling, 'The Making of Colonial Elite'; Jeanne Cilliers, Johan Fourie and Christie Swanepoel, ''Unobtrusively into the Ranks of Colonial Society': Intergenerational Wealth Mobility in the Cape Colony Over the Eighteenth Century', in: *Economic History of Developing Regions* 34:1 (2019), 48–71.

[30] Fourie and Swanepoel, ''Impending Ruin''.

[31] Johan Fourie and Jan-Luiten van Zanden, 'GDP in the Dutch Cape Colony: The National Accounts of a Slave-based Society', in: *South African Journal of Economics* 81:4 (2013), 467–490.

the network. What I will further study is how his portfolio differs from other individuals, identified through network analysis. The description of the Cape's credit market is followed by my network analysis. Networks can further be used to distinguish between the two types of credit transactions that took place in the Cape Colony. The characteristics of the Cape Colony's credit market highlighted in part one will inform why it is important to introduce networks for the analysis of credit markets. Some reasons include the building of trust and the elimination of asymmetric information.[32] A final part of the chapter will conclude and interpret the Cape Colony's credit market in comparison to other regions. The aim here is to place the Cape Colony into the other works developed in this edited volume.

2 Probate Inventories and Financial Markets in Pre-industrial Societies

The probate inventories from the Orphan Chamber of the Cape Colony, known as the MOOC8 series,[33] between 1700 and 1795 provide the bulk of data for this analysis. The data from the inventories has been widely used by both historians and economic historians to study the Cape's individuals and economic outcomes. This series captures all the assets, credits, and debts of members of Cape households after death. The households included in the series are those with children younger than 25, those with no last will and testament, or those where heirs were overseas or absent. While the combined data are useful for exploring aspects like age, gender, marriage, and occupation, it is not key to describing the network. Here I only focus on the inventories and data on credit transaction in them.

The main concern with the use of probate records to research credit markets is their representativeness. This concern is threefold: which debts are excluded, are many debts repaid before death, and are those without assets excluded? These concerns are mitigated if the role of the Orphan Chamber at the Cape is considered. The Orphan Chambers followed

[32] Martin Ruef, Howard E. Aldrich and Nancy M. Carter, 'The Structure of Founding Teams: Homophily, Strong Ties and Isolation among US Entrepreneurs', in: *American Sociological Review* 68:2 (2003), 195–222.

[33] The full series is available at the Western Cape Archives and Record Services (from here on: WCARS), Master of Orphan Chamber (hereafter, MOOC) Probate Inventories and Estate Records, Series 8, Volumes 1–75.

the Company to the various regions where the Dutch settled and were responsible for the legal and financial care of orphans in these regions.[34] The Orphan Chamber's role in taking probate inventories was wider than in Europe, as it included the task of locating any heir(s) absent from the Cape.

Some evidence exists that suggests the open frontier and the lack of geographic barriers meant if settlers felt pressured to repay debts, they would simply leave and move inward from the coastal regions.[35] But there are also many insolvency records and civil court records that have not been systematically studied which suggest otherwise. One way to estimate which debts are excluded is to measure it against wages which would often be paid more regularly than debts. Which debts are included or excluded in the probate inventories has not been thoroughly investigated at the Cape, but wages at the Cape were high and sustained high living standards.[36] A cursory look at probate inventories provides examples of wage debts and suggests not many debts were not recorded. For example, Hendrik Willem Plooy and his wife, Regina, probated on March 21, 1781, owed Frederik Wolff Ruberg 25 Dutch *rijksdaalder* (rds) for *knechtsgagie* (servant's wage).[37] That debts were not excluded is further supported by Fourie, who notes that the "Cape was a landholder and slave society, with very low numbers of wage labourers" and these assets were likely captured in the probates.[38]

The second concern about the repayment of debts is more difficult to address. However, the extensive number of transactions observed in the probate inventories suggests that at least some remained and were not repaid before death. This means the results below should be considered a lower bound rather than a complete or upper bound estimate

[34] Josje Schnitzeler, 'Financial Care for the Vulnerable: Rise and Decline of Holland Orphan Chamber' (dissertation, Utrecht University, 2022).

[35] Susan Newton-King, *Masters and Servants on the Cape Frontier* (Cambridge, 1999).

[36] Stan du Plessis and Sophia du Plessis, 'Happy in the Service of the Company: The Purchasing Power of VOC Salaries at the Cape in the Eighteenth Century', in: *Economic History of Developing Regions* 27:1 (2012), 125–149; Pim de Zwart, 'South African Living Standards in a Global Perspective, 1835–1910', in: *Economic History of Developing Regions* 26:1 (2011), 49–74.

[37] WCARS, MOOC8, Vol. 18 No. 15.

[38] Johan Fourie, 'The Remarkable Wealth of the Dutch Cape Colony: Measurements from Eighteenth-Century Probate Inventories', in: *Economic History Review* 66:2 (2013), 419–448, there 425.

of the transactions at the Cape. As for the representativeness of assets and wealth in the probate records, there are two ways to address the concern: either compare the probates to other series or investigate who are included in the probates. Like Ogilvie, Küpker, and Maegraith, Fourie compared the Orphan Chamber probate inventories to those of Stellenbosch—the wealthiest region at the Cape. He concluded that the Orphan Chamber inventories were more representative of the population and that the Stellenbosch inventories included more gentry. He concluded that the probate inventories were not as biased as expected and capture many wealthy individuals as well.[39] Some examples of these landed gentry in the probates are Hendrik Oostwald Eksteen, Jan Meindert Kruywagen, and Johannes Groenewald.[40]

Another limitation is the limited information on familial connections and occupations between the individuals. Groenewald and Baartman have shown familial and business links as key to network building at the Cape.[41] This might be possible to add in the future if more sources and information on the individuals are gathered.

Given that the probate records are concerned with assets, there is the further concern that the poor are excluded. This does not seem to be the case with the probates of the Cape Colony either. The Orphan Chamber was extensively involved in the lives of the poor and there are inventories of individuals with only clothes listed. There are also a select few inventories of freed slaves with few assets.

Before I discuss some descriptive statistics from the inventories, a note on the currency used. I follow Fourie and Swanepoel in the conversion of exchange rates.[42] There were various specie circulating in the Cape Colony at the time. The two most common for the eighteenth century were the Dutch *rijksdaalder* and *gulden*. It is possible to convert these currencies to grams of silver which is useful for comparison to other

39 Ogilvie, Küpker and Maegraith, 'Household Debt'; Fourie, 'The Remarkable Wealth'.

40 WCARS, MOOC8, Vol. 3 No. 93; WCARS, MOOC8, Vol. 5 No. 19; WCARS, MOOC8, Vol. 15 No. 23.

41 Gerald Groenewald, 'Dynasty Building, Family Networks and Social Capital: Alcohol Pachters and the Development of a Colonial Elite of the Cape of Good Hope, c. 1760–1790', in: *New Contree* 62:10 (2011), 23–53; Teun Baartman, 'Fighting for the Spoils: Cape Burgerschap and Faction Disputes in Cape Town in the 1770s' (unpublished dissertation, University of Cape Town, 2011).

42 Fourie and Swanepoel, "Impending Ruin", 12.

countries. Further, while it is possible to adjust for inflation, I follow Du Plessis and Du Plessis and Fourie and Swanepoel who discuss that prices at the Cape during this time were stagnant or deflating and use nominal values.[43] Despite this, the results remain similar and there are no significant differences between the nominal and real values.

3 The Cape's Credit Market

Before I focus on the network of credit at the Cape Colony, I will use this section to describe the market. It will discuss the volume of transactions, who were involved, and other aspects like the type of contacts that were used and will briefly note on the size of the credit market. While Fourie and Swanepoel study the whole period of 1652 until 1834, I will focus on only the eighteenth century here, until 1795 when the first British occupation occurred.[44] This excludes the initial period of establishment when the networks and markets were still forming and excludes any institutional changes that British control might have brought. To illustrate the settlers' reliance on trading on credit, I compare the total debt and credit transactions' value from the inventories to the GDP data compiled by Fourie and Van Zanden.[45]

From Fig. 1, debt and credit transactions played a vital role in the Cape Colony's economy. The log-values on a moving average basis of the two series are consistently higher than the GDP growth of the colony.[46] This indicates that the settlers relied on these transactions to trade, produce, and consume more. But despite the high reliance on debt, the use of both small and large debts with and without contracts suggests that the Cape's credit market was widely used. One of the problems that the Cape market needed to solve was that it was a small market with less than 10,000 individuals spread over an increasingly large geographic region. It did this by including various individuals from spheres of the population as seen by the occupations, the values of the transactions, and the number of inventories that had at least one transaction.

[43] Du Plessis and du Plessis, 'Happy in the Service'; Fourie and Swanepoel, "Impending Ruin".

[44] Fourie and Swanepoel, "Impending Ruin".

[45] Fourie and van Zanden, 'GDP in the Dutch Cape Colony'.

[46] The moving average used two years to remove the widest swings of the data.

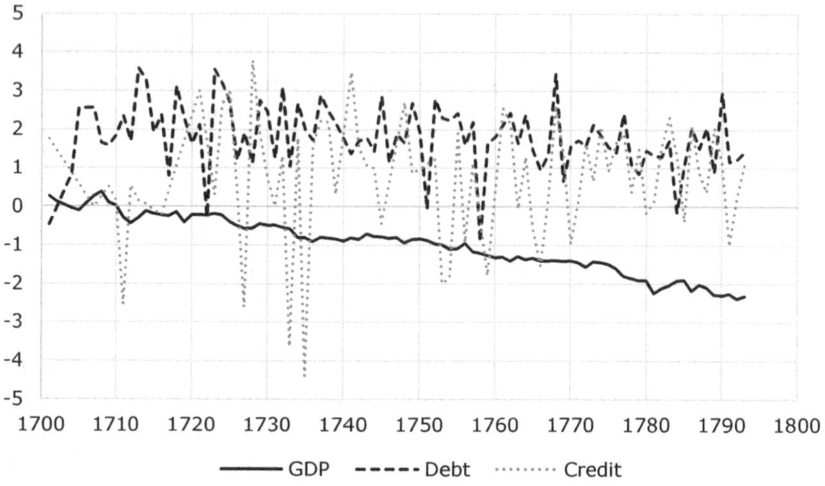

Fig. 1 GDP per capita versus financial transactions per capita (*Note* Credit and debt values were converted to gulden to be comparable to Fourie and van Zanden, 'GDP in the Dutch Cape Colony' and log-normalized per capita. The moving average removes missing years with the probate inventories and some of the wide swings in the values from one year to the next. The y-axis can be interpreted similar to a growth trend using the moving averages. *Source* See text)

Table 1 Panel A provides the initial descriptive data for the inventories between 1700 and 1795. There are some interesting things to note: first, the importance of the two most common assets at the Cape—landed property and slaves. Land is reported in 56.54% of the inventories, at an average of 1.56 properties per inventory. Even more individuals owned slaves at the Cape as reported in 72% of the inventories, at a mean of five slaves and a median of two slaves. Of the 1,622 inventories, 576 or 35.51% were taken of women who are often understudied in these contexts.

Panel B of Table 1 shows the specific financial observations from the inventories. 30% of inventories include credits (that is debts owed to the individual whose inventory it is) and 63% of inventories have debt (that is the estate owed money to someone at the time when the inventory was taken). The probates reveal wide differences in the values that settlers borrowed and lent. The smallest cumulative value is 3rds per probate in real values while the largest is over 180,000rds. There are also differences

Table 1 Descriptive statistics of inventories between 1700 and 1790

	Obs	*% of inventories*	*Mean*	*Median*	*Min*	*Max*
Panel A: Summary statistics on inventories						
Number of inventories	1,622.00					
Number of female inventories	576.00	35.51%				
Number of landed properties	917.00	56.54%	1.56	1.00	1.00	10.00
Number of slaves	1,178.00	72.62%	4.88	2.00	0.00	61.00
Number of inventories who dealt with an institution	278.00	17.13%	2.60	3.00	1.00	3.00
Number of inventories with both credit and debt transactions	425.00	26.19%				
Number of inventories without credit or debt transactions	121.00	7.46%				
Panel B: Summary statistics on financial aspects of inventories						
Real value of cash	381.00	23.49%	676.44	140.00	1.00	36,651.64
Real value of credits	482.00	29.72%	2,210.02	328.94	3.00	180,679.40
Real value of inventories with only credits	83.00	5.11%	2,200.94	411.10	17.83	14,398.99
Real value of debts	1,019.00	62.82%	1,615.19	565.00	4.00	164,640.80
Real value of inventories with only debts	619.00	38.16%	1,007.83	427.09	3.99	17,105.20
Panel C: Summary statistics on credit/debt transactions in the inventories						
Total number of transactions on credit or debt	8,993.00		103.00	5.00	1.00	1,307.00

(continued)

Table 1 (continued)

	Obs	*% of inventories*	*Mean*	*Median*	*Min*	*Max*
Number of transactions with a contract (debt)	314.00	3.49%	1.89	2.00	1.00	4.00
Real value of transactions with a contract (debt)			842.02	341.78	2.84	9,340.62
Number of transactions with a contract (credit)	827.00	9.19%	1.98	2.00	1.00	4.00
Real value of transactions with a contract (credit)			589.57	257.93	1.67	23,213.44

Source See text
Note There are some years for which the inflation-adjusted values are not available to maintain balance between the nominal and real values, these are ignored. The base-year for real value conversion is 1699.

in the mean and median, probably explained by this widespread of values. The mean value of lending among the probated individuals is 2,210.02rds and for borrowing the value is lower at 1,615.19rds, while the median of lending is 328.94rds and 565rds for borrowing.

The final panel, Panel C of Table 1, provides more information on all the observed transactions in the inventories. There is also evidence of how formal debt transactions were at the Cape. We observe 1,141 probates where some debt contract is recorded—either as a debt or a credit. These contracts are most comparable with a bond or *obligatie (privaat, secretarieel,* or *onderhandsche*[47]). These contracts were often signed with eyewitnesses present, with lawyers or notaries involved. Most of the information on interest rates at the Cape are observed from these as well—ranged between 3 and 6%. We can already see the importance of the VOC, the Orphan Chamber and the Church here too. These three

[47] There is evidence that *privaat* and *onderhandsche obligaties* amount to the same contract. However, given the lack of research into the contracts at the Cape, I chose to remain to the original terms as recorded in the probates.

institutions were often involved in financial transactions, and at least 17% of the inventories recorded transactions on debt with these institutions.

It also bears to mention what this documentary source reveals about women in the eighteenth century economy and society. As shown in Table 1: Panel A, there are 36% of inventories of women and Table 2 shows the values for the various measures between genders. What is surprising is that the mean and median values of the men and women are close to each other. The median[48] credit value of probates of women is 350rds and for males its 295rds, and 430rds versus 587rds in debt. As in Europe, the United States, and the Americas, women played a significant role in the economy, but this has not received the full attention of researchers in South Africa yet.

There were 8,993 transactions on credit over the period from the inventories with a median of 5 contracts per inventory. Again, the difference between the minimum and maximum drives up the average to 103 per inventory, which makes the median a more reflective measure. The individual with 1,307 transactions (Table 1: Panel C) is Tobias Christiaan Rönnenkamp. I discuss his portfolio in more detail below. Overall,

Table 2 Comparison of values between males and females

		Obs	*Mean*	*Median*	*Min*	*Max*
Females	Real value of cash	126	537.66	145.45	0.89	11,278.25
	Real value of credits	167	2,738.18	350.14	6.01	148,021.50
	Real value of debts	360	1,697.76	429.52	3.99	134,881.90
Males	Real value of cash	239	781.57	149.26	0.36	46,781.50
	Real value of credits	314	1,696.39	295.23	2.40	36,030.77
	Real value of debts	655	1,496.65	586.80	5.80	33,052.86

Source See text
Note The values might not add up to the values of Table 1 because of missing information on the genders of some inventories and because of overlap between the three groups

[48] Due to some outliers in terms of the size of the debt, I use the median rather than the average value.

3% of debt transactions indicate that a contract was involved, while 9% of credit transactions indicate this. This suggests those with a surplus who lent other money were more inclined to make sure they can reclaim their money. What remains to be investigated in future research is the difference between the two—why are there these differences?

One way to identify the match makers and identify whether they were mostly notaries is to look in the probate inventories to see who were involved in both credit and debt transactions. I use the occupations from the matched data from Fourie and Swanepoel to find the occupations of the individuals involved in both credit and debt transactions.[49] From this matched sample, there are 39 occupations descriptions and 522 transactions. These are shown in Table 3.

The small sample shows "farmers" most recorded in the probates in line with the description of Cape society. But there are also many traders like bookkeeper, woodcutter, wheelwright, butcher, baker, carpenter, and cobbler (all contained under Other). This suggests that there were few match makers but that it was an entwined society. Besides these traders there are also individuals from the higher echelons like the orphan-master, physician and medical doctors, district councilor, deacons, and magistrate.

Table 3 Major occupations of individuals with both credit and debt transactions

Occupation	*Frequency*	*Total number of transactions*	*Credit transactions*		*Debt transactions*	
			Average value	*Median value*	*Average value*	*Median value*
Farmer	11	68	428.32	72.67	98.00	426.32
Soldier	5	68	72.61	32.67	40.00	109.67
Laborer	1	8	666.67	666.67	30.00	111.19
Smith	1	12	1,116.13	502.50	771.75	1,269.22
Physician	1	94	23.54	14.00	450.00	1,179.29
Assistant	1	50	80.09	29.25	260.00	841.42
Captain	1	4	33.33	33.33	1,000.00	2,210.29
Other	18	218	389.62	93.50	317.13	549.92
Total	39	522				

Source See text

[49] Fourie and Swanepoel, "Impending Ruin".

But it does not answer the question on whether notaries or these individuals from the higher echelons played the role of match makers in the credit market at the Cape. One reason why notaries might not have played this role at the Cape is the structure of the Cape's economy and reliance on agriculture. Often very wealthy farmers played key roles in the economy and their networks were key to connect the other occupations and classes at the Cape. To investigate this further, I use network analysis below to help us identify the key match makers in the Cape's credit market.

4 Networks and Credit Transactions at the Cape Colony

Early literature on South African society by Robertson shows that even under Van Riebeeck before settlement, credit already played a vital role in the Cape's society. The first settlers organized private lending to "create a more closely-knit society at the Cape, where people would be bound together by their interlocking interest as debtors and creditors".[50] In more recent work, Fourie and Swanepoel[51] show how one prominent settler, Johannes Fredrik Kirsten, wrote to the British government before their takeover of the Cape Colony in 1795 about the economic conditions in which he described debilitating debt level for farmers.[52] However, once his motives are further interrogated it becomes clear that his brother, Jan Pieter Kirsten, was the source of his grievance. They further show how both brothers could be considered wealthy within the context of the Cape Colony with connections to other well-known families, like Van Reenen and Van Rheede van Oudtshoorn.

To support and further investigate this anecdotal evidence of networks in the credit market, I rely on network analysis to study how information might have flowed and how sanctions were implemented between individuals. More data is required but the initial results with the connections

[50] H.M. Robertson, 'The Economic Development of the Cape under Van Riebeek: Part III', in: *The South African Journal of Economics* 13:3 (1945), 170–184, there 175.

[51] Fourie and Swanepoel, "Impending Ruin".

[52] C.F.J. Muller, *Johannes Frederik Kirsten oor die Toestand van die Kaapkolonie in 1795: 'n Kritiese Studie* (Pretoria, 1960).

show that the parties at least knew each other.[53] The timing of the transactions problematic in the probate records as these are only recorded at death, while the probate records cannot tell us if there were any sanctions placed on individuals who did not repay their debts.[54]

The results here show the widespread use of credit at the Cape Colony by all individuals, both poor and rich, and individuals from different occupations and social ranks. Dooling points to the role of social networks, including marriage, as key to gaining access and influence in the credit market.[55] It is the aim to further investigate the role of these networks here. I will use two aspects of network analysis to do this. First, I will discuss the overall network statistics, the diameter and average path length, of the credit market at the Cape over the eighteenth century. Second, I identify some individuals through the network to show how individuals were connected.

The diameter of a network is the largest distance between any two nodes, while the average path length is the average of these distances.[56] In my case nodes are individuals and connections are credit transactions. It should be noted that the network measured here is a directed network, because we know whether the transaction was a credit or debt. A credit is therefore a flow into the node, while a debt is a flow to the opposite node. The distance between the nodes is the number of connections it takes to move from one node to the next. For example, if Smith was in debt with De Beer, but not to Fourie, but De Beer was in debt with Fourie, the network distance between Smith and Fourie is two. Figure 2 illustrates this example while Table 4 discusses the network diameter and average path length over time. These values from this table are not affected by the directionality of the network.

Because of the long period over which the inventories were captured, it is illogical to assume a single time period. Given other limitations with dynamic networks, I will use static network analysis here and divide the research period into sub-periods. The inventories were observed at death, so no new transactions with the person could be noted afterward; but it

[53] Burt, 'The Gender of Social Capital'.

[54] Further investigation into the timing and sanctions from transactions would require additional sources like insolvency records, court cases, or account books.

[55] Dooling, 'Slavery'.

[56] Jackson, *Social and Economic Networks,* 38.

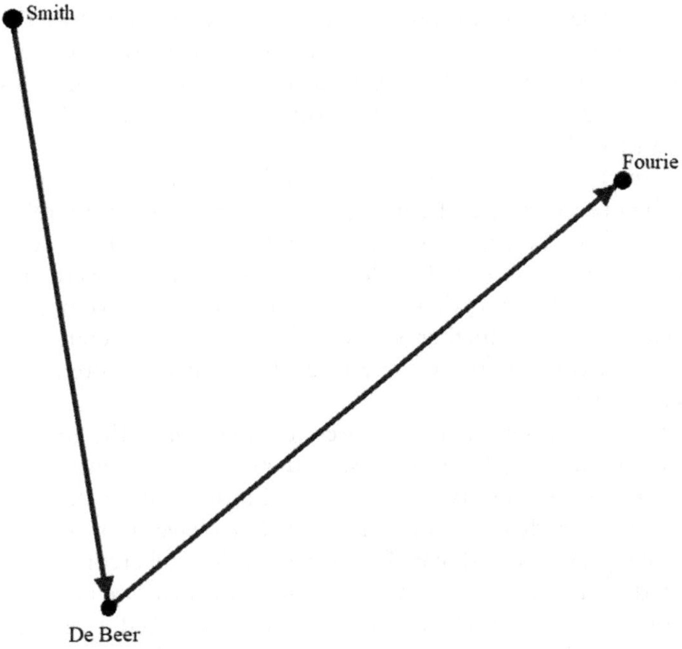

Fig. 2 An example of the directed credit network (*Source* See text)

Table 4 Descriptive statistics of the credit network at the Cape Colony with population

Period	*Diameter*	*Average path length*
1700–1724	9	4.35
1725–1749	16	6.36
1750–1774	15	6.22
1775–1795	13	4.10

Source See text

cannot be excluded that individuals at the Cape did not trade with individuals younger than themselves. The younger individuals' transactions would only be captured later in the inventories. It is also likely that individuals traded with individuals older than themselves, who may have died before them. This transaction would have been recorded before the individual's own probate inventory was taken. For these reasons, the period is divided into 25-year intervals. This is likely to capture one generation of "trading partners". The periods are 1700 to 1724, 1725 to 1749, 1750 to 1774, and 1775 to 1795.

The diameter and average path length increase over the period observed before slowing in the final period. If nodes are randomly added and connected to the previous nodes, the diameter should increase over time as we observe here too. The slower growth likely means the network at the Cape was became denser over time—or more connected than before. This could be further support for the other literature on the reliance on networks at the Cape and evidence of the entrenchment of the market over time.

The three commonly used measures for identifying the most central individuals are degree, betweenness, and eigenvector centrality. These measures allow us to identity more important individuals relative to others and show the individuals who are more likely to have information about others. While previous work has shown that wealth and credit transactions were related,[57] it is not necessary that these individuals are also central to the network. Degree centrality describes how connected a certain node, in this case an individual listed in the inventories, is. In the case of social network analysis, a node is defined as either an individual or a household connected to others in the network and is an element of $N = \{1, 2, 3, \ldots\}$. The degree of centrality for a node is $\frac{d_i(g_{ij})}{n-1}$, where g is an $n \times n$ matrix for individuals and g_{ij} are all the possible relationships between i and j.[58] This measure would tell us how many connections an individual at the Cape had to other individuals, but not how important the individual was within the network. Degree is only an indication of the number of connections or transactions an individual has or was involved in.

The second measure is betweenness centrality. For betweenness centrality, the shortest path between two individuals (k and j) is calculated, and the number of paths on which individual i lies is counted. The betweenness centrality of individual i is calculated by $Ce_i^{B(g)} = \sum_{k \neq j : i \notin k, j} \frac{\left(\frac{P_i(kj)}{P(kj)}\right)}{\frac{(n-1)(n-2)}{2}}$. The closer this ratio is to one, the more i lies on

[57] Fourie and Swanepoel, "Impending Ruin".

[58] Jackson, *Social and Economic Networks,* 37–38.

paths connecting others (k and j defined here) to one another, and thus the more central i becomes to the network. It is often an important node for information.[59] If an individual has a higher betweenness centrality, they likely have more information about others and could be match maker in the market.

The next measure of centrality considered for the Cape's credit network is eigenvector centrality. Eigenvector centrality for individual i is proportional to the relative position of the connection with j, or $C_i = a \sum_j g_{ij} C_j$. Eigenvector centrality gives an indication of the relative importance of individual i in the network. Eigenvector centrality increases as the node is connected to more influential and central nodes, that is i becomes proportionally more important if j is more important.[60] Eigenvector centrality will give an indication of the nodes with the most influence over others in the network. More influential individuals would likely have more wealth, so eigenvector centrality and wealth are expected to be correlated.

Figure 3 shows the betweenness centrality network for the second period. It is possible to use shorter or longer periods for cutoff dates or individual inventories to construct an individual's network. The first observation to note from Fig. 3 is the interconnectedness of Cape society. This graph shows the giant graph of the transactions between 1725 and 1749 and includes only the nodes that are connected to the whole graph. For example, those with a debt to another individual who is not connected to others are be excluded. This does not mean that those with few debts are excluded. The white nodes show the individuals with few transactions that might be connected to only one other individual that is connected in the network. The gray nodes have more connections and are on more paths between individuals, while the black nodes are individuals with the highest betweenness centrality. These black nodes are the individuals who are most likely to have the most information about others.

Table 5 shows the top individuals by the highest degree, betweenness, and eigenvalue centrality and by time period. What is immediately apparent from Table 5 is how a few of the central individuals identified by historians are identified in these networks as well. The more familiar

[59] Jackson, *Social and Economic Networks*, 39.

[60] Jackson, *Social and Economic Networks*, 39.

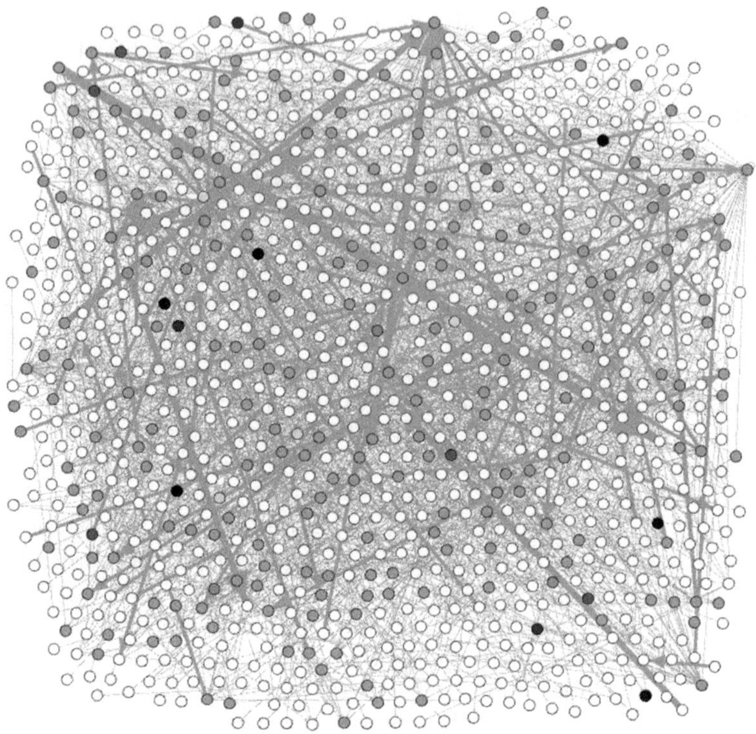

Fig. 3 Credit network with betweenness centrality between 1725 and 1749 (*Source* See text; *Note* Darker nodes have higher betweenness centrality. The same graphs can be drawn for all time periods and centrality measures)

Cape settlers include Jan van der Swyn[61] (an alcohol *pachter*), Jan Meindert Kruywagen[62] (son of a main creditor), and Jacob van Reenen[63] (a meat *pachter*; his sons are noticeably absent). These individuals were likely

[61] WCARS, MOOC8, Vol. 5 No. 110; Groenewald, 'Dynasty building'.

[62] WCARS, MOOC8, Vol. 5 No. 19; Leonard Guelke and Ross Shell, 'An Early Landed Gentry: Land and Wealth in the Cape Colony, 1652–1731', in: *Journal of Historical Geography* 52:2 (1983), 293–306.

[63] WCARS, MOOC8, Vol. 11 No. 45a; Roy Havemann and Johan Fourie, 'The Cape of Perfect Storms: Colonial Africa's First Financial Crash, 1788–1793' (ERSA working paper 511, 2015).

market makers with not only vast volumes of trading but also various contracts and both credits and debts (albeit more credit than debts). The apparent absence of the wealthiest does not mean none of the wealthy are identified here.

A key example of this is Tobias Christiaan Rönnenkamp,[64] whose inventory was taken in 1793. Born in 1730 in Hamburg, Germany, he was the son of a needle maker. He came to the Cape Colony in 1754 as a soldier with the VOC—as many others had too. He quickly rose through the ranks and by 1788 he was secretary of the Orphan Chamber.[65] There is no doubt about his wealth—his estate was worth over 24,000rds or over 600,000 grams of silver. The Dutch National Archives[66] lists his full salary over the years and shows an annual salary of 480 gulden, and a total of 10,003 gulden (or assuming a 1:3 exchange rate; Sect. 2 details exchange rate use), 3,334rds or 83,000 grams of silver. He was chosen due to the vast number of transactions that he was involved in. Listed in his probate are 1,234 transactions that were taken on behalf of the Orphan Chamber, I ignore these here and focus only on the transactions that were made in his personal capacity. At the time of his death, he owed 33,816rds in debt, but 67,571rds of credit was owed to him from 248 transactions (162 debt transactions and 86 credit transactions). This included transactions for landed property, slaves, and wages, with some supported by and recorded through bonds. He furthermore had 37 slaves, two properties in Cape Town, and volumes of books on religion, law, and history. His wealth is in no doubt, as his probate is over 100 pages long (transcribed). Although he may be an exception, the results should not be disregarded as a network which excluded the gentry or *pachters*.

I have been able to locate five of these bond records in the notaries' ledgers that involve Rönnenkamp. One of these was for capital (probably land) offered to a settler, Isaac de Vlamming, with Johannes Daniel Karnespek as the notary, and his lawyer, Willem Kolver present. The

[64] WCARS, MOOC8, Vol. 46 No. 28.

[65] J. Hoge, *Personalia of the Germans at the Cape, 1652–1803* (Pretoria, 1946); W.J. de Kock and D.W. Kruger Kruger (eds.), *Dictionary of South African Bibliography* volume 2 (Tafelberg, 1972); Anatonia Malan, 'Households of the Cape, 1750 to 1850: Inventories and the Archaeological Record' (dissertation, University of Cape Town, 1993).

[66] Dutch National Archives, 1.04.02 VOC archive, inv. nr. 6308 f222. Available at: https://www.nationaalarchief.nl/onderzoeken/archief/1.04.02/invnr/6308/file/NL-HaNA_1.04.02_6308_0474 (accessed on: 19 October 2022).

Table 5 Identified individuals from various centrality measures

	1700–1724	*1725–1749*	*1750–1774*	*1775–1795*
	Eigenvalue centrality			
1.	Pieter Meyer	Judith Kuyp	Jacob van Reenen	Tobias Christiaan Rönnenkamp
2.	Barend van den Brink	Jan de Wit	Roelof Laubscher	Jan Jacob Meyer
3.	Willem de Ruiter	Gerrit Olivier	Michiel Smuts	Josua Joubert
4.	Wynand Bezuidenhout	Jan Meidert Kruywagen	Hermanus Keeve	Christoffel Lombaard
5.	Martin Godlieb Eckard	Jasper Raats	Johannes Henricus Blankenberg	Johannes Matthias Bletterman
6.	Joost Reinard Schenk	Jacob de Villiers	Theodorus Kriel	Jacobus Scheepers
7.	Jan Dirk de Beer	Claas Kuyp	Frans Adam Carelson	Joseph de Klerk
8.	Christina Does	Gideon Slabbert	Fredrik Sparman	Anna Bock
9.	Johannes Bocklenbergh	Susanna Joubert	Johanna Siekermans	Francois Smit
10.	Christiaan Bock	Geertruida de Wit	Joachim Nicolaas von Dessin	Johannes Mattheus Hartzog
	Betweenness centrality			
1.	Pieter Meyer	Jan Meindert Kruywagen	Jacob van Reenen	Tobias Christiaan Rönnenkamp
2.	Wynand Bezuidenhout	Jacob de Villiers	Johanna Siekermans	Pieter Terblanche
3.	Barend van den Brink	Jan van der Swyn	Roelof Laubscher	Josua Joubert
4.	Willem Ruiter	Judith Kuyp	Daniel van Reenen	Maria Johanna Hugo
5.	Johannes Bocklenbergh	Jan Christoffel Bek	Christiaan Victor	Stephanus Stroh
6.	Jean Roy	Andries Bruyns	Hermanus Keeve	Gabriel Stoltz
7.	Engela Lambert	Lukas Meyer	Fredrik Sparman	Daniel Hugo
8.	Dina Willems	Geertruida de Wit	Salomon Bosch	Jan Jacob Jarling
9.	Jacob Bisseux	Johannes Ernst Heger	Jurgen Jansen	Hendrik Christiaan Herholdt
10.	Anna Bockelenberg	Jasper Raats	Hendrik Ras	Jacobus Scheepers
	Degree centrality			

(continued)

Table 5 (continued)

	1700–1724	*1725–1749*	*1750–1774*	*1775–1795*
1.	Pieter Meyer	Judith Kuyp	Hermanus Keeve	Tobias Christiaan Rönnenkamp
2.	Wynand Bezuidenhout	Jan van der Swyn	Jacob van Reenen	Josua Joubert
3.	Barend van den Brink	Jan Meindert Kruywagen	Fredrik Sparman	Johan Adam Raubenheimer
4.	Maria de Peronne	Hendrik Thomas van Hoesum	Joachim Nicolaas von Dessin	Abraham de Haan
5.	Anna Retief	Aletta van der Storm	Cornelis van Rooyen	Andries Brink
6.	Jacques Pinard	Gelyn van Gogh	Johanna Siekermans	Jan Martin Vogel
7.	Jan Dirk de Beer	Geertruida de Wit	Johannes Henricus Blankenberg	Johannes Albertus Laubscher
8.	Martin Meckelenberg	Jan Jacob Grandam	Jurgen Jansen	Michiel Otto
9.	Engela Lambert	Hendrik Hoppe	Christiaan Ackerman	Johannes Matthias Bletterman
10.	Maria le Febre	Emma Martha van der Byl	Maria Knoetse	Jan Jacob Meyer

Source See text

contract is for the value of 3,466.32rds with a 6% interest—the maximum interest rate allowed under usury laws at the Cape Colony. There are also conditions that the loan could be recalled in case of non-payment. Based on the sample from the archives, these were standardized contracts and not individualized, and similar statements are observed elsewhere. What is interesting to note here is that this debt is not noted in Rönnenkamp's inventory but there are other debts to De Vlamming for goods bought on auction. This suggests that the large debt was repaid but that the relationship between the two men continued after the initial debt. This is further support for the evidence provided by Dooling and Mitchell that networks at the Cape were important for the settlers.[67]

Despite the sheer number of transactions in Rönnenkamp's inventory, the question remains if and how his portfolio differed from others. To answer this, I compare his portfolio to those of persons identified through

[67] Dooling, 'Slavery'; Mitchell, 'Belongings'.

the historiography and who are in the inventories named above. The results are shown in Table 6. All four individuals were involved in both credit and debt transactions. They have properties, slaves, and cash. One difference is the number of transactions that Rönnenkamp was involved in. This suggests that some individuals especially the wealthy individuals had similar portfolios and used the credit market in the same manner.

A second result from Table 5 is to note the role of women in the Cape's financial market and economy. There are six women identified in the centrality measures. This provides further support for the literature on the role of widows within the Cape. For example, Von Fintel, Du Plessis, and Jansen found widows were often very wealthy and used their share of inheritances to become socially mobile.[68] Although beyond the scope here, these women identified here warrant further biographical and scholarly attention. One example is Johanna Siekermans.[69] She was the mother of Jacob van Reenen, and yet is not mentioned when the legacy of the Van Reenens is discussed. She had no less than nine properties in

Table 6 A comparison of portfolios between various identified individuals

Name	*Number of properties*	*Number of Slaves*	*Cash (rds)*	*Number of transactions*	*Number of bonds*	*Credits (rds)*	*Debts (rds)*
Tobias Christiaan Rönnenkamp	2	37	160.20	248	35	67,571.90	33,816.50
Jan van der Swyn	4	21	2,276.00	50	3	2,723.10	13,462.70
Jan Meindert Kruywagen	4	2	5,015.00	40	29	28,622.40	269.20
Jacob Van Reenen	3	10	1,699.00	52	26	36,378.00	945.90

Source See text

[68] Dieter von Fintel, Sophia du Plessis, and Ada Jansen, 'The Wealth of Cape Colonial Widows: Inheritance Laws and Investment Responses Following Male Death in the Seventeenth and Eighteenth Century', in: *Economic History of Developing Regions* 28:1 (2013), 87–108.

[69] WCARS, MOOC8, Vol. 7 No. 48.

Cape Town, nineteen slaves, and the net value of her estate stood over 10,000rds when she died in 1756.

A final consideration for this chapter is the central role of institutions in the credit market at the Cape. As mentioned above, there were three major institutions at the Cape—the Company, the Orphan Chamber and the church. The Cape was not unique in that these institutions were involved in the provision of credit. In other Dutch colonies, like Makassar and Batavia, these institutions also played a role.[70] Gelderblom and Jonker showed how institutional investors in Amsterdam were key in Dutch financial development.[71] At the Cape, they provided initial loans for capital (mainly farms) and labor (imported slaves).

More important for the structure of the network are the eigenvector and betweenness centralities. The Company and the Orphan Chamber both had high eigenvector centrality rankings. A reason for this is that Company employees often borrowed from them. For example, Rönnenkamp used his position as Secretary at the Orphan Chamber and had almost 13,000rds in his records owed to the Orphan Chamber and 3,200rds to the Company; Hendrik Oostwald Eksteen owed 800rds to the Company; Nicolaas Laubscher owed 800rds to the Orphan Chamber. These are just a few examples. Borrowing from the Company happened almost exclusively to purchase land, again a case for why it became influential in the market, while the Orphan Chamber and church were involved in lending for production purposes.

5 Conclusion

This chapter placed the Cape Colony's credit market into international perspective and used network analysis to identify the central individuals in the Cape's credit network. The Cape's credit market had elements that coexisted together. There was peer-to-peer lending, some of which was done by market makers. While many other regions and case studies have the two elements as well, focus is often placed on one or the other. At

[70] Schnitzeler, 'Financial Care for the Vulnerable'.

[71] Oscar Gelderblom and Joost Jonker, 'With a View to Hold: The Emergence of Institutional Investors on the Amsterdam Securities Market During the Seventeenth and Eighteenth Century', in: Jeremy Atack and Larry Neal (eds.), *The Origin and Development of Financial Markets and Institutions: From the Seventeenth Century to the Present* (Cambridge, 2009).

the Cape, the elements are more entwined, making it difficult to separate the roles played by individuals. This structure of the credit market was caused by the smallness of the markets and the reliance on each other. This familiarity between parties, with the contracts and sanctions suggests that the Cape's credit markets was a network + market.

I used network analysis to further investigate this network structure and identified the key market makers through the centrality measures. Networks are important for credit markets in most cases as the structure of them can be informative of the information and knowledge infrastructure. Using the centrality measures, especially betweenness centrality that measures who shares information, I could find the market makers. While many of these individuals were already well-documented in the Cape's historiography, I also identified some new prominent players like Tobias Christiaan Rönnenkamp and Johanna Siekermans. The centrality measures further enabled me to distinguish who the most influential individuals in the network were, and whether the individuals identified in the network here are the same individuals identified in the existing historiography of the Cape. The results show that many of the individuals identified by the existing historiography as important economic agents are also identified when social network analysis is used.

The chapter makes two important contributions to the literature on non-bank credit markets: First, it offers an interesting case study where there are elements of both peer-to-peer lending and transactions with intermediation that were present in the market. It characterizes the Cape credit market and shows how the two elements of peer-to-peer lending and market makers were important for the expansion of the market. The limited size of Cape society made the presence of these elements vital for the market and it was one way in which the credit market solved problems of cash scarcity and resource allocation. Secondly, it expands our understanding of credit markets outside of Europe and America and how to identify the market types developed in this volume. The Cape's credit market was a network + market with the reliance on familiarity between parties, with sanctions, and contracts. The network uses various centrality degrees to identify the key players in the network. The betweenness centrality is a measure of information flow and can be used to identify the market makers in the network. One avenue for future research is to investigate these individuals in more detail and how some have been overlooked by historians.

References

Baartman, Teun, 'Fighting for the Spoils: Cape Burgerschap and Faction Disputes in Cape Town in the 1770s' (unpublished dissertation, University of Cape Town, 2011).

Burt, Ronald S., 'Structural Holes versus Network Closure as Social Capital', in: Nan Lin, Cook, Karen, and Ronald S. Burt (eds.), *Social Capital: Theory and Research* (New York, 2001).

Cilliers, Jeanne and Johan Fourie, 'New Estimates of Settler Life Span and Other Demographic Trends in South Africa, 1651–1948', in: *Economic History of Developing Regions* 27:2 (2012), 61–86.

Cilliers, Jeanne, Johan Fourie, and Christie Swanepoel, ''Unobtrusively into the Ranks of Colonial Society': Intergenerational Wealth Mobility in the Cape Colony Over the Eighteenth Century', in: *Economic History of Developing Regions* 34:1 (2019), 48–71.

De Kiewiet, Cornelis, *A History of South Africa: Social and Economic* (Oxford, 1941).

De Kock, W.J. and D.W. Kruger (eds.), *Dictionary of South African Bibliography* volume 2 (Tafelberg, 1972).

De Zwart, Pim, 'South African Living Standards in a Global Perspective, 1835–1910', in: *Economic History of Developing Regions* 26:1 (2011), 49–74.

Dermineur, Elise M., 'Peer-to-Peer Lending in Pre-industrial France', in: *Financial History Review* 26:3 (2019), 359–388.

Dooling, Wayne, 'The Decline of the Cape Gentry, 1838–c.1900', in: *The Journal of African History* 40:3 (1999), 215–242.

Dooling, Wayne, *Slavery, Emancipation and Colonial Rule in South Africa* (Pietermaritzburg, 2005).

Dooling, Wayne, 'The Making of a Colonial Elite: Property, Family and Landed Stability in the Cape Colony, c.1750–1834', in: *Journal of Southern African Studies* 31:1 (2005), 147–162.

Du Plessis, Stan and Sophia du Plessis, 'Happy in the Service of the Company: The Purchasing Power of VOC Salaries at the Cape in the 18th Century', in: *Economic History of Developing Regions* 27:1 (2012), 125–149.

Dutch National Archives, 1.04.02 VOC archive, inv. nr. 6308 f222. Available at: https://www.nationaalarchief.nl/onderzoeken/archief/1.04.02/invnr/6308/file/NL-HaNA_1.04.02_6308_0474 (accessed on: 19 October 2022).

Ekama, Kate, 'Bondsmen: Slave Collateral in the 19th-Century Cape Colony', in: *Journal of Southern African Studies* 47:3 (2021), 437–453.

Fourie, Johan. 'The Remarkable Wealth of the Dutch Cape Colony: Measurements from Eighteenth-Century Probate Inventories', in: *Economic History Review* 66:2 (2013), 419–448.

Fourie, Johan and Christie Swanepoel, "'Impending Ruin' or 'Remarkable Wealth'? The Role of Private Credit Markets in a Settler Colony', in: *Journal of Southern African Studies* 44:1 (2018), 7–25.

Fourie, Johan and Jan Luiten van Zanden, 'GDP in the Dutch Cape Colony: The National Accounts of a Slave-based Society', in: *South African Journal of Economics* 81:4 (2013), 467–490.

Gelderblom, Oscar and Joost Jonker, 'Completing a Financial Revolution: The Finance of the Dutch East India Trade and the Rise of the Amsterdam Capital Market, 1595–1612', in: *The Journal of Economic History* 64:3 (2004), 641–672.

Gelderblom, Oscar and Joost Jonker, 'With a View to Hold: The Emergence of Institutional Investors on the Amsterdam Securities Market During the Seventeenth and Eighteenth Century', in: Jeremy Atack and Larry Neal (eds.), *The Origin and Development of Financial markets and Institutions: From the Seventeenth Century to the Present*, (Cambridge, 2009), 71–98.

Gelderblom, Oscar, Joost Jonker and Mark Hup, 'Public Functions, Private Markets: Credit Registration by Aldermen and Notaries in the Low Countries, 1500–1800', in: Marcella Lorenzini, Cinzia Lorandini and D'Maris Coffman (eds.), *Financing in Europe: Evolution, Coexistence and Complementarity of Lending Practices from the Middle Ages to Modern Times* (London, 2018), 163–194.

Groenewald, Gerald, 'Dynasty Building, Family Networks and Social Capital: Alcohol Pachters and the Development of a Colonial Elite of the Cape of Good Hope, c. 1760–1790', in: *New Contree* 62:10 (2011), 23–53.

Guelke, Leonard and Ross Shell, 'An Early Landed Gentry: Land and Wealth in the Cape Colony, 1652–1731', in: *Journal of Historical Geography* 52:2 (1983), 293–306.

Havemann, Roy and Johan Fourie, 'The Cape of Perfect Storms: Colonial Africa's First Financial Crash, 1788–1793' (ERSA working paper 511, 2015).

Hoffman, Philip, Gilles Postal-Vinay, and Jean-Laurent Rosenthal, *Priceless markets: The Political Economy of Credit in Paris, 1660–1870* (Chicago, 2000).

Hoffman, Philip, Gilles Postal-Vinay, and Jean-Laurent Rosenthal, *Dark Matter Credit: The Development of Peer-to-Peer Lending and Banking in France* (Princeton, 2019).

Hoge, J. (ed.), *Personalia of the Germans at the Cape, 1652–1803* (Pretoria, 1946).

Holderness, B.A., 'Credit in English Rural Society Before the Nineteenth Century, with Special Reference to the Period 1650–1720', in: *The Agricultural History Review* 24:2 (1976), 97–109.

Jackson, Matthew O., *Social and Economic Networks* (Princeton, 2008).

Lamoreaux, Naomi R., Daniel M.G. Raff, and Peter Temin, 'Beyond Markets and Hierarchies: Toward a New Synthesis of American Business History', in: *The American Historical review* 108:2 (2003), 404–433.

Malan, Antonia, 'Households of the Cape, 1750 to 1850: Inventories and the Archaeological Record' (dissertation, University of Cape Town, 1993).

Merton, Robert C. and Zvi Bodie, 'A Conceptual Framework for Analyzing the Financial Environment', in: Dwight B. Crane et al. (eds.), *The Global Financial System: A Functional Perspective* (Boston [MA]., 1995).

Mitchell, Laura Jane, *Belongings: Property, Family, and Identity in Colonial South Africa (An Exploration of Frontiers, 1725–c.1830)* (Columbia, 2008).

Muldrew, Craig, *The Economy of Obligation: The Culture of Credit and Social Relations in Early Modern England* (New York, 1998).

Muldrew, Craig, 'Debt, Credit and Poverty in Early Modern England', in: Ralph Brubaker, Robert M. Lawless, and Charles J. Tabb (eds.) *A Debtor World: Interdisciplinary Perspectives on Debt* (Oxford, 2012), 10–23.

Muller, C.F.J., *Johannes Frederik Kirsten oor die Toestand van die Kaapkolonie in 1795: 'n Kritiese Studie* (Pretoria, 1960).

Newton-King, Susan, *Masters and Servants on the Cape Frontier* (Cambridge, 1999).

Ogilvie, Sheilagh, Markus Küpker, and Janine Maegraith, 'Household Debt in Early Modern Germany: Evidence from Personal Inventories', in: *Journal of Economic History* 72:1 (2012), 134–167.

Pagett, John F. and Christopher K. Ansell, 'Robust Action and the Rise of the Medici, 1400–1434', in: *American Journal of Sociology* 98:6 (1993), 1259–1319.

Pagett, John F. and Paul D. McLean, 'Economic Credit in Renaissance Florence', in: *The Journal of Modern History* 83:1 (2011), 1–47.

Robertson, H. M., 'The Economic Development of the Cape under Van Riebeek: Part III', in: *The South African Journal of Economics* 13:3 (1945), 170–184.

Rothenberg, Winifred B., 'The Emergence of a Capital Market in Rural Massachusetts, 1730–1838', in: *The Journal of Economic History* 45:4 (1984), 781–808.

Ruef, Martin, Howard E. Aldrich and Nancy M. Carter, 'The Structure of Founding Teams: Homophily, Strong Ties and Isolation among US Entrepreneurs', in: *American Sociological Review* 68:2 (2003), 195–222.

Schofield, Thijs and Philip Lambrecht, 'Introduction', in: Thijs Schofield and Philip Lambrecht (eds.), *Credit and the Rural Economy in North-Western Europe, c. 1200–1850* (Brepols, 2009), 1–18.

Schnitzeler, Josje, 'Financial Care for the Vulnerable: Rise and Decline of Holland Orphan Chamber' (dissertation, Utrecht University, 2022).

Stiglitz, J. E. and A. Weiss, 'Asymmetric Information in Credit Markets and its implications from Macro-Economics', in: *Oxford Economic Papers* 44:4 (1992), 694–724.
Van Bochove, Christiaan and Heleen Kole, 'Uncovering Private Credit Markets: Amsterdam, 1660–1809', in: *Low Countries Journal* 11:3 (2014), 39–72.
Van Bochove, Christiaan and Ton van Velzen, 'Loans to Salaried Employees: The Case of the Dutch East India Company, 1602–1794', in: *European Review of Economic History* 18:1 (2014), 19–38.
Verwaaij, Daan and Christiaan van Bochove, 'Credit Without Banks: The Amsterdam Water Bailiff's Ledger of 1856', in: *Financial History Review*, 26:2 (2019), 171–195.
Vickers, Daniel, 'Credit and Misunderstanding on Nantucket Island, Massachusetts (1683–1763)', in: *Quaderni Storici* 46:2 (2011), 415–440.
Von Fintel, Dieter, Sophia du Plessis, and Ada Jansen, 'The Wealth of Cape Colonial Widows: Inheritance Laws and Investment Responses Following Male Death in the 17th and 18th Century', in: *Economic History of Developing Regions* 28:1 (2013), 87–108.
Western Cape Archives and Record Services, Master of the Orphan Chamber, MOOC8/1-MOOC8/75, Inventories.

An Enslaved Credit Market: Slavery, Deeds, and Litigation in Nineteenth-Century Rio de Janeiro's Financial Landscape

Clemente G. Penna

1 Introduction

During the first half of the nineteenth century, a series of economic changes set the stage for Brazil to become the world's leading coffee exporter. Rio de Janeiro, as Brazil's capital and main commercial hub, experienced significant urban development along with an economic and demographic boom, with its population more than doubling in three decades. This period of expansion fueled a high demand for investment, and the residents, known as Cariocas, witnessed the establishment of numerous new stores and businesses. These economic transformations happened under a very underdeveloped banking infrastructure.

The Bank of Brazil, opened in Rio de Janeiro in 1808, was the nation's first and only bank until its liquidation in 1829. The Brazilian

C. G. Penna (✉)
Fundação de Amparo à Pesquisa e Inovação do Estado de Santa Catarina (Fapesc), Florianópolis, Brazil
e-mail: clemente.penna@gmail.com

Laboratório de História Social do Trabalho e da Cultura, Universidade Federal de Santa Catarina, Florianópolis, Brazil

C. van Bochove and J. Levy (eds.), *Beyond Banks*,
Palgrave Studies in the History of Finance,
https://doi.org/10.1007/978-3-031-75819-5_5

capital then remained without a single bank until late 1838, and significant banking development did not emerge until the early 1860s. In the interim, borrowing and lending money was predominantly conducted by private individuals and commercial firms. Companies and ordinary people issued and circulated numerous negotiable loan titles while also successfully pursuing legal action to collect on them, navigating a highly formal lending environment. To elucidate these dynamics, this chapter provides an overview of Rio's credit market, detailing the most common financial instruments and the legal and institutional frameworks that supported the high level of credit circulation necessary to sustain the largest urban and commercial bankless center in South America.

The chapter also explores how Brazilian authorities played an active role in stimulating peer-to-peer loans. They passed legislation aimed at increasing the supply of capital to meet the growing demand for investment and to facilitate debt collection. This new financial legislation, coupled with an effective and extensive legal system, fostered an interconnection between loans and private property. In the largest slave society in the Americas, the property of enslaved people, one of the most valuable assets at the time, played a significant role in the city's financial landscape. The transatlantic and domestic slave trades generated thousands of negotiable titles that were used in other businesses and transactions, increasing credit circulation. At the same time, the ownership of enslaved men, women, and children served as one of the main guarantors for defaulted loans when they reached the courts of law.

2 Entangled Stories of Credit and Private Property

Valongo Street (see Fig. 2) was one of the busiest areas in nineteenth-century Rio de Janeiro, running alongside the docks and warehouses of South America's largest port. The street was always teeming with sailors, stevedores, merchants, street vendors, policemen, and city officials, all engaged in the bustling activity typical of any Atlantic port city at the time. On Monday, October 14, 1833, an oxcart carrying two chairs, a table, and a wooden box containing two overcoats and an adorned cotton blanket moved slowly across Valongo's uneven, rutted pavement. In the cart's lift rode the driver and a bailiff from Rio's second civil court. João Angola, an African enslaved man, sat alongside the other items in the cargo bed.[1] They were heading to the Depósito Público (Public Warehouse), or simply Depósito, as the locals used to call it. It was the legal and official entity in charge of receiving and storing assets seized by civil and commercial courts to secure payment on outstanding loans.

Every month, judges in Rio de Janeiro heard dozens of debt litigation cases, and mandatory seizure of a debtor's property was a common legal avenue for resolving such disputes. In addition to impounded assets, the Depósito stored items seized by the criminal courts, police department, and city administration. However, most of the goods and assets stored within the walls of the Public Warehouse were there to guarantee the payment of outstanding loans contracted mainly with unsecured credit titles.[2] Between 1830 and 1859, the Depósito received seized items from 2,275 debt litigation cases,[3] and as we will see, the number of court proceedings over unpaid loans steadily increased over time.[4]

One of those court cases led the oxcart in this story to Valongo Street. When it reached the Depósito in 1833, Francisco Teixeira de Lira, the manager, did what he had done numerous times before. Lira opened the gates, reviewed the court documents, inspected the shipments, labeled its contents, and directed the warehouse employees to unload and store the items safely. João Angola may have helped with unloading, but he was not there to work; he was part of the cargo. Between 1830 and 1859, Rio's law courts ordered the seizure of 2,487 enslaved people as security for unpaid loans. Like João, they found in the Public Warehouse a temporary home until their litigation proceedings were completed.

João Angola and the few pieces of furniture and clothing entering the Depósito on that Monday of 1833 underscore a typical yet fundamental event, marking the legal conclusion of a credit cycle well-known to anyone living in Rio de Janeiro at that time. The monetary value of these items and enslaved individuals sustained a thriving market for short-term and

[1] Arquivo Público do Estado do Rio de Janeiro, Collection Depósito Público (collection code Fundo DP), volume 002, documents 163 and 208.

[2] These unsecured loans were covered by a general lien—allowing legal recourse in case of default, but a collateral was not explicitly defined in the document.

[3] Arquivo Público do Estado do Rio de Janeiro, Collection Depósito Público (collection code Fundo DP).

[4] For a list of Rio de Janeiro's legal courts and their respective number of debt litigation, see: Arquivo Nacional, Base de Dados Acervo Judiciário (available at: http://www.an.gov.br/Basedocjud/MenuDocJud/MenuDocJud.php).

unsecured credit titles, due to a unique legal and institutional framework with the Depósito as one of its cornerstones. Teixeira de Lira, as the manager, was one of the gatekeepers of credit circulation in the city. The courts of law and the Depósito ensured that the money from unpaid loans would quickly return to the market by seizing and auctioning off a debtors' furniture, clothing, household appliances, books, tools, and most prominently, enslaved people. Like many other commercial centers in the modern era, the authorities of newly independent Brazil could not meet the ever-growing demand for currency. These circumstances created a background in which Rio's economy relied heavily on the more elastic peer-to-peer credit, most notably on the private issuance of an endorsable and uncomplicated deed known as *letras da terra*.[5] These *letras* became a very popular negotiable short-term credit instrument and circulated widely and almost as fiduciary money among individuals and commercial firms.

Archival sources reveal that one of the cornerstones of Rio's market for *letras da terra* was the intertwined relationship between credit and private property, a relationship that in Rio de Janeiro extended far beyond the links observed in mortgage contracts commonly seen across the Atlantic.[6] The multitude of assets entering daily into the Depósito Público due to unpaid *letras* point to a thriving credit market dominated by unsecured titles, contracted without *ex ante* collateral. The story of João Angola, along with many other enslaved individuals who passed through the Depósito, illustrates that in Rio de Janeiro, slavery's role in credit circulation extended far beyond using enslaved people as collateral in mortgage

[5] "*Letras da terra*" ("bills of the land" in a literal translation) does not have a direct English equivalent. As the chapter will show, they were unsecured short-term credit instruments that, although bearing some similarities to promissory notes and British domestic bills of exchange, were a distinct financial instrument used throughout Brazil since the late-colonial period.

[6] Linda Greenow, *Credit and Socioeconomic Change in Colonial Mexico: Loans and Mortgages in Guadalajara, 1720–1820* (Boulder, 1983); Richard Holcombe Kilbourne, *Debt, Investment, Slaves: Credit Relations in East Feliciana Parish, Louisiana, 1825–1885* (Tuscaloosa, 1995); Renato Leite Marcondes, *A Arte de Acumular na Economia Cafeeira: Vale do Paraiba Seculo XIX* (Lorena, 1998); Joseph James Ryan Jr., 'Credit Where Credit is Due: Lending and Borrowing in Rio de Janeiro, 1820–1900' (unpublished dissertation, Los Angeles, 2007); Luis Felipe Zegarra, 'Private Lenders, banks and mortgage credit in Peru: Evidence from notarised loans', in: *Journal of Iberian and Latin American Economic History* 35:1 (2017), 105–146.

contracts. João Angola's brief tenure as a "resident" of the Public Warehouse offers a novel perspective on the impact of slavery on Brazilian nineteenth-century financial markets. As for the Depósito, it reveals a swift and effective institutional apparatus for enforcing loan contracts and facilitating peer-to-peer transactions, primarily through negotiable, unsecured instruments.

As an example of how entangled the *letras da terra* were with slavery and credit circulation, let me briefly describe a civil litigation court case. In 1829, the clerk and accountant Possidônio Martins de Mendonça sued his former boss, the merchant Joaquim de Mattos Costa, for unpaid wages[7] of approximately 110 pounds sterling (962$271).[8] The businessman claimed he did not pay the wages because Possidônio had cooked the company's account books and embezzled £591. According to Costa, the clerk received that amount on a *letra da terra* that he discounted at another commercial firm but did not write down in his own company's financial logs. That particular *letra* was given to the clerk by one Pedro José Viana, who received it as payment "for four slaves he had sold," and Possidônio would later discount that same *letra* for money and a few yards of fabric.

Costa had a diverse business portfolio. He owned a partnership in a metalworking company, was one of the directors of the insurance company Tranquilidade, exported coffee and imported tea, and brought slave ships from Africa to the port of Rio de Janeiro at least twice.[9] However, Costa's commercial firm primarily dealt in *letras da terra*, acquiring them for a fee (5% was the usual market rate) through

[7] Arquivo Nacional, Supremo Tribunal de Justiça (collection code BU), 1836, reference code BU.0.RCI.0900, number 7397, box 17.

[8] The Brazilian currency throughout the post-independence years was the *mil-réis*, expressed as 1$000. One thousand *mil-réis* amounted to a *conto de réis* (*conto* for short) and expressed as 1:000$000. The exchanges rates of the *mil-réis* against the dollar and the pound sterling fluctuated during the nineteenth century. For the period covered by this chapter one *mil-réis* (1$000) would correspond on average (based on the yearly exchange rates variations and inflation) to 8.8 pounds sterling and 1.5 dollars. See: Heitor P. de Moura Filho, 'Câmbio de longo prazo do mil-réis: Uma abordagem empírica referente às taxas contra a libra esterlina e o dólar (1795–1913)', in: *Cadernos de História* 11:14 (2009), 9–34.

[9] The information on Costa's businesses was taken from the two most popular newspapers at time, *Jornal da Commercio* and *Diário do Rio de Janeiro* over the years of 1826 until 1830. The collection of nineteenth-century Brazilian newspapers can be found at Biblioteca Nacional, available at: http://memoria.bn.br.

discounting. In 1829, his company's account books registered £14,659 in such transactions, and he was far from unique in this practice. Many commercial firms at the time specialized in this form of credit intermediation, trading unsecured instruments like *letras da terra*.[10]

This legal dispute over unpaid wages[11] helps illustrate how the market for discounts on *letras* worked as a multiplier of credit. Costa became suspicious of Possidônio during a creditors' meeting for negotiating the bankrupt estate of Francisco Lima's commercial firm, a common practice in Brazilian credit market at the time.[12] While auditing the failed company's records, Costa noticed that his clerk discounted small amounts of that infamous *letra da terra* several times for cash and some yards of fabric and remained with a balance of £57. That is to say that the sale of just four enslaved human beings generated a negotiable title that soon began to circulate, with the capital invested in slavery quickly returning to the market. Apart from its sketchy discount, the story behind Pedro and Possidônio's *letra da terra* is not much different from other *letras* circulating in Rio de Janeiro at the time. As the reader will soon see, even when the links between a credit title and slavery were not as straightforward as in this particular *letra* (issued for the sale of four captives), enslaved property still played a crucial role in credit circulation.

The intertwined stories of João Angola, Costa, Possidônio, and Pedro, caught in a web of credit, property, and slavery, unfolded against a backdrop of significant economic transformation in Rio de Janeiro. Before exploring the nuances of Rio's peer-to-peer credit market, which will help explain how their stories eventually met at the Depósito, it is important to highlight two pivotal moments in the city's history.

[10] From 1821 to 1859, the newspapers *Jornal do Commercio and Diário do Rio de Janeiro* published advertisements from 208 *casas de comissão* (comission houses in a literal translation), the popular term for firms specializing in credit intermediation. See: Clemente Gentil Penna, *Economias urbanas: Capital, créditos e escravidão na cidade do Rio de Janeiro, c.1820–1860* (São Paulo, 2023), 287–290.

[11] The verdict was in Possidônio's favor: the courts decided that the illegal discount did not serve as an excuse for Costa to withhold the clerk's wages.

[12] Hanna Sonkajärvi, 'A aplicação do Código Comercial brasileiro entre 1850 e 1860: Análise das evidências de um caso de falência culposa', in: *Tempo* 21:37 (2015), 170–186; Penna, *Economias urbanas, 89–95.*

3 Credit and the Economy of Rio de Janeiro Before 1850

The first decisive moment dates to 1763, when the discovery of gold in the hinterlands of Brazil led the Portuguese colonial authorities to move the Brazilian capital from Salvador—once the pinnacle of colonial sugar production in the northwest of Brazil—to Rio de Janeiro, then a small port city but much closer to the mining region in what is today the state of Minas Gerais. This pragmatic decision by the Portuguese Crown led to a rapid increase in the political and economic power of Rio de Janeiro's merchant community, especially toward the end of the eighteenth century, when they began to control one of the most lucrative businesses of the time: the slave trade with Africa.[13] Between 1792 and 1807, the number of ships docking in its port more than doubled, and the commercial firms operating in the city grew more than threefold.[14]

The second pivotal date was 1808. With the Napoleonic Wars raging in Europe, Dom João VI of Portugal made an unexpected political decision by literally moving the Portuguese Royal Court from Lisbon to Rio de Janeiro. That voyage forever changed the life and economy of the Brazilian capital—from that moment onward, a once modest colonial city became the center of the Portuguese Empire and home to its vast legal and bureaucratic apparatus.[15] This event drastically transformed the city's infrastructure. Significant urban developments followed the royal family's arrival, including the construction of numerous roads linking Rio to other parts of the country, as well as several urban improvements.[16]

The Crown implemented yet other significant change by ending the Portuguese trade monopoly. From 1808, Brazilian ports and markets

[13] Luiz Felipe de Alencastro, *O Trato dos Viventes: Formação do Brasil no Atlântico Sul, Séculos XVI e XVII* (São Paulo, 2000); Manolo Florentino, *Em costas negras: Uma história do tráfico de escravos entre a África e o Rio de Janeiro (séculos XVIII e XIX)* (São Paulo, 1997); João Luís Ribeiro Fragoso, *Homens de grossa aventura: Acumulação e hierarquia na praça mercantil do Rio de Janeiro, 1790–1830* (São Paulo, 1998).

[14] José Jobson de Adrade Arruda, *Uma colônia entre dois impérios: A abertura dos portos brasileiros, 1800–1808* (Bauru, 2008); Théo Lobarinhas Piñero, *Os "simples comissários": Negociantes e política no Brasil Império* (Niterói, 2014), 55.

[15] José Murilo de Carvalho, 'D. João e as histórias dos Brasis', in: *Revista Brasileira de História* 28:56 (2008), 551–572.

[16] Kristen Schultz, *Tropical Versailles: Empire, Monarchy, and the Portuguese Royal Court in Rio de Janeiro, 1808–1821* (New York, 2001).

were opened for business to all nations with diplomatic relations with Portugal, leading to an intense commercial boom and increasing foreign investment, mostly British.[17] Local merchant communities gained greater autonomy following the end of colonial monopolies, especially when they began to control the lucrative transatlantic slave trade. The bustling activity at the port of Rio de Janeiro facilitated a level of capital circulation that sustained economic growth, outshining the recession affecting other areas of the country during those years.[18] This transformation became even more noticeable in the decades following Brazil's independence from Portugal in 1822, as the new nation experienced continuous increases in agricultural exports produced with enslaved labor. Additionally, a robust consumer market emerged, with an ever-growing variety of domestic and imported goods flowing through the city's docks and its many merchant warehouses.

An intense commercial and demographic boom followed this economic growth. In 1808, the arrival of the Portuguese royal fleet alone was responsible for an instant 25% increase in the city's population, adding up to 15,000 new residents.[19] By 1821, the number of the city's inhabitants jumped to 112,695, with 79,321 residing within the urban perimeter. Less than 30 years later, in 1849, the city's population grew by an impressive 138%, reaching 268,386 individuals, and these numbers do not consider the transient population typical of a port city.

As Table 1 illustrates, Rio de Janeiro boasted a significant consumer market during this period. Providing food, clothing, housing, and services for the city's residents put a significant amount of capital into circulation and employed a large labor force.

It is also important to note that all these individuals and businesses were concentrated in an area spanning just over four square kilometers. In Fig. 1, the area within the continuous lines corresponds to the

[17] Richard Graham, *Britain & the Onset of Modernization in Brazil 1850–1914* (Cambridge, 1968); Arruda, *Uma colônia*; Carlos Gabriel Guimarães, *A presença inglesa nas finanças e no comércio no Brasil imperial: Os casos da Sociedade Bancária Mauá, MacGregor & Cia. (1854–1866) e da firma inglesa Samuel Phillips & Cia. (1808–1840)* (Rio de Janeiro, 2012).

[18] Nathaniel H. Leff, *Underdevelopment and Development in Brazil* volume 1: *Economic Structure and Change, 1822–1947* (Boston, 1982).

[19] Jurandir Malerba, *A corte no exílio: Civilização e poder no Brasil às vésperas da Independência (1808 a 1821)* (São Paulo, 2000), 234.

Table 1 Demographic evolution of Rio de Janeiro, 1799 to 1872

	1799	*1821*	*1834**	*1838*	*1849*	*1872*
Households	n/a	13,901	n/a	17,056	27,024	30,918
Free born	19,578 (46%)	57,605 (51%)	39,743	78,525 (57%)	144,403 (54%)	226,033 (82%)
Freed slaves	8,812 (20%)	n/a	14,507	n/a	13,361 (5%)	n/a
Slaves	14,986 (34%)	55,090 (49%)	n/a	58,553 (43%)	110,622 (41%)	48,939 (18%)
Total	43,376	112,695	n/a	137,078	268,386	274,972

Source Mary C. Karasch, *Slave Life in Rio de Janeiro, 1808–1850* (Princeton, 1987), 111; Thomas H. Holloway, *Policing Rio de Janeiro: Repression and Resistance in a 19th-Century City* (Stanford, 1993), 26–27; Manolo Florentino, 'Alforrias e etnicidade no Rio de Janeiro oitocentista: Notas de pesquisa', in: *Topoi* 3:5 (2002), 9–40, there 10–11; Luís Carlos Soares, *O "Povo de Cam" na capital do Brasil: A escravidão urbana no Rio de Janeiro do século XIX* (Rio de Janeiro, 2007), 362–375

urban neighborhoods (*freguesias*) of Santana, Santa Rita, Candelária, Sacramento, and São José. These neighborhoods contained the residential addresses of most of the city's households. The area inside the dotted lines is where most of the commercial activity took place and where one would find the bulk of the city's stores, offices, and warehouses, as well as most public buildings, notaries, and courts of law. The star pinpoints the location of the Depósito Público.

It was a densely populated city, and the commercial and demographic booms following 1808 led to a striking rise in demand for credit and investment, a need the Crown was well aware of. Dom João VI took a series of measures to increase the money supply. The most significant of them dates from October 1808, when just a few months after his arrival the king established the Bank of Brazil, the first and only bank in the country at that time.[20] Unlike the predominantly private banks operating in the North Atlantic, which focused on commercial lending and operated mostly independently from state governments,[21] the Bank of Brazil had a monopoly on currency issuance and was heavily used to finance government spending. Due to persistent deficits, it became insolvent and

[20] Angelo Alves Carrara, *As Finanças do Estado Brasileiro, 1808–1898* (Belo Horizonte, 2022).

[21] Youssef Cassis and Philip L. Cottrell, *Private Banking in Europe: Rise, Retreat, and Resurgence* (Oxford, 2015).

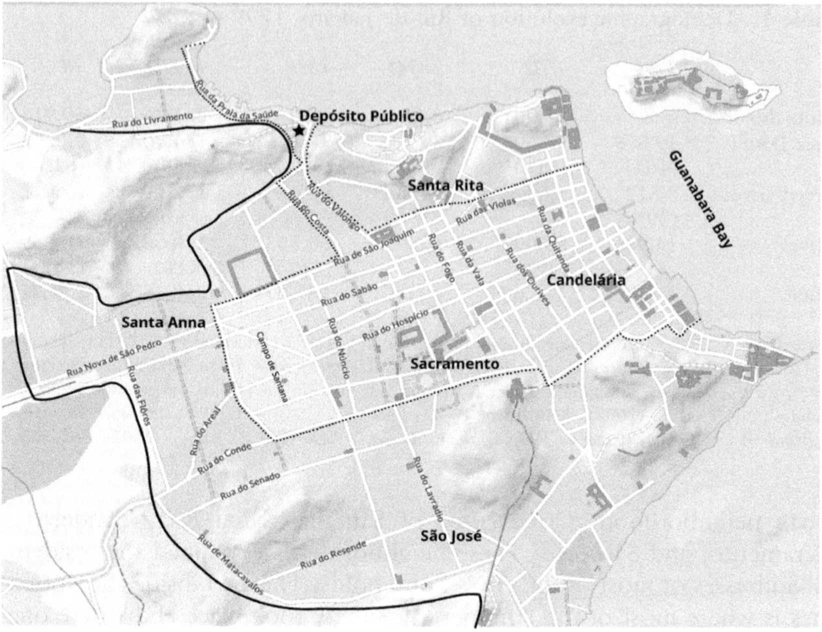

Fig. 1 Map of Rio de Janeiro, c.1840 (*Source* Author's elaboration of ImagineRio https://imaginerio.org)

closed its doors in 1829.[22] For many economic and financial historians, the bank's excessive ties to the Brazilian Treasury and its short lifespan, along with the government's hesitation in implementing new banks in the following decade, portrayed the first half of the nineteenth century as a time of credit shortage and financial archaism.[23] This picture, however, can be misleading when one does not take into account the impact of the credit reforms of the 1830s, the widespread use and practicality of

[22] José Luis Cardoso, 'Novos elementos para a história do Bank of Brazil (1808–1829): Crónica de um fracaso anunciado', in: *Revista Brasileira de História* 30:59 (2010), 167–192; Afonso Arinos de Melo Franco and Claudio Pacheco, *História do Banco do Brasil: história financeira do Brasil desde 1808 até 1951* (Brasília, 1979); Carlos Manuel Peláez and Wilson Suzigan, *História monetária do Brasil* (Brasília, 1981).

[23] Stephen Haber (ed.), *How Latin America Fell Behind: Essays on the Economic Histories of Brazil and Mexico, 1800–1914* (Stanford, 1997).

the *letras da terra*, and the role of the Depósito and the law courts in guaranteeing contracts and a smooth credit circulation.

4 The Bankless Decades

By the end of 1822, the newly independent Brazil found itself navigating treacherous economic waters. The tumultuous political landscape in Portugal after the Liberal Revolution led to Dom João VI's return to his home country, leaving his son, Dom Pedro I, as the ruler of Brazil. Along with the Brazilian throne, Pedro I inherited the nation's only bank with an empty safe, as all its funds accompanied Dom João to Lisbon. The considerable expense of setting up the Portuguese Royal Court in Rio de Janeiro and the Independence Wars meant that the economic foundation of the new nation was built over a substantial deficit. Furthermore, maintaining a stable exchange rate emerged as a crucial issue following the 1808 commercial openings, when contracts started being denominated in pounds sterling.[24] The fierce global competition for tobacco, cotton, and sugar, the country's main exports at the time, posed a significant risk to a nation whose fiscal stability relied heavily on export duties, a tax infrastructure and tariff system rooted in the long colonial tradition of rigorously controlling the wealth extracted from the New World.[25]

To make matters worse, the new country inherited preferential tariffs for British goods in addition to a sizable debt of about one and a half million pounds sterling that the Portuguese Crown contracted in London. Another potentially earth-shattering issue loomed over the Brazilian productive sector: the impending end of the slave trade with Africa. Amidst the Napoleonic Wars, to secure his throne and maintain his ruling status, Dom João signed a series of treaties with British authorities aiming to terminate the transatlantic slave trade.[26] Although risky, this trade was arguably the most lucrative and liquid business of

[24] Fernando Cerqueira Lima, 'Da moeda metálica à moeda fiduciária: As transformações do meio circulante na construção do Império do Brasil (1808–1840)', in: *História Econômica & História de Empresas* 25:1 (2022), 118–140.

[25] Michael D. Bordo and Roberto Cortés Conde (eds.), *Transferring Wealth & Power from the Old to the New World: Monetary and Fiscal Institutions in the 17th through the 19th Centuries* (Cambridge, 2001).

[26] Leslie Bethell, *The Abolition of the Brazilian Slave Trade: Britain, Brazil and the Slave Trade Question 1807–1869* (Cambridge, 1970); Beatriz G. Mamigonian, 'In the Name of Freedom: Slave Trade Abolition, the Law and the Brazilian Branch of the African

the time.[27] Despite opposition from slave traders and those exploiting enslaved workers, British pressure ultimately led to the enactment of a law in November 1831 that formally ended the slave trade with Africa.

The Law of 1831 soon encountered fierce resistance from both the Brazilian rural elites:[28] and the urban middling classes, who were heavily reliant on enslaved labor[29] and whose capital and investments were tied to slavery. Consequently, that law was soon blatantly disregarded. Brazil continued to receive and maintain over 900,000 illegally enslaved Africans from 1831 until the mid-1850s. It was only with the enactment and strict enforcement of a second and definitive law in 1850 that the transatlantic slave trade in Brazil was finally brought to an end.[30]

These factors contributed to a high level of uncertainty during the bankless decades after independence—years of fiscal crises, economic downturns, and infrastructural challenges.[31] It was only by the mid-nineteenth century that the domestic slave trade and European immigration alleviated the labor issues faced by the new and lucrative coffee plantations, providing some financial respite to the Brazilian Treasury until the Paraguayan War in 1864.[32] By mid-century, the Brazilian Conservative Party decisively rose to power,[33] stabilizing the political

Emigration Scheme (Brazil–British West Indies, 1830s-1850s)', in: *Slavery & Abolition* 30:1 (2009), 41–66.

[27] Florentino, *Em costas negras*.

[28] Jeffrey D. Needell, *The Party of Order: The Conservatives, the State, and Slavery in the Brazilian Monarchy, 1831–1871* (Stanford, 2006); Rafael Marquese, Tâmis Parron, and Márcia Berbel, Slavery and Politics: Brazil and Cuba, 1790–1850 (Albuquerque, 2016).

[29] Zephyr L. Frank, *Dutra's World: Wealth and Family in Nineteenth-Century Rio de Janeiro* (Albuquerque, 2004).

[30] Bethell, *Abolition*; Tâmis Parron, *A política da escravidão no Império do Brasil 1826–1865* (Rio de Janeiro, 2011).

[31] Leff, *Underdevelopment*; Stephen Haber and Herbert S. Klein, 'The Economic Consequences of Brazilian Independence', in: Stephen Haber (ed.), *How Latin America Fell Behind: Essays on the Economic Histories of Brazil and Mexico, 1800–1914* (Stanford, 1997), 243–266; Marcelo de Paiva Abreu and Luiz Aranha Correa do Lago, 'A economia brasileira no Império, 1822–1889', in: *Texto para discussão* 584 (2010), 1–44.

[32] For a recent and detailed overview of the Brazilian political landscape in the nineteenth century, see Thiago Nascimento Krause and Rodrigo Goyena Soares, *Império em disputa: Coroa, oligarquia e povo na formação do Estado brasileiro (1823–1870)* (Rio de Janeiro, 2022).

[33] Needell, *The Party of Order*.

landscape and gaining enough influence to pass institutional reforms that stimulated the banking sector,[34] but also placed it under the strict control of the new conservative administration.[35]

Undoubtedly, Brazil's emergence as the leading global producer of coffee, a commodity in high demand across Europe and the United States, contributed to fiscal stability and helped balance the national budget. The increased banking activity in the 1850s likely improved the flow of credit. However, the absence of these two factors—coffee money and banks—did not necessarily mean an overall lack of credit availability or a slowdown in credit circulation before that time. Independent Brazil had already shown a surprising capability of raising capital, both within the international banking system and through the issuance of domestic bonds.[36] In Rio de Janeiro, peer-to-peer credit proved to be another strong avenue for economic agents to access idle private savings to invest in new business ventures.

After the Bank of Brazil failed, the nation's capital (and the rest of the country) went almost ten years without having a single bank in operation, and a more robust banking system would only emerge by the end of the 1850s. As a contemporary observer wrote about the banks operating until 1853: "They were simple discount and deposit establishments, without issuing rights, and none of them excelled as a supplier of credit."[37] In other words: the city's commercial expansion during the first half of the nineteenth century was sustained chiefly by peer-to-peer and merchant credit.

[34] Guimarães, *A presença inglesa*.

[35] William R. Summerhill, *Inglorious Revolution: Political Institutions, Sovereign Debt, and Financial Underdevelopment in Imperial Brazil* (New Haven, 2015).

[36] Summerhill, *Inglorious Revolution*. Summerhill points out that Brazil's success in raising money abroad and at home resulted from an institutional framework that placed the national budget and the servicing of loans under the strict supervision of parliament. This oversight, in essence, lowered default risk, improved tax collection, and made sovereign borrowing easier and cheaper. However, as the author shows, this institutional framework also fostered a powerful and centralized government capable of controlling other aspects of the capital markets—one that was quick to intervene and raise barriers to the creation of joint-stock companies and the development of banking. Thus, Brazil's strong sovereign debt performance did not translate into broader financial development.

[37] Sebastião Ferreira Soares, *Elementos de estatistica comprehendendo a theoria da sciencia e a sua applicação à estatistica commercial do Brasil* volume 1 (Rio de Janeiro, 1865), 168 [author's translation].

The absence of a solid banking system in the decades following Brazilian independence is often attributed to political turmoil between liberals and conservatives[38] and its many controversies over the adoption of hard currency versus paper money.[39] Additionally, these were years of global financial turbulence, such as the Panic of 1819, which affected the American banking system until 1821 and was dubbed the first Great Depression by some authors.[40] The subsequent crises and growing animosity toward banking in North America during the 1830s[41]—including President Andrew Jackson's "declaration of war" against the Second Bank of the United States, which ultimately led to an emission bubble and burst culminating in the Panic of 1837 that spread globally[42]—likely contributed to Brazil's cautious approach toward implementing new banks.[43]

As this edited volume so aptly shows, the lack of banking activity was a feature that Rio de Janeiro shared with many other late eighteenth and early-nineteenth-century cities and rural areas worldwide. Like the Brazilian capital, several regional economies throughout the globe developed highly complex and effective credit markets[44] even without the institutional changes deemed responsible for sustaining the economic and financial development seen in the North Atlantic after the Glorious

[38] Needell, *The Party of Order*; Gladys Sabina Ribeiro and Vantuil Pereira, 'O Primeiro Reinado em revisão', in: Keila Grinberg and Ricardo Salles (eds.), *O Brasil Imperial* volume 1: *1808–1831* (Rio de Janeiro, 2010), 137–173.

[39] Thiago Fontelas Rosado Gambi, *O banco da Ordem: Política e finanças no Império brasileiro (1853–1866)* (São Paulo, 2015).

[40] Andrew H. Browning, *The Panic of 1819: The First Great Depression* (Columbia, 2019).

[41] Jeffrey Sklansky, *Sovereign of the Market: The Money Question in Early America* (Chicago, 2017).

[42] Jessica M. Lepler, *The Many Panics of 1837: People, Politics, and the Creation of a Transatlantic Financial Crisis* (New York, 2013).

[43] Penna, *Economias urbanas*.

[44] Gareth Austin and Kaoru Sugihara, *Local Suppliers of Credit in the Third World, 1750–1960* (London, 1993); Juliette Levy, *The Making of a Market: Credit, Henequen, and Notaries in Yucatán, 1850–1900* (University Park, 2012); Marcella Lorenzini, Cinzia Lorandini, and D'Maris Coffman, *Financing in Europe: Evolution, Coexistence and Complementarity of Lending Practices from the Middle Ages to Modern Times* (Cham, 2018).

and Industrial Revolutions of the seventeenth and eighteenth centuries.[45] Sound fiscal and monetary policies, strict observance of property rights, and intense banking activities are undeniably critical factors for economic development. However, merely pointing to the absence or unstable adherence to these elements, along with the relative underdevelopment of supposedly institutionally backward nations, does little to explain how credit circulated in such places.

In any case, regardless of the reasons for the delay in the emergence of banking in Brazil compared to developed nations, the economic growth in Rio de Janeiro created new investment opportunities that generated a large demand for capital. In the absence of banks, this demand was met by an expansion of peer-to-peer credit officially sanctioned by Brazilian authorities. In 1832, the national chambers enacted the Law of October 24th,[46] allowing parties in a transaction to mutually agree on interest rates instead of adhering to the previously set annual rate of 5% enforced by early usury laws.[47] However, these agreements had to be documented in a written contract, either public or private. Oral agreements, without credible witnesses, no longer carried legal value. In contracts (or any credit tittle) that did not mention interest rates the courts would enforce a standard yearly rate of 6% after maturity.

The attempts to stimulate private loans did not stop there. Brazilian legislators acted directly to boost private credit circulation during these bankless decades, enacting, less than a year later, Law Number 46 of August 30, 1833.[48] This piece of legislation abolished various previous decrees and royal executive orders that prohibited the seizure of mines, sugar mills, farms, as well as the enslaved workforce and tools within, to settle unpaid debts. Such prohibitions dated back to the 1600s, the

[45] Douglas C. North, *Institutions, Institutional Change, and Economic Performance* (Cambridge, 1990).

[46] *Coleção de Leis do Império do Brasil* volume 1.1 (1832), 129 (available at: https://www2.camara.leg.br/legin/fed/lei_sn/1824-1899/lei-37337-24-outubro-1832-563868-publicacaooriginal-87920-pl.html).

[47] Usury laws in Brazil were regulated by title LXVII of the fourth book of the Philippine Ordinances (available at: https://www2.senado.leg.br/bdsf/handle/id/242733).

[48] Available at: https://www.planalto.gov.br/ccivil_03/leis/lim/LIM46.htm.

heyday of sugar production in the Brazilian northeast,[49] and were also prevalent during the peak of gold mining in the province of Minas Gerais, in southeastern Brazil. The most famous of these was the Trintena Law, which forbade the courts from seizing enslaved workers and tools from production units with more than 30 captives.[50]

Impounding slaves as safeguard for debt payments was a common legal recourse at the time. The Trintena Law aimed to ensure that the region's largest and most productive gold mines retained the necessary workforce for extracting precious minerals for the Portuguese Crown. In a similar vein, during his reign from Brazil, Dom João enacted a series of royal decrees expanding the reach of asset seizure prohibitions regardless of the number of captives within a given production unit.[51] Mines, mills, and sugarcane farms, along with their respective equipment and enslaved workers, were safe from legal arrest.[52] These actions coincided with intense British pressure for the abolition of the slave trade with Africa. Royal policymakers believed that the end of the transatlantic slave trade would not only disrupt the workforce supply but also trigger a rush to the courts to collect debts from owners of enslaved workers, thereby exacerbating an eventual Brazilian export production crisis and Dom João likely enacted these preemptive measures to avoid a potential economic collapse.

Such legislation represented a significant state intervention in property rights, yet it was justified by the economic imperatives of a slave-based economy. Other slave societies grappled with similar dilemmas, leading to legal measures that reflected the complex interplay of economic interests and the brutal realities of slavery. These included instances such as the British Empire forcing debtors in Jamaica and Virginia to accept produce for debt payment, the French Code Noir of 1685, which declared slaves as

[49] Stuart B. Schwartz, *Sugar Plantations in the Formation of Brazilian Society: Bahia, 1550–1835* (Cambridge, 1985).

[50] Paul Ferrand, *O ouro em Minas Gerais* (Belo Horizonte, 1998).

[51] Available at: https://www2.camara.leg.br/atividade-legislativa/legislacao/colecao-anual-de-leis/copy_of_colecao1.html.

[52] These decrees, however, maintained several possibilities for collecting loans in default: the creditor had the right to confiscate a share of the unit's future production or even the estate as a whole when the debt surpassed the value of the entire property, but not the breaking of the property in parts for debt collection. It was forbidden, for instance, to seize only a plantation's sugar mills or its enslaved workforce.

personal property but included provisions to protect family units and limit the seizure of slaves for debts,[53] and the erratic state legislation in the US South that constantly changed the classification of enslaved individuals between real and personal property, impacting their availability to satisfy certain types of debt.[54]

Nevertheless, very few studies have examined how this seizure-restricting legislation actually worked on the ground, affecting debt disputes in Brazilian courts of law. Those that have, indicate that such prohibitions proved hard to enforce and had a limited scope during the eighteenth and early nineteenth centuries.[55] It also seems unlikely that Brazil could have sustained slavery, the most brutal of property systems, until 1888 without a legal, political, and institutional mechanisms to effectively enforce property rights. Notably, none of the decrees and laws prior to 1833 forbade the legal seizure of assets other than mines, mills, crop farms, and their respective enslaved workers and tools. Seeking court intervention to seize other types of property from defaulting debtors was legal and regularly enforced in the Brazilian judiciary system throughout the eighteenth and nineteenth centuries. As the reader will see, judges in Rio did not hesitate to issue seizure orders for a wide variety of items to ensure debt payment from loans made with unsecured titles that had no *ex ante* collateral, unlike collateralized debt contracts, such as mortgage deeds, which were also commonly used in Brazil since colonial times.[56] Yet, Dom João's decrees created some legal instability, which would only be addressed by Brazilian legislature some fifteen years later.

With the reforms of the 1830s, the Brazilian lawmakers took the first steps to improve debt collection legislation, aiming to enhance contract

[53] Jacob Price, 'Credit in the slave trade and plantation economies', in: Barbara L. Solow (ed.), *Slavery and the rise of the Atlantic System* (Cambridge, 1991), 293–339.

[54] Sharon Ann Murphy, *Banking on Slavery: Financing Southern Expansion in the Antebellum United States* (Chicago, 2023).

[55] Carlos Leonardo Kelmer Mathias, 'O movimento do crédito: O papel dos escravos nas relações de crédito, Rio de Janeiro e Minas Gerais (c.1711-c.1756)', in: *Revista de História Regional* 13:2 (2008), 46–69; Angelo Alves Carrara, *À vista ou à prazo: Comércio e crédito nas Minas setecentistas* (Juiz de Jora, 2010).

[56] Schwartz, *Sugar Plantations*; João Fragoso, 'Hierarquias sociais e formas de acumulação no Rio de Janeiro (Brasil), século XVII', in: *Colonial Latin American Review* 6:2 (1997), 151–164; Antonio Carlos Jucá de Sampaio, *Na encruzilhada do império: Hierarquias sociais e conjunturas econômicas no Rio de Janeiro (c.1650-c.1750)* (Rio de Janeiro, 2003).

negotiability. These changes allowed and stimulated private savings and idle capital to circulate primarily in the form of unsecured credit titles, helping to address the high demand for investments generated by population growth and the increase in commercial activities. From that moment onward, the courts could once again issue seizure orders for any type of asset, including enslaved people, and such legal recourse became the norm to resolve debt disputes.[57] With these credit reforms, the Brazilian government sent a clear message to all economic agents: make your investments and the law will not create obstacles to freedom of contract and loan collection.

During the bankless decades, the Brazilian legislators built a new legal framework that favored the emergence of increasingly extensive, complex, and impersonal credit networks. In Rio de Janeiro, the *letras da terra*—an unsecured, simple, and negotiable title moved vast amounts of capital among the Cariocas. These *letras* were a vital part of this new engine of credit that would later sustain the comeback of a national banking system.

5 *Letras da terra*, Rio de Janeiro's Credit Instrument of Choice

Most commercial centers in the early modern Atlantic and Indian oceans dealt in bills of exchange to circumvent the chronic problems of money supply and the many predicaments of long-distance trade.[58] In eighteenth- and nineteenth-century Brazil, bills of exchange also played a significant commercial role. Similar to those in Europe and North America, the Brazilian bill of exchange (*letras de câmbio*) circulated widely among merchant firms and was also commonly used as payment order,

[57] Penna, *Economias urbanas*.

[58] Fahad Ahmad Bishara, *A Sea of Debt: Law and Economic Life in the Western Indian Ocean, 1780–1950* (Cambridge, 2017); Jeremy Baskes, *Staying Afloat: Risk and Uncertainty in Spanish Atlantic World Trade, 1760–1820* (Stanford, 2013).

also facilitating the transfer of goods and capital between regions and countries worldwide.[59]

José da Silva Lisboa, the viscount of Cairu, a highly influential political figure with direct access to the Portuguese king, authored the first legal study on these instruments in Brazil as part of his extensive seven-volume series on Portuguese commercial law.[60] His compendium was popular among the Luso-Brazilian merchant and legal communities.[61] The fourth volume comprises of a comprehensive description of bills of exchange and the many and intricate legal aspects surrounding this complex commercial instrument,[62] and the viscount's definition sets the tone for future legislation regarding their use in Brazil. According to Cairu, bills of exchange are distinct from loan titles or mutual arrangements and serve chiefly as means of payment. He argued that legitimate bills of exchange were primarily for commercial negotiations between different trading posts, with detailed values, deadlines, and parties involved.

Regardless of the viscount's view that bills of exchange should be exclusively employed in commercial transactions, by the time he wrote his study, the adoption of multiple endorsements had long transformed

59 Raymond de Roover, *L'Evolution de la lettre de change: XIVe-XVIIIe siècles* (Paris, 1953); James Steven Rogers, *The Early History of the Law of Bills and Notes: A Study of the Origins of Anglo-American Commercial Law* (Cambridge, 2004); Francesca Trivellato, *The Promise and Peril of Credit: What a Forgotten Legend about Jews and Finance Tells Us about the Making of European Commercial Society* (Princeton, 2019); Penna, *Economias urbanas*.

60 With the very long title of *Principios de direito mercantil, e leis da marinha: Para uso da mocidade portugueza, destinada ao commercio, divididos em oito tratados elementares, contendo a respectiva legislaçaõ patria, e indicando as fontes originaes dos regulamentos maritimos das principaes praças da Europa: de ordem de sua alteza real, o principe regente nosso senhor, por José da Silva Lisboa, Deputado, e Secretario da Meza da Inspecçaõ da Agricultura e Commercio da Cidade da Bahia*. Cairu's study comprises of seven volumes, with the first edition dating from 1801. All the volumes are available at: https://digital.bbm.usp.br/handle/bbm/5313 and https://digital.bbm.usp.br/handle/bbm/5315.

61 Antonio Penalves Rocha, *A economia política na sociedade escravista: Um estudo dos textos econômicos de Cairu* (São Paulo, 1996); Arno Wehling, 'Cairu e o "Comércio Franco e Legítimo"', in: *Revista Interdisciplinar do Direito* 18:1 (2020), 59–74.

62 José da Silva Lisboa, *Principios de direito mercantil, e leis de marinha: Para uso da mocidade portugueza, destinada ao comercio* volume 4: *Das letras de cambio; De ordem de sua alteza real, o principe regente nosso senhor* (Lisbon, 1811).

European bills of exchange, that had already lost their mostly mercantile nature and were widely used as credit instruments.[63] The textual composition, laws, and traditional rules governing the use of bills of exchange were very similar throughout global mercantile communities,[64] which helped the bills to retain their status as the most common long-distance payment medium and a well-established credit title long into the nineteenth century.[65]

As a nobleman and a member of the Portuguese *ancien régime*, the viscount of Cairu championed the moral virtues of commerce and insisted on the pure mercantile nature of the traditional bills of exchange, cautiously advocating against their use as credit instruments. However, he acknowledged the existence of some local Luso-Brazilian variations. In Rio de Janeiro, the most prominent and broadly used of these local variants were the *letras da terra*. According to Cairu,[66] they were payment orders or credit documents issued by a person to be paid to themselves or another designated party within a specified time frame, even if both resided in the same location. These local bills, like English promissory notes, could also be negotiated and transferred by endorsement. In January 1793, a royal decree crafted the legal definition that would regulate their use: "the so called '*Letras da Terra*,' are bills issued and accepted in the same locality, and they have all the effects of a Bill of Exchange."[67] Despite the alleged lack of commercial virtue in the much more credit-inclined *letras da terra*, the viscount, albeit unwillingly, admitted and recognized that they facilitated commerce and the circulation of credit within the country.

[63] Edwin S. Hunt and James M. Murray, *A History of Business in Medieval Europe, 1200–1550* (Cambridge, 1999); Trivellato, *The Promise*.

[64] Roover, *L'Evolution de la lettre de change*; Larry Neal, *The Rise of Financial Capitalism: International Capital Markets in the Age of Reason* (Cambridge, 1993); Rogers, *The Early History*; Sushil Chaudhury and Markus A. Denzel, *Cashless Payments and Transactions from the Antiquity to 1914* (Stuttgart, 2008).

[65] Trivellato, *The Promise*.

[66] José da Silva Lisboa, *Principios de direito mercantil, e leis de marinha: Para uso da mocidade portugueza, destinada ao commercio, divididos em oito tratados elementares, contendo a respectiva legislção patria, e indicando as fontes originaes dos regulamentos maritimos das principaes parças da Europa* (Lisbon, 1811), 18–19.

[67] Joaquim José Caetano Pereira e Sousa, *Esboço de hum diccionario juridico, theoretico, e practico, remissivo ás leis compiladas, e extravagantes* volume 2: *F-Q* (Lisbon, 1827), [author's translation].

Cairu's reluctant acquiescence underscores a crucial aspect of the *letras da terra*: their practical role in Rio de Janeiro's economy. These instruments frequently functioned merely as loan certificates that accepted endorsement and were constantly negotiated in the market. The Commercial Code of 1850, in its article 425, ratified the previous idea that the *letras da terra* were in every way legally equal to regular bills of exchange, with the sole difference being that they are issued and accepted within the same province.[68]

Title XVI of the Code listed the elements both instruments had to contain to be of legal value. As with regular bills of exchange, *letras da terra* followed a precise textual pattern, beginning with the place of issue, date, and value stated in the opening line, with this formal directive usually following: "In [x days or months] Your Mercy is required to pay, through this only and original copy of this *letra*, to myself or at my designated order, the sum of [specified amount in mil-réis], for the value you have received from me in [currency, goods, services, etcetera]. This amount is expected to be paid punctually upon its due date. To [name and signature of the issuer/creditor]. Accepted, [name and signature of the acceptor/debtor]."

It is important to note that, unlike regular bills of exchange that did not mention interest rates, the *letras da terra* could specify conditions regarding the accrual of interest, especially after the law of 1832 favored negotiability between those partaking in credit transactions. Interest rates could be charged either from the *letra*'s date of acceptance or only after its maturity. Once the *letra* was issued, it lost *any* connection with the original transaction that brought it into existence. For instance, if the *letra* in the case of Possidômio v. Costa, drawn on the sale of four slaves, was not paid for, the holder could not simply cancel the transaction and get the sold enslaved workers back. He would need to seek recourse in the courts of law, as the four captives were not automatically considered collateral for that *letra*. This is especially relevant for transactions after 1810, when new legislation changed the formalities for installment sales, decoupling the act of sale from its object. After that date a seller could

[68] Brazilian Commercial Code, Law number 556 of July 25, 1850, available at: https://www2.camara.leg.br/legin/fed/leimp/1824-1899/lei-556-25-junho-1850-501245-publicacaooriginal-1-pl.html.

no longer reclaim the sold item in the event of payment default; only a litigation court case would settle a sale debt.[69]

After issuance, a *letra da terra* could be endorsed and traded freely in the market, with no legal constraints on the number of endorsements. Whether printed[70] or handwritten, the *letras da terra* generally followed a similar structure and wording; maintaining these elements was necessary for them to hold legal value in the courts. Figures 2 and 3 show this consistency in their layout and language, depicting their standardized nature. The printed *letra* has a one-month payment term and specifies a monthly interest rate of 1% after maturity, while the handwritten one has a five-month payment term and no mention of interest rates.

Unlike regular bills of exchange, which had four copies, *letras da terra* typically had only one, which the drawer could endorse to others, often

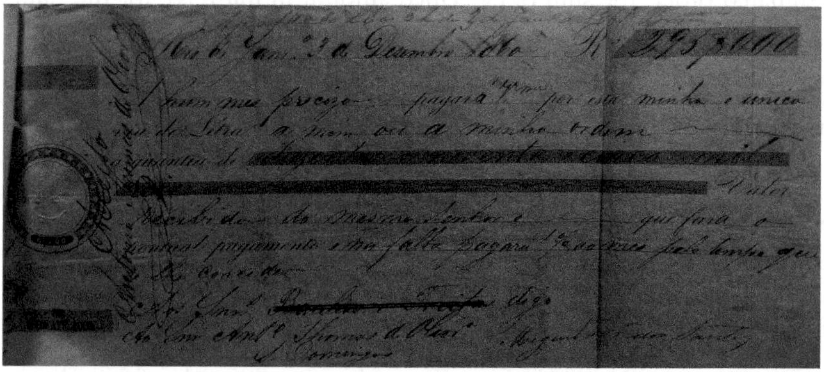

Fig. 2 Printed letra da terra (*Source* Arquivo Nacional, Juízo Especial do Comércio (collection code JD), 1864, appeal (*apelação*), number 114, box 151)

[69] The Royal Decree of September 4, 1810, also impacted Rio's mortgage practices. After that date, many such contracts began to be signed in notary books immediately following a sale's deed. These contracts used the sold item as collateral for the mortgage, functioning literally as a type of secured installment sale. The decree is available at: https://www2.camara.leg.br/atividade-legislativa/legislacao/colecao-anual-de-leis/copy_of_colecao1.html.

[70] The printed *letras* were commonly sold in booklets available in many stores or printed on demand for commercial firms, featuring the logo art of choice. Firms' booklets usually came with the companies' names pre-filled and the *letras* were numbered for easier accounting control.

Rio de Janeiro 14 de Dezembro de 1821

A cinco mezes precizos da data pagara V.S. por esta minha unica Letra a mim ou a minha ordem a quantia de dous Contos de reis, Valor Recebido

A o Snr. Antonio Joze Leite Lobo
na Rua da Candelaria

Fig. 3 Handwritten letra da terra (*Source* Arquivo Nacional, Juízo de Fora (collection code ZK), 1828, ten-day summon (*ação de dez dias*), number 2484, box 2301)

at a discount. This restricted the original acceptor's control over subsequent endorsements, creating a complex credit dynamic. Market agents had to be extra vigilant about their loans and transactions, as acceptors might not always have known who held one of their endorsed *letras*. This led to a multitude of newspaper advertisements about *letras* and loans in general, often sparking heated credit disputes in the press, with lenders publicly calling in outstanding debts, followed by the borrowers' rebuttals and justifications. This made the *letras da terra* a matter of literal public interest among the Cariocas in the nineteenth century.[71] As one would expect from a short-term title, the overall individual value of the *letras* in circulation was small, making them accessible to most market agents, regardless of the depth of their pockets.

Although extensively used in Rio de Janeiro, few studies have paid attention to their relevance for Brazilian credit markets. In Fernando Saraiva and Théo Piñero's analysis of 279 debt litigation cases from 1821 to 1850, albeit not a study on *letras da terra*, the authors shed light on the predominant use of these instruments. Remarkably, they found that 96% of the loan disputes in their sample reached the courts due

[71] Penna, *Economias urbanas*.

to unpaid *letras*.[72] However, they only looked into court cases labeled as "debt litigation" in the Brazilian Arquivo Nacional's database.[73] Yet, there were many judicial avenues to collect an unpaid loan. The Depósito, for instance, held assets seized as a result of a variety of legal responses to debt default. Between 1820 and 1850, the first civil court of Rio de Janeiro alone ruled on approximately 2,500 cases arising from debt non-payment and contract breaches via different legal instruments, such as ten-day summon, appearance day, conciliation, garnishment, legal attachment, and civil petitions. The city also hosted an extensive judiciary system comprising four civil courts, three municipal courts, the British conciliatory court, multiple judges of peace courts, parish courts, two family courts, and, post-1850, two commercial courts and a state treasury court. All of them issued seizure orders sending assets/items to the Depósito due to unpaid loans. This clearly indicates that the actual number of legal proceedings concerning default and contract compliance during 1820–1850 far exceeds the 279 labeled as "debt litigation" in the Brazil's Arquivo Nacional. Nevertheless, this does not detract from the validity of Piñero and Saraiva's findings and the high percentage of litigation initiated by unpaid *letras da terra* indicates that they were indeed the Carioca's credit title of choice.

The records from the first and second notary offices of Rio de Janeiro for the years 1835 to 1855, further demonstrate the relevance of the *letras da terra* for Rio's credit market. The 2,668 *letras* registered in notarial books amounted to a considerable sum of £489,090, suggesting a vibrant financial activity centered around the *letras*. The multiple endorsements provided the flexibility needed for a short-term credit title. Despite their similarity with promissory notes and IOUs circulating at the same time in North America and Europe, the Brazilians innovated in their credit dealings by creating a short-term unsecured title based on the rules and laws governing the well-known and long-established bills of exchange. By following the latter's rigid formal structure and drawing on the consolidated legal reasoning and tradition regulating both their use and litigation, the *letras da terra* acquired a well-founded recognition in

[72] Théo Lobarinhas Piñeiro and Luiz Fernando Saraiva, 'O mercado de crédito no Rio de Janeiro (1821–1850)', in: *Locus – Revista de História* 20:2 (2016), 129–151, there 146.

[73] Arquivo Nacional, Base de Dados Acervo Judiciário (available at: http://www.an.gov.br/Basedocjud/MenuDocJud/MenuDocJud.php).

Rio's credit market and circulated virtually as fiduciary money. More than mere financial instruments, they were integral components of the city's economic fabric in the nineteenth century.

However, it is important to acknowledge that the sample of *letras da terra* used in this chapter represents just a tiny fraction of their actual circulation volume. Rio's notary offices maintained specific books for registering and protesting bills of exchange and *letras da terra*. Registration served two main purposes: creating a legal copy of a *letra* (especially useful for single-issued *letras da terra*) and allowing its protest. The notarial act of protesting a *letra* was the issuer/creditor's first formal step to collect on an overdue one. To register a *letra*, the issuer would present it to the notary, who would copy its entire contents into the Book of Registration and Protests of *Letras*, sign this copy, and charge stamp fees and taxes. When a *letra* was not paid on time, its issuer/holder could initiate a formal protest by providing the book and page numbers where the *letra* was registered. After verifying this information, the notary would write and register a protest letter, detailing the *letra*'s amount, payment terms, interest rates, and the known addresses of the acceptor/debtor, and charge the corresponding fees and taxes. The notary officer would then deliver the protest letter to the defaulting party, either personally or by mail, and record the response (or lack thereof) in the books, concluding the protest phase. It was only with protest papers in hand that the holder of an unpaid *letra* could litigate in court. By fulfilling their legal and official role of registering and delivering protest letters for the city's most popular short-term title, Rio's notarial clerks acquired the status of bona fide experts in credit and the market of *letras da terra*—they knew the financial health and dealings of many people and commercial firms intimately. They played a relevant role as credit intermediaries, like what many scholars have shown regarding notaries throughout Europe and the Americas.[74]

[74] Philip T. Hoffman, Gilles Postel-Vinay, and Jean-Laurent Rosenthal, *Priceless Markets: The Political Economy of Credit in Paris, 1660–1870* (Chicago, 2001); Donna Merwick, *Death of a Notary: Conquest & Change in Colonial New York* (Ithaca, 2002); Levy, *The Making of a Market*; Giuseppe de Luca, 'Informal Credit and Economic Modernization in Milan (1802–1840)', in: *Journal of European Economic History* 42:1 (2013), 211–236; Lorenzini, Lorandini, and Coffman, *Financing in Europe*; Philip T. Hoffman, Gilles Postel-Vinay, and Jean-Laurent Rosenthal, *Dark Matter Credit: The Development of Peer-to-Peer Lending and Banking in France* (Princeton, 2019).

To be deemed valid, a *letra* did not have to be notarized, but registration was always necessary to protest a *letra da terra*. This rule changed in 1843 when the Brazilian government decided the Treasury should share in the successful results of the 1830s reforms in increasing credit circulation. The law setting the national budget for that fiscal year made registration in notary books mandatory for a *letra* to be valid and imposed fines for dealing with unregistered ones, leading commercial firms and banks to no longer discount *letras* without proof of notarial registration.[75] Particularly opposed by small commercial ventures and individual agents, the new tax system for *letras* (and credit titles in general) sparked heated debates in the press and congress whenever yearly deliberations for the budgetary law began during the 1840s, until the matter was settled in 1850 with the first Brazilian Commercial Code.[76]

This is one reason the sample shows a striking increase in registered *letras* in the 1850s. Since *letras da terra* had only one copy, those paid on time never made it into the notary books; instead, the parties to the transaction simply discarded them. In other words, before 1843, the Books of Registration and Protests of Letras mostly show defaults. Afterward, as the new rules took effect, they begin to reflect the market for discounting *letras*, indicating a high volume in circulation in the 1850s.

To further illustrate this point, let's revisit the case of Possidônio v. Costa. The commercial firm's account book for 1829 was audited during court proceedings, and the total value of discounted *letras* in Costa's firm alone (a medium-sized one by Rio's standards) amounted to £13,233—more than all those registered in the notary books for 1835 and 1836 combined.

Given Rio de Janeiro's status as a major commercial hub and home to the largest and busiest port in the South Atlantic during the nineteenth century, and as Costa's account books suggest, the sample used here shows just the tip of the iceberg (see Fig. 4). The total volume of *letras* circulating in the city was much higher than the notarial records display. This not only points to a robust and functional short-term market for unsecured credit titles but also suggests that default was remarkably

[75] Law number 317 of October 21, 1843 (available at: http://www.planalto.gov.br/ccivil_03/leis/lim/LIM317.htm).

[76] For a more detailed description of the registration and protest of *letras*, as well as the implementation and effects of 1843's new tax system for credit titles, see Penna, *Economias urbanas*, 198–215.

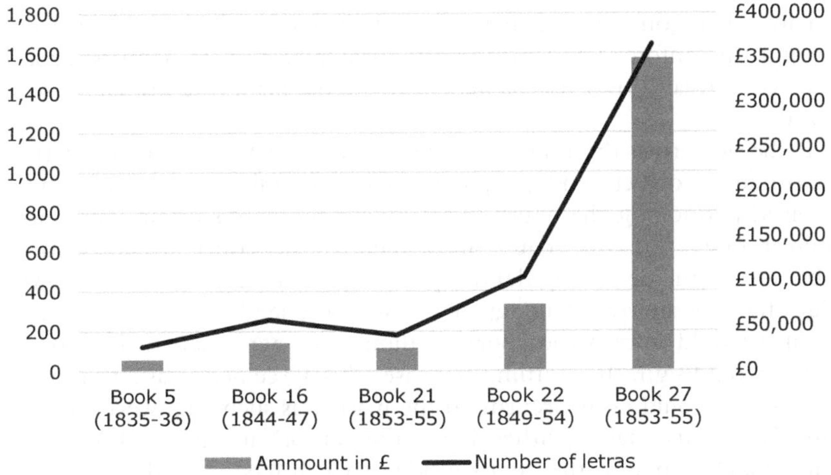

Fig. 4 Total amount of letras da terra in pounds sterling by book/years (*Source* Arquivo Nacional, Livros de Registro e Protestos de letras, numbers 5, 16, 21, 22, and 27)

low. A closer look at the Depósito, the pervasive reach of the judiciary system, and the capital literally embodied in thousands of enslaved men, women, and children explains this surprising stability.

6 Depositing Human Beings, Securing Credit

João Angola, introduced earlier in this chapter, was among the 108 enslaved individuals who were held at the Depósito in 1833. He spent nearly a month there during a particularly busy October, with 38 enslaved men, women, and children forcibly residing within the facility. The Depósito also received an eclectic assortment of goods that month: fifteen pieces of furniture, 40 yards of Portuguese cotton, six bottles of gouache paint, 415 bottles of ordinary red wine, 684 bottles of fine Portuguese wine, ten empty wine bottles, and a brown horse. Additionally to the complete contents of a typography business—printing presses, type cases, composing sticks, galley trays, 45 paper boxes, an ink roller—in essence, everything needed to establish a nineteenth-century printing enterprise. While *letras da terra* facilitated credit transactions, the judicial system played a pivotal role in ensuring the smooth operation of a credit market heavily reliant on short-term unsecured loan titles. This was achieved through the enforced and mandatory collateralization of debtors' property, with enslaved individuals like João Angola being the primary assets seized.

In broad terms, the litigation disputes that led to the seizure of this multitude of objects and people unfolded as follows: the initial step involved petitioning the court and detailing the debt's origin, amounts, interest rates, and due date. Subsequently, the court would send a subpoena to the defaulting debtor, granting them three days to acknowledge the debt and reach an agreement with the lender. If successful, the plaintiff would inform the court, outlining the agreement, which both parties would sign, thus settling the case (this agreement was a valid title in itself and could even circulate in the market as such). However, if this conciliatory phase failed, either due to the debtor's inability to honor the loan or a challenge to the debt's validity (which was never the case with the *letras da terra*, as notarial protest had already proven that), the judge would grant the plaintiff and defendant an additional ten days to present arguments and evidence. The judge would then rule on the matter, either dismissing the claim and charging the plaintiff for legal costs or ordering a *penhora* for debts deemed valid. Regularly used in Brazil since colonial times,[77] the *penhora*, akin to common law's writs of execution and judicial attachments, were a well-established legal recourse in Luso-Brazilian law to collect from defaulting debtors.[78] With this seizure order in hand, a court officer would go to the defendant's known home and business address to seize assets necessary to cover the nominal debt, incurred interest rates, and legal costs. These assets would then be placed in the Depósito awaiting the court's final rule, after which the judge would sign its release order.

The Depósito Público was a Portuguese legal and bureaucratic institution created by a royal decree in 1751.[79] Its purpose was to regulate two cumbersome aspects of public and legal administration: the handling of assets apprehended by fiscal and executive authorities and those under

[77] Carrara, *À vista ou à prazo.*

[78] Elizabeth Santos de Souza, *Dos litígios da obrigação de crédito: A ação judiciária do Tribunal da Suplicação do Brasil (1808–1821)* (Rio de Janeiro, 2021); Penna, *Economias urbanas.*

[79] Antonio Delgado da Silva, *Collecção da legislação Portugueza desde a ultima compilação das ordenações: Legislação de 1750 a 1762* (Lisbon, 1830), 62–67.

legal dispute. Previous legislation had required that all such goods and assets be placed under the care of legal guardians, citizens of upright reputation appointed at the discretion of local civil or judicial authorities.[80] However, from a public administration standpoint, this morality-based system proved ineffective. Dom João V, the king at the time, implemented the public Depósito because, as the royal decree states, private guardianship practices were being conducted "with grave scandal to the public faith, and with intolerable detriment to the inner Commerce of My Kingdoms."[81] In 1757, another decree would outright forbid private guardianship in Lisbon,[82] granting the new Depósito Público of that city a monopoly over court-seized and apprehended items. This innovation in public and legal administration of assets soon spread to other corners of the Portuguese kingdoms.[83]

It is worth reminding the reader that, in the mid-eighteenth century, the American territories of Dom João's kingdoms were mining vast quantities of gold and precious stones—highly valuable and easily smuggled commodities.[84] Removing fiscal apprehensions from the hands of private guardians and placing them under direct royal authority appears to have played a significant role in the creation of the Depósito. This was particularly true in Brazil, where, as discussed earlier, colonial law enacted several barriers to asset seizure. If the argument for weak protection of Brazilian creditors holds true, there was no urgency in addressing the legal aspect of that problem in the South Atlantic colony. However, such limitations

[80] The Philippine Ordinances of 1603, but primarily a series of later decrees and norms, regulated legal guardianship of assets. A comprehensive compilation of these later regulations can be found in Paschoal José de Mello Freire's 1789 study on Portuguese civil law, first published in 1828 in Latin and later translated to Portuguese. See Pascoal José de Melo Freire, 'Instituições de Direito Civil Português: Tanto Público Como Particular', in: *Boletim do Ministério da Justiça, Portugal* 163 (1967) (available at: https://www.fd.unl.pt/Anexos/Investigacao/1563.pdf).

[81] Da Silva, *Collecção*, 62 [author's translation].

[82] Da Silva, *Collecção*, 530–531.

[83] For a comprehensive list of Portuguese legislation in the period, see: www.governodosoutros.ics.ul.pt.

[84] For the problem of contraband and fiscal evasion in Brazilian mining regions, see Charles R. Boxer, *The Golden Age of Brazil: Growing Pains of a Colonial Society 1695–1750* (New York, 1995); André Figueiredo Rodrigues, 'Os "extravios que tão continuados têm sido...": Contrabando e práticas comerciais ilícitas nas atividades do contratador João Rodrigues de Macedo', in: *Locus – Revista de História* 11:1–2 (2005), 117–136.

were exclusive to Brazilian territory and did not apply to the European part of the kingdoms. Direct government supervision of the storage and management of assets under litigation in Lisbon, the commercial center controlling the Portuguese trade monopoly, was crucial for ensuring a functioning trade inside Dom João V's kingdoms.

The Depósito Público in Rio de Janeiro mirrored its Lisbon counterpart, serving as the institution responsible for receiving and safeguarding virtually everything apprehended by the police, city inspectors, and fiscal authorities. It also functioned as the city's lost and found department, receiving stray livestock (mainly horses, cattle, and pigs) and cargo fallen from ships or accidentally dropped on the streets by oxcarts and wagons. However, in Rio, its primary purpose was to safeguard assets from *penhoras*, particularly after the credit reforms of the 1830s, which not only favored negotiability and debt collection but also made their legal costs more predictable.

The eighteenth-century legal guardianship system was not *pro bono*; legal guardians received compensation through an intricate and varying system of gratifications based on the volume and type of items under their care. This led to numerous accusations of corruption and collusion with legal and civil authorities, causing "grave scandal to the public faith." To address the ethical aspect of this problem, the Depósito would answer to both congress and the modern-day equivalents of the Treasury and Justice Departments. On the financial side, the Depósito had clearer rules for the costs of storing and safeguarding assets. Initially, it imposed a 2% tax on the value of assets going to auction and a 1% tax on currency, metals, precious stones, jewelry, and treasury bonds. Later, the law introduced fixed fees for items that did not go to auction, along with daily charges for feeding and boarding enslaved individuals and tending to livestock. Later decrees also authorized the auctioning of unclaimed items within a specific time frame and allowed the Depósito's manager to rent out enslaved workers under his watch to offset their owner's expenses for food, clothing, and medical care.[85]

[85] The rules governing the Depósito's operations evolved throughout the nineteenth century as the number of litigation cases grew, increasing the demand and cost of storage. See: Penna, *Economias urbanas*. For the decrees, laws, and executive orders regarding the Depósito Público, see Francisco Maria de Souza Furtado de Mendonça, *Repertorio geral, ou, Indice alphabetico da leis do imperio do Brasil publicadas desde o começo do anno de 1808 até o presente: em seguimento ao Repertorio geral do Desembargador Manuel Fernandes Thomaz* volume 2 (Rio de Janeiro, 1849), 337–342.

In loan disputes involving *letras da terra*, enslaved individuals were typically held in the Depósito for no more than fifteen days, but in more complex legal cases, their stay could extend for months. For instance, in an 1839 inheritance dispute, enslaved Africans Francisco Congo and Joanna Cabinda lived under the roofs of the Depósito for 290 days. Between meals, straw mats, medical care, and prescription drugs, the losing side in that dispute incurred a bill amounting to roughly one-third the average price of an unskilled adult enslaved male worker at the time.[86]

A sample of 2,275 court proceedings with assets seized in loan disputes between 1833 and 1859[87] sheds light on how the *penhoras* and the Depósito sustained a close relationship between credit and private property in Rio, and how slavery was one of its key elements. In 35% of such cases, a wide array of items was seized: furniture, clothes, artworks, housewares, boats, oxcarts, fabric, jewelry, sacred art, tools, musical instruments, wine, liquor, livestock, books—the list is extensive. Most of these items went to public auction and quickly returned to the city's thriving retail and second-hand market.[88] However, it was slavery that held together the system created by the 1830s credit reforms. In 65% of the court seizures (1,535 cases), at least one enslaved person was placed in the Depósito to secure payment of a defaulted loan, from a total of 2,487

86 Arquivo Nacional, Juízo de Órfão e Ausente (collection code ZN), 1840, number 3969, box 558, gallery A.

87 The surviving archival sources regarding Rio's Depósito Público, spanning from 1829 to 1888, primarily consist of documents from the final stage of legal disputes involving seized assets—specifically, the judge's release order. These documents typically contain the issuing court and case number, the names of the plaintiff and defendant (in this case, the creditor and debtor), a list of items held in the Depósito, and the court's ruling. The ruling could be a conciliation, resulting in the assets being returned to the defendant; an adjudication, where the creditor accepts the assets as direct payment for the debt; or an order releasing the assets to the highest bidder following a public auction. In some cases, the documents may indicate that a third party obtained a court injunction voiding the seizure, usually when the defendant was not the sole owner of the asset or if it had been previously used as collateral in a mortgage contract. After handing the release order to the Depósito's manager, its bearer could retrieve the listed asset. Part of the Arquivo Público do Estado do Rio de Janeiro's collection, the individual orders are bound in numbered books that follow a loose chronological order. Book 1 begins in 1829 with only ten release orders for that year and then jumps to 1834; there are no records from 1830 to 1832. Book 2 has release orders beginning in 1833, and the remaining books have no records for the years 1839; 1845 to 1847; 1849; and 1850 to 1851.

88 Penna, *Economias urbanas*.

enslaved individuals forcibly living under its roof because their owners did not pay their debts (Fig. 5).

The expansion of Brazilian financial markets in the nineteenth century is often linked to two interconnected events: the wealth created by growing international demand for coffee, Brazil's main export, and a sudden influx of capital previously tied to the transatlantic slave trade before its prohibition in 1850.[89] Together, these factors are often cited as the main explanations for the mid-nineteenth-century banking resurgence that led to a modernization of the country's financial system. However, the credit reforms that effectively increased the circulation of *letras* and the role of the Depósito tell a considerably different story about the development of the Brazilian financial market.

Enslaved human beings were essential to support short-term credit circulation, usually for loan amounts not exceeding the average price of an adult unskilled enslaved worker. In 76% of the 1,535 *penhoras* backed by

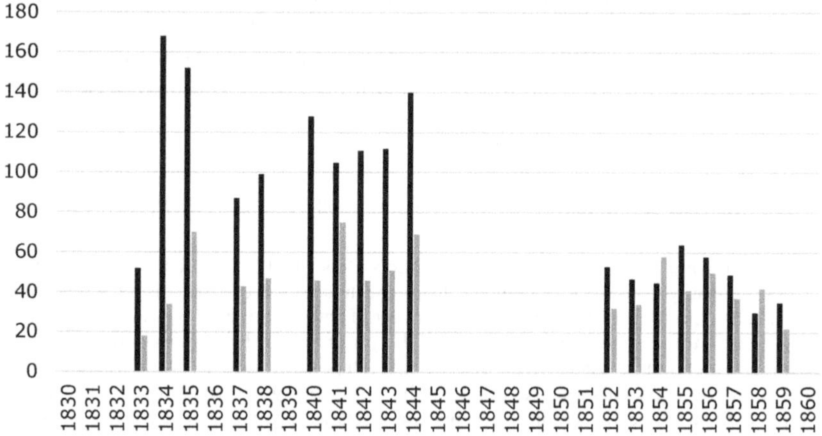

Fig. 5 Yearly distribution of penhoras by type of property seized (*Source* Arquivo Público do Estado do Rio de Janeiro, Collection Depósito Público (collection code Fundo DP), volumes 001 to 017)

[89] Carlos Eduardo Valencia Villa, *Ao Longo Daquelas Ruas: A Economia dos Negros Livres em Richmond e Rio de Janeiro, 1840–1860* (Jundiaí, 2016).

slavery, only one enslaved person was seized and sent to the Depósito, indicating loans of small amounts, as slave prices before the abolition of the transatlantic slave trade were relatively low and enslaved ownership was widespread in the city. The toil and suffering of thousands of Africans and their descendants were not only among the free population's main and most lucrative investments until the 1850s,[90] but also proved essential for the overall stability of the financial environment of a country that, during the first half of the 19th century, became the world's coffee powerhouse.

The bankless decades financed the dawn of Brazilian coffee production, a labor-intensive crop that requires high initial investments and at least five years to yield returns, the time it takes for plants to become fully productive. This suggests that the country's coffee plantations benefited from the capital that began to circulate more effectively after the laws were enacted to boost and regulate peer-to-peer credit. The data also show that the sudden influx of capital in the 1850s was not tied solely to a realignment of money previously tied in the nefarious trade. As slave ships from Africa ceased to land on Brazilian shores, the prices of enslaved workers skyrocketed, along with a proportional rise in the overall value of *letras* in circulation (Figs. 6 and 7).

Discounting *letras* was one of the most profitable operations for the newly established banks that began to dominate the credit market in the mid-1850s.[91] Like coffee production, banking also tapped into the resulting increase in credit circulation after the 1830s reforms. This created a backdrop in which slavery proved even more essential to the country's economy and finances. Enslaved workers were not only the primary labor force behind the nation's increasing integration with the industrial capitalist nations of the north,[92] but also the most significant asset sustaining credit circulation in Rio.

The crude reality of using enslaved human beings as financial assets was a common feature in other Atlantic slave societies. In the US South, for instance, close to 60% of mortgage deeds had enslaved property as the

[90] Frank, *Dutra's World*.

[91] Guimarães, *A presença inglesa*.

[92] Rafael Marquese and Ricardo Salles, *Escravidão e capitalismo histórico no século XIX: Cuba, Brasil e Estados Unidos* (Rio de Janeiro, 2016).

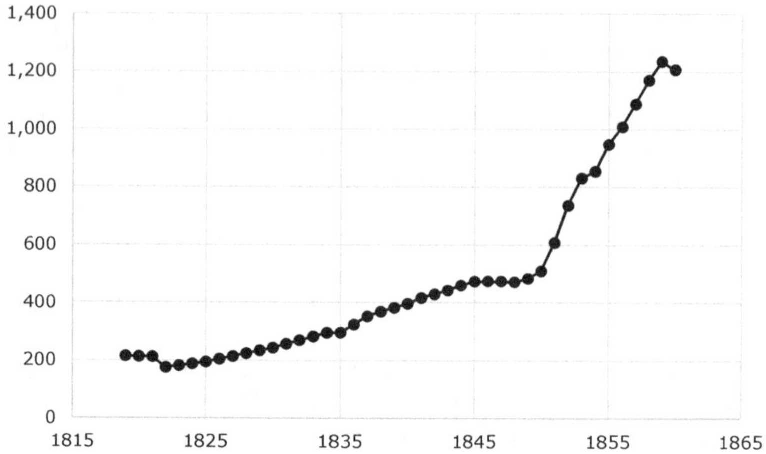

Fig. 6 Annual average prices of slaves (in mil-réis) (*Source* Stanley J. Stein, *Vassouras: A Brazilian Coffee County, 1850–1900: The Roles of Planter and Slave in a Plantation Society* (Princeton, 1985); Kátia M. de Queirós Mattoso, Herbert S. Klein, and Stanley L. Engerman, 'Research Note: Trends and Patterns in the Prices of Manumitted Slaves: Bahia, 1819–1888', in: *Slavery & Abolition* 7:1 (1986), 59–67; Mieko Nishida, 'Manumission and Ethnicity in Urban Slavery: Salvador, Brazil, 1808–1888', in: *The Hispanic American Historical Review* 73:3 (1993), 361–391; Pedro Carvalho de Mello, *Slavery and the Economics of Labor in Brazilian Coffee Plantations, 1850–1888* (São Paulo, 2016))

main collateral for a loan.[93] However, in Rio de Janeiro, individual slaves secured only 6% of all mortgage transactions.[94] Rural and primarily urban real estate comprised the vast majority of mortgage loans in Rio's notarial offices, obscuring the impacts of slavery ownership on Brazilian credit

[93] Kilbourne, *Debt*; Bonnie Martin, 'Slavery's Invisible Engine: Mortgaging Human Property', in: *The Journal of Southern History* 76:4 (2010), 817–866; Bonnie Martin, 'Neighbor-to-Neighbor Capitalism: Local Credit Networks and the Mortgaging of Slaves', in: Sven Beckert and Seth Rockman (eds.), *Slavery's Capitalism: A New History of American Economic Development* (Philadelphia, 2016), 107–121.

[94] Ryan, 'Credit Where Credit Is Due'. The percentage would be 18% when considering mortgage contracts in which enslaved people were used as collateral alongside real estate, which was usually done for higher loan amounts and longer maturities, types of loans commonly seen in mortgages backed by entire production units such as coffee or sugar plantations.

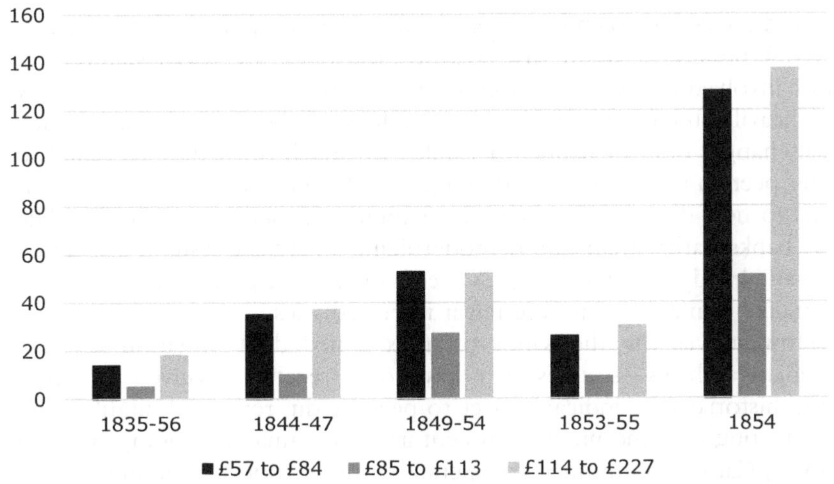

Fig. 7 The number of registered bills per amount category (in pounds sterling) (*Source* Arquivo Nacional, Livros de Registro e Protestos de letras, numbers 5, 16, 21, 22, and 27)

history. The swiftness of the courts in forcibly turning enslaved property into collateral for unsecured yet more flexible short-term loans made with *letras da terra*, and the role of the Depósito in aptly managing these *penhoras*, help to explain the difference in the mortgaging of enslaved property between these two large American slave societies. In Rio de Janeiro, both the transatlantic and domestic slave trades generated thousands of negotiable *letras* that fostered credit circulation backed by the ownership of enslaved human beings. The story of João Angola and the Depósito reveals how the inequalities of a slave society interacted with and influenced the emergence of a modern financial market, showing us how its interconnections to slavery are more robust than many care to admit.

7 Conclusion

Peer-to-peer credit played a crucial role in nineteenth-century Brazilian society, sustaining an urban economy of vast proportions. For this system to function effectively, Brazilian lawmakers created a set of rules that allowed the courts to enforce negotiability and loan payments more effectively. Whenever a credit title was deemed valid, the social standing of those involved in the transaction was usually of little concern. In a society still heavily influenced by the social values of the *ancien régime*, such legal changes did not happen naturally. In Brazil, the state intervened to foster peer-to-peer credit by adapting longstanding rules, laws, and traditions to new demands in a rapidly changing financial environment. The later banks, rather than simply modernizing an archaic system, integrated into an already vast and complex credit market, helping to organize and centralize transactions among fewer intermediaries.

However, as the thousands of unexamined debt litigation cases in Brazilian archives—sources that have only recently received attention from historians[95]—indicate, peer-to-peer credit remained highly relevant throughout the nineteenth century. Even amid expanding banking activity, Cariocas continued to operate within a robust legal and institutional apparatus that proved highly effective in facilitating debt collection. This effectiveness was unexpected in a nation often considered to have a comparatively underdeveloped legal and institutional framework.[96] Enslaved individuals played a central role in this financial system: their coerced labor generated wealth, while the institution of slavery and the trafficking of enslaved men, women, and children enabled the creation of unsecured credit instruments, such as *letras da terr*a. These negotiable titles circulated widely and were backed by the enslaved people themselves. Such credit systems likely functioned similarly in other urban centers across Portuguese America.

The Depósito Público also maintained its role as the guardian of credit security. In 1900, plans were being made to move it to a larger and remodeled building near Campo de Santana, on the western limits of the

[95] Rita Almico conducted the first comprehensive study on Brazilian credit history to address debt litigation cases, although her research covers a later period, starting in 1850. See Rita de Cássia da Silva Almico, *Em nome da palavra e da lei: Relações de crédito em Minas Gerais no Oitocentos* (Rio de Janeiro, 2015). For more recent studies addressing the first half of the nineteenth century, see De Souza, *Dos litígios da obrigação*; Penna, *Economias Urbanas*.

[96] The difference between common law and civil law systems, with the latter often considered less efficient in dealing with property rights and debt litigation, is frequently presented as an explanation for Latin America's comparative legal and institutional weakness. See, Rafael La Porta, Florencio Lopez-de-Silanes, Andrei Shleifer, and Robert W. Vishny, 'Law and Finance', in: *Journal of Political Economy* 106:6 (1998), 1113–1155.

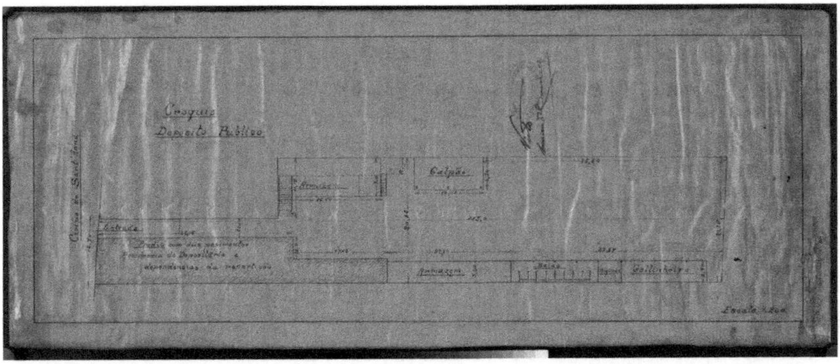

Fig. 8 Floor plan sketch of the new Depósito Público building, Rio de Janeiro, 1900 (*Source* Arquivo Nacional, Ministério da Justiça e Negócios Interiores, 1900, Croquis [do] Depósito Público reference BR-RJANRIO-4T.0.MAP.60 (available at: http://imagem.sian.an.gov.br/acervo/derivadas/BR_RJANRIO_4T/0/MAP/0060/BR_RJANRIO_4T_0_MAP_0060_d0001de0001.pdf))

city (see Fig. 8). The most significant change was that this new facility would no longer include slave quarters.

Acknowledgment The author expresses his gratitude to the volume editors, along with Christian Robles and Luiz Fernando Saraiva, for their careful reading and suggestions.

Archival Sources and Literature

Abreu, Marcelo de Paiva, and Luiz Aranha Correa do Lago, 'A economia brasileira no Império, 1822–1889', in: *Texto para discussão* 584 (2010), 1–44.

Alencastro, Luiz Felipe de, *O Trato dos Viventes: Formação do Brasil no Atlântico Sul, Séculos XVI e XVII* (São Paulo, 2000).

Almico, Rita de Cássia da Silva, *Em nome da palavra e da lei: Relações de crédito em Minas Gerais no Oitocentos* (Rio de Janeiro, 2015).

Arinos, Afonso de Melo Franco and Pacheco, Cláudio, História do Banco do Brasil: história financeira do Brasil desde 1808 até 1951 (Brasília, 1979).

Arquivo Nacional, Base de Dados Acervo Judiciário (available at: http://www.an.gov.br/Basedocjud/MenuDocJud/MenuDocJud.php).

Arquivo Nacional, Juízo Especial do Comércio (collection code JD), 1864, appeal (*apelação*), number 114, box 151.

Arquivo Nacional, Juízo de Fora (collection code ZK), 1828, ten-day summon (*ação de dez dias*), number 2484, box 2301.

Arquivo Nacional, Juízo de Órfão e Ausente (collection code ZN), 1840, number 3969, box 558, gallery A.

Arquivo Nacional, Livros de Registro e Protestos de letras, numbers 5, 16, 21, 22, and 27.

Arquivo Nacional, Ministério da Justiça e Negócios Interiores, 1900, Croquis [do] Depósito Público reference BR-RJANRIO-4T.0.MAP.60 (available at: http://imagem.sian.an.gov.br/acervo/derivadas/BR_RJANRIO_4T/0/MAP/0060/BR_RJANRIO_4T_0_MAP_0060_d0001de0001.pdf).

Arquivo Nacional, Supremo Tribunal de Justiça (collection code BU), 1836, reference code BU.0.RCI.0900, number 7397, box 17.

Arquivo Público do Estado do Rio de Janeiro, Collection Depósito Público (collection code Fundo DP), volumes 001 to 017.

Arruda, José Jobson de Adrade, *Uma colônia entre dois impérios: A abertura dos portos brasileiros, 1800–1808* (Bauru, 2008).

Austin, Gareth, and Kaoru Sugihara, *Local Suppliers of Credit in the Third World, 1750–1960* (London, 1993).

Baskes, Jeremy, *Staying Afloat: Risk and Uncertainty in Spanish Atlantic World Trade, 1760–1820* (Stanford, 2013).

Bethell, Leslie, *The Abolition of the Brazilian Slave Trade: Britain, Brazil and the Slave Trade Question 1807–1869* (Cambridge, 1970).

Biblioteca Nacional, *Diário do Rio de Janeiro*, 1826–1830 (available at http://memoria.bn.br).

Biblioteca Nacional, *Jornal da Commercio*, 1826–1830 (available at http://memoria.bn.br).

Bishara, Fahad Ahmad, *A Sea of Debt: Law and Economic Life in the Western Indian Ocean, 1780–1950* (Cambridge, 2017).

Bordo, Michael D., and Roberto Cortés Conde (eds.), *Transferring Wealth & Power from the Old to the New World: Monetary and Fiscal Institutions in the 17th through the 19th Centuries* (Cambridge, 2001).

Boxer, Charles R., *The Golden Age of Brazil: Growing Pains of a Colonial Society 1695–1750* (New York, 1995).

Browning, Andrew H., *The Panic of 1819: The First Great Depression* (Columbia, 2019).

Cardoso, José Luis, 'Novos elementos para a história do Bank of Brazil (1808–1829): Crónica de um fracasso anunciado', in: *Revista Brasileira de História* 30:59 (2010), 167–192.

Carrara, Angelo Alves, *À vista ou à prazo: Comércio e crédito nas Minas setecentistas* (Juiz de Jora, 2010).

Carrara, Angelo Alves, *As Finanças do Estado Brasileiro, 1808–1898* (Belo Horizonte, 2022).

Carvalho, José Murilo de, 'D. João e as histórias dos Brasis', in: *Revista Brasileira de História* 28:56 (2008), 551–572.

Cassis, Youssef, and Philip L. Cottrell, *Private Banking in Europe: Rise, Retreat, and Resurgence* (Oxford, 2015).

Chaudhury, Sushil, and Markus A. Denzel, *Cashless Payments and Transactions from the Antiquity to 1914* (Stuttgart, 2008).

Coleção de Leis do Império do Brasil volume 1.1 (1832), 129 (available at: https://www2.camara.leg.br/legin/fed/lei_sn/1824-1899/lei-37337-24-outubro-1832-563868-publicacaooriginal-87920-pl.html).

Ferrand, Paul, *O ouro em Minas Gerais* (Belo Horizonte, 1998).

Florentino, Manolo, *Em costas negras: Uma história do tráfico de escravos entre a África e o Rio de Janeiro (séculos XVIII e XIX)* (São Paulo, 1997).

Florentino, Manolo, 'Alforrias e etnicidade no Rio de Janeiro oitocentista: Notas de pesquisa', in: *Topoi* 3:5 (2002), 9–40.

Fragoso, João, 'Hierarquias sociais e formas de acumulação no Rio de Janeiro (Brasil), século XVII', in: *Colonial Latin American Review* 6:2 (1997), 151–164.

Fragoso, João Luís Ribeiro, *Homens de grossa aventura: Acumulação e hierarquia na praça mercantil do Rio de Janeiro, 1790–1830* (São Paulo, 1998).

Frank, Zephyr L., *Dutra's World: Wealth and Family in Nineteenth-Century Rio de Janeiro* (Albuquerque, 2004).

Freire, Pascoal José de Melo, 'Instituições de Direito Civil Português: Tanto Público Como Particular', in: Boletim do Ministério da Justiça, Portugal 163 (1967) (available at: https://www.fd.unl.pt/Anexos/Investigacao/1563.pdf).

Gambi, Thiago Fontelas Rosado, *O banco da Ordem: Política e finanças no Império brasileiro (1853–1866)* (São Paulo, 2015).

Graham, Richard, *Britain & the Onset of Modernization in Brazil 1850–1914* (Cambridge, 1968).

Greenow, Linda, *Credit and Socioeconomic Change in Colonial Mexico: Loans and Mortgages in Guadalajara, 1720–1820* (Boulder, 1983)

Guimarães, Carlos Gabriel, *A presença inglesa nas finanças e no comércio no Brasil imperial: Os casos da Sociedade Bancária Mauá, MacGregor & Cia. (1854–1866) e da firma inglesa Samuel Phillips & Cia. (1808–1840)* (Rio de Janeiro, 2012).

Haber, Stephen (ed.), *How Latin America Fell Behind: Essays on the Economic Histories of Brazil and Mexico, 1800–1914* (Stanford, 1997).

Haber, Stephen, and Herbert S. Klein, 'The Economic Consequences of Brazilian Independence', in: Stephen Haber (ed.), *How Latin America Fell Behind: Essays on the Economic Histories of Brazil and Mexico, 1800–1914* (Stanford, 1997), 243–266.

Hoffman, Philip T., Gilles Postel-Vinay, and Jean-Laurent Rosenthal, *Priceless Markets: The Political Economy of Credit in Paris, 1660–1870* (Chicago, 2001).

Hoffman, Philip T., Gilles Postel-Vinay, and Jean-Laurent Rosenthal, *Dark Matter Credit: The Development of Peer-to-Peer Lending and Banking in France* (Princeton, 2019).

Holloway, Thomas H., *Policing Rio de Janeiro: Repression and Resistance in a 19th-Century City* (Stanford, 1993).

Hunt, Edwin S., and James M. Murray, *A History of Business in Medieval Europe, 1200–1550* (Cambridge, 1999).

Karasch, Mary C., *Slave Life in Rio de Janeiro, 1808–1850* (Princeton, 1987).

Kilbourne, Richard Holcombe, *Debt, Investment, Slaves: Credit Relations in East Feliciana Parish, Louisiana, 1825–1885* (Tuscaloosa, 1995).

Krause, Thiago Nascimento, and Rodrigo Goyena Soares, *Império em disputa: Coroa, oligarquia e povo na formação do Estado brasileiro (1823–1870)* (Rio de Janeiro, 2022).

La Porta, Rafael, Florencio Lopez-de-Silanes, Andrei Shleifer, and Robert W. Vishny, 'Law and Finance', in: *Journal of Political Economy* 106:6 (1998), 1113–1155.

Leff, Nathaniel H., *Underdevelopment and Development in Brazil* volume 1: *Economic Structure and Change, 1822–1947* (Boston, 1982).

Lepler, Jessica M., *The Many Panics of 1837: People, Politics, and the Creation of a Transatlantic Financial Crisis* (New York, 2013).

Levy, Juliette, *The Making of a Market: Credit, Henequen, and Notaries in Yucatán, 1850–1900* (University Park, 2012).

Lima, Fernando Cerqueira, 'Da moeda metálica à moeda fiduciária: As transformações do meio circulante na construção do Império do Brasil (1808–1840)', in: *História Econômica & História de Empresas* 25:1 (2022), 118–140.

Lisboa, José da Silva, *Principios de direito mercantil, e leis de marinha: Para uso da mocidade portugueza, destinada ao commercio, divididos em oito tratados elementares, contendo a respectiva legislcaõ patria, e indicando as fontes originaes dos regulamentos maritimos das principaes parças da Europa* (Lisbon, 1811).

Lisboa, José da Silva, *Principios de direito mercantil, e leis de marinha: Para uso da mocidade portugueza, destinada ao comercio* volume 4: *Das letras de cambio; De ordem de sua alteza real, o principe regente nosso senhor* (Lisbon, 1811).

Lorenzini, Marcella, Cinzia Lorandini, and D'Maris Coffman, *Financing in Europe: Evolution, Coexistence and Complementarity of Lending Practices from the Middle Ages to Modern Times* (Cham, 2018).

Luca, Giuseppe de, 'Informal Credit and Economic Modernization in Milan (1802–1840)', in: *Journal of European Economic History* 42:1 (2013), 211–236.

Malerba, Jurandir, *A corte no exílio: Civilização e poder no Brasil às vésperas da Independência (1808 a 1821)* (São Paulo, 2000).

Mamigonian, Beatriz G., 'In the Name of Freedom: Slave Trade Abolition, the Law and the Brazilian Branch of the African Emigration Scheme (Brazil-British West Indies, 1830s–1850s)', in: *Slavery & Abolition* 30:1 (2009), 41–66.

Marcondes, Renato Leite, *A Arte de Acumular na Economia Cafeeira: Vale do Paraiba Seculo XIX* (Lorena, 1998).

Marquese, Rafael, Tâmis Parron, and Márcia Berbel, *Slavery and Politics: Brazil and Cuba, 1790–1850* (Albuquerque, 2016).

Marquese, Rafael, and Ricardo Salles, *Escravidão e capitalismo histórico no século XIX: Cuba, Brasil e Estados Unidos* (Rio de Janeiro, 2016).

Martin, Bonnie, 'Slavery's Invisible Engine: Mortgaging Human Property', in: *The Journal of Southern History* 76:4 (2010), 817–866.

Martin, Bonnie, 'Neighbor-to-Neighbor Capitalism: Local Credit Networks and the Mortgaging of Slaves', in: Sven Beckert and Seth Rockman (eds.), *Slavery's Capitalism: A New History of American Economic Development* (Philadelphia, 2016), 107–121.

Mathias, Carlos Leonardo Kelmer, 'O movimento do crédito: O papel dos escravos nas relações de crédito, Rio de Janeiro e Minas Gerais (c.1711–c.1756)', in: *Revista de História Regional* 13:2 (2008), 46–69.

Mattoso, Kátia M. de Queirós, Herbert S. Klein, and Stanley L. Engerman, 'Research Note: Trends and Patterns in the Prices of Manumitted Slaves: Bahia, 1819–1888', in: *Slavery & Abolition* 7:1 (1986), 59–67.

Mello, Pedro Carvalho de, *Slavery and the economics of labor in Brazilian coffee plantations, 1850–1888* (São Paulo, 2016).

Mendonça, Francisco Maria de Souza Furtado de, *Repertorio geral, ou, Indice alphabetico da leis do imperio do Brasil publicadas desde o começo do anno de 1808 até o presente: em seguimento ao Repertorio geral do Desembargador Manuel Fernandes Thomaz* volume 2 (Rio de Janeiro, 1849).

Merwick, Donna, *Death of a Notary: Conquest & Change in Colonial New York* (Ithaca, 2002).

Moura Filho, Heitor P. de, 'Câmbio de longo prazo do mil-réis: Uma abordagem empírica referente às taxas contra a libra esterlina e o dólar (1795–1913)', in: *Cadernos de História* 11:14 (2009), 9–34.

Murphy, Sharon Ann, *Banking on Slavery: Financing Southern Expansion in the Antebellum United States* (Chicago, 2023).

Neal, Larry, *The Rise of Financial Capitalism: International Capital Markets in the Age of Reason* (Cambridge, 1993).

Needell, Jeffrey D., *The Party of Order: The Conservatives, the State, and Slavery in the Brazilian Monarchy, 1831–1871* (Stanford, 2006).

Nishida, Mieko, 'Manumission and Ethnicity in Urban Slavery: Salvador, Brazil, 1808–1888', in: *The Hispanic American Historical Review* 73:3 (1993), 361–391.

North, Douglas C., *Institutions, Institutional Change, and Economic Performance* (Cambridge, 1990).

Parron, Tâmis, *A política da escravidão no Império do Brasil 1826–1865* (Rio de Janeiro, 2011).

Peláez, Carlos Manuel, and Wilson Suzigan, *História monetária do Brasil* (Brasília, 1981).

Penna, Clemente Gentil, *Economias urbanas: Capital, créditos e escravidão na cidade do Rio de Janeiro, c.1820–1860* (São Paulo, 2023).

Piñero, Théo Lobarinhas, *Os "simples comissários": Negociantes e política no Brasil Império* (Niterói, 2014).

Piñeiro, Théo Lobarinhas, and Luiz Fernando Saraiva, 'O mercado de crédito no Rio de Janeiro (1821–1850)', in: *Locus – Revista de História* 20:2 (2016), 129–151

Price, Jacob, 'Credit in the Slave Trade and Plantation Economies', in: Barbara L. Solow (ed.), *Slavery and the rise of the Atlantic System* (Cambridge, 1991), 293–339.

Ribeiro, Gladys Sabina, and Vantuil Pereira, 'O Primeiro Reinado em revisão', in: Keila Grinberg and Ricardo Salles (eds.), *O Brasil Imperial* volume 1: *1808–1831* (Rio de Janeiro, 2010), 137–173.

Rocha, Antonio Penalves, *A economia política na sociedade escravista: Um estudo dos textos econômicos de Cairu* (São Paulo, 1996).

Rodrigues, André Figueiredo, 'Os "extravios que tão continuados têm sido...": Contrabando e práticas comerciais ilícitas nas atividades do contratador João Rodrigues de Macedo', in: *Locus – Revista de História* 11:1–2 (2005), 117–136.

Rogers, James Steven, *The Early History of the Law of Bills and Notes: A Study of the Origins of Anglo-American Commercial Law* (Cambridge, 2004).

Roover, Raymond de, *L'Evolution de la lettre de change: XIVe-XVIIIe siècles* (Paris, 1953).

Ryan Jr., Joseph James, 'Credit Where Credit is Due: Lending and Borrowing in Rio de Janeiro, 1820–1900' (unpublished dissertation, Los Angeles, 2007).

Sampaio, Antonio Carlos Jucá de, *Na encruzilhada do império: Hierarquias sociais e conjunturas econômicas no Rio de Janeiro (c.1650–c.1750)* (Rio de Janeiro, 2003).

Schultz, Kristen, *Tropical Versailles: Empire, Monarchy, and the Portuguese Royal Court in Rio de Janeiro, 1808–1821* (New York, 2001).

Schwartz, Stuart B., *Sugar Plantations in the Formation of Brazilian Society: Bahia, 1550–1835* (Cambridge, 1985).

Silva, Antonio Delgado da, *Collecção da legislação Portugueza desde a ultima compilação das ordenações: Legislação de 1750 a 1762* (Lisbon, 1830).

Sklansky, Jeffrey, *Sovereign of the Market: The Money Question in Early America* (Chicago, 2017).

Soares, Luís Carlos, *O "Povo de Cam" na capital do Brasil: A escravidão urbana no Rio de Janeiro do século XIX* (Rio de Janeiro, 2007).

Soares, Sebastião Ferreira, *Elementos de estatistica comprehendendo a theoria da sciencia e a sua applicação à estatistica commercial do Brasil* volume 1 (Rio de Janeiro, 1865).

Sonkajärvi, Hanna, 'A aplicação do Código Comercial brasileiro entre 1850 e 1860: Análise das evidências de um caso de falência culposa', in: *Tempo* 21:37 (2015), 170–186.

Sousa, Joaquim José Caetano Pereira e, *Esboço de hum diccionario juridico, theoretico, e practico, remissivo ás leis compiladas, e extravagantes* volume 2: *F-Q* (Lisbon, 1827).

Souza, Elizabeth Santos de, *Dos litígios da obrigação de crédito: A ação judiciária do Tribunal da Suplicação do Brasil (1808–1821)* (Rio de Janeiro, 2021).

Stein, Stanley J., *Vassouras: A Brazilian Coffee County, 1850–1900: The Roles of Planter and Slave in a Plantation Society* (Princeton, 1985).

Summerhill, William R., *Inglorious Revolution: Political Institutions, Sovereign Debt, and Financial Underdevelopment in Imperial Brazil* (New Haven, 2015).

Trivellato, Francesca, *The Promise and Peril of Credit: What a Forgotten Legend about Jews and Finance Tells Us about the Making of European Commercial Society* (Princeton, 2019).

Villa, Carlos Eduardo Valencia, *Ao Longo Daquelas Ruas: A Economia dos Negros Livres em Richmond e Rio de Janeiro, 1840–1860* (Jundiaí, 2016).

Wehling, Arno, 'Cairu e o "Comércio Franco e Legítimo"', in: *Revista Interdisciplinar do Direito* 18:1 (2020), 59–74.

Zegarra, Luis Felipe, 'Private Lenders, Banks and Mortgage Credit in Peru: Evidence From Notarised Loans', in: *Journal of Iberian and Latin American Economic History* 35:1 (2017), 105–146.

From Peer-to-Peer Credit to Banks: A Study of Credit Networks in Uppsala (1810–1910)

Elise M. Dermineur

1 Introduction[1]

Before banks operated in the Swedish kingdom, the allocation and deployment of financial funds was mainly ensured by private lenders.[2] Sweden lacked intermediaries like notaries, who could connect lenders to borrowers. Swedes borrowed and lent from and to each other, mostly at the local level, in small circles. Households financed investment in real estate, land, livestock, shop stocks, or even international trade via the allocation of capital from their peers. They also made ends meet, paid their

[1] The author would like to acknowledge the generous support of the Riksbankens Jubileumsfond via a Pro Futura Scientia fellowship, the Jan Wallanders och Tom Hedelius stiftelse via grant P17-0040 and the Stiftelsen Marcus och Amalia Wallenbergs Minnesfond (MAW2018-0015). The author would like to thank Martin Almbjär and Robert Eklund for their help with the source material.

[2] See especially Håkan Lindgren, 'Parish Banking in Informal Credit Markets: The Business of Private Lending in Early Nineteenth-Century Sweden', in: *Financial History* Review 24:1 (2017), 83–102; Håkan Lindgren, 'The Evolution of Secondary Financial Markets, 1820–1920', in: Anders Ögren (eds.), *The Swedish Financial Revolution* (New York, 2010), 95–112; Håkan Lindgren, 'The Modernization of Swedish Credit Markets,

E. M. Dermineur (✉)
Stockholm University, Stockholm, Sweden
e-mail: elise.dermineur@ekohist.su.se

C. van Bochove and J. Levy (eds.), *Beyond Banks*, Palgrave Studies in the History of Finance,
https://doi.org/10.1007/978-3-031-75819-5_6

taxes, and fed their families with small loans from family members, friends, and neighbors and by deferring payments. These interpersonal loans, or peer-to-peer transactions, were ubiquitous.

In the nineteenth century, however, Sweden experienced what historians have labeled a "financial revolution".[3] In a relatively short time span, between roughly the 1850s and 1870s, major changes in institutional and organizational structures led to a rapid increase in liquidity and financial services. In particular, the creation of several banking establishments boosted both monetization and financial services.[4] As a result, growth ensued, and the industrial sector overtook agriculture as the largest part of GDP by the end of the nineteenth century.[5]

Against this backdrop, what happened to peer-to-peer lending? How did the new banking institutions compete with non-intermediated lending? And how were households affected by these new developments in the banking sector? Not a lot of attention has been devoted to the transition from peer-to-peer lending to commercial bank lending so far.[6] We know that peer-to-peer lending was dynamic and popular in pre-industrial Sweden, even in the absence of traditional intermediaries like notaries. Anders Perlinge, for example, has shed light on the pre-industrial

1840–1905: Evidence from Probate Records', in: *The Journal of Economic History* 62:3 (2002), 810–832; Anders Perlinge, *Sockenbankirerna: kreditrelationer och tidig bankverksamhet: Vånga socken i Skåne 1840–1900* (Stockholm, 2005); Hilda Hellgren,, 'Fasta förbindelser: en studie av låntagare hos sparbanken och informella kreditgivare i Sala 1860–1910', in: *Acta Universitatis Upsaliensis: Univ bibldistributör* (dissertation, 2003); Kristina Lilja, 'Marknad och hushåll: Sparande och krediter i Falun 1820–1910 utifrån ett. livscykelperspektiv' (thesis, Uppsala University, 2004).

[3] Savings banks were established in the 1820s followed by commercial banks in the 1830s. But it is not until the mid-nineteenth century that a real take off took place. Cooperative banking is excluded from this study as it did not start in Sweden until 1915. See Ingemar Nygren, 'Svensk kreditmarknad 1820–1875: översikt av det institutionella kreditväsendets utveckling' (Univeristy of Gothenburg, 1981).

[4] Oskar Broberg and Anders Ögren, 'Names, Shares and Mortgages: The Formalisation of Swedish Commercial Bank Lending, 1870–1938', in: *Financial History Review* 26:1 (2019), 81–108. See also Mats Larsson, Kristina Lilja, and Tom Petersson, *Risk Management in Early Banking: An International Perspective of Swedish Saving Banks, 1820–1910 (London, 2021).*

[5] Anders Ögren, 'Financial Revolution and Economic Modernisation in Sweden', in: *Financial History Review* 16:1 (2009), 47–71.

[6] Youssef Cassis, *City Bankers, 1890–1914 (Cambridge, 1994)*; Youssef Cassis, *Capitals of Capital: The Rise and Fall of International Financial Centres, 1780–2009* (Cambridge, 2010).

"parish bankers", those individuals able to allocate significant amounts of money to their community members.[7] For the nineteenth century, several scholars have underlined the dynamism of credit markets via several case studies.[8] For Kalmar and its region, for example, Håkan Lindgren showed that promissory notes were of utmost importance.[9] He also pointed to the persistence of the peer-to-peer lending markets well into the twentieth century. We may wonder if Kalmar was an isolated case or representative of a more general trend.

To answer the questions highlighted above, this chapter uses a selection of probate inventories for the city of Uppsala from 1810 to 1910. Uppsala is located 70 kilometers north of Stockholm. In the pre-industrial period, Uppsala was known for being a commercial center surrounded by fertile agricultural lands. It was the seat of both the archbishopric and the oldest university in the country. In the nineteenth century Uppsala was a dynamic city with a diversified economy made up of manufacturers, service-oriented labor, retailers, and highly skilled artisans. The city then witnessed the development of new industries, such as the food and brick industries, with the particularity that no single employer dominated the local economy.[10] Commerce and trade benefitted from both the proximity of the capital and the inauguration of a railway station in 1866.[11] As a result of this economic and cultural dynamism, the population of the city doubled between 1870 and 1900. The diversified population of a middling town like Uppsala lent itself well to the study of peer-to-peer

[7] Anders Perlinge, *Sockenbankirerna*. See also Lindgren, 'Parish Banking'; Marja Erikson, *Krediter i Lust Och Nöd: Skattebönder i Torstuna Härad, Västmanlands Län, 1770–1870 (Uppsala, 2018)*.

[8] Ingemar Nygren, 'Göteborgs kreditmarknad 1820–1913' (report from the economic-historic department of the University of Gothenburg, 1987); Lilja,'Marknad och hushåll'; Per Hallén, Lili-Annè Aldman, and Martin Fritz, *Krona eller klave: utvecklingen av kreditmarknaden i Göteborg under 1800 (Malmö, 2015)*.

[9] Lindgren, 'The Modernization', Lindgren's greatest contribution lies in the use of the inverted mortality rate applied to probate inventories. He was able to estimate the size of the peer-to-peer lending market for the entire living population in Kalmar.

[10] Jakob Molinder and Martin Söderhäll, 'Did Industrialisation Lead to Segregation in Cities of the Nineteenth Century? The Case of Uppsala 1880–1900', in: *Scandinavian Economic History Review* 68:1 (2020), 24.

[11] Hans Westlund, 'Kommunikationer, tillgänglighet, omvandling: en studie av samspelet mellan kommunikationsnät och näringsstruktur i Sveriges mellanstora städer 1850–1970' (unpublished dissertation, Umeå University, 1992).

transactions and networks. Uppsala resembles many northern cities in the nineteenth century that featured the same type of diversified economy. In addition, the city has a large and continuous collection of well-preserved probate inventories and, to a lesser extent, well-kept church records with which it is possible to draw a picture of financial transactions before and after banks, and also reconstruct peer-to-peer networks.

To shed light on the impact of the financial revolution on Swedish non-intermediated credit markets, this chapter first examines the characteristics of peer-to-peer lending in Sweden, before turning more specifically to the city of Uppsala from 1810 to 1910. The chapter studies in detail the tools and contracts at the heart of these exchanges as well as their users. Most peer-to-peer lending featured promissory notes and deferred payments. Second, this chapter is concerned with the transition from non-intermediated to intermediated transactions. It studies the development of interpersonal credit markets over a long period of time. And finally, the last section of this chapter offers hypotheses to explain the shift that occurred from non-intermediated financial transactions to banking transactions on the eve of World War I.

2 Peer-to-Peer Lending in Sweden

2.1 Probate Inventories

Probate inventories are a great source for the analysis of peer-to-peer lending in Scandinavia.[12] In 1734 the Swedish crown issued a decree enforcing the need for probate inventories and making their use mandatory upon an individual's death. Thanks to the systematization of such legal procedures, reliable, and continuous data are available regarding debt and credit transactions from 1734 onward.[13] Swedish probate inventories, just like most of their European counterparts, featured information about the decedent and his estate. Real estate, movables, cash, and other assets were listed along with claims and liabilities. For our purpose, the

[12] See in particular Lindgren, 'The Modernization'; Jan Kuuse, 'The Probate Inventory as a Source for Economic and Social History', in: *Scandinavian Economic History Review* 22:1 (1974), 22–31; Erkki Markkanen, 'The Use of Probate Inventories as Indicators of Personal Wealth during the Period of Industrialization: The Financial Resources of the Finnish Rural Population 1850–1911', in: *Scandinavian Economic History Review* 26:1 (1978), 66–83; Anders Perlinge, *Sockenbankirerna*.

[13] Kuuse, 'The probate inventory'.

list of debtors and creditors is of significance. This list featured the name, place of residence, and profession of lenders and borrowers (note that part of this information was often not registered properly and was often missing), but also the amount, the nature of the contract and/or the purpose of the transaction. Yet, probate inventories were often vague regarding the nature and purpose of the liabilities and the claims listed. Often, assessors did not properly record the type of contract used, the interest rate, the deadline for repayment, or the purpose of the loan. For example, C.G. Brolan, a spice grocer, died in 1830.[14] His probate inventories listed a total of 100 transactions, 78 liabilities, and 22 claims. Most of these transactions stipulated an amount but no purpose.[15]

While probates are the most suitable source with which to examine interpersonal credit, this type of document is not without its flaws. First, the age distribution may appear problematic. Decedents tended to be older than the rest of the population and are consequently not representative of the living population.[16] This bias can be addressed thanks to the inverted mortality rate methodology, which projects the data to the living population at large, thus correcting the age bias.[17]

Second, the representativeness of such source material in terms of wealth distribution and socio-professional categories is also problematic. Not everyone had property worth listing after their death.[18] In the 1770s, only 10% of Stockholm's inhabitants had estate inventories preserved.[19] But in the 1830s, this rate exceeded 50%. In Skåne, Anders Perlinge has found that more than half of the individuals who died between 1840

[14] A spice grocer, or "kryddkramhandlare" in Swedish, was a grocer who had the right to sell dry spices and goods such as tea, coffee, sugar, salt and even porcelain and newspapers.

[15] Uppsala city hall court and magistrate 1831–1840, FIIa:45. All prices are in the fixed monetary value for 1914.

[16] Livio Di Matteo, 'Patterns and Determinants of Wealth Inequality in Late-Nineteenth Century Ontario—Evidence from Census-Linked Probate Data', in: *Social Science History* 25:3 (2001), 347–380.

[17] Lindgren, 'The Evolution', 95–112; Carole Shammas, 'Constructing a Wealth Distribution from Probate Records', in: *The Journal of Interdisciplinary History* 9:2 (1978), 297–307.

[18] Sebastiaan Keibek, 'Correcting the Probate Inventory Record for Wealth Bias', Working Paper (University of Cambridge, 2017).

[19] Lindgren, 'The Modernization'.

and 1900 had a probate written up.[20] In Uppsala, about a third of the decedents' estates were probated in 1810, while this proportion increased to more than 50% after 1850 (see Table 1). In 1910, 55% of Uppsala decedents were to have their estates probated. The rest of the population might have been too poor to have anything to pass over to the next generation and/or to be able to pay the tax on gross assets. Similarly, the list of claims and liabilities of the decedents featured in probate inventories might not correspond to the living, especially if one assumes that decedents were wealthier in general. We might also suppose that non-probated estates did not feature any debt to be repaid. But if these estates featured no valuable assets worth listing, existing liabilities could not be repaid anyway.

Additionally, probate inventories list the estate of the decedent but do not distinguish between the assets of a married couple. Therefore, it is impossible to estimate the wealth or the credit relations of married women or married men. To some extent, it is also difficult to know if a widow initiated the credit transactions herself or if the ones featured in her inventory were in fact from her late husband. Gender representativity thus presents another bias while examining probate inventories.[21]

For the period studied here, the household was not only at the center of consumption but also of production. Probate inventories, therefore, featured both debts incurred for the household's private consumption, but also debts related to the decedent's entrepreneurial activities. No clear distinction between the two was made. This aspect is troublesome as the professions of some decedents can bias the sample. Shopkeepers and merchants, for example, often featured a long list of claims and liabilities directly connected to their business (see Figs. 2 and 3). When Carl Christian Jacobsson, a grocer from Uppsala, died in 1851, his probate inventory featured a long list of claims. It is very likely that the 409 deferred payments listed there were related to the sale of his products to individuals and households.[22]

[20] Perlinge, *Sockenbankirerna*.

[21] See Elise M. Dermineur, 'The Wealth of the Swedish Nobility: The Case of the Never-Married Women, 1850–1910', in: Anna Nilsson Hammar, Daniel Nyström and Martin Almbjär (eds.), *Gender, Materiality and Politics: Essays on the Making of Power* (Lund, 2022), 101–121; Matteo Pompermaier, 'A Complicated Puzzle: Spinsters, Widows and Credit in Sweden (1790–1910)', in: *Financial History Review* 29:1 (2021), 1–23.

[22] Uppsala town hall court and magistrate 1851–1860, FIIa:52.

2.2 *The Ubiquity of Peer-to-Peer Lending in Sweden*

In the absence of notaries and notarial ledgers, probate inventories tell us that peer-to-peer lending remained popular throughout the nineteenth century, especially in small towns and rural areas. Their popularity only started to decline toward the end of the century to the benefit of institutional lending provided by commercial banks.[23] A recent study shows that in Askersund, a small town located between Gothenburg and Stockholm, more than 90% of the debt owed by the living population in 1865 was private, that is, between private individuals. In 1900, the percentage dropped to 70%. In Filipstad, a town located in the middle of Sweden, the same pattern can be observed. In 1865, 89% of household debt there was owed to private individuals. The amount dropped to 63% in 1900.[24] In Gothenburg, the proportion was 99% in 1800 before decreasing to 77% in 1900.[25] In 1840, in the town of Kalmar, promissory notes accounted for more than half the total credit market. But in 1905, commercial credit surpassed the non-intermediated transactions.[26] In Uppsala, peer-to-peer lending also remained popular in the nineteenth century. Throughout the period, about a third of the living population there constantly turned to the interpersonal market to borrow money. Even if borrowers progressively turned to banks to finance their activities and projects, private lenders continued to provide them with capital.[27] Here and there throughout Sweden, peer-to-peer lending dominated financial transactions until the eve of World War I.

How can the resilience of peer-to-peer lending in nineteenth-century Sweden be explained? First, interpersonal transactions were the traditional means of finance. Households and individuals had turned to their family, friends, and acquaintances to finance investment and/or to make

[23] Lindgren, 'The Modernization'; Lilja, 'Marknad och hushåll'; Hellgren, 'Fasta förbindelser'.

[24] I would like to thank Axel Hagberg for sharing his data with me. Axel Hagberg, 'Households Assets and Liabilities in Sweden 1800–1900', (paper presented at the symposium *Wealth and Debt Accumulation in Early Financial Markets,* Stockholm, 2018).

[25] Hallén, Aldman, and Fritz, *Krona eller klave,* 177.

[26] Lindgren, 'The Modernization'.

[27] Hellgren, 'Fasta förbindelser'.

ends meet for centuries.[28] This practice was well-established and ritualized in traditional communities and tight-knit societies.[29] This partly explains the slow penetration of banking services in these communities in the nineteenth century. Second, there was a chronic shortage of cash as a medium of payment, even in the nineteenth century.[30] Demand often far exceeded supply. To alleviate this lack of cash, households exchanged fungible promissory notes, practiced reciprocal exchange, lent in kind (often grain), and expected repayment in cash whenever it became available again. Third, wages and income were irregular, especially in rural areas. Households often needed to turn to their networks to find enough resources for their projects or simply for their survival. And finally, the nineteenth century witnessed significant economic developments. In particular, the intensification of production and the development of trade and commerce meant new manufactured items flooded the market, prompting a rise in consumption.[31] Such items were often purchased on credit. Households did not turn to banking institutions for small purchases but relied on traditional financial networks instead and on deferred payments in particular.

2.3 *Main Characteristics and Actors*

In the nineteenth century, the Swedish capital market counted several actors able to allocate and deploy funds to households. Private lenders alongside institutions were the two main categories of credit providers. Each of these categories filled a different purpose.

[28] Christopher Pihl, 'Learning to bring dead capital to life': The Riksens Ständers Bank and the Credit Market in Seventeenth-Century Sweden', in: *Continuity and Change* 34:2 (2019), 209–230; Tiina Hemminki, 'Långa listor med fordringar och skulder. Om förtroende- förhållanden i Ilmola och Nordmaling i början av 1800-talet', in: *Historisk Tidskrift för Finland* 97:3, (2012).

[29] On previous periods, see for instance Maria Ågren, 'Land and Debt: On the Process of Social Differentiation in Rural Sweden, circa 1750–1850', in: *Rural History* 5:1 (1994), 23–40; Maria Ågren, *Jord och gäld: Social skiktning och rättslig konflikt i södra dalarna ca 1650–1850* (Uppsala, 1992).

[30] Anders Ögren, 'Free or Central Banking? Liquidity and Financial Deepening in Sweden, 1834–1913', in: *Explorations in Economic History* 43:1 (2006), 72.

[31] Jan De Vries, *The Industrious Revolution: Consumer Behavior and the Household Economy, 1650 to the Present* (Cambridge 2008).

First, borrowers could turn to private individuals. There were different categories of private lenders. Some lenders with accumulated wealth invested their savings from time to time in peer-to-peer lending to make a profit. Others extended credit to kin and acquaintances upon cash availability because of the prevailing norms of solidarity and cooperation within the community.[32] Another category of lenders consisted of semi-professional providers of credit such as merchants, shopkeepers, innkeepers, and parish bankers, who often accumulated enough cash via their activities to redistribute it at interest.[33] Some of these actors could also act as brokers.[34] Among those brokers, one often finds women.[35] These actors often favored the promissory note to acknowledge the debt; the contract stipulated the transfer of capital from one party to another secured by a pledge, often a piece of land in rural areas.

Finally, a fair number of private individuals simply allowed delayed payment for the purchase of items and services. The debt would be paid later in time with or without interest. Such debt was often registered in a private ledger. In fact, deferred payments were extremely common. In pre-industrial Sweden, individuals delayed the payment for small amounts either because of a lack of cash in circulation or because of a lack of disposable cash or income. In fact, throughout the period, about 60% of decedents in Uppsala left no cash behind.[36]

Peer-to-peer lending was characterized by highly personalized transactions and entailed de facto a social dimension. Contracting parties often knew each other, worked alongside each other, frequented the same places of sociability. This social proximity in tight-knit networks featured strong social norms, which governed credit exchanges; solidarity, reciprocity,

32 Laurence Fontaine, *L'économie morale: Pauvreté, crédit et confiance dans l'Europe préindustrielle* (Paris, 2008); Craig Muldrew, *The Economy of Obligation: The Culture of Credit and Social Relations in Early Modern England* (London, 1998). For Sweden see especially Ögren, 'Financial Revolution'; Perlinge, *Sockenbankirerna*.

33 Anders Perlinge, 'Sockenbankirerna'. Tony Kenttä, Kristina Lilja, and Dan Bäcklund,, 'The Necessity of Small Loans: The Borrowing and Lending among Low-Income Earners in Early 20th Century Sweden', in: *The History of the Family* 27:2 (2022), 268–292.

34 Nygren, 'Svensk kreditmarknad', 13.

35 Ågren, 'Providing Security'.

36 71.5% of decedents in 1810 did not leave any cash behind. The proportion decreased gradually throughout the period. In 1910, 49.1% of the probates did not feature any cash.

cooperation, and fairness, the main social features of local communities, were at the heart of most exchanges. Economic transactions were strongly embedded in the social fabric of local communities, prompting the preservation and reproduction of these social ties.[37]

Evidently, some of these transactions featured a relation of power between a wealthy creditor and his debtor in which difference of social and economic status mattered. Large and small investors used the credit market for their savings to thrive. They were less concerned with norms of solidarity, albeit profit and solidarity were not mutually exclusive. Additionally, some transactions were brokered by intermediaries. These brokers could locate available funds on the behalf of potential borrowers; they could also reduce information asymmetries for lenders.

The trust and the norms of solidarity at work in such transactions did not prevent an occasional breach of trust or contract. In these cases, enforcement of mutual agreements could take place informally or at court. We still know very little about informal enforcement of financial transactions, but it is likely that the strong social norms at work acted as a deterrent to non-compliance. In case of default, parties could certainly renegotiate their agreement and resolve their contention privately. Regarding enforcement, lenders could petition the court to coerce a defaulting borrower into payment of his obligation. Written documents such as promissory notes bore legal validity and were easily enforceable at court. There is currently no exhaustive study regarding the proportion of default for non-formalized transactions.[38]

Alongside these private lenders, pawnshops, mutual aid associations, foundations, and funds (e.g., church and professional funds such as the seamen's fund) offered lending and saving possibilities as well.[39] Workers' associations (*arbetarföreningar*), for example, could lend money

[37] See for example Marcel Fafchamps, 'Formal and Informal Market Institutions: Embeddedness Revisited', in: Jean-Marie Baland et al. (eds.), *The Handbook of Economic Development and Institutions* (Princeton, 2020), 375–413. See also Samuel Bowles, *The Moral Economy: Why Good Incentives Are No Substitute for Good Citizens* (London, 2016).

[38] On the issue of bankruptcy see especially Karl Gratzer, Mats Hayen, and Klas Nyberg, 'The Swedish bankruptcy system, 1734–1849', in: Klas Nyberg and Håkan Jakobsson (eds.), *Luxury, Fashion and the Early Modern Idea of Credit* (Abingdon, 2020), 51–61. See also Ågren, *Jord och gäld*.

[39] See for instance Göran Ulväng and Sofia Murhem, 'Church Endowments Used for Credit in 18th and 19th Century Rural Sweden' (paper presented at the ESSHC, 2021).

to their workers and accept their deposits.[40] In the late nineteenth century, insurance companies also began to propose long-term savings placements.[41]

The emerging savings and commercial banks established respectively in the 1820s and 1830s offered deposit and credit facilities to households.[42] Savings banks aimed at facilitating savings for households of slender means while extending loans to households that could offer personal sureties.[43] In 1850, 82 savings banks could be found throughout Sweden, their number jumped to 388 in 1900. However, savings banks had mixed results. One has to wait until the end of the nineteenth century to witness an increase in both the number of accounts and the volume of deposits. In 1900, about 55% of these accounts contained at most 100 kronor, the equivalent of a male worker's earnings for six weeks.[44] The first commercial banks began to emerge in the 1850s, and in 1856, the Stockholm Enskilda Bank (SEB, still active today) was established. It was one of the first private commercial banks with a broad range of activities.[45] Commercial banks did not seem to privilege lending to households up until the late nineteenth century. Then, banks' lending capacities almost tripled from 1895 to 1910 (see Fig. 1).[46] In the 1860s, mortgage institutes specialized in lending for households wishing to purchase real estate emerged as well.

[40] Anne Berg, 'The Market and 'the Making': The Economics of the First Workers' Associations in Nineteenth-Century Sweden', in: *Social History* 45:2 (2020), 167–192.

[41] Lars Fredrik Andersson, Liselotte Eriksson, and Magnus Lindmark, 'Life Insurance and Income Growth: The Case of Sweden 1830–1950', in: *Scandinavian Economic History Review* 58:3 (2010), 203–219; Mike Adams et al., 'Commercial Banking, Insurance and Economic Growth in Sweden between 1830 and 1998', in: *Accounting, Business & Financial History* 19:1 (2009), 21–38.

[42] Kristina Lilja and Dan Bäcklund, 'Savings Banks and Working-class Saving during the Swedish Industrialisation', in: *Financial History Review* 23:1 (2016), 111–132; Kristina Lilja, 'The Deposit Market Revolution in Sweden', in: Anders Ögren (eds.), *The Swedish Financial Revolution* (London, 2010), 41–63; Broberg and Ögren, 'Names, Shares and Mortgages'.

[43] Gradually savings Banks Financed Entrepreneurial Activities for Better-off Individuals. See Lilja and Bäcklund, 'Savings Banks'.

[44] G. Bagge, E. Lundberg, and I. Svennilson (eds.), *Wages, Cost of Living and National Income in Sweden 1860–1930* volume 2: *Wages in Sweden 1860–1930* (London, 1935), 260.

[45] Lars Magnusson, *An Economic History of Sweden* (London, 2000), 99.

[46] Ingemar Nygren, 'Transformation of Bank Structures in the Industrial Period. The Case of Sweden 1820–1913', in: *Journal of European Economic History* 12:1 (1983), 60.

Banks had the capacity to extend larger loans than private individuals, albeit they might have suffered more from information asymmetry.

Overall, households could choose which credit provider or saving opportunity filled their needs best. But depending on level of income and assets available to offer as security, certain credit channels remained inaccessible. While savings and commercial banks relied on personal sureties to grant loans, private lenders tended to privilege personal knowledge and information. Overall, individual and household preferences remained largely inclined to the peer-to-peer transactions throughout the period studied here, even though bank lending gradually increased.

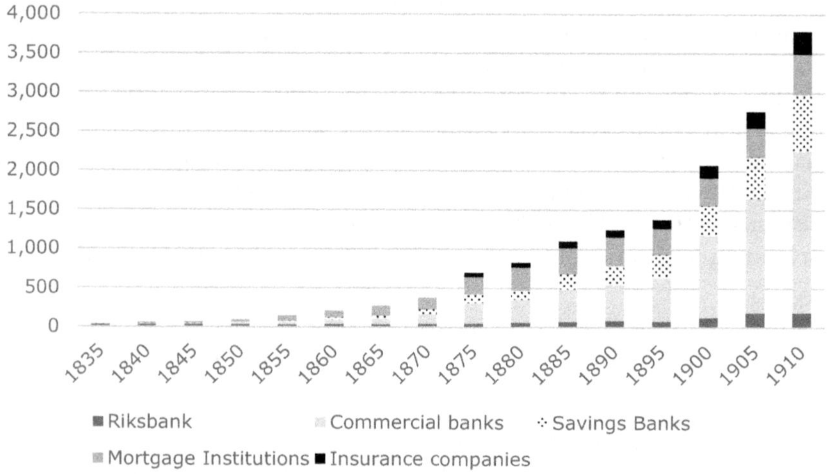

Fig. 1 Advances by credit institutions in millions of kronor in Sweden, 1835–1910 (*Source* Nygren, 'Transformation of Bank Structures')

3 Peer-to-Peer Lending in Uppsala

3.1 An Overview

The probate inventories of Uppsala illustrate peer-to-peer lending in nineteenth-century Sweden well.[47] In 1810, the town had roughly 4,000 inhabitants. In 1850, their number had increased to 7,000. And in 1910, this had jumped to approximately 26,000. For the years 1810 to 1910, the sample collected includes 720 probate inventories, gathered every twenty years and accounting for all probated adults above twenty years old (see Table 1). The focus here is on those who left claims and/or liabilities in their estate (N = 634).

The inverted mortality rate methodology applied to probate inventories in Uppsala allows an estimation of both private and institutional debt for the entire living population of Uppsala (Table 2). In the beginning of the nineteenth century, 94% of the transactions were private. A century later, they had dropped to 50%. Through the period, peer-to-peer transactions receded to the profit of institutions, in particular banking services (see also Figs. 1, 2, and 3). Commercial and savings banks' activities

Table 1 Overview of the probate inventories dataset, Uppsala 1810–1910

	No. of probates	*% of probated estates*	*No. of probates with claims or liabilities*	*Men*	*Women*
1810–1812	116	36.9	98	61	37
1830–1831	90	40.2	79	45	34
1850–1851	117	56.5	94	47	47
1870	81	59.5	71	34	37
1890	141	69.1	129	68	61
1910	175	55.2	163	72	91
Total	720	52.9	634	327	307

Source See text

[47] Uppsala town hall court and magistrate, FIIa:34, 35, 36, 37, 38, 39, 40, 41, 42, 43, 44, 45, 46, 47, 48, 49, 50, 51, 52, 53, 54, 55, 56, 57, 70, 90; Uppsala University Archive, FXI/8, 10; Uppsala University Archive, EIII:204, 205. Hereafter the dataset.

Table 2 Debt volume in the living population of Uppsala, 1810–1910 (fixed monetary value for 1914)

	Total per capita debt of living population (kronor)	*Private debt*(%)*	*Institutional debt**(%)*
1810–1812	752.2	93.9%	6.1%
1830–1831	1,398.9	93.3%	6.7%
1850–1851	1,459.3	75.3%	24.7%
1870	1,092.6	77.3%	22.7%
1890	2,021.6	77.4%	22.6%
1910	387.8	50%	50%

Source See text
Note (*) Interpersonal debt consists of promissory notes, deferred payments, other loans, interpersonal transactions of unknown nature, services to natural persons, interest, pawnbroking between natural persons, and auction. (**) Institutional debt consists of bank loans, insurance, and funds

progressed especially between 1890 and 1910. In the meantime, the total debt per capita rose until the mid-nineteenth century and then fell.[48]

3.2 The Popularity of Promissory Notes

Between 1810 and 1910, most financial transactions took place between private individuals. These exchanges were either promissory notes or deferred payments. In Kalmar, for example, in 1841–1845, 51% of transactions were promissory notes and 29.7% were credit sales.[49] In 1901–1905, promissory notes still represented 30.5% of debts. In Uppsala, the proportion of decedents using promissory notes in 1810 was at least about 20%, 34.5% in 1870 and 28.6% in 1910, figures comparable to Kalmar.[50]

Promissory notes thus accounted for a large part of the peer-to-peer transactions in pre-industrial Sweden and Uppsala in particular. Called *revers* or sometimes *skuldsedel*, *sedel*, or *förskrivning*, a promissory note, as we have seen, was a private contract acknowledging a debt between

[48] The year 1890 is an exception. Several wealthy outliers skew the sample for that year.

[49] The rest was made up of institutional debts. Lindgren, 'The Modernization', 827.

[50] Note that this proportion could be more important because many transactions lack specification.

a lender and a borrower, an IOU. A promissory note was fungible and transmissible, and as such could circulate as a means of currency. It was usually secured with a pledge, often a piece of land in a rural area, or other valuable assets, and/or a guarantor. Witnesses attesting the validity of the transaction could also be added to the deed.[51] The authorities did not provide any infrastructure for the conclusion of these contracts. There were no notaries for instance. But in the nineteenth century, it was theoretically possible to register such a deed at court by paying a fee. Most contracts remained only secured by personal guarantees because of the high transaction costs. In most instances, lenders, and borrowers negotiated and contracted privately. Terms and conditions, including the exchange of promises and repayment and compensation modes, were included in the initial agreement. Renegotiation and mitigation of the initial agreement might occur *ex post* if both parties agreed, and in the absence of notaries, private intermediaries could broker some of these transactions.[52] We know very little about such intermediation, but it is safe to assume, that a good proportion of promissory notes were highly personalized and entailed a social dimension. Contracting parties often knew each other, lived in the same town, worked with each other, and frequented the same places of sociability. Professionals such as wholesale merchants also widely used promissory notes for their business with customers and suppliers. Personal ties also existed among them, but might have been looser.

Promissory notes did not necessarily entail the absence of trust between parties. They were widely used for at least three reasons. First, merchants have used this instrument of credit for generations, to conduct their business and to extend loans within their circles. The use of promissory notes then spread to the rest of society. Second, the success of promissory notes also resides partly in Swedish monetary history, which witnessed many impractical innovations such as huge copper plate money of several kilos or banknotes in the seventeenth century.[53] Meanwhile, in the nineteenth century—before 1873—several currencies circulated at

[51] Hellgren, 'Fasta förbindelser', 62.

[52] For the role of women in loan brokerage see, for instance, Ågren, 'Providing Security'.

[53] In the early modern period, currency in the form of huge copperplate money of several kilos circulated. This was obviously not practical to carry around and hindered commerce and trade. Gunnar Wetterberg, *Money and Power: From Stockholms Banco 1656*

once, which is nothing short of impractical.[54] And finally, the rise in consumption in the nineteenth century also meant an increase in transactions as well as an increase in coins and paper notes. With a shortage of coins, households could turn to promissory notes.[55]

In general, a promissory note was designed to be reimbursed in the short term, often within six months. From 1800, promissory notes older than ten years were legally no longer collectable.[56] But in practice some of these obligations could drag on over several generations. Probate inventories do not systematically give the date of the *revers*, but they are sometimes specified. For example, Daniel Boëthius, a professor in Uppsala, borrowed money in 1792 via a promissory note from the recently widowed Christina Groth. She died in 1795 and Groth's heirs were now collecting the interest.[57] Upon Boëthius' death in 1810, the debt had not yet been repaid in full.[58] Lars August Backman extended 2,181 kronor to a relative living in Västerås in 1908 with 5% interest. A year later, a new loan contract for 436 kronor was made with the same person. Six months later, a new contract for 218 kronor was signed, again with the same relative.[59] It is likely that the original loan was not repaid in full after a year. Catharina Gustava Günther died in 1830. Her household had borrowed money via a promissory note in 1800. Upon her death, 30 years later, the capital and the interest (at least in part) remained outstanding.[60]

to Sveriges Riksbank today (Stockholm 2009) https://www.riksbank.se/en-gb/about-the-riksbank/history/money-and-power--the-history-of-sveriges-riksbank/.

54 Rodney Edvinsson, 'Swedish Monetary Standards in a Historical Perspective', in: *Scandinavian Working Papers in Economics* (2009). https://swopec.hhs.se/suekhi/abs/suekhi0006.htm.

55 Rodney Edvinsson and Anders Ögren,'Swedish Money Supply, 1620–2012", in: Rodney Edvinsson, Tor Jacobson, and Daniel Waldenström (eds.) *Historical Monetary and Financial Statistics for Sweden* volume 2: *House Prices, Stock Returns, National Accounts, and the Riksbank Balance Sheet, 1620–2012* (Stockholm, 2014), 293–338.

56 Håkan Lindgren, 'Over-indebtedness'—or not? Household Debt Accumulation and Risk Exposure in Nineteenth Century Sweden', in: *Scandinavian Economic History Review* 70:1 (2022), 9.

57 Uppsala city court hall and magistrate, Bouppteckningar 1795–1797, FII a:31.

58 Uppsala University Archive, FXI:8.

59 Uppsala city court hall and magistrate 1910–1910, FIIa:90.

60 Uppsala city court hall and magistrate 1821–1830, FIIa:42.

Promissory notes usually carried an interest rate, negotiated by the contracting parties. One knows very little regarding how this decision was made and on what basis. The nature of their relationship, the reputation of the borrower, and the degree of risk taken by the lender certainly played a role. In theory, in Sweden, interest rates were free on the privately arranged loan market.[61] But, up until 1864, institutions such as banks were, on the other hand, constrained not to exceed 6% on their loans. In practice, however, individuals did not seem to charge more than 6%. Parties could decide on a rate below this ceiling. Interest rates of 5% were common. Lower interest such as 4% or 3.5% could also be found but remained more unusual. In even fewer cases, no interest rate was applied on promissory note contracts. In 1864, the interest rate ceiling was abolished.

Promissory notes were secured either via a security or a guarantor or both. In rural areas, land was a common security. Real estate, movables, and other valuable assets could also be used to back loans. Gradually, new types of securities were introduced. In 1889, the merchant August Littorin signed a promissory note with J. Johansson for 268 kronor. The deal was secured with shares in the Mälareprovinsernas Enskilda Bank.[62] In 1809, A. Cederström backed a loan from farm owner Karl Erik Andersson on a Thule life insurance policy, along with two guarantors.[63] In 1907, professor Knut Blomberg borrowed 2,726 kronor, quite a significant amount, from his colleague Maths Falk. Blomberg secured the transaction by offering the usufruct of shares in two banks.[64] It is unclear whether the security was also used as a payment to cover the interest.

It is difficult to draw an exact picture of promissory notes via the lens of probate inventories. Many transactions elude us as no specific nature or characteristic was recorded. In many cases, only the name of the creditor or debtor appeared along with the amount due. How many of these transactions were in fact promissory notes? It is impossible to say. In Uppsala, the number of such agreements per probate inventory oscillated between 1 and 1.3 throughout the period. A promissory note

[61] Nygren, 'Transformation of Bank Structures', 34.

[62] Uppsala city court hall and magistrate 1890–1890, FIIa:70.

[63] Uppsala city court hall and magistrate 1910–1910, FIIa:90.

[64] Uppsala city court hall and magistrate 1910–1910, FIIa:90.

remained a binding contract featuring an amount of money to be repaid in the short or medium term. Therefore, most households did not multiply such contractual commitments and the average promissory note either extended or due per household remained below two. Meanwhile, the mean per contract multiplied by four from 1810 to 1910 (see Table 3). Households seemed to have used promissory notes for larger investments and the purchase of dearer, durable goods.

In the beginning of the nineteenth century, mostly the upper class and the bourgeoisie of Uppsala used promissory notes (about 30% of all the transactions). The bourgeoisie, in particular the merchants and grocers, used them to exchange with the better-off, but also with unskilled workers (see Fig. 2). This pattern remains more or less the same throughout the period. In 1910, the upper strata of the population, especially the merchants, used promissory notes the most (about 35% for all promissory notes). The bourgeoisie often practiced exchanges among themselves, mostly to conduct business.

Promissory notes could be used for substantial amounts, usually a business-related transaction between professionals. More than half of the promissory notes dealt with amounts worth several weeks or months of salaries for a male worker. While some promissory notes could concern trivial amounts, over 75% dealt with substantial sums. Those featuring the largest amounts were mostly all business related. In 1910, the mean value of promissory notes that either the bourgeoisie or the upper class exchanged was worth twice the mean of those of skilled workers and was ten times larger than that of unskilled workers (see Table 3). Interestingly, the spread between the socio-professional categories did actually grow throughout the period.

3.3 The Significance of Deferred Payments

Lydia Kristina Kihl died in 1909. Her probate inventory featured a list of 69 claims related to the sewing workshop she ran with her husband. The couple seem to have specialized in uniforms as many of their customers were military. Their claims amounted to 4,405 kronor, about 63 kronor on average per customer.[65] The spice grocer I.P. Lennqvist died in 1830 at 38 years old. He left 337 pending credit sales for more than 30,000

[65] Uppsala city court hall and magistrate 1910–1910, FIIa:90.

Table 3 Overview of the (percentile) distribution of promissory notes in Uppsala

	(% interpersonal transaction)	*Sum (% interpersonal transaction)*	*Mean*	*StDev*	*P5*	*P25*	*P50*	*P75*	*P95*	*P99*
1810–1812	122 (1 s%)	83,060.3 (28.6%)	680.8	1,037.5	29.8	119.3	334.8	837.1	2,233	7,582.4
1830–1831	174 (11.4%)	107,570.6 (19.5%)	618.2	1,491.5	11.8	44.74	122.3	489.2	2,446.2	11,089.4
1850–1851	192 (8%)	188,584.2 (40.8%)	982.2	2,659.3	12.6	47.3	217.6	735.9	3,812.1	22,872.8
1870	201 (28.9%)	127,127 (39.4%)	632.5	1,275	6.5	25.9	118.8	777.5	2,591.7	12,440
1890	429 (18.8%)	2,414,233.6 (64.7%)	5,627.6	16,007.1	67.2	604.8	2,688.1	5,376.3	13,440.9	222,806.7
1910	229 (17.2%)	573,204.3 (50.2%)	2,503	5,628.4	59.9	327.2	817.9	2,181.2	10,906.3	43,038.5

Source See text
Note In 1910, P25 means that 25% of the promissory notes equaled 327 kronor or less

kronor. His customers came from all social classes and even included 20% of women pledging to reimburse in their own name.[66] Like many grocers and artisans, the seamstress and the spice grocer granted their clients time to pay their dues.

Either because of shortage of cash in circulation, reduced income in the household, or increased expenditure, deferred payments often prevailed to delay the payment of crafted, subsistence items or services. This type of credit was especially sought from local grocers, shopkeepers, artisans, and doctors. Durable goods suppliers, for example, had to sell on credit because most households did not have enough liquid savings to pay for expensive items outright. Incidentally, these suppliers often sold their items on credit via a promissory note. Private individuals could also implement credit sales for their small transactions.

Deferred payments, often called *leveratörskrediter* or *kontokrediter*, usually featured small amounts of money to be repaid in the short term. This type of credit did not compete with that offered by institutions like banks because they were too small. While promissory notes averaged between 600 and 2,500 kronor per transaction over the period, deferred payments only averaged about 360 kronor. Before 1850, the average per transaction was even lower (see Table 4). Here, there is a clear difference with the amounts stipulated for promissory notes indicating thus the different purposes of these transactions.

This type of transaction was prevailing especially among shopkeepers. Some of these wholesale grocers had a large portfolio. Carolina Sahlin died in 1850 at 28 years old. Her husband was an important grocer in Uppsala. Her probate inventory mentioned 1,031 claims and liabilities. Most of these were in fact claims (98.9%). The couple's clients lived in and around Uppsala. In another example, the grocer Carl Christian Jacobsson died in 1851 at 39 years old.[67] He left behind a long list of claims. His probate inventory listed 410 clients who owed him 16,070 kronor (mean per household = 39,2 kronor). His clients belonged to various social class; one can find soldiers, artisans, civil servants, and university professors. 36 s women (8.8%) figured among the customers in their own name. Some of these people certainly had the means to pay outright for the items bought. These shopkeepers' large networks made them de

[66] Uppsala city court hall and magistrate 1831–1840, FIIa:46.

[67] Uppsala city court hall and magistrate 1851–1860, FIIa:52.

Table 4 Overview of the (percentile) distribution of deferred payments in Uppsala

	N (% interpersonal transaction)	*Sum (% interpersonal transaction)*	*Mean*	*StDev*	*P5*	*P25*	*P50*	*P75*	*P95*	*P99*
1810–1812	478 (41.3%)	83,948.77 (28.9%)	175.6	994.5	3.4	13.4	38.6	99	447.2	20,268.1
1830–1831	475 (31.2%)	83,328.32 (15.1%)	175.4	722.3	1.6	7.2	28.4	100.6	495.8	10,175.3
1850–1851	638 (26.6%)	35,756.21 (7.7%)	56	318.8	1.4	5.6	13.4	29.9	201.9	7,557,94
1870	69 (9.9%)	73,941.49 (23%)	1,071.6	5,090.1	2.6	10.1	20.6	140.7	4,772.3	39,143.4
1890	574 (25.1%)	209,524.25 (5.6%)	365	3830	1.1	4	16.2	76.6	863.8	89,773.2
1910	127 (9.5%)	41,465.54 (3.6%)	326.5	1,351.1	4.4	13.9	49.6	102.8	799.9	11,724.3

Source See text

facto local bankers. How did shopkeepers finance such large outstanding claims? Very little information about this is currently available. We can hypothesize that they financed credit sales out of their own pockets as well as by borrowing themselves for the goods they sold. Such long chains of credit are visible in Figs. 6.2 and 6.3. It seems reasonable also to assume that they inserted a premium in the price of the goods sold to compensate for the time awaiting repayment.

Most of the deferred payments were registered informally in account books. Shopkeepers and artisans kept these books with care; they were legal proof of ongoing transactions. Carl Erik Herman Holmberg was a shopkeeper in Uppsala. He died in 1890 leaving behind a *handelsbok*, an account book, featuring several clients owing him money.[68] Private individuals also kept such proofs of dues. When the soldier Wilhelm Blixt died in 1889, his probate listed several people living in Uppsala owing his household money for the delivery of milk.[69] Maria Margareta Hesselgren, the widow of a doctor, died in 1910. Her probate inventory featured a book listing her household's dues to several individuals.[70]

The pervasiveness of credit sales can be explained by several factors. Like promissory notes, the lack of cash in circulation, the irregularities of salaries, and recurrent problems of resource availability within households made deferred payments popular. One could add to the list simple force of habit. The practice of credit sales has been documented well beyond the Middle Ages. Within the framework of the moral economy, of neighborliness, in which norms of solidarity and Christian charity applied, shopkeepers were expected to show empathy and forbearance to their customers. Well-anchored in social habits, deferred payment was therefore a widespread practice. Even better-off households, which could certainly afford to pay outright, delayed payments of their expenditure at local stores.

Could deferred payments carry an interest rate? The thorny question of interest rates applied to credit sales continues to divide historians. Probate inventories remain silent on this issue. There is no indication that shopkeepers charged a fee for the delayed payment. But there is no evidence either that they did not hide a surplus in the price. Craig Muldrew

[68] Uppsala city court hall and magistrate 1890–1890, FIIa:70.

[69] Uppsala city court hall and magistrate 1890–1890, FIIa:70.

[70] Uppsala city court hall and magistrate 1910–1910, FIIa:90.

argues that these transactions were not subject to any interest rate in early modern England.[71] But recently, James Shaw has demonstrated that interest rates were often hidden in any sort of transaction, notarized, and non-intermediated ones.[72] He argues that shopkeepers and artisans could account for the deferred payment in the price. And in France, Natacha Coquery estimates that interest for deferred payments could vary between 10 and 14% a year, based on her examination of a jeweler's account books of the eighteenth century.[73] It is therefore reasonable to assume that retailers' forbearance came with a price. An immobilization of capital required a form of compensation, either as disguised interest included in the price or in the form of moral interest (for example service, moral debt), especially in tight-knit communities. A shopkeeper had leverage to indemnify himself for the delay in payment. Similarly, movements in the price level, especially for foodstuffs, surely needed to be accounted for.

Sellers and shopkeepers practicing credit sales had no guarantee the required payment would be completed at all. Contrary to promissory notes, and in most cases, no security backed such agreements, especially if the good or item bought were edible and/or could be consumed. Anders Theodor Brawallius, a 29-year-old spice grocer from Uppsala, died in 1811. He left a long list of claims and liabilities after him. As a shopkeeper, he allowed the deferred payments of items he sold to his customers. Out of the 353 pending claims featured in his probate inventory, 332 were deferred payments, averaging 71.48 kronor per claim and amounting 23,731 kronor. In total, a small fortune. The grocer took risks in allowing his customers to defer the payments for his products; 89 out of 332 (26.8%) deferred payments were considered *ösaker* (uncertain), in other words those were bad debts. The grocer Carl Christian Jacobsson, who died in 1851, had 34% of his dues considered unsecure.[74] The spice grocer Lennqvist had 30% of these bad credit sales upon his death in

[71] Muldrew, *Economy of Obligation*.

[72] James E., Shaw, 'The Informal Economy of Credit in Early Modern Venice', in: *The Historical Journal* 61:3 (2018), 1–20.

[73] Natacha Coquery, Vente, troc, crédit: les livres de comptabilité d'un joaillier-bijoutier à la fin du XVIIIe siècle. Association française de comptabilité. *6èmes journées d'histoire de la comptabilité et du management, Faculté Jean Monnet-Pésor*, Faculté Jean Monnet-Pesor, (Conference proceedings, 2000), 12.

[74] Uppsala city hall court and magistrate 1851–1860, FIIa:52.

1830.[75] Probate inventories are full of small deferred transactions labeled as "uncertain" whose origin dated far beyond a few years. With such high levels of non-repayment, we can hypothesize that these shopkeepers probably concealed some fees in the price to account for these problems.

The incentive for repayment was strong in tight-knit communities with repeated interactions. And that is precisely what replaced securities in credit sales: social networks, long-lasting relationships, the prospect of repeated future interactions and mutual trust. Yet, uncertain debts were common. It was generally the smallest ones which remained unpaid. In Uppsala, out of all the deferred payments 21.6% were considered unsecure (7% of the total volume). In Sweden, the shopkeepers with insolvent customers could nonetheless deduce those unsecured debts from the net wealth of their estate, thus diminishing the mandatory fees to be paid.

4 The Evolution of Peer-to-Peer Lending in Nineteenth-Century Uppsala

4.1 The Emergence of Banks

The development of financial institutions in the nineteenth century contributed greatly to the modernization and development of the economy.[76] Capital creation helped businesses to develop their activities and households to acquire real estate. Meanwhile, the number of banks rose, especially after the 1860s, reaching its climax before World War I when the large number of banking institutions began to merge.[77] In 1850, eight commercial banks and 85 saving banks existed. In 1910, one counts more than 80 commercial banks with 600 local branches, and 440 saving banks with more than 800 branches throughout the kingdom.[78] In this context, the banks' balance sheets rose from 12% of GDP in 1860 to 75% in 1910.[79] And the total amount of mortgages multiplied by six

[75] Uppsala city hall court and magistrate 1831–1840, FIIa:46.

[76] Anders Ögren, 'Financial Revolution'.

[77] Henric Häggqvist et al., 'The Development of Swedish Commercial Banking, from Establishment to Consolidation: A Presentation of a New Database, 1866–1938', in: *Uppsala Papers in Financial and Business History* 24 (2019), 49.

[78] Lilja,'Marknad och hushåll', 49.

[79] Broberg and Ögren, 'Names, Shares and Mortgages', 91.

between 1868 and 1938.[80] Historians often characterize the nineteenth century in Sweden as a period of "financial revolution".[81]

In Uppsala, households had several possibilities to invest their savings with the new institutions. The Uppsala Sparbank opened its doors in 1830. Additionally, the Upplands Enskilda Bank (in 1865 in Uppsala) and the Mälareprovinsernas Enskilda Bank (founded in 1847 in Västerås) became the two main commercial banks in the area.[82] In 1910, those three banking institutions held more than 66% of the decedents' deposits in Uppsala and had extended almost 70% of the loans among all banking institutions (see Table 5).

Yet, banks extended only 5.8% of the total loans recorded for decedents in Uppsala in 1910 in terms of volume, meaning that only a handful of households had access to these loans. Uppsala Sparbank, the savings bank, on the other hand, extended more loans in terms of number and of less value to households. This can be explained because savings banks targeted mainly workers. Despite the growing formalization of the transactions, the

Table 5 Representation of the main banking institutions in the probate inventories of Uppsala, 1870–1910

	1870		*1890*		*1910*	
	Deposits	Loans	Deposits	Loans	Deposits	Loans
Total volume	30,218.7	36,944.4	115,252.7	150,781.8	474,627.1	66,487.5
Mälareprovinsernas Enskilda Bank	26.6%	30.7%	37.5%	16.3%	18%	11.6%
Upplands Enskilda Bank	29.6%	30.1%	29.3%	13.3%	28%	19.3%
Uppsala Sparbank	43.8%	27.7%	26.7%	67.2%	20.6%	38%

Source See text

[80] Broberg and Ögren, 'Names, Shares and Mortgages', 90.

[81] Anders Ögren, *The Swedish Financial Revolution.*

[82] K. W Herdin, *Uplands enskilda bank, 1865–1915: minnesskrift* (Uppsala, 1915); Tom Petersson, Petersson, Tom,'Mälareprovinsernas Enskilda Bank', in: *It All Began in Old Town: A Swedish Banking History*, Avseende Bankirfirmor Och Banker, Sveriges Riksbank, SEB, Handelsbanken och Nordea i samband med Stockholms 750-årsjubileum (Stockholm, 2002).

personal lending market resisted the advent of banking institutions well, as suggested by Håkan Lindgren.[83]

4.2 *The Persistence of Peer-to-Peer Lending and the Competition with Banks in Uppsala: A Network Analysis*

Despite the emergence and rapid success of banking institutions, peer-to-peer lending persisted well into the twentieth century. In Askersund, 70% of debts were still private in 1900. The same proportion can be found in Filipstad (63%), Rönö (71%), the rural parish of Askim (71%) and Östra Hising (82%), for example.[84] In Uppsala in 1910, 50% of debts were still contracted via peer-to-peer lending. Banks did not compete with the peer-to-peer credit market. Their market segment was different as peer-to-peer loans were smaller.

In the 1810s, in the absence of banks, peer-to-peer transactions represented most transactions. In Uppsala, about 94% of debts were private. Figure 6.2 shows the network of financial transactions based on the probate inventories of decedents in Uppsala for the period 1810–1812 (116 probate inventories, 886 nodes, and 1,157 transactions). Decedents and their creditors or debtors are represented on the graph as nodes and colored according to their socio-professional categories.[85] The most interesting feature for our purpose is that most of the credit transactions took place in the so-called giant component in which the bourgeoisie and the upper class dominated the exchanges. It means that members of the bourgeoisie and the upper class showed both dependency on each other and their connection was good. As the graph shows, these nodes exhibit high eigenvector centrality measures, meaning they were connected to the most well-connected nodes in the network. They were not necessarily important lenders as most of them did not exhibit a large number of transactions, but they could act as "brokers", putting people in touch with each other and spreading information. Such an individual was the director of postal service Per Magnus Bartels, for example. It is likely that

[83] Lindgren, 'The Modernization'.

[84] Axel Hagberg, 'Household Assets'.

[85] For married women, I have considered the socio-professional category of their husbands.

his professional activity provided him with information, connections, and opportunities of all kinds.

Information inside this local credit network seems to have traveled fast as the diameter was nine; it took only nine steps to link the furthest apart nodes in the network. In comparison, in 1910, the diameter was fifteen. The average path length, which determines the average number of steps separating all the possible pairs of nodes, is 3.44. This low figure tends to indicate a "small world" in which strangers are linked by a short chain of acquaintances.[86] In such a world, it is theoretically possible to easily find credit via one's social network.

Most of the households featured in Fig. 2 were from the upper class and the bourgeoisie. Running a similar exercise for data from a century later, these individuals have largely, but not completely, been replaced by banking institutions, as seen in Fig. 3.

As established earlier and confirmed in the network analysis, in 1910, peer-to-peer lending still prevailed, as shown by Fig. 3 (1,225 nodes, 1,369 transactions). A giant component featured most of the transactions. Differently to 1810, the diameter is fifteen and the average path length is 6.62, making information to travel slower (due partly to the effects of outliers). Just like a century before, a few nodes feature a large amount of connections (the biggest nodes on the graph). Those were mostly grocers and merchants featuring long lists of deferred payments in their inventories. These actors were often poorly connected to their local community. Their network often extended beyond Uppsala.

But now, contrary to the 1810s, the three main banks in Uppsala are at the center of the exchanges with the highest score for betweenness centrality (featured in black on the graph). The Uppsala Sparbank, for example, has only a degree of 67 (in-degree of 62). But it has one of the highest eigencentrality levels (or prestige scores) in the network. The bank is directly connected to people who also score high, thus exhibiting influence. Its betweenness centrality is also among the highest, meaning the bank finds itself on paths between actors in the network. Theoretically, it also means that the bank had control over information passing between others and played a "bridge spanning" role in the network.[87]

[86] Duncan J. Watts and Steven H. Strogatz, 'Collective Dynamics of 'Small-World' Networks', *Nature* 393:6684 (1998), 440–442.

[87] Derek L. Hansen et al., "Chapter 6—Calculating and Visualizing Network Metrics," in *Analyzing Social Media Networks with NodeXL: Insights from a Connected World*

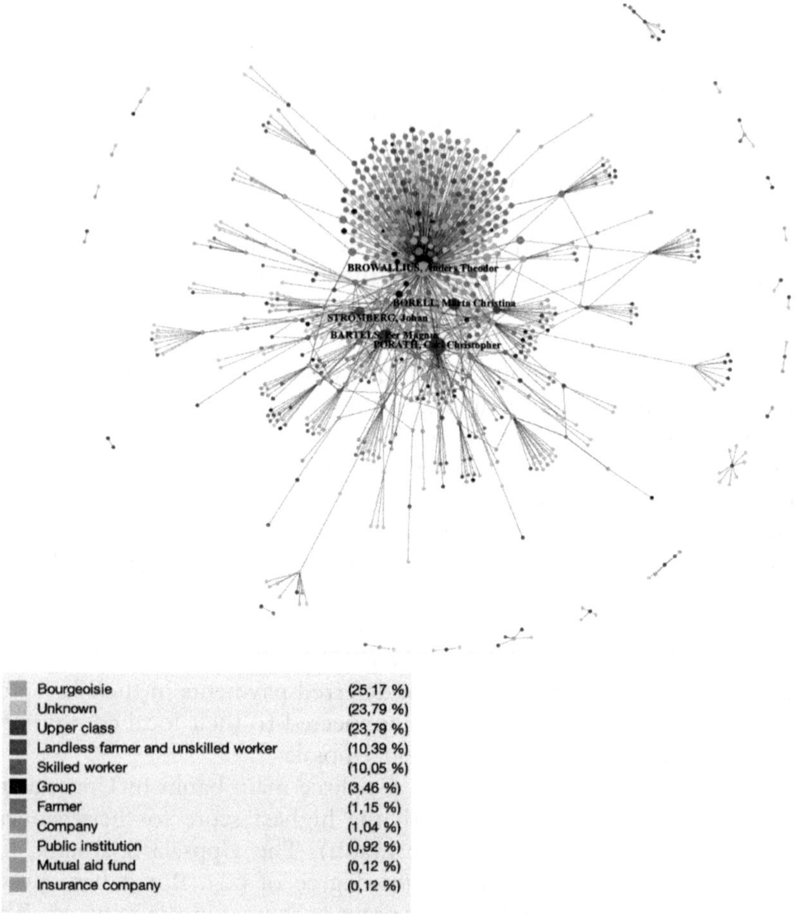

Fig. 2 Interpersonal network in Uppsala, 1810–1812 (nodes weighted according to their eigenvector centrality and colored according to their socio-professional categories) (*Source* See text)

(Second Edition), ed. Derek L. Hansen et al. (Morgan Kaufmann, 2020), 79–94; Elise Dermineur and Matteo Pompermaier, "Credit Networks in Renaissance Florence: Revisiting the Catasto of 1427," *Rivista Di Storia Economica e Sociale*, 2022.

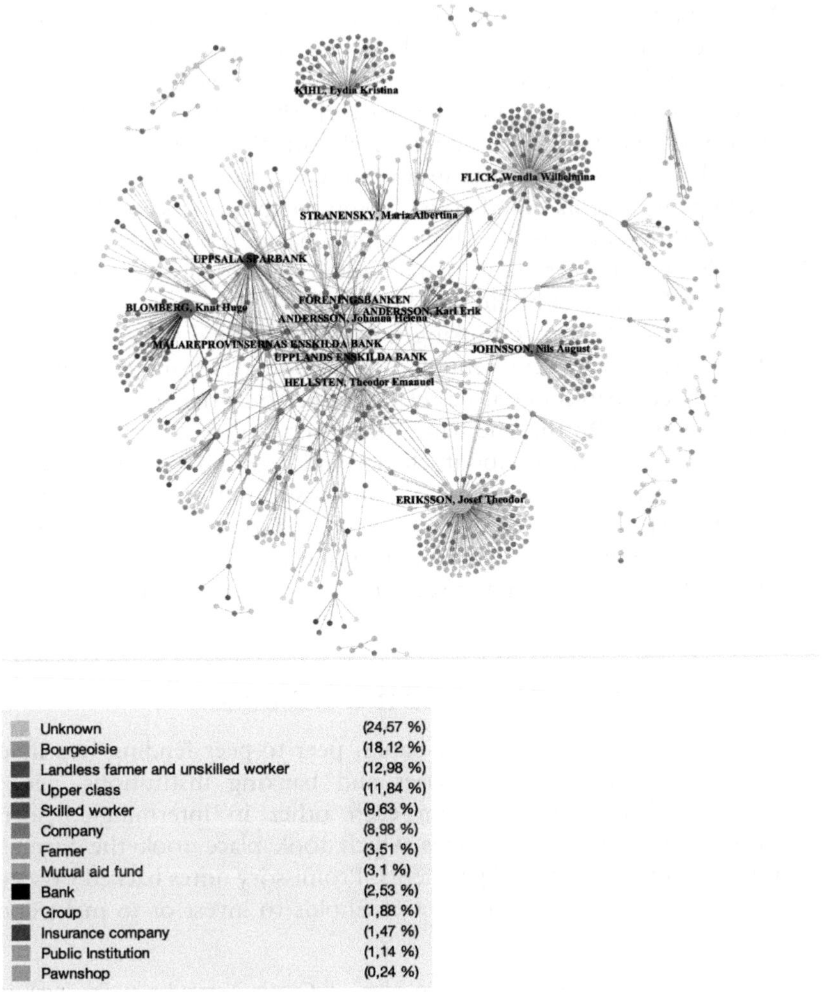

Fig. 3 Network of interpersonal and banking relations in Uppsala in 1910 (nodes weighted according to their eigenvector centrality and colored according to their socio-professional categories) (*Source* See text)

As this network analysis shows, and as we know from other historical research, commercial, and savings banks competed with each other for wealthy clients' savings. Not much research is available on how the banks recruited their customers, but the network shows that they shared the same pool of clients.[88] Lars August Backman, the owner of a farm, for example, had placed his savings in four different banks and one life insurance company. Clients could have chosen to spread risks and put their deposits in different banks. Such prudent behavior was clearly a feature in the strictly peer-to-peer credit market where individuals were connected to several individuals either for credit or debt.

But it is also likely that banking institutions chased the same wealthy clients.[89] The network representation of 1910 tends to suggest that client sharing between banks might be related to personal ties between bankers at those banks.[90] On the one hand, these personal ties might have facilitated information access about clients and reduced transaction costs. Clients were certainly not shared randomly. But on the other, the importance of these personal ties might have excluded some potential customers who were newcomers and/or not well connected. As a result, these individuals might have continued to seek credit within their own personal and private network.

5 Concluding Remarks

In Sweden, before the advent of banks, peer-to-peer lending was ubiquitous. In the absence of notaries and banking institutions, people borrowed and lent money from each other in intermingled social networks. Most of the exchanges which took place took the form of promissory notes or deferred payments. Promissory notes backed by securities and/or a guarantor allowed households to invest or to make ends

[88] See Elise M. Dermineur, "The Evolution of Credit Networks in Pre-Industrial Finland," *Scandinavian Economic History Review* 0:0 (2021), 57–86.

[89] Noble, Aurelius, 'Business Among Friends: Personal Connections and Client-Sharing in Merchant Banking, c-1900' (Paper given at the *Early financial markets: Strategies, Behaviour and Networks* symposium, Stockholm, 2022).

[90] Accominotti et al. show that the amount of information needed about borrowers could be significantly reduced via the role of personal relations. Olivier Accominotti, Delio Lucena-Piquero, and Stefano Ugolini, "The Origination and Distribution of Money Market Instruments: Sterling Bills of Exchange during the First Globalization" *The Economic History Review* 74: 4 (2021), 892–921.

meet. These contracts were the favorite tool of the bourgeoisie and the upper class. Deferred payments, a less well-known credit instrument, allowed households from all classes to delay the payment of their expenditures in order to juggle with unsteady budgets and various economic hazards.

This pattern of peer-to-peer lending began to change in the late nineteenth century when banking institutions slowly entered the picture. Yet, the rise of bank-intermediated credit did take a long time. In the 1860s, banking institutions started to target private customers. Yet, their client base was made up mainly of wealthy individuals who deposited their savings in several banking establishments. Before the democratization of credit and banking in the second half of the twentieth century, banks shared the same pool of clients.

On the eve of World War I, despite the presence of many banks, most financial transactions continued to be interpersonal. This can be explained because households sought credit constantly for a wide range of reasons in personal settings. The well-anchored deferred payments resisted the penetration of banks particularly well. Peer-to-peer lending and institutionalized credit did not compete with each other and continued for a while to serve different types of customers and various purposes for borrowing. Interestingly, network analysis indicates that banks shared the same pool of clients. These clients were certainly not shared randomly. We can hypothesize that via their social relations and tight networks, just as with peer-to-peer lending, bankers exchanged information about their clients and were able to reduce transaction costs.

Archival Sources and Literature

Accominotti, Olivier, Delio Lucena-Piquero, and Stefano Ugolini. 'The Origination and Distribution of Money Market Instruments: Sterling Bills of Exchange during the First Globalization', in: *The Economic History Review* 74:4 (2021), 892–921.

Adams, Mike et al. 'Commercial Banking, Insurance and Economic Growth in Sweden between 1830 and 1998', in: *Accounting, Business & Financial History* 19:1 (2009), 21–38.

Ågren, Maria, *Jord och gäld: Social skiktning och rättslig konflikt i södra dalarna ca 1650–1850* (Uppsala, 1992).

Ågren, Maria, 'Land and Debt: On the Process of Social Differentiation in Rural Sweden, circa 1750–1850', in: *Rural History* 5:1 (1994), 23–40.

Ågren, Maria, 'Providing Security for Others: Swedish Women in Early Modern Credit Networks', in: Elise M. Dermineur (eds.), *Women and Credit in Pre-Industrial Europe* (Turnhout, 2018), 121–142.

Andersson, Lars Fredrik, Liselotte Eriksson, and Magnus Lindmark, 'Life Insurance and Income Growth: The Case of Sweden 1830–1950', in: *Scandinavian Economic History Review* 58:3 (2010), 203–219.

Bagge, G., E. Lundberg, and I. Svennilson (eds.), *Wages, Cost of Living and National Income in Sweden 1860–1930* Volume 2: *Wages in Sweden 1860–1930* (London, 1935).

Berg, Anne, 'The Market and 'The Making': The Economics of the First Workers' Associations in Nineteenth-Century Sweden', in: *Social History* 45:2 (2020), 167–192.

Bowles, Samuel, *The Moral Economy: Why Good Incentives Are No Substitute for Good Citizens* (London, 2016).

Broberg, Oskar, and Anders Ögren, 'Names, Shares and Mortgages: The Formalisation of Swedish Commercial Bank Lending, 1870–1938', in: *Financial History Review* 26:1 (2019), 81–108.

Cassis, Youssef, *City Bankers, 1890–1914* (Cambridge, 1994).

Cassis, Youssef, *Capitals of Capital: The Rise and Fall of International Financial Centres, 1780–2009* (Cambridge, 2010).

Coquery, Natacha. Vente, troc, crédit: les livres de comptabilité d'un joaillier-bijoutier à la fin du XVIIIe siècle. Association française de comptabilité. *6èmes journées d'histoire de la comptabilité et du management, Faculté Jean Monnet-Pésor*, Faculté Jean Monnet-Pesor, (Conference proceedings, 2000), 133–144.

De Vries, Jan, *The Industrious Revolution: Consumer Behavior and the Household Economy, 1650 to the Present* (Cambridge 2008).

Dermineur, Elise M., 'The Evolution of Credit Networks in Pre-industrial Finland', in: *Scandinavian Economic History Review* 70:1 (2022), 57–86.

Dermineur, Elise M., 'The Wealth of the Swedish Nobility: The Case of the Never-Married Women, 1850–1910', in: Anna Nilsson Hammar, Daniel Nyström and Martin Almbjär (eds.), *Gender, Materiality and Politics: Essays on the Making of Power* (Lund, 2022), 101–121.

Dermineur, Elise and Matteo Pompermaier, 'Credit Networks in Renaissance Florence: Revisiting the Catasto of 1427', in: *Ricerche di storia economica e sociale* VIII (2022), 89–110. https://doi.org/10.17426/R08C08

Di Matteo, Livio, 'Patterns and Determinants of Wealth Inequality in Late-Nineteenth Century Ontario—Evidence from Census-Linked Probate Data', in: *Social Science History* 25:3 (2001), 347–380.

Edvinsson, Rodney, 'Swedish Monetary Standards in a Historical Perspective', in: *Scandinavian Working Papers in Economics* (2009). https://swopec.hhs.se/suekhi/abs/suekhi0006.htm

Edvinsson, Rodney and Anders Ögren, 'Swedish Money Supply, 1620–2012', in: Rodney Edvinsson, Tor Jacobson, and Daniel Waldenström (eds.) *Historical Monetary and Financial Statistics for Sweden* volume 2: *House Prices, Stock Returns, National Accounts, and the Riksbank Balance Sheet, 1620–2012* (Stockholm, 2014), 293–338.

Erikson, Marja, *Krediter i Lust Och Nöd: Skattebönder i Torstuna Härad, Västmanlands Län, 1770–1870* (Uppsala, 2018).

Fontaine, Laurence, *L'économie morale: Pauvreté, crédit et confiance dans l'Europe préindustrielle* (Paris, 2008).

Fafchamps, Marcel. 'Formal and Informal Market Institutions: Embeddedness Revisited', in: Jean-Marie Baland et al. (eds.), *The Handbook of Economic Development and Institutions* (Princeton, 2020), 375–413.

Gratzer, Karl, Mats Hayen, and Klas Nyberg, 'The Swedish Bankruptcy system, 1734–1849', in: Klas Nyberg and Håkan Jakobsson (eds.), *Luxury, Fashion and the Early Modern Idea of Credit* (Abingdon, 2020), 51–61.

Hagberg, Axel, 'Households Assets and Liabilities in Sweden 1800–1900', (paper presented at the symposium *Wealth and Debt Accumulation in Early Financial Markets,* Stockholm, 2018).

Häggqvist, Henric et al., 'The Development of Swedish Commercial Banking, from Establishment to Consolidation: A Presentation of a New Database, 1866–1938', in: *Uppsala Papers in Financial and Business History* 24 (2019).

Hallén, Per, Lili-Annè Aldman, and Martin Fritz, *Krona eller klave: utvecklingen av kreditmarknaden i Göteborg under 1800* (Malmö, 2015).

Hansen, Derek L. et al., 'Chapter 6—Calculating and Visualizing Network Metrics', in: Derek L. Hansen et al. (eds.), *Analyzing Social Media Networks with NodeXL: Insights from a Connected World (Second Edition)* (Burlington, 2020), 79–94.

Herdin, K.W., *Uplands enskilda bank, 1865–1915: minnesskrift* (Uppsala, 1915).

Hellgren, Hilda, 'Fasta förbindelser: en studie av låntagare hos sparbanken och informella kreditgivare i Sala 1860–1910', in: *Acta Universitatis Upsaliensis : Univ-bibldistributör* (dissertation, 2003).

Hemminki, Tiina, 'Långa listor med fordringar och skulder. Om förtroendeförhållanden i Ilmola och Nordmaling i början av 1800-talet', in: *Historisk Tidskrift för Finland* 97:3 (2012).

Keibek, Sebastiaan, 'Correcting the Probate Inventory Record for Wealth Bias', Working Paper (University of Cambridge, 2017).

Kenttä, Tony, Kristina Lilja, and Dan Bäcklund, 'The Necessity of Small Loans: The Borrowing and Lending among Low-Income Earners in Early 20th Century Sweden', in: *The History of the Family* 27:2 (2022), 268–292.

Kuuse, Jan, 'The Probate Inventory as a Source for Economic and Social History', in: *Scandinavian Economic History Review* 22:1 (1974), 22–31.

Larsson, Mats, Kristina Lilja, and Tom Petersson, *Risk Management in Early Banking: An International Perspective of Swedish Saving Banks, 1820–1910* (London, 2021).
Lilja, Kristina, 'Marknad och hushåll : Sparande och krediter i Falun 1820–1910 utifrån ett livscykelperspektiv' (thesis, Uppsala University, 2004).
Lilja, Kristina, 'The Deposit Market Revolution in Sweden', in: Anders Ögren (ed.), *The Swedish Financial Revolution* (London, 2010), 41–63.
Lilja, Kristina, and Dan Bäcklund, 'Savings Banks and Working-class saving during the Swedish Industrialisation', in: *Financial History Review* 23:1 (2016), 111–132.
Lindgren, Håkan, 'The Modernization of Swedish Credit Markets, 1840–1905: Evidence from Probate Records', in: *The Journal of Economic History* 62:3 (2002), 810–832.
Lindgren, Håkan, 'The Evolution of Secondary Financial Markets, 1820–1920', in: Anders Ögren (ed.), *The Swedish Financial Revolution* (New York, 2010), 95–112.
Lindgren, Håkan, 'Parish Banking in Informal Credit Markets: The Business of Private Lending in Early Nineteenth-Century Sweden', in: *Financial History* Review 24:1 (2017), 83–102.
Lindgren, Håkan, 'Over-indebtedness'—or not? Household debt Accumulation and Risk Exposure in Nineteenth Century Sweden', in: *Scandinavian Economic History Review* 70:1 (2022), 33–56.
Magnusson, Lars, *An Economic History of Sweden* (London, 2000).
Markkanen, Erkki, 'The Use of Probate Inventories as Indicators of Personal Wealth during the Period of Industrialization: The Financial Resources of the Finnish Rural Population 1850–1911', in: *Scandinavian Economic History Review* 26:1 (1978), 66–83.
Molinder, Jakob, and Martin Söderhäll, 'Did Industrialisation lead to Segregation in Cities of the Nineteenth Century? The Case of Uppsala 1880–1900', in: *Scandinavian Economic History Review* 68:1 (2020), 23–44.
Muldrew, Craig, *The Economy of Obligation: The Culture of Credit and Social Relations in Early Modern England* (London, 1998).
Noble, Aurelius, 'Business Among Friends: Personal Connections and Client-Sharing in Merchant Banking, c-1900' (Paper given at the *Early financial markets: Strategies, Behaviour and Networks* symposium, Stockholm, 2022).
Nygren, Ingemar, 'Svensk kreditmarknad 1820–1875: översikt av det institutionella kreditväsendets utveckling' (Announcements from the Department of Economic History at University of Gothenburg, Univeristy of Gothenburg, 1981).
Nygren, Ingemar, 'Transformation of Bank Structures in the Industrial Period. The Case of Sweden 1820–1913', in: *Journal of European Economic History* 12:1 (1983).

Nygren, Ingemar, 'Göteborgs kreditmarknad 1820–1913' (report from the economic historic department of the University of Gothenburg, 1987).
Ögren, Anders, 'Free or Central Banking? Liquidity and Financial Deepening in Sweden, 1834–1913', in: *Explorations in Economic History* 43:1 (2006), 64–93.
Ögren, Anders, 'Financial Revolution and Economic Modernisation in Sweden', in: *Financial History Review* 16:1 (2009), 47–71.
Ögren, Anders, *The Swedish Financial Revolution*. (New York, 2010).
Perlinge, Anders, *Sockenbankirerna: kreditrelationer och tidig bankverksamhet : Vånga socken i Skåne 1840–1900* (Stockholm, 2005).
Petersson, Tom, 'Mälareprovinsernas Enskilda Bank', in: *It All Began in Old Town: A Swedish Banking History*, Avseende Bankirfirmor Och Banker, Sveriges Riksbank, SEB, Handelsbanken och Nordea i samband med Stockholms 750-årsjubileum (Stockholm, 2002).
Pihl, Christopher, 'Learning to Bring Dead Capital to Life': The Riksens Ständers Bank and the Credit Market in Seventeenth-Century Sweden', in: *Continuity and Change* 34:2 (2019), 209–230.
Pompermaier, Matteo, 'A Complicated Puzzle: Spinsters, Widows and Credit in Sweden (1790–1910)', in: *Financial History Review* 29:1 (2021), 1–23.
Shammas, Carole, 'Constructing a Wealth Distribution from Probate Records', in: *The Journal of Interdisciplinary History* 9:2 (1978), 297–307.
Shaw, James E., 'The Informal Economy of Credit in Early Modern Venice', in: *The Historical Journal* 61:3 (2018), 1–20.
Uppsala town hall court and magistrate, FIIa:34–57, 70 and 90.
Uppsala city court hall and magistrate 1910–1910, FIIa:90.
Uppsala city court hall and magistrate 1890–1890, FIIa:70.
Uppsala town hall court and magistrate 1851–1860, FIIa:52.
Uppsala city hall court and magistrate 1831–1840, FIIa:45–46.
Uppsala city court hall and magistrate 1821–1830, FIIa:42.
Uppsala city court hall and magistrate, Bouppteckningar 1795–1797, FIIa:31.
Uppsala University Archive, EIII: 204, 205.
Uppsala University Archive, FXI:8.
Uppsala University Archive, FXI: 10.
Ulväng, Göran and Sofia Murhem, 'Church Endowments Used for Credit in 18th and 19th Century Rural Sweden' (paper presented at the ESSHC, 2021).
Westlund, Hans, 'Kommunikationer, tillgänglighet, omvandling: en studie av samspelet mellan kommunikationsnät och näringsstruktur i Sveriges mellanstora städer 1850–1970' (unpublished dissertation, Umeå University, 1992).

Wetterberg, Gunnar, *Money and Power: From Stockholms Banco 1656 to Sveriges Riksbank today* (Stockholm 2009) https://www.riksbank.se/en-gb/about-the-riksbank/history/money-and-power--the-history-of-sveriges-riksbank/
Watts, Duncan J., and Steven H. Strogatz, 'Collective Dynamics of 'Small-World' Networks', *Nature* 393:6684 (1998), 440–442.

Consumer Credit in Early Modern Venice: The Lending Activity of Innkeepers and *Bastioneri*

Matteo Pompermaier

1 Introduction

The traditional narrative about the evolution of credit markets throughout history often resorts to the argument of formalization or modernization. Following this idea, markets characterized by informal relationships have been gradually replaced by modern and more efficient ones, dominated by banks and other specialized institutions. A world in which transactions were "embedded in personal interactions and [in] the intimate bonds inherent in family or community", is opposed to

M. Pompermaier (✉)
Department of Economics and Management, University of Brescia, Brescia, Italy
e-mail: matteo.pompermaier@unibs.it

C. van Bochove and J. Levy (eds.), *Beyond Banks*, Palgrave Studies in the History of Finance,
https://doi.org/10.1007/978-3-031-75819-5_7

another one where they were "normalized and left to specialized institutions".[1] Therefore, the role and significance of pre-bank credit markets, which are considered to rely almost completely upon interpersonal relations, have often been undervalued: they are usually considered small and fragmented, as well as risky and expensive.

This chapter challenges this skepticism about pre-bank institutions and shows that organized and bureaucratized credit developed and flourished also before the introduction of banks. It proves that the pre-bank credit markets responded to a broad set of clients and was very inclusive: there were lenders specialized in providing credit to the lower strata of the population, those individuals who sometimes suffer from financial exclusion even in our contemporary world. More specifically, the chapter focuses on early modern Venice and on the rather unique pawnbroking activity of Venetian innkeepers and *bastioneri*—managers of the *bastioni*, warehouses where wine was sold to the local population. The analysis of this type of credit allows us to assess how an early modern city like Venice was able to support the popular classes and provide access to low-cost credit.

This chapter traces the process of formalization of what can be defined as a traditional activity. More specifically, it studies the evolution of innkeepers and *bastioneri* from simple wine sellers to public pawnbrokers, supervised and controlled by a specific magistracy. This was a highly regulated, hierarchically defined, and increasingly bureaucratized supply of credit: at the same time, the nature of the places involved—inns and *bastioni*—suggests that transactions were often characterized by personal relations between lenders and borrowers, in the context of almost daily interactions. The large number of loans supplied every year by innkeepers and *bastioneri* also shows that this hybrid solution, in which the line separating credit from barter is not always well discernible, was efficient and

[1] Claire Lemercier and Claire Zalc, 'For a New Approach to Credit Relations in Modern History', in: *Annales. Histoire, Sciences Sociales* 67:4 (2012), 663–691, there 664–665; for the concept of 'economic identification' and on the role of social institutions in credit relationships, see Gilles Laferté, 'L'identification économique', in: *Genèses* 79:2 (2010), 2–5; about the embeddedness, see Mark Granovetter, 'Economic Action and Social Structure: The Problem of Embeddedness', in: *American Journal of Sociology* 91:3 (1985), 481–510; about the moral and social nature of credit transactions, see Laurence Fontaine, *L'économie morale: Pauvreté, crédit et confiance dans l'Europe pré-industrielle* (Gallimard, 2008) and Craig Muldrew, *The Economy of Obligation: The Culture of Credit and Social Relations in Early Modern England* (Basingstoke, 1998).

represented an advantageous solution for both creditors and debtors. It is a very interesting case that sheds more light on the variety of actors and solutions available in pre-bank credit markets.

The role played by different shopkeepers in the credit market has already been highlighted by the literature. In the early modern period, due to coin shortage and irregularity of income, shopkeepers often allowed their customers to buy their products on credit. There are many examples that certify the important role of local retailers as lenders all over Europe. For instance, French bakeries were centers of sociability at the core of the daily life of the population, as well as places where people could ask for a loan.[2] In eighteenth-century Amsterdam, shopkeepers often sold their items—including alcoholic beverages—on credit to the seafarers in a way that overcame problems of moral hazard and adverse selection.[3] It was not only in Venice that innkeepers and *bastioneri* had an important role in the credit market: in an article devoted to the material culture in sixteenth-century Siena, Paula Hohti traced the role of the local innkeepers as pawnbrokers, underlining the importance of pawnbroking for individuals with limited means. Innkeepers had a similar role also in the Prince-Bishopric of Trent, as stated in the *Clesiani* statutes of 1528.[4]

Those lending activities that involved shopkeepers were usually characterized by some common features. In many cases, it was not direct lending but rather sales with deferred or cumulative payments. It was usually informal credit, in the sense that public authorities did not control or monitor their functioning (an exception to that is the already mentioned case of shopkeepers in Amsterdam). Transactions were based on personal knowledge between borrowers and lenders, and the overall volume and number of operations were typically quite limited. As we will see, the Venetian case proves to be very different and it contributes to reshaping

[2] Angleraud Bernardette, 'Le pain quotidien: la boutique boulangère au cœur de sociabilités de quartier au XIXe siècle', in: Natasha Coquery (eds.), *La Boutique et La Ville. Commerces, Commerçants, Espaces et Clientèles, XVIe-XXe Siècle* (Tours, 2000), 368–380, there 377.

[3] Christiaan van Bochove, 'Seafarers and Shopkeepers: Credit in Eighteenth-Century Amsterdam' in: *Eighteenth-Century Studies* 48:1 (2014), there 67–88.

[4] Paula Hohti, 'The Innkeeper's Goods: The Use and Acquisition of Household Property in Sixteenth-Century Siena', in: Evelyn S. Welch and Michelle O'Malley (eds.), *The Material Renaissance* (Manchester, 2007), 242–259; Giovanni Libera, 'Vini e osterie trentini', in: *Strenna Trentina* 14:1 (1934), 101–103.

our ideas about shopkeepers' credit in the early modern period, giving us a totally different and unexpected picture of pre-bank credit markets as a whole.

The chapter is organized as follows: the next section contextualizes the research and briefly describes eighteenth-century Venice from a political and economic point of view. Then, it focuses on the credit activity of innkeepers and *bastioneri*: it analyses their role as market-makers and describes the main characteristics of their pawnbroking service. It also provides some information about the overall volume of transactions, highlighting its importance in the context of the city. The third section provides insights into the judicial framework regulating this credit activity, highlighting its evolution over time. The fourth section takes a step back and considers the structure of the Venetian credit market as a whole, focusing on the institutional supply of consumer credit. It analyses how the market performed during the phase of economic distress and traces the main causes of its fragility. The final section summarizes the main findings.

2 Innkeepers and *Bastioneri*: Pre-Bank Lenders in Early Modern Venice

2.1 *A Declining Economy: Venice in the "Short" Eighteenth Century*

Even though the unique pawnbroking activity of innkeepers and *bastioneri* accompanied the Republic of Venice for a long part of its history, this chapter mainly focuses on the eighteenth century. The source material for this period is very abundant, and we cannot say the same for previous centuries. This is the consequence of the increasing bureaucratization of the whole Venetian society and of the accentuated growth in the demand for consumer credit.

The eighteenth century can certainly be considered a contradictory period for Venice. It is a "short" century, which started with the de facto exclusion of the Republic from European diplomacy after the second Morea war (1714–1718) and ended in May 1797.[5] During this "short

[5] There is scholarly debate on the importance of the second Morea war. Piero del Negro does not consider it as a decisive episode in Venetian history since the political marginalization of the Republic began at least 70 years earlier. See Piero del Negro, 'Introduzione' in: Piero Del Negro and Paolo Preto (eds.), *Storia di Venezia dalle origini alla caduta*

century", Venice was still the city of the Carnival and home of some of the most famous painters and playwrights of the time and its monuments and arts were widely celebrated. It also still was the crossroads of the European nobility as well as one of the obliged stops for the numerous travelers that visited the Italian peninsula each year. However, it was not the pre-eminent maritime and commercial power of the eastern Mediterranean anymore. The *doge* Paolo Renier (1779–1789) openly admitted the weakness of the Republic saying that "we don't have land forces, we don't have maritime forces, we don't have alliances, we live at the mercy of destiny and fate, without other concern but prudence".[6]

Even if the Rialto market retained "a certain dynamism and the possibility of appropriately allocating the available resources", the city was no longer at the center of the trade networks linking the Middle East with central and northern Europe.[7] The role of Venice in international trade was definitively reduced and the city could not compete with the much more advanced economies of the north, especially the Netherlands and England.[8] Some of the most important sectors of Venetian manufacturing were declining, such as wool production, and the dynamism that characterized the previous centuries seemed to be lost. Real wages decreased during the eighteenth century, pushed down by the increase in the price of basic goods such as wheat and wine, further limiting the purchasing power of poor households.[9]

della Serenissima volume 7: 'La Venezia Barocca' (Rome, 1997), 1–80. However, many scholars still emphasize the relevant military and economic consequences of the war, the last conflict in which the Republic of Venice took part.

[6] Indro Montanelli and Roberto Gervaso, *L'Italia del Settecento: (1700–1789)* (Milan, 1970), there 223; all translations are mine unless otherwise noted.

[7] Walter Panciera, 'L'economia: imprenditoria, corporazioni, lavoro' in: Piero Del Negro and Paolo Preto (eds.), *Storia di Venezia: dalle origini alla caduta della Serenissima* volume 8: 'L'ultima fase della Serenissima' (Rome, 1999), 479–553, there 506.

[8] Luciano Pezzolo, 'L'economia', in: Gino Benzoni and Gaetano Cozzi (eds.), *Storia di Venezia dalle origini alla caduta della Serenissima*, volume 7: 'La Venezia Barocca' (Rome, 1997), 369–433; Richard T. Rapp, *Industria e decadenza economica a Venezia nel XVII secolo* (Rome, 1986); Walter Panciera, *La Repubblica di Venezia nel Settecento* (Rome, 2014); Richard Mackenney, *Tradesmen and Traders: The World of the Guilds in Venice and Europe: c.1250–c.1650* (London-Sidney, 1987).

[9] For wages in the northern part of the Italian peninsula, see Paolo Malanima, 'The Long Decline of a Leading Economy: GDP in Central and Northern Italy, 1300–1913' in: *European Review of Economic History* 15:1 (2010), 169–219, there 177; the prices of basic products grew throughout the eighteenth century: for the price of wine, see

In such a context, providing the urban population with access to low-cost credit was of crucial importance. This was even more critical considering that Venice was one of the few cities in the Italian peninsula without a municipal pawnshop, which would not be established until the 1820s. It is not easy to explain why the Venetian public authorities had always hindered the foundation of a *monte di pietà*, but this does not mean they were not aware of the importance of providing access to consumer credit to the urban population. As we will see, the Republic intervened several times in regulating the market to safeguard the rights of borrowers and make sure that the social purposes of credit prevailed over the "greed" of lenders. The strict supervision had two main objectives, protecting the rights of borrowers, and increasing public revenues. In so doing, the Republic influenced the evolution of the urban credit market, improving its strengths but amplifying some of its weaknesses.

2.2 Innkeepers and Bastioneri as Public Market-Makers

In pre-industrial Europe, access to drinking water was a major problem for the urban population, and the management of rivers and springs was carefully regulated by public authorities.[10] This situation seemed to be even more complicated in Venice because of the atypical position of the city, located in the middle of a lagoon. From its origins, the city built a network of wells and cisterns to accumulate potable rainwater. Maintaining these infrastructures was difficult and costly. A study that dates back to 1796 mentions that there were more than 5,000 wells scattered across the city but only about 2,000 of them were still working, while the others, often due to negligence, were unusable or salted because of infiltrations.[11] The water was mainly imported from the rivers that flew into the lagoon—one of the tasks of the *acquaroli*'s guild. However, there

Matteo Pompermaier, *L'économie du mouchoir: crédit et microcrédit à Venise au XVIIIe siècle* (Rome 2022), there 57; for the price of wheat (Venice) and corn (Udine), see Jean Georgelin, *Venise au siècle des Lumières* (Paris, 1978), annexes 46 and 54.

[10] Daniel Roche, 'Le temps de l'eau rare du Moyen Age à l'époque modern', in: *Annales. Histoire, Sciences Sociales* 39:2 (1984), 383–399, there 393.

[11] Federico Gaspare, *Topografia fisico-medica della città di Venezia delle sue isole, estuarj e lagune, dei cangiamenti nati e dei mezzi profilattici d'igiene del dott. Gaspare Federigo* (Padova, 1831), there 57. See also David Gentilcore, 'The Cistern-System of Early Modern Venice: Technology, Politics and Culture in a Hydraulic Society', in: *Water History* 13:1 (2021), 375–406.

were many problems linked to its preservation, especially during the hot and dry summer months.[12]

Wine played a decisive role in the daily diet of people, both as a source of liquid and calories. Its consumption was not limited to the higher social strata and the difference between rich and poor only concerned the quality of the product.[13] Between the medieval and early modern periods, wine consumption in Venice was very high. In 1730, the Republic estimated the average quantity of wine drunk by its inhabitants, dividing them into different gender and age groups.[14] The average consumption for men under eighteen years old was 0.67 liters a day; between eighteen and 50 years old it rose to 1.34 liters, and 1.79 liters for those over 50. For women we only have information about the quantity of wine drunk between eighteen and 50 years old, amounting to 0.67 liters a day: this figure, although much lower than that of men, confirms the general high per capita consumption.[15]

The relevance of the wine trade and the high demand favored the development of a complex retail system, at the heart of which there were inns and *bastioni*.[16] Inns were located exclusively in the area around the Rialto bridge and St. Mark's square, respectively the commercial and

[12] For a more detailed analysis, see Virgilio Giormani, 'Acqua Potabile per Venezia', in: *Studi Veneziani* 60 (2010), 325–374.

[13] Massimo Montanari, *L'alimentazione contadina nell'alto Medioevo* (Napels, 1979), 381–384. The daily diet of a worker in the Venetian Arsenal at mid-seventeenth century included 0.7 liters of wine, see Luciano Pezzolo, *Il fisco dei veneziani. Finanza pubblica ed economia fra XV e XVII secolo* (Verona, 2003), there 156.

[14] Ugo Tucci, 'Commercio e consumo del vino a Venezia in età moderna', in: *Il vino nell'economia e nella società italiana medioevale e moderna*, conference proceedings, Greve in Chianti, 21–24 May 1987 (Florence, 1987), 185–202, there 186.

[15] Foreigners did not seem to like Venetian wine. A French traveler claimed that it was harmful to drink because it was "adulterated with a kind of wine which comes [...] from Dalmatia, and whose use is dangerous", and also because "the sailors drink it during the journeys, and replace it by the water of the lagoon, which is unhealthy", even if the same author recognizes that it "tastes like water of seltzer". See Houssaye Arsène, *Voyage à Venise* (Paris, 1850), there 105–106. Another traveler said that "wine merchants cannot really be visited in Venice, because the indigenous wines that they drunk (the so-called *vino nostrano*) is an odious beverage that doesn't deserve the name by which it is called". *Venise. Guide historique-topographique et artistique* (Trieste, 1861), there 49.

[16] While the *hostarie* (inns) seems to have always been part of Venetian history, the term *bastione* appeared in the sources only starting from the beginning of the sixteenth century. For a general overview on the issue, see Matteo Pompermaier, *L'économie du mouchoir*, there 39–42.

administrative center of the city. The innkeepers provided their customers with a complete hospitality service, offering them accommodation and rooms where to stay to eat and drink. As specified in the statutes of the innkeepers' guild and confirmed by their specific geographical location, inns' services were not meant for the majority of the Venetian population, but mainly for foreigners and wealthy people.[17]

On the contrary, the public authorities assigned a different role to the *bastioni*. They were scattered across the city, except in the areas reserved for the inns, and were exclusively concerned with supplying wine to the popular classes, selling it to take away. It was forbidden—at least in theory—to stay in a *bastione* to drink and eat, as it happened in the inns: the public authorities were well aware of the importance of wine for the daily diet of the popular classes, but they specified "that those who buy such wines"—the one sold by the *bastioneri*—"[had to] drink them in their homes with their families".[18] Safer domestic consumption was encouraged, limiting as far as possible the public episodes of excessive drinking and the gathering of people in crowded places, where potentially dangerous ideas could easily circulate.[19] The *bastioni* were, together with the wells and the bakeries, at the core of the daily life of ordinary individuals in early modern Venice. By providing their inhabitants with access to all basic services, they characterized each of the 70 Venetian parishes, making them autonomous units.[20]

Therefore, inns and *bastioni* were different in the way they sold wine, the volume of sales, and the kind of customers they targeted. However, among all these differences there were also some similarities. First, they were both short-term professions. They were organized in two professional groups, the guild of innkeepers and the consortium of *mercanti*

[17] "According to an ancient institution, which is based on the most venerable decrees of the *Serenissimo* Prince, the inns of this city have been divided and separated from the *bastioni*, each having its own particular laws, and neither one has to abuse the privileges of the other. The public mind ordered the establishment of the inns for the need of foreigners and for the comfort of wealthy and *morbinose* (happy) people". Venice State Archive (henceforth ASVe), *Arti*, b. 430, f. 95r, 31 August 1701.

[18] ASVe, *Giustizia Nuova* (henceforth GN), b. 2 r. 3, f. 88.

[19] ASVe, *Governatori alle Entrate*, b. 448, "Ristretto dell'obbligo del consumo delle anfore"; The *bastione* played an important role in the wine market; between 1694 and 1698, the 45 *bastioni* active in the city sold 17.64 million liters of wine to the Venetian population.

[20] Ennio Concina, *Venezia nell'età moderna. Strutture e funzioni* (Venice, 1989), 168.

bastioneri da vin (wine merchants *bastioneri*). As members of these two institutions, they had the right to participate in specific public auctions through which the Republic sold the right to run an inn or a *bastione* for a period between two and four years called *condotta*.[21] At the end of it, those who wanted to continue with the same activity had to participate in another auction and buy a new license. For this reason, innkeepers and *bastioneri* were often considered "temporary brothers ... only for the period in which they were effectively employed in that activity".[22] The second important similarity between these two professions concerned the fact that they were also both pawnbrokers. In fact, innkeepers and *bastioneri* offered loans to their customers with items of personal property used as collateral.

The centrality of inns and *bastioni* in the daily economy of the lower classes and, more broadly, the role of various kinds of wine sellers in the credit market is not just a Venetian feature. However, among the many examples that prove the economic and social role of inns in pre-industrial societies, the Venetian case proves to be rather unique. The first crucial trait of this lending lies in its relationship with the public authorities. They did not just tolerate or perfunctorily regulate it, as happened in many cases with the various forms of shopkeepers' credit, but they made it public and completely formal. It was placed under the supervision of a specific magistracy, the *Provveditori and Sopraprovveditori alla Giustizia Nuova*.[23]

The reasons why the Republic decided to regulate and recognize the role of lenders of innkeepers and *bastioneri* are stated very clearly in the primary sources. In the first place, they wanted to support the popular

[21] The *Giustizia Nuova* auctioned the license for the inns, while the *Governatori delle Entrate* those for the *bastioni*.

[22] Literally, "fratelli a scadenza". See Giuseppe Tassini, *Curiosità Veneziane ovvero delle denominazioni stradali di Venezia* (Venice, 1872), there 78.

[23] From 1502, this activity was also supervised by the *Collegio dei Sette Savi sopra Provveditori alla Giustizia Nuova*, the *Giustizia Nuova*'s court of appeal and controlling body. Before 1513, the *Provveditori and Sopraprovveditori alla Giustia Nuova* where called *Giustizieri Nuovi*. In this chapter I will make no distinction between *Giustizieri* and *Provveditori*, I will refer to both of them as the *Giustizia Nuova* (and *Collegio dei Sette Savi* or *Savi*).

classes, giving them access to credit.[24] As we will see in the following section, this was crucial to support the lower strata, those characterized by low wages and irregular income. The public authorities were also well aware that allowing those who did not have cash to buy wine on credit favored the retailing activity, thus increasing the turnover of inns and *bastioni*.[25] At the same time, the more wine was sold, the more had to be imported into the city, increasing the public income from the duty it levied on this.[26] Therefore, promoting this activity was very profitable for the Republic as well.[27] It was this sort of virtuous circle that probably pushed the public authorities to formalize and support this credit activity.

Another characteristic that makes this credit activity rather unique concerns the cost of capital. Loans were officially supplied free of charge, except for a small tax that borrowers had to pay on each object pawned (one *soldo* per each loan).[28] However, several nineteenth-century authors claimed that at least one-third of each loan was supplied in wine. In this way, all transactions involved at least one part in kind and lenders could profit from the difference between the price of wine bought and sold.[29] Comparing the wholesale price of wine on the Venetian mainland with the retailing price established monthly by the Republic, it has been possible to

[24] "The sums supplied by innkeepers and *bastioneri* in exchange for pledges [aim to] help the poor in their daily hardships, [and this is] the only reason for the public authorization of this type of commerce" ASVe, *GN*, b. 2 r. 4, f. 205r. Before they could start running their activities, innkeepers and *bastioneri* were also obliged to swear that their participation in the credit market "aims at the benefit of the poor". ASVe, *GN*, b. 2 r. 4, f. 49v, 10 June 1604.

[25] "By the *bastioneri* and innkeepers are accepted pledges from the poor in order to stimulate the sales of wine". ASVe, *GN*, b. 2 r. 4, f. 191r, 6 July 1743.

[26] "It is necessary to take every precaution so that the innkeepers do not have to send people away, because the duty depends on it [...] many times it happened that some people go to the inns to eat, and drink, and not having cash they leave a pledge". ASVe, *GN*, b. 1, f. 117r, 26 October 1531.

[27] In the eighteenth century, import duties on wine represented on average 6% or 7% of all annual revenue. See Tucci, 'Commercio', 192.

[28] 1 *soldo* was 1/20th of a *lira*.

[29] Pierluigi Bembo, *Delle istituzioni di beneficienza nella città e provincia di Venezia* (Venice, 1859), there 135. This information finds a direct correspondence in the *Dizionario del dialetto veneto*, which specifies that the *bastioni* "received objects in pawn, on which it was possible to obtain two thirds of the value in money, and one third in very bad wine, known as *pledges wine* (*vin da pegni*)". Giuseppe Boerio and Daniele Manin, *Dizionario del dialetto veneziano di Giuseppe Boerio* (Venice, 1829), see term *Magazèn*.

estimate that the interest rate was about 28% a year (1780s). This figure is obviously only approximate, as it was linked to several variables, such as the wholesale price of wine and its quality.[30] However, it gives us an idea of the profit margin of the lenders. This feature surely contributes to characterizing this credit activity, further linking credit to consumption.

2.3 *Average Value and Frequency of Loans*

Loans usually involved quite small amounts. The analysis of a sample of more than 30,000 transactions confirms that the mean value of a loan was about three *lire*, while the median one was slightly lower, just two *lire*.[31] Even though the data includes credits ranging from one *soldo* (1/20 of a *lira*) up to more than 200 Venetian *lire*, a quite wide range of the loans, more than 96%, were lower than ten Venetian *lire*, and in seven cases out of ten even lower than three *lire* (see Fig. 1).[32]

In the 1730s, the average monthly salary of a *bastionere* was about 130–150 *ducati* a year, or 70 to 85 *lire* a month. It is difficult to estimate the number of working days a week, but we can expect him to have earnt between three and four *lire* a day, more or less the average value of a loan they provided to their customers in the same period (3.6 *lire* in 1739).[33] Between 1767 and 1771, when the median value of a loan was about 2.9

[30] We know that the *vin da pegni* was of very bad quality, which increases, therefore, the gain of the lenders. See Bembo, *Delle Istituzioni*, 139; Boerio and Manin, *Dizionario*, there 382.

[31] ASVe, GN, b. 3 r. 5 and 6, b. 6, b. 7, b. 9, b. 16, b. 17, b. 18, b. 22, b. 35 b. 40, b. 41, b. 42, b. 43. All values have been corrected for inflation using wheat price in Venice. See Georgelin, *Venise*, annex 46.

[32] The low average value of loans increases the relative weight of fixed charges on the total cost of the operation. In fact, fixed costs, although limited, have a high weight in the case of small, short-term loans. Considering the median value of a loan of 3 *lire*, the fee of 1 *soldo* per operation would bring the interest rate from 28% to about 30% a year.

[33] ASVe, governatori alle entrate, b. 447: "Costituti dei *bastioneri* sul numero degli uomini impiegati in ogni *bastione*, e loro salario" ("Declarations made by the *bastioneri* concerning the number of men employed in every *bastione*, and their wages"). In many cases, an investor called *conduttore* or *capitalista* bought the licenses to manage several bastioni: each of them was then conducted by a bastionere, who was only an employee. This never happened in the case of the inns, and the innkeeper was both the manager and the investor. See Pompermaier, *L'économie du mouchoir*, there 73–74.

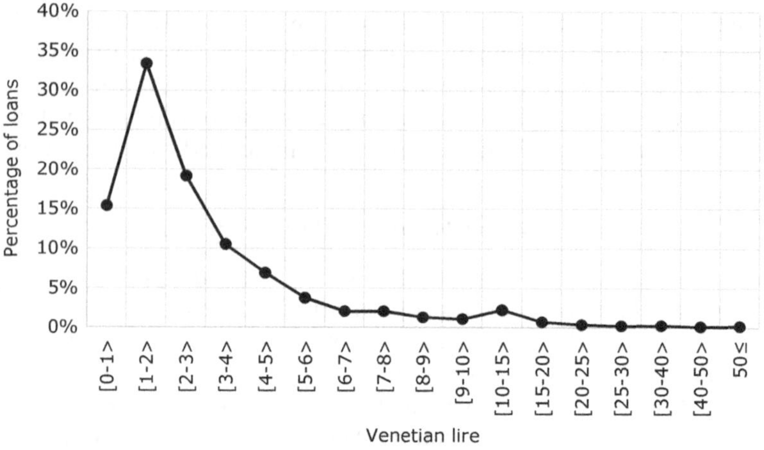

Fig. 1 Percentage of loans per range of value (Venetian lire), eighteenth century (expressed in lire of 1739 using wheat prices in Venice) (*Source* ASVe, Giustizia Nuova, b. 3 r. 5 and 6, b. 6, b. 7, b. 9, b. 16, b. 17, b. 18, b. 22, b. 35 b. 40, b. 41, b. 42, b. 43. For wheat prices, see Georgelin, Venise, annex 46)

lire (1767), the average salary of an unskilled construction worker was about 40.9 *soldi* a day, a little over two *lire*.[34]

On average, the median value of a loan supplied by innkeepers and *bastioneri* corresponded to half a day of work for a *bastionere* and about the daily wage of an unskilled worker. However, we have to consider that, as stated above, at least one-third of each credit was supplied in wine. Therefore, to have a better idea about the real value of the average loan, we should perhaps compare it with the price of wine and the level of consumption. During the eighteenth century with about two *lire*, it was possible to buy between five and nine liters of wine. The average consumption per capita was about 0.8 liters per day, including every man, woman, and child living in the city.[35] Considering that each household consisted on average of about five individuals, the daily consumption was

[34] Andrea Zannini, 'L'economia veneta nel Seicento. Oltre il paradigma della "crisi generale"', in: Società Italiana di Demografia Storica, 'La popolazione nel Seicento', conference proceedings, Florence, 28–30 November 1996, (Bologna, 1999), 473–502, there 490.

[35] Tucci, 'Commercio', 186.

around 3.9 liters of wine per day; consequently, a loan of two *lire* would purchase a sufficient quantity for about two days.

The small amounts supplied were compensated by the high frequency of transactions. Figure 2 gives us an idea of the enormous quantity of objects that were not redeemed in time by their owners and were therefore auctioned every year. Moreover, the sources suggest that the rate of redemption of pledges was rather high, which means that the total volume of transactions was even higher. This helps us assess the importance of this credit activity in the context of the city, and it also testifies to the high frequency with which the population resorted to the services of these lenders.

Through different methods, it has been possible to calculate that between 1745 and 1762 about two-thirds of the loans were repaid, and therefore only one-third of the objects pawned were sold through

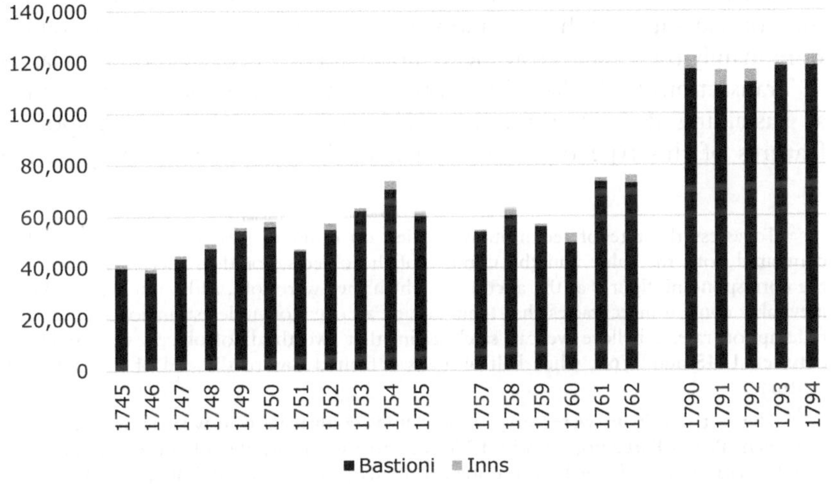

Fig. 2 Number of objects sold through ordinary public auctions during the second half of the eighteenth century in Venice (*Source* ASVe, Giustizia Nuova, b. 13 r. 13 and 14, b. 40–43)

auctions.[36] Over the course of the century, the redemption rate decreased, and in the 1790s about half of the loans defaulted. Applying these values to the number of pawned objects sold during the auctions, we estimate an average of about 170,000 loans a year between 1745 and 1762 and something less than 240,000 loans in the early 1790s. During the eighteenth century, the Venetian population remained at a roughly stable level of about 150,000, divided into 25,000 to 30,000 households. This means that every year *bastioneri* and innkeepers provided an average of between 1.1 and 1.6 loans per capita and between seven and ten per household.[37]

Figure 2 also shows us the different roles that inns and *bastioni* played in the credit market. Innkeepers and *bastioneri* did not have many things in common: they offered different services, they were located in diverse parts of the city, and they were likely targeted toward different customers. It is very likely that their specific characteristics also had consequences for their role as lenders, given that 96.6% of the credit transactions took place in the *bastioni* and just 3.4% in the inns.[38] The major role of *bastioneri* in this context suggests that the individuals involved in the credit operations were mainly their usual customers, mostly members of the popular classes.

Transactions took place frequently and at least part of them was aimed at sustaining daily consumption. This is one of the most important features of this type of credit, which made it just an ordinary part of

[36] To assess the rate of redemption I relied on different strategies. When possible, I compared both the value and the number of the objects stored in specific *bastioni* with the corresponding figures at the auction in which they were sold. Although these estimates inevitably contain inaccuracies that tend toward an over- or underestimation of the actual redemption rate, I believe we can safely claim that two-thirds of objects were redeemed between 1745 and 1762, while half of loans defaulted toward the end of the eighteenth century.

[37] The fact that loans were very frequent finds confirmation in what is declared by the *bastionere* Pietro Bareggio, who in 1730 said to the magistrates of the *Giustizia Nuova* that the *bastioneri* did not have registers of items pawned that indicated the money they lent to each borrower because once an object was pawned "in one or two days they [the borrowers] come and redeem their stuff". ASVe, *GN*, b. 33, unnumbered documents, 30 July 1731. See Matteo Pompermaier, 'Credit and Poverty in Early Modern Venice', in: *The Journal of Interdisciplinary History*, 52:4 (2022), 513–536. These figures are probably also underestimated because there are no data about the "extraordinary" auctions. Data about the population in early modern Venice can be found in Daniele Beltrami, *Storia della popolazione di Venezia dalla fine del secolo 16 alla caduta della* Repubblica (Padua, 1954) and in Angus Maddison, *The World Economy. A Millennial Perspective* (Paris, 2001).

[38] On the other hand, the quality of objects used as pledges was the same. See Pompermaier, 'Credit and Poverty'.

the daily life of individuals. Thanks to the centrality of their premises, innkeepers and *bastioneri* were fully inserted in the local social network. They probably got to know their clients, where they lived, the profession they practiced, and had easy access to all the information they needed. All of this contributed to the establishment of strong ties between lenders and borrowers. The literature suggests that in the context of repeated transactions between individuals who know each other well, collateral is usually superfluous. Not by chance, shopkeepers seemed to have provided unsecured loans to their neighbors throughout Europe. This is not true in the case of Venetian innkeepers and *bastioneri*.

There are many reasons that could explain this difference. First, it is likely that in some cases customers knew they would not be able to repay their loans, and they bartered some of their cheap possessions in exchange for some wine. Many borrowers belonged to the poorest strata of society, they had no cash and they perfectly knew it would have been impossible for them to redeem their objects: they pawned them anyway because it was the only way through which they could access the food and wine they needed in order to survive. This was the case in one-third of pledges in the first half of the century, and two-thirds in the 1790s. Second and most important, a shopkeeper usually worked in the same place for years, while a *bastionere* and an innkeeper have a two-to-four-year contract (*condotta*) and then they had to renew it or move somewhere else in the city. By selling the pledges immediately before or after the end of their *condotta* they were able to quickly recover the amount they invested before moving elsewhere.

Innkeepers and *bastioneri* supplied petty credit, small amounts usually aimed at sustaining consumption. The recourse to credit was quite frequent, to such an extent that it seems to have been part of the daily routine of individuals. The lending activity of inns and *bastioni* was clearly one of the most important sources of funding for the lower classes of Venetian society. The analysis gradually highlighted some of the main characteristics of this activity that can be ascribed to what I have called the "handkerchief economy".[39]

[39] Named after the most-pawned object, handkerchief.

3 "Formalizing" Informal Lenders

The credit activity of innkeepers and *bastioneri* accompanied the Republic for a good part of its history. It is not possible to precisely trace its origins, nor when it was formalized in the first place, but the earliest mention dates back to the second half of the fourteenth century. In 1368, innkeepers and generic tavernkeepers were obliged to ask for a pledge for every sale on credit of wine for an amount of more than 100 *soldi* (five Venetian *lire*).[40] A few years later, the *Giustizia Nuova* clarified how to store and preserve the pledges and the procedures to follow in order to sell them (1388).[41] The public authorities wanted to establish clear procedures in order to safeguard borrowers and lenders, who were previously involved in what probably was an informal and unregulated activity. These norms certainly regulated only details, but they certify that the lending activity was already ongoing.

At the beginning of the seventeenth century, the *Savi* introduced several new rules because, by their own admission, the existing regulations at that time were inadequate.[42] The attention of the public magistracies focused primarily on two subjects that were perceived as the most urgent, the safeguarding of the debtors and the efficient organization of the public auctions in which unredeemed pledges were sold. The protection of borrowers was implemented through a progressive bureaucratization of transactions. In 1603, innkeepers and *bastioneri* were obliged to keep a register in which they had to indicate the name of the customer, the date, and the amount of the loan. Moreover, they had to attach to each pledge a ticket called *bollettino* reporting the same information, in order to rationalize the organization of the warehouses and to avoid the risk that pledges were mixed up.[43] In 1630, a second ticket was introduced (the *bollettino rosso,* red ticket) as a receipt that the borrowers had to show when they wanted to redeem their objects.[44] In order to standardize these operations, in 1698 both the registers and the tickets assumed a

[40] ASVe, *GN,* b. 2 r. 4, f. 143v, 29 April 1368.

[41] ASVe, *GN,* b. 2 r. 4, f. 140v, 2 April 1388.

[42] They openly admitted that "the old regulations are not enough". ASVe, *GN,* b. 2 r. 4, f. 35r–40v, 21 March 1603; for more information about the *savi,* see footnote 23.

[43] ASVe, *GN,* b. 2 r. 4, f. 35r–40v, 21 March 1603.

[44] ASVe, *GN,* b. 2 r. 4, f. 73r–74r, 26 September 1630.

pre-printed form.[45] Those *bollettini* contained the emblem of the St. Mark's Lion—the symbol of the Republic—and a reference to the sacred nature of this activity (*In nome di Dio*, "In the name of God"). The red ticket also included some general information about the functioning of the whole system, with deadlines and procedures to follow.[46]

The fact that these rules were introduced during the seventeenth century suggests that for a long time the entire lending activity was exclusively based on oral agreements between the two parties, or perhaps on simple notes taken by the lenders. This is a common development of informal activities: when the turnover increases and the number of transactions grows beyond a certain threshold, written contracts are usually introduced. Therefore, the interventions of the public authorities testify to the first strong development of this credit circuit at least from the beginning of the seventeenth century. A century later, this form of pre-bank credit was highly bureaucratized and involved formal written contracts that were embedded in the legal system and fully enforceable in court. In the event of a dispute concerning, for instance, the value of a pledge or its quality, the law always protected the interest of the debtors and their simple testimonies were considered truthful, even without any other evidence. To further safeguard the borrowers and in order to limit the number of conflicts and trials, during the eighteenth century a new set of rules obliged the lenders to write both in the register and on the tickets a brief description of the pledge that specified its quality.[47]

The public authorities clearly wanted to protect the property rights of borrowers under all circumstances: the pledges remained their exclusive

[45] ASVe, *GN,* b. 2 r. 4, f. 81r–86r, 22 August 1698.

[46] In a red ticket issued by the *bastionere* of the *bastione* San Pantalon in 1792 we can read "In the name of God // *Collegio dei Sette Savi* // *Cond[otta]* started 1 March 1790, will end the last of February 1793 [...]. Before three months starting from this day included the *strida*, the poor will have to redeem the pledge, after that term it will be irremediably sold; and those who want to ask for the *sopravanzo* (surplus) of the auctioned pledge had to come to the office of the *Giustizia Nuova* on Monday, Wednesday and Friday at Terce (third hour) and this will be given to them". *Bastion de la Crosera*; ASVe, *Governatori delle Entrate*, b. 448, r. "Inventario nel *bastion* di San Pantalon", 28 September 1792.

[47] Starting from 1732, the amount of the loan had to be indicated both in numbers and letters. ASVe, *GN,* b. 2 r. 4, f. 143r. To avoid that objects were exchanged with similar objects of less value, from 1760 innkeepers and *bastioneri* were obliged to write in their registers also a short description of each pledge, which indicated its quality, whether it was new or used, etc. ASVe, *GN,* b. 2 r. 4, f. 246r.

property during the entire process, from the moment they pawned them until their redemption or their auctioning. It is not by chance that the law established that any surplus gained from the sales of the pledges—any positive difference between the value of a loan provided in exchange for a specific pledge and its selling price—had to be returned to the debtors, their legitimate owners. Innkeepers and *bastioneri* had to simply safeguard these objects, and they were responsible in case of theft, fire, or anything else that could happen to them.[48]

Besides the protection of borrowers, public authorities devoted a great deal of attention to regulating public auctions. The analysis of how the content and the number of rules concerning these public sales evolved over time proves to be a fairly reliable measure of the volume of credit provided by innkeepers and *bastioneri*. In 1505, there were just two auctions every month, lasting three days each.[49] During the seventeenth century, the number of days on which those sales took place gradually increased, and in 1702 the *Giustizia Nuova* claimed that, although auctions were held on a daily basis, they were not enough to handle the large volume of objects waiting to be sold. The number of pledges awaiting to be auctioned did not stop to rise, and in the middle of the eighteenth century the public authorities had to intervene again: in 1750, *bastioni* and inns were allowed to sell their pledges even during the three days per month previously reserved for the sale of the Jewish moneylenders.[50] Between 1761 and 1764, a list was drawn up to clarify the order that each *bastione* and inn had to follow to participate in the auctions, as well as the maximum number of days available to each of them for selling their pledges. In fact, it often happened that the sales of every single *bastione* took up so many days that other *bastioneri* were unable to participate in the auctions before the end of the *condotta*. However, these interventions proved to be inadequate, since in 1773 the Venetian Senate

[48] For instance, see the case of theft in the inn of the Red Lion (*Lion Rosso*), on 24 April 1771: the innkeepers had to repay the entire value of the pledges stolen since the *Giustizia Nuova* found no signs of forced entry in the room where objects were stocked. ASVe, *GN*, b. 35, unnumbered documents, 24 April 1771.

[49] ASVe, *GN*, b. 2 r. 4, f. 11r–12r, 17 April 1505. Auctions took place at the middle and at the end of every month. ASVe, *GN*, b. 2 r. 4, f. 15r–17r, 10 November 1506.

[50] "15 *bastioni* have a large number of objects pawned in the previous *condotte*". ASVe, *GN*, b. 2 r. 4, f. 220v–221r, 30 January 1749. Just to highlight the difference between the volume of loans supplied by the two activities, Jews needed just 3 days a month to sell all their unredeemed pledges.

approved the institution of new extraordinary auctions (to be held in the *campi*, squares, of San Polo and Santi Apostoli) dedicated to the pledges that remained unsold during the "ordinary" ones.[51]

The increasing number of loans and pledges corresponded to a larger amount of money that the officers of the *Giustizia Nuova* had to manage. After several frauds and thefts, in 1743 their activity started to be strictly monitored. The *Savi* decided that all the accounting produced by the *masser*, the officer who organized and supervised the public auctions, had to be verified every six months by an external accountant.[52] The high number of pledges pushed also for tighter supervision of the registers of the *bastioneri* and innkeepers, which began to be checked on a monthly basis. The increased turnover obliged the public authorities to intervene to establish stricter supervision of the lending activity and all the actors involved in it. The need for further control affected the entire system negatively because it implied a growing bureaucratization that made the whole activity more complicated and less profitable for innkeepers and *bastioneri*.

The evolution of this traditional credit activity into a public institution certainly affected its development, surely favoring it. We could wonder why the Republic intervened in the case of innkeepers and *bastioneri*, while it did not do the same in the case of other shopkeepers who were highly involved in the credit market, such as for instance the goldsmiths.[53] They had many skills that were particularly useful, mainly in the pawnbroking of jewels: they could quickly evaluate their price and, if the borrowers did not repay their loans, they could easily resell or melt them in order to create something different. At the core of the uniqueness of innkeepers and *bastioneri* in the Venetian context probably lies the already mentioned importance of the wine duty for the finances of the Republic, as well as the importance of this beverage in the daily diet of individuals.

[51] ASVe, *GN*, b. 2 r. 4, f. 363r, 25 August 1773.

[52] ASVe, *GN*, b. 2 r. 4, f. 191r–194r, 6 July 1743.

[53] Jewels and other precious objects were very often accepted as pledges by goldsmiths. For example, see the trials Zanetti vs Venturini (ASVe, *Signori di Notte al Civil*, b. 342, 22 August 1731); Guglielmini vs Zarlin (ASVe, *Signori di Notte al Civil*, b. 345, 22 August 1731); Guadagnin vs Gavazzi (ASVe, *Signori di Notte al Civil*, b. 342, 09 September 1718); Gasparina vs Benavicchi (ASVe, *Signori di Notte al Civil*, b. 342, 19 September 1703). Goldsmiths offered the same service in almost all European cities. For the French case, see Fontaine, *L'économie morale*, 120–125.

4 Public Needs, Private Interest, and the Credit Market

During the eighteenth century, Venice experienced a period of economic and political inertia, which eventually culminated in the fall of the Republic in May 1797. The crisis of key sectors of Venetian manufacturing, the reduction of commerce with the Middle East, and the decrease in the real value of wages contributed to a gradual growth in the demand for consumer credit, further amplified by the increasing number of vagrants who moved from the mainland to the capital and begged in the streets of the city.[54] This situation is clearly reflected in the data regarding the lending activity of innkeepers and *bastioneri*.

This section analyzes how the economic context affected the demand and supply of consumer credit. More specifically, it aims to understand how well the credit system, shaped by the Republic and strictly under its control, reacted to the crisis as a whole. It is therefore a matter of studying the relationship between public needs and private interest, highlighting its consequences on the credit market. To this end, this section focuses on two of the main actors in the Venetian credit market, which represent the institutional supply of consumer credit in eighteenth-century Venice: innkeepers and *bastioneri* on the one hand and the Jewish moneylenders on the other. How did their credit activity react to the period of economic distress? Were they well-suited to manage the growing need for credit? These questions delve deeper into the structure of a pre-bank credit market: they allow us to explain why the system collapsed and was replaced, at the beginning of the nineteenth century, by a new institution in the Venetian credit landscape, the *monte di pietà*.

The three Jewish *banchi* (banks) in the Ghetto were among the main suppliers of consumer credit available in the city. The Jewish community, which settled in Venice for the first time in 1382, had the right and the requirement of funding and managing three *banchi* that offered secured credit to the Venetians.[55] Dissimilarly to what happened in the rest of

[54] Casarin Meneghetti, 'La repressione dei vagabondi alla fine del XVIII secolo: il caso della Repubblica di Venezia', *Società e storia* 18:1 (1982), 781–830.

[55] The Jews were exiled shortly after they arrived in the city and were allowed to settle in Venice again only at the beginning of the sixteenth century. See Reinhold C. Mueller, 'The Jewish moneylenders of late Trecento Venice: A revisitation', in: *Mediterranean Historical Review* 10:1–2 (1995), 202–217.

the Italian peninsula, they were obliged to follow a strict set of rules that regulated their activity, limiting the interest rate as well as the maximum amount of loans. As in the case of inns and *bastioni*, the public authorities intervened and influenced their development, affecting the structure of the entire credit supply. These restrictions were introduced to make sure that the social purposes of this credit activity always prevailed over the financial needs and the greed of the lenders. Attilio Milano claimed that this was the result of the influence of new Franciscan ideas in the socio-economic field, which, starting from the end of the fifteenth century, had particular appeal and rapidly spread across the Italian peninsula. In Venice, this attempt of giving new and more equal economic possibilities to the lower strata of the population had not resulted in the foundation of a municipal pawnshop: they "were channeled into Jewish lending" transforming it from a "place of small-scale profit-making operations to [...] a public bank for the poor".[56]

The analysis of the lending activity of the Jewish moneylenders confirms that the urban credit market was experiencing some trouble in the eighteenth century. In this period, the three *banchi* nearly went bankrupt, crushed by a growing indebtedness: due to the strict conditions imposed by the Republic, the pawnbroking activity was not profitable and the Jewish community was obliged to borrow in order to cover the expenses and continue supplying loans.[57] This crisis reached its peak in the 1720s and it took almost until the end of the eighteenth century before the *banchi* started making some profit. In the meantime, their activity was likely affected by the lack of capital.

At the same time, the demand for consumer credit increased considerably: the Jewish moneylenders were only partially operative, and part of the demand deviated toward inns and *bastioni* (that explains the trend we saw in Fig. 2). Although data confirms that innkeepers and *bastionieri*'s activity continued smoothly up to December 1794, in May 1795 the situation changed dramatically. They suddenly declared to the public authorities that they did not have pledges to sell anymore.[58] This radical and sudden change raises many doubts, since the same lenders who in

56 Attilio Milano, 'I 'banchi dei poveri' a Venezia', in: *La rassegna mensile di Israel* 17:6 (1951): 250–265, there 256.

57 ASVe, *Inquisitori sopra l'Università degli ebrei*, b. 43, f. 53v. See also Milano 'I 'banchi dei poveri', 263.

58 ASVe, *Giustizia Nuova*, b. 2 r. 4, f. 451r.

1794 supplied about 240,000 loans, a few months later informed the public authorities that they did not want to participate in the public auctions because they did not have any items to sell. What could explain such a sudden change?

The basis for the success of pawnbroking, especially when it concerns small loans based on everyday textile objects, rests in the great number of objects pawned and in their frequent turnover.[59] Not by chance, the long duration of loans (one year) and the ceiling on the interest rate imposed by the Republic made the activity of the Jewish moneylenders very unprofitable, obliging them to borrow to supply new loans. At the same time, an economic crisis does not create the most favorable climate for pawnbroking. Although the increase in unemployment and the consequent drop in average income leads to an increase in the volume of items pawned, it is not sustainable in the long run. The lenders are forced to accept an increasing quantity of pledges, while the number of borrowers who manage to redeem them progressively decreases. In the case of innkeepers and *bastioneri*, it is likely that the reduction of the redemption rate meant that their resources became more and more illiquid, while they were accumulating objects in their warehouses.[60]

A dynamic second-hand market is also of critical importance for pawnbroking. The numerous and efficient auctions held every day should have guaranteed a quick return on the capital they invested, ready to be used again in other operations. However, the system seems to have collapsed in 1795 when, unexpectedly, all innkeepers and *bastioneri* refused to participate in public auctions and declared they did not have any unredeemed pledges to sell.[61] The introduction of extraordinary auctions in 1773 suggests that many pledges were not sold during the ordinary ones. It is likely that the number of these objects, which increased proportionally to the total number of loans, reached an unsustainable level in the late 1790s. Even though these were cheap second-hand objects, there were not a lot of individuals with ready cash and willingness to invest it. A complicated normative framework and a cumbersome and costly bureaucracy surely did not incentivize lenders to continue with their

[59] Aron L. Minkes, 'The decline of pawnbroking', in: *Economica* 20:77 (1953), 10–23, there 16.

[60] Minkes, 'The decline', 17.

[61] ASVe, *Giustizia Nuova*, b. 2 r. 4, f. 451r.

activity: they probably stopped lending, at least officially, to reduce costs and, perhaps, to send a clear message to the public authorities.

The Republic strongly regulated the credit market over the years, favoring its bureaucratization and limiting in many ways the activity of the lenders in order to protect the borrowers. Eventually, all of this contributed to determining the fragility of the urban credit market. In the context described above, characterized by an increase in the demand for credit and a reduction in the rate of redemption, a municipal pawnshop could certainly have played a major role. It would have absorbed part of the demand, thus relieving the pressure on *bastioneri* and innkeepers, as well as on the Jewish moneylenders. However, such an institution was not established in Venice before the 1820s.

The first attempts to create a *monte* date back to the sixteenth century, but the public authorities refused to approve and support these plans: it is very likely that the Republic did not want to create an institution that would have competed with the Jewish moneylenders that on many occasions lent money to the state. On the other hand, the wine duty—critical for the annual budget of the Republic—was closely linked to the credit activity of innkeepers and *bastioneri*, which would have suffered from the presence of a municipal pawnshop. Other attempts followed in the 1730s and 1760s when some noblemen again proposed the foundation of a *monte*, but both of them eventually failed.[62] This is a good example of the tension between interests and needs, both of public and private nature, and how it could affect the credit market. It also proves that lenders in Venice were inserted into a system that was strictly regulated by the public authorities.

The formalization of the credit supply of inns and *bastioni*, the strict regulation of the activities of Jewish moneylenders, and the absence of a *monte* in Venice emphasize the important role that the Venetian state played in shaping the urban credit market. The structure of the Venetian credit market was not the outcome of a predetermined plan, but it was the result of choices aimed at meeting two different needs, the safeguarding of the social aims of credit and the stability of fiscal revenues. The fact that the municipal pawnshop was never established also suggests that this

[62] Another (failed) attempt was made during the period of the regency of a pro-French *Municipalità provvisoria* (Provisional Municipality) immediately after the fall of the Republic in 1797.

structure managed for a long time to satisfy the demand for credit, or at least to maintain a general equilibrium.

Bastioni and inns were of critical importance in Venice, functioning like small branches of a municipal pawnshop, independent from each other but kept together by the fact of belonging to the same professional context and regulatory framework. They also offered the advantage of increasing the annual public revenue, something that a pawnshop could not do. At the same time, they proved to be too fragile to resist the political and economic crisis of the eighteenth century. At that time, the equilibrium of the credit market was definitively broken.

5 Concluding Remarks

Pawnbroking is a specific form of credit that today plays only a marginal role, at least in the European context. A more stable labor market and mass production, with its stores that sell relatively cheap clothing and other goods, have contributed to making this type of credit almost obsolete.[63] However, we rediscover the importance of pawn lending on a cyclical basis, each time our national economies struggle and unemployment rates rise. This tells us a lot about the importance of such a form of credit in pre-industrial societies, where work was not stable, households' incomes were irregular and the real value of wages fluctuated according to the prices of basic commodities: societies in which there were practically no social policies or any form of pensions, support for families in difficulty, and so forth.

Innkeepers and *bastioneri* were at the center of what I have called the "handkerchief economy", characterized by a need for frequent small loans aimed at sustaining consumption. This was not informal and risky credit left to the arbitrariness of unscrupulous usurers; on the contrary, it was publicly recognized, supervised by specific magistracies, and characterized by the existence of written contracts enforceable in court. It was part of a broader organized system. The formal nature of this lending activity certainly assured it a stunning development, especially in the eighteenth century, but innkeepers and *bastioneri* were public lenders since at least the fourteenth century, about three centuries earlier. Over time, lending operations became strictly regulated, in the context of a hierarchically

[63] Minkes, 'The decline', 21.

defined and bureaucratized activity. However, transactions preserved a personal dimension since they continued to be characterized by strong relations between lenders and borrowers.

From a broader perspective, the case study of the Venetian credit market—the role played by innkeepers and *bastioneri*, as well as by the Jewish moneylenders, and the absence of a municipal pawnshop—highlights that the Republic strongly intervened in regulating the rights and duties of each lender. This fact leaves us with some questions about the real structure of pre-bank credit markets, especially about their level of formalization and bureaucratization, the relation existing between different lenders, as well as the major role that public authorities could have played in determining the presence and absence of particular credit arrangements. Focusing on the Venetian case, this chapter provides a first case study, waiting for others to follow.

Archival Sources and Literature

Venice State Archive, *Arti*, b. 430.
Venice State Archive, *Giustizia Nuova*, b. 1.
Venice State Archive, *Giustizia Nuova*, b. 2 r. 3.
Venice State Archive, *Giustizia Nuova*, b. 2 r. 4.
Venice State Archive, *Giustizia Nuova*, b. 33.
Venice State Archive, *Giustizia Nuova*, b. 35.
Venice State Archive, *Giustizia Nuova*, b. 3 r. 5.
Venice State Archive, *Giustizia Nuova*, b. 3 r. 6.
Venice State Archive, *Giustizia Nuova*, b. 6.
Venice State Archive, *Giustizia Nuova*, b. 7.
Venice State Archive, *Giustizia Nuova*, b. 9.
Venice State Archive, *Giustizia Nuova*, b. 16.
Venice State Archive, *Giustizia Nuova*, b. 17.
Venice State Archive, *Giustizia Nuova*, b. 18.
Venice State Archive, *Giustizia Nuova*, b. 22.
Venice State Archive, *Giustizia Nuova*, b. 35.
Venice State Archive, *Giustizia Nuova*, b. 40.
Venice State Archive, *Giustizia Nuova*, b. 41.
Venice State Archive, *Giustizia Nuova*, b. 42
Venice State Archive, *Giustizia Nuova*, b. 43.
Venice State Archive, *Inquisitori sopra l'Università degli ebrei*, b. 43.
Venice State Archive, *Signori di Notte al Civil*, b. 342.
Venice State Archive, *Governatori alle Entrate*, b. 448.
Arsène, Houssaye, *Voyage à Venise* (Paris, 1850).

Beltrami, Daniele, *Storia della popolazione di Venezia dalla fine del secolo 16 alla caduta della Repubblica* (Padua, 1954).

Bembo, Pierluigi, *Delle istituzioni di beneficienza nella città e provincia di Venezia* (Venice, 1859).

Bernardette, Angleraud, 'Le pain quotidien: la boutique boulangère au cœur de sociabilités de quartier au XIXe siècle', in: Natasha Coquery (eds.), *La Boutique et La Ville. Commerces, Commerçants, Espaces et Clientèles, XVIe-XXe Siècle* (Tours, 2000), 368–380.

Bochove, Christiaan van, 'Seafarers and Shopkeepers: Credit in Eighteenth-Century Amsterdam', in: *Eighteenth-Century Studies*, 48:1 (2014).

Boerio, Giuseppe and Daniele Manin, *Dizionario del dialetto veneziano di Giuseppe Boerio* (Venice, 1829).

Concina, Ennio, *Venezia nell'età moderna. Strutture e funzioni* (Venice, 1989), 168.

Fontaine, Laurence, *L'économie morale: Pauvreté, crédit et confiance dans l'Europe pré-industrielle* (Paris, 2008).

Gaspare, Federico, *Topografia fisico-medica della città di Venezia delle sue isole, estuarj e lagune, dei cangiamenti nati e dei mezzi profilattici d'igiene del dott* (Padova, 1831).

Gentilcore, David, 'The Cistern-System of Early Modern Venice: Technology, Politics and Culture in a Hydraulic Society', in: *Water History* 13:1 (2021), 375–406.

Georgelin, Jean, *Venise au siècle des Lumières* (Paris, 1978).

Giormani, Virgilio, 'Acqua potabile per Venezia', in: *Studi Veneziani* 60:1 (2010), 325–374.

Granovetter, Mark, 'Economic Action and Social Structure: The Problem of Embeddedness', in: *American journal of sociology* 91:3 (1985), 481-510.

Hohti, Paula, 'The Innkeeper's Goods: The Use and Acquisition of Household Property in Sixteenth-Century Siena', in: Evelyn S. Welch and Michelle O'Malley (eds.), *The Material Renaissance* (Manchester, 2007), 242–259.

Laferté, Gilles, 'De l'interconnaissance sociale à l'identification économique: vers une histoire et une sociologie comparées de la transaction à crédit', in: *Genèses* 79:2 (2010).

Lemercier, Claire and Claire Zalc, 'For a New Approach to Credit Relations in Modern History', in: *Annales. Histoire, Sciences Sociales* 67:4 (2012), 663–691.

Libera, Giovanni, 'Vini e osterie trentini', in: *Strenna Trentina*, 14:1 (1934), 101-103.

Mackenney, Richard, *Tradesmen and Traders: the World of the Guilds in Venice and Europe: c.1250–c.1650* (London-Sidney, 1987).

Maddison, Angus, *The World Economy: A Millennial Perspective* (Paris, 2001).

Malanima, Paolo, 'The Long Decline of a Leading Economy: GDP in Central and Northern Italy, 1300–1913', in: *European Review of Economic History* 15:1 (2010), 169–219.

Meneghetti, Casarin, 'La repressione dei vagabondi alla fine del XVIII secolo: il caso della Repubblica di Venezia', in: *Società e storia* 18:1 (1982), 781-830.

Milano, Attilo, 'I 'banchi dei poveri' a Venezia', in: *La rassegna mensile di Israel* 17:6 (1951), 250–265.

Minkes, A. L., 'The decline of pawnbroking', in: *Economica* 20:77 (1953), 10-23.

Montanari, Massimo, *L'alimentazione contadina nell'alto Medioevo* (Napels 1979), 381–384.

Montanelli, Indro and Roberto Gervaso, *L'Italia del Settecento: (1700–1789)* (Milan, 1970).

Mueller, Reinhold C., 'The Jewish Moneylenders of Late Trecento Venice: A Revisitation', in: *Mediterranean Historical Review* 10:1-2 (1995), 202-217.

Muldrew, Craig, *The Economy of Obligation: The Culture of Credit and Social Relations in Early Modern England* (Basingstoke, 1998).

Negro, Piero del, 'Introduzione', in: Piero Del Negro and Paolo Preto (eds.), *Storia di Venezia dalle origini alla caduta della Serenissima* volume 7: 'La Venezia Barocca' (Rome, 1997) 1–80.

Panciera, Walter, 'L'economia: imprenditoria, corporazioni, lavoro', in: Piero Del Negro and Paolo Preto (eds.), *Storia di Venezia: dalle origini alla caduta della Serenissima* volume 8: 'L'ultima fase della Serenissima' (Rome, 1999), 479–553.

Panciera, Walter, *La Repubblica di Venezia nel Settecento* (Rome, 2014).

Pezzolo, Luciano, 'L'economia', in: Gino Benzoni and Gaetano Cozzi (eds.), *Storia di Venezia dalle origini alla caduta della Serenissima*, volume 7 'La Venezia Barocca' (Rome, 1997), 369–433.

Pezzolo, Luciano, *Il fisco dei veneziani. Finanza pubblica ed economia fra XV e XVII secolo* (Verona, 2003).

Pompermaier, Matteo, 'Credit and Poverty in Early Modern Venice', in: *The Journal of Interdisciplinary History* 52:4 (2022), 513–536.

Pompermaier, Matteo, *L'économie du mouchoir: crédit et microcrédit à Venise au XVIIIe siècle*, (Rome, 2022).

Rapp, Richard T., *Industria e decadenza economica a Venezia nel XVII secolo* (Rome, 1986).

Roche, Daniel, 'Le temps de l'eau rare du Moyen Age à l'époque modern', in: *Annales. Histoire, Sciences Sociales* 39:2 (1984), 383–399.

Tassini, Giuseppe, *Curiosità Veneziane ovvero delle denominazioni stradali di Venezia* (Venice, 1872).

Tucci, Ugo, 'Commercio e consumo del vino a Venezia in età moderna', in: *Il vino nell'economia e nella società italiana medioevale e moderna*, conference proceedings, Greve in Chianti, 21–24 May 1987 (Florence, 1987), 185–202.
Venise. Guide historique-topographique et artistique (Trieste, 1861).
Zannini, Andrea, 'L'economia veneta nel Seicento: Oltre il paradigma della "crisi generale"', in: *Società Italiana di Demografia Storica*, 'La popolazione nel Seicento', conference proceedings, Florence, 28–30 November 1996, (Bologna, 1999), 473–502.

Lender Classifications and Contracts: Categorization in the All-India Surveys (1951–2012) and Evidence From the Account Books of a Moneylender in Rajasthan (1982–2015)

J. Howard M. Jones

1 Introduction[1]

Using a number of binary oppositions, financial agents are commonly divided into two broad sectors of provision such as formal and informal, institutional and non-institutional, official and unofficial, organized and

[1] This chapter refers to data on livelihoods and migration, including those gathered in 2011 facilitated by a research grant from the British Academy for which I would like to express my gratitude. Thanks are due to Mahendra Joshi for his long-standing assistance in these areas of research. I would also like to thank Joseph Chiriyankandath for his help with the moneylender data input and analysis, and Dr. Marylin Williams for her much-valued comments in revising the chapter. I would like to thank Dr. Chris Phillips for her thoughts on the themes explored in the chapter and Pallavi Chavan for her clarifications regarding the All-India surveys. I am very grateful for being able to benefit from the considerable expertise, at both the theoretical and policy levels, of Dr. Yashwant Thorat, Usha Thorat, and Professor Sriram, in the area of financial services in India.

J. H. M. Jones (✉)
Institute of Commonwealth Studies, School of Advanced Study, University of London, London, UK
e-mail: howard.jones@sas.ac.uk

C. van Bochove and J. Levy (eds.), *Beyond Banks*, Palgrave Studies in the History of Finance,
https://doi.org/10.1007/978-3-031-75819-5_8

unorganized.[2] None of the binary classifications are completely clear cut; they each have shortcomings and definitional complexities. As a consequence, emphasis tends to be placed on identifying the defining characteristics of the two financial sectors in terms of their respective scale, structure, regulatory status, market niche, rather than on the exact definitions of the two sectors as such.[3] A continuum of financial agents with graduated degrees of these characteristics, rather than two separate and discrete financial enclaves, has also been proposed.[4]

The binary divisions each contain a variety of financial agents, with the informal/non-institutional/unofficial/unorganized sector being characterized by a greater heterogeneity of financial service providers. Using various criteria, these providers are commonly divided into different kinds of financial agents, including commercial and non-commercial agents,[5] individual lenders and groups of individuals organized mutually,[6] and combinations of both of these.[7] As with the two-fold binary classification, definitions and boundaries are not always clearly distinguishable, especially when financial agents can combine different positions and roles.[8]

Despite their shortcomings and imperfections, the binary oppositions (particularly the formal finance/informal finance dichotomy) continue

[2] Prabhu Ghate, *Informal Finance: Some Findings from Asia* (Oxford, 1992); J. Howard M. Jones, 'Informal Finance and Rural Finance Policy in India: Historical and Contemporary Perspectives', in: *Contemporary South Asia* 16:3 (2008), 269–285.

[3] Anand G. Chandavarkar, 'The Non-Institutional Financial Sector in Developing Countries: Macroeconomic Implications for Savings Policies', in: *Savings and Development* 9:2 (1985), 129–141; Dimitri Germidis, 'Interlinking the Formal and Informal Financial Sectors in Developing Countries', in: *Savings and Development* 14:1 (1990), 5–21; Ghate, *Informal Finance.*

[4] Ghate, *Informal Finance.*

[5] Avishay Braverman and J. Luis Gausch, *The Theory of Rural Credit Markets*, Department of Economics, Discussion Paper 19 (University of California, 1990).

[6] Chandavarkar, 'The Non-Institutional Financial Sector'; Germidis, 'Interlinking the Formal'.

[7] Ghate, *Informal Finance.*

[8] Clive Bell, 'Interactions between Institutional and Informal Credit Agencies in Rural India', in: Karla Hoff, Avishay Braverman, and Joseph E. Stiglitz (eds.) *The Economics of Rural Organization: Theory, Practice and Policy* (Oxford, 1993), 186–213.

to be used by national governments, financial authorities, and national and international development agencies. As a consequence, how financial agents, especially lending agents, are classified, is not just a matter of academic interest and debate. The classifications have had, and continue to have, a major influence on financial services provision, particularly when they are differentially perceived by policymakers in terms of suitability and desirability.[9]

With few exceptions[10] the assumptions that the formal/institutional financial sector is inherently superior to its informal/non-institutional counterpart, and that moneylenders are fundamentally exploitative, remain largely unquestioned, and far too readily accepted, by many of those concerned with financial services planning, provision, and research. This chapter questions these assumptions by reference to India, a country, where, using the binary distinction between institutional and non-institutional finance, it has long been government policy to enhance the role of the former, in order, among other objectives, to diminish and replace the latter.

Following this Introduction, Section 2 addresses the development of the lender classification system used in the All-India credit/debt/investment surveys from 1951/1952 to 2012/2013 and identifies the credit agencies (the official term used to denote lenders) included in these surveys over time. Section 3 examines the attitudes and perceptions associated with the division of credit agencies into institutional and non-institutional loan providers. How the relative importance of the different credit agencies is measured, and their respective shares assessed, are outlined in Section 4. Section 5 examines criticisms leveled against the macro-level surveys since their inception—these have included advocating the use of other research approaches. Examples of such alternative research approaches, micro-level studies on the demand side (the borrowers) and on the supply side (the moneylenders), are given.

[9] F.J.A. Bouman, 'Informal Rural Finance: an Alladin's Lamp of Information', in: F.J.A. Bouman and Otto Hospes (eds.) *Financial Landscapes Reconstructed: The Fine Art of Mapping Development* (Boulder, 1994), 105–122.

[10] For instance, Bouman, 'Informal Rural Finance'; Ghate, *Informal Finance*; J. Howard M. Jones, 'Good Businesses and Good Archives: Perspectives from the Records of a Moneylender in Rural India', in Anna Cantaluppi et al. (eds.), *Social Aims of Finance. Rediscovering Varieties of Credit in Financial Archives* (Frankfurt, 2020), 274–290.

Turning to the micro-level research of this author, Sections 6, 7, 8, and 9 provide a more detailed example of a "professional" moneylender's loan provision and contracts[11] in rural Rajasthan based on access to his lending records over time. The contributions of such micro-level investigations to the classification of financial service providers and to financial services policy are included in the Conclusion (Section 10) to the chapter.

2 The Development of the Classification of Credit Agencies in the All-India Surveys

The ways in which credit agencies have been classified in the Government of India decennial national credit surveys since the early 1950s are shown in Table 1.

The first of these surveys, the All-India Rural Credit Survey (AIRCS), conducted during 1951/1952, made a distinction between credit sourced from Government and Co-operatives, and credit sourced from "private" credit agencies (Relatives, Landlords, Agriculturist Moneylenders, Professional Moneylenders, Traders and Commission Agents, Commercial Banks, and Others).[12] Commercial banks were regarded as a credit agency in their own right, but also part of the "financial superstructure" of other private credit agencies. Loans from relatives qualified as such if they were interest-free, Agriculturist Moneylenders were those where the "major" profession was agriculture, while Professional Moneylenders were those earning a "substantial" part of their income from moneylending—these three distinctions have remained the same in subsequent surveys. Similarly, the All-India Rural Debt and Investment Survey

[11] Contracts are commonly defined, and contrasted with agreements, in terms of their legal enforceability. However, enforceability is not necessarily secured through a civil court, but through custom and social sanctions. Moreover, there may not be a clear distinction between agreement and contract. *Iqraar* (of Persian/Urdu origin), for instance, has a dictionary definition of 'consent, promise, pledge, agreement, compact' while *iqraar-naama* (in current use in Pakistan) is defined as a 'written bond, contract, indenture, agreement' (www.rekhtadictionary.com, consulted 09.12.2021). For this chapter, the term 'contract' is used in this broader sense of signifying a binding agreement and understanding, between two or more parties, even though, from a strictly 'legal' perspective, for an agreement to be a contract, enforceability should be through a court of law. Also, in the case of moneylending, there can be enforcement mechanisms built into the loan contract itself, by the taking of collateral for example.

[12] Reserve Bank of India, *The General Report of the Committee of Direction, All-India Rural Credit Survey, Abridged Edition* (Bombay, 1955).

Table 1 Lender classifications in the All-India Credit/Debt/Investment surveys 1951/1952–2012/2013

AIRCS	AIRDIS	AIDIS				
1951/1952	1961/1962	1971/1972	1981/1982	1991/1992	2002/2003	2012/2013
Credit Agencies		***Institutional Credit Agencies***				
Government	Government	Government >				
Co-ops.	Co-ops.	Co-operatives		Co-operative Society/Bank >		
Relatives	Com. Banks	Com. Banks	Commercial Banks + Regional Rural Banks >			
Landlords	Landlords	Insurance >				
Agric. MLs	Agric. MLs	Provident Funds >				
Prof. MLs	Prof. MLs				Financial Corporation/Institution	
Traders/CAs	Traders/CAs				Financial Company	
Com. Banks	Relatives					SHGs Bank*
Others	Others					SHGs NBFI**
		Other Institutional Agencies >				
		Non-Institutional Credit Agencies				
		Landlord >				
		Agriculturist Moneylender*** >				
		Professional Moneylender >				
		Trader				Input Supplier
		Relatives and Friends >				
					Doctors, Lawyers & Other Prof.	
		Other Non-Institutional Agencies >				

Source All-India Rural Credit Survey (Reserve Bank of India, 1955), All-India Rural Debt and Investment Survey (Reserve Bank of India, 1965), All-India Debt and Investment Survey (various issues)
Note (*) Self-Help Group-bank linked. (**) Self-Help Group-Non Banking Financial Companies (***) The terms Agriculturist Moneylender and Agricultural Moneylender are used interchangeably in some of these surveys

(AIRDIS), conducted during 1961/1962, did not classify credit agencies along an institutional/non-institutional divide, though in accompanying tables Commercial Banks were listed just below Government and Co-operatives.[13] The AIRCS and the AIRDIS had a rural focus and both were conducted by the Reserve Bank of India (RBI)—the Central Bank. The subsequent surveys investigated both rural and urban credit provision and were conducted by the National Sample Survey Office, though the RBI made some contributions to the 1971/1972 and 1981/1982 surveys.[14]

With the All-India Debt and Investment Survey (AIDIS, 1971/1972 onward) the binary distinction between institutional and non-institutional credit agencies became explicit, and the constituent parts of each, identified. Table 1 shows a proliferation of institutional credit agencies after 1971/1972, reflecting a succession of policy measures to boost the market share of this sector.

Initially, co-operatives were the institutional vehicle of choice to compete with the moneylender.[15] This was evident before the AIRCS—by 1925, 21 years after the Co-operative Societies Act of 1904, some 50,000 rural co-operatives had been established. Following the recommendations of the AIRCS, state partnership with rural co-operatives resulted in a rapid expansion of their numbers; they were federated into district-level and then state-level co-operative banks.[16] But, by the mid-1960s, successive committees had identified problems in the

[13] Reserve Bank of India, 'All-India Rural Debt and Investment Survey, 1961–2', in: Reserve Bank of India Bulletin December (1963), 1512–1520; Reserve Bank of India, 'All-India Rural Debt and Investment Survey, 1961–62: Outstanding Loans, Borrowings and Repayments of Rural Households', in: Reserve Bank of India Bulletin September (1965), 1296–1393.

[14] For details see: Pallavi Chavan, 'Debt of Rural Households in India: A Note on the All-India Debt and Investment Survey', in: *Review of Agrarian Studies* 2:1 (2012), 151–160.

[15] J. Howard M. Jones, Marylin Williams, and Yashwant Thorat, 'Pro-poor Rural Financial Services in India: Institutional Imperatives and Responses', International Conference on Rural Finance Research: Moving Results into Policies and Practice, FAO Headquarters, Rome, Italy, 19–21 March, 2007.

[16] M.S. Sriram, *Talking Financial Inclusion in Liberalised India: Conversations with Governors of the Reserve Bank of India* (New Delhi, 2018).

co-operatives: mounting overdues, politicization, weak governance, and failure to achieve effective lending to the rural poor.[17]

The nationalization of the major commercial banks in 1969 signaled a major shift toward rural banking. Unlike co-operatives, which were mutual organizations and a state-level concern, banking policy and operations came under the direct control of the central government, initiating the most significant period, the 1970s to the 1980s, of taking banking to unbanked areas and to the unbanked.[18] This period included the introduction of a new kind of rural bank—the Regional Rural Bank (RRB), designed to combine the local knowledge and feel of co-operatives with the professionalism and resources of commercial banks. However, in turn, weaknesses (largely financial) became evident in these institutions too.[19]

The financial sector reforms initiated in 1991 marked a shift away from social banking toward a concern with institutional sustainability and performance. This heralded what Sriram terms the "fourth phase" of financial inclusion in India, financial inclusion being commonly perceived by national and international policymakers as synonymous with access to institutional finance.[20] Sriram provides a detailed account of these developments. For the purposes of this chapter, we can note that the 2012/2013 AIDIS listed agencies that qualified as institutional credit agencies, though they formed *indirect* rather than *direct* channels for institutional lending—Self-Help Groups linked to banks and Self-Help Groups linked to Non-banking Financial Companies.

For Sriram, these groups "broke" a number of banking orthodoxies: they were largely women-oriented, focused on livelihoods (not just cultivation) and were sympathetic toward consumption credit, had a "savings first" approach, shifted from sporadic individual transactions to regular group-based transactions, did not require business to be conducted on bank premises, provided financial services locally, and moved from paper-based collateral to social collateral.[21] An example of such groups is given later in this chapter when identifying loan purposes for credit advanced by the Rajasthan moneylender.

[17] Jones, Williams and Thorat, 'Pro-poor Rural Financial Services'.

[18] Sriram, *Talking Financial Inclusion.*

[19] Jones, Williams and Thorat, 'Pro-poor Rural Financial Services'.

[20] Sriram, *Talking Financial Inclusion.*

[21] Sriram, *Talking Financial Inclusion.*

3 Perceptions of Credit Agencies in the All-India Surveys

The classification of credit agencies in the All-India surveys is not neutral; it has not been value-free. Moreover, perceptions of the relative worth and appropriateness of different credit agencies is closely linked to the policy focus of these surveys. This was most clearly detailed in the 1951/1952 AIRCS. The survey emphasized that it was "concerned with the collection of only such data as will enable it to recommend practicable policies for the future".[22] The AIRCS was to be "policy-oriented", in keeping with "national policy on increasing agricultural production".[23]

Although the AIRCS touched upon problems existing within co-operatives and the co-operative structure since the passing of the 1904 Co-operative Act, particular censure was reserved for the whole nexus of private sector agencies (credit, trade, industry) operating within and between the rural and urban economies, which, in collaboration with village leaders and subordinate government officials, placed the co-operative societies at considerable disadvantage.[24] Even so, particular attention and criticism was directed toward moneylenders.

In the view of the AIRCS, restrictions on moneylending were commonly evaded; interest rates were largely unrestrained, moneylenders held "different kinds and degrees of hold" on borrowers, and many moneylenders operated without a proper license and had a near-monopoly of rural credit. The AIRCS acknowledged the adaptability and flexibility of moneylenders, along with their unrivaled local knowledge and ability to provide funds promptly.[25] Nonetheless, with the view that the moneylenders were "part of the problem which has to be solved",[26] the conclusion was that there was to be no role for them in any future scheme.

Negative perceptions of moneylenders in the AIRCS and in the subsequent All-India surveys did not come out of the blue; they were no doubt influenced by Malcolm Darling's powerful condemnation of usury

[22] Reserve Bank of India, *The General Report*, 4.

[23] N.S.R. Sastry, 'The All-India Rural Credit Survey Viewed as a Scientific Enquiry: A Reply', in: *The Economic Weekly* 12:37 (1960), 1379–1380.

[24] Reserve Bank of India, *The General Report*.

[25] Reserve Bank of India, *The General Report*, 64.

[26] Reserve Bank of India, *The General Report*, 166–167.

in the 1920s Punjab. Darling's views in turn were informed by nineteenth century reports attributing unrest and disturbances to the exploitative nature of moneylenders and their practices—peasant indebtedness being a major preoccupation throughout colonial rule in the Punjab.[27] Darling's belief that usury was more acceptable "with the comparatively impersonal organization of the banker", resonates throughout the institutional/non-institutional divide.[28]

Likewise, the enthusiasm for co-operatives in the AIRCS was unsurprising. The suggestion for the AIRCS came from a conference, largely of "cooperators", convened by the Reserve Bank of India early in 1951.[29] Darling had been a "central figure" in the diagnosis of rural poverty in the Punjab and in the establishment of credit co-operatives to address this concern; he later became a "global authority" and advocate of cooperation across many parts of the world.[30]

Darling's views of moneylenders as distinct from, and alien to, their cultivator clients, added a further and very potent layer of condemnation to these credit agencies. Apart from the agriculturist moneylenders, he noted that moneylending in the Punjab was in the hands of three "castes"—the Aggarwal, the Khatri and the Arora, all differing, in his view, in their degree of rapaciousness and nefarious ways.[31] On an All-India basis (pre-independence), using data from the 1921 Census, Jain identified the population densities of the different banking and moneylending communities across the whole country and in Burma.[32] While all these moneylending communities were distinct from their clients in various ways, whether they were *alien* to their clients is a rather different matter. This is a point explored later with respect to the community of the Rajasthan moneylender.

While the enthusiasm for particular institutional forms to compete with the moneylender has waxed and waned with successive All-India

[27] Atiyab Sultan, 'Malcolm Darling and Developmentalism in Colonial Punjab', in: *Modern Asian Studies*, 51:6 (2017), 1891–1921.

[28] Malcolm Lyall Darling, *The Punjab Peasant in Prosperity and Debt* (Oxford, 1928, 2nd ed.), 197.

[29] Sastry, 'The All-India', 1379.

[30] Sultan, 'Malcolm Darling', 1905.

[31] Darling, *The Punjab Peasant*, 210–212.

[32] Lakshmi Chandra Jain, *Indigenous Banking in India* (London, 1929).

surveys, the hope throughout has been to see an expanding share in the provision of institutional credit agencies and the opposite result for their non-institutional counterparts, especially for credit sourced from moneylenders.

4 Measuring and Assessing the Relative Importance of Credit Agencies in the All-India Surveys

Although the initial 1951/1952 AIRCS included interviews on the supply side—with the credit agencies themselves—the relative *quantitative* importance of these agencies was determined through household interviews on the demand side, by estimating the proportion of outstanding household debt sourced from different credit providers at one- point-in-time. This methodology has remained in place for the subsequent surveys, hence the reference to specific years in Table 2. While the 1951/1952 and 1961/1962 surveys did not report these proportions along an institutional/non-institutional divide, for comparative purposes, retrospectively, as shown in Table 2, they can be adjusted to do so.

Three main trends are discernible in Table 2. First, there has been a very substantial growth in the share of credit sourced from institutional agencies and a corresponding decrease in the share of credit sourced from non-institutional agencies. Second, the combined share of rural household debt sourced from all institutional agencies increased dramatically up to 1991 and declined thereafter, while the total share sourced from non-institutional agencies shows an opposite trajectory. Third, by far the greatest share of institutionally sourced debt derives from co-operatives and banks (notably after 1981), while moneylenders, especially professional moneylenders, are the main suppliers of non-institutional credit.

In a notable change to decades of strategies to replace moneylenders with institutional alternatives, in 2007, the Reserve Bank of India produced a report on Moneylender Legislations. This allowed for the creation of a new category of moneylender, accredited loan providers, these being eligible for bank finance which they could then on-lend to their clients.[33] So far, no state in India (moneylender legislation being a state-level concern) has adopted these measures. It seems that the negative attitudes toward moneylenders are just too strong, and/or politically unpalatable, to be overcome, at least for the present. The policy prescriptions of this report were based not just on the macro-level findings of the All-India credit/debt/investment surveys, but also on a synthesis of a number of micro-level investigations of moneylender credit in the country. Suggestions for such research approaches had earlier formed part of critiques of the AIRCS and of the subsequent macro-level survey methodologies and findings.

Table 2 Percentage shares of the major institutional and non-institutional credit agencies in rural household debt in India, 1951–2012

Credit agencies	*1951*	*1961*	*1971*	*1981*	*1991*	*2002*	*2012*
Institutional Credit Agencies							
Government	3.3	5.3	6.7	4.0	5.7	2.3	1.2
Co-operatives	3.1	9.1	20.1	28.6	18.6	27.3	24.8
Commercial Banks (incl. RRBs* since 1981)	0.8	0.4	2.2	28.0	29.0	24.5	25.1
Other Institutional Agencies	–	–	0.2	0.6	10.7	3.0	4.9
All Institutional Agencies	**7.2**	**14.8**	**29.2**	**61.2**	**64.0**	**57.1**	**56.0**
Non-Institutional Credit Agencies							
Agriculturist Moneylender	24.9	45.9	23.1	8.6	6.3	10.0	5.0
Professional Moneylender	44.8	14.9	13.8	8.3	9.4	19.6	28.2
Relatives & Friends	14.2	6.8	13.8	9.0	6.7	7.1	8.0
Input Supplier	5.5	7.7	8.7	3.4	7.1	2.6	0.1
Other Non-Institutional Agencies	3.4	9.8	11.4	8.9	6.5	3.6	2.6
All Non-Institutional Agencies	**92.8**	**85.2**	**70.8**	**38.8**	**36.0**	**42.9**	**44.0**

Source All-India Rural Credit Survey (Reserve Bank of India, 1955), All-India Rural Debt and Investment Survey (Reserve Bank of India, 1965), All-India Debt and Investment Survey (various issues); Sriram, *Talking Financial Inclusion*
Note (*) Regional Rural Banks

[33] Reserve Bank of India, The Report of the Technical Group to Review Legislations on Money Lending (Mumbai, 2007).

5 Criticisms Leveled Against the All-India Surveys

Not long after the findings of the 1951/1952 AIRCS were made public, Daniel Thorner, an American scholar of Indian history, economy, and society, pioneering in the scope and methodology of his research, published a trenchant critique of this survey.

Rather than being designed to objectively determine the structure and functioning of existing rural credit markets, he felt that the design of the survey was unduly influenced by "preconceptions" of how the credit system should be reconstructed through the expansion of a favored credit agency—co-operatives.[34] The AIRCS assumed that households were willing to furnish information on their indebtedness, that households were able to provide the required detail of their indebtedness and of other aspects of their livelihoods, and that borrowers could clearly distinguish between the lending agencies and apportion the share of their debt accordingly. In Thorner's view, all three assumptions were questionable.[35]

He was also critical of the way that clients, the borrowers, were categorized and perceived as "cultivators". Not only did everyone in possession of a "bit of land which he cultivated" qualify as a cultivator, such cultivators, regardless of the proportion of family income derived from this activity, were viewed as operating a "farm business", a conceptual framework developed in the UK and the USA, but inappropriate, he thought, for the majority of "peasants" in India for whom "farming is [...] a hereditary occupation carried on chiefly with family labour for family subsistence".[36]

Such criticisms were subsequently leveled against the later All-India Debt and Investment Surveys (AIDIS): the reliance on borrower recall to estimate the relative importance of different credit agencies, the assumption of clearly differentiated credit agents with distinguishable market shares, and the classification of client households into broad categories of cultivating and non-cultivating households.[37] As a consequence, Bell noted that the stated composition of debt owed to individual lenders

[34] Daniel Thorner, 'The All-India Rural Credit Survey Viewed as a Scientific Enquiry', in: *The Economic Weekly*, Special Number 12:23–25 (1960), 949–963.

[35] Thorner, 'The All-India'.

[36] Thorner, 'The All-India, 956.

[37] Jones, 'Informal finance'.

should be viewed with caution.[38] He further noted how the moneylender could adopt a different "guise" according to the exigencies of the times.[39]

In his critique of the 1951/1952 AIRCS, Thorner advocated the use of different research approaches. On the demand side, rather than using interview questionnaires based on respondent recall at one point in time, he argued for "stationing investigators with small groups of households *throughout* the period of enquiry".[40] On the supply side, having criticized the AIRCS for abandoning hope that quantitative data could be secured from the moneylenders themselves, he argued for obtaining quantitative data from these very agents—the principal suppliers of credit at that time.

On the demand side, Ruthven and Kumar used a research approach similar to that suggested by Thorner.[41] Their studies, in North India, one in a rural and another in an urban setting, employed periodic interviews with clients, the most intensive of which were held every two weeks, over extended time periods—a year for the rural study, four months for the urban study. These were supplemented by interactions with a larger number of respondents, conducted less frequently, but nonetheless, constituting more than just a one-off interview. Such close engagement with clients yielded insights into the diversity of livelihoods, the links between different kinds of expenses and the sourcing of credit from particular types of credit providers, and the financial arrangements embedded within different forms of social relations.

On the supply side, while it was not unreasonable for the 1951/1952 AIRCS to emphasize the difficulties in obtaining quantitative information directly from moneylenders, it was perhaps a little unwise for the survey authorities to abandon this altogether. Such information may be obtained *indirectly*, as with Jeromi's study of 97 "balance sheets" lodged

[38] Bell, 'Interactions'.

[39] In Bell's view Professional Moneylenders adopting the guise of Agriculturist Moneylenders to avoid legislation could explain the reported increase in the share of debt sourced from the latter credit agents between 1951 and 1961 (see Table 2).

[40] Thorner, 'The All-India', 959.

[41] Orlanda Ruthven and Sushil Kumar, *Fine-Grain Finance: Financial Choice and Strategy Among the Poor in Rural North India*, Working Paper No. 57, IDPM (University of Manchester, 2002); Orlanda Ruthven, 'Money Mosaics: Financial Choice and Strategy in a West Delhi Squatter Settlement', in: *Journal of International Development* 14:2 (2002), 249–271.

by moneylenders with the supervising authorities.[42] While this approach was necessarily confined to registered moneylenders, estimated to be around half of the 12,000 moneylenders in Kerala, the records nonetheless added quantitative information to a wider literature-based analysis of moneylender operations in the state.

Patole and Ruthven worked *directly* with moneylenders, in the same squatter settlement in West Delhi,[43] where research, noted above, was conducted with the clients of financial services.[44] While their supply side study was not based on day-to-day loan records, "several" interviews were conducted with each of the respondent moneylenders. Moreover, these interactions took place within a context of a detailed understanding of residents and of their lives and livelihoods built up over the course of a full year's field-level investigation. Another example of working directly with moneylenders, this time with access to a "diary" in which the moneylender's loans were recorded from 1981 to 2004, is provided by Reddy.[45] The moneylender, a village landowner in the southern state of Andra Pradesh, provided loans only to those with whom he had economic relations—agricultural laborers, and tenants. For each loan, the diary recorded name and caste of borrower, date advanced, the amount provided, and for what purpose the loan was taken—information recorded in the event of any future dispute.

For Jeromi, at the time a RBI Assistant Adviser in Kerala, data from the 97 moneylender ledgers, in conjunction with a literature review, led him to conclude that the ideal policy outcome would be to reduce the role of moneylenders and the dependence on them—the conventional policy perspective in India. Reddy did not really address the issue of the conflicting negative and positive images of moneylenders, posed at the beginning of his paper, but he proposed that data from the moneylender's diary provide useful insights for institutional financial service providers. This point is addressed in greater detail, more broadly, and more forcibly

[42] P.D. Jeromi, 'Regulation of Informal Financial Institutions: A Study of Money Lenders in Kerela', in: *Reserve Bank of India Occasional Papers* 28:1 (2007), 1–32.

[43] Meenal Patole and Orlanda Ruthven, 'Metro Moneylenders: Microcredit Providers for Delhi's Poor', in: *Small Enterprise Development* 12:2 (2002), 36–45.

[44] Ruthven, 'Money Mosaics'.

[45] S.T. Somashekhara Reddy, 'Diary of a Moneylender', in: *Economic and Political Weekly* 42:29 (2007), 3037–3043.

by Patole and Ruthven.[46] They note that maligning moneylenders remains a convenient justification for the agendas of policymakers and development practitioners, that few microfinance organizations make an effort to study the role of moneylenders prior to their market entry, and that the products microfinance institutions provide, complement rather than replace, the products of the local moneylenders.

6 Records and Contracts: The Moneylender in Rural Rajasthan

Sultan, in her detailed study of the links between colonial and post-colonial welfare policies in the Punjab, described how, for Malcolm Darling, co-operatives were a means of freeing "peasants" from "oppressive contracts".[47] The macro-level surveys in India show that the replacement of moneylender credit by institutional credit agencies has been only partially successful. At the micro-level, while Reddy was able to gain rare access to a moneylender's records, the lender concerned was not a *professional* moneylender—since the start of this century, by far the most important of the non-institutional credit agencies in the country. Access to the lending records of a professional moneylender, a distinctive feature of the research discussed in the rest of this chapter, provides a unique evidence-based longitudinal perspective on the position and contracts of moneylenders, and on their clients' financial service needs.

For the professional moneylender referred to below, contracts are recorded, and new account books started, from Diwali to Diwali—a festival celebrated by Hindus, Jains and Sikhs in India around October/November each year. For each loan, the moneylender records the client's name and village, the amount of money advanced, the date of the transaction, and the type and weight of jewelry left as collateral—such collateralized loans being subsumed under credit sourced from moneylenders in the decennial All-India credit/debt/investment surveys. At the request of the researcher, for certain years, two additional pieces of information, loan purpose and repayment date, were also recorded for each contract.[48]

46 Patole and Ruthven, 'Metro moneylenders'.

47 Sultan, 'Malcolm Darling', 1902.

48 Jones, 'Good business'.

The moneylender, who, like the majority of such lenders in the village is unlicensed, has been running his business for over 40 years, with the researcher having access to his records for much of this period. This access came about through prolonged periods of residence with the moneylender's family, though two conditions were attached.[49] First, that the researcher should not discuss any of the loans with the clients themselves. Second, the moneylender's name and village should not be disclosed in any publications. It was taken for granted that his records would not be discussed with other moneylenders in the village.

7 State-Level, District-Level, and Village-Level Contexts of the Moneylender Study

Contracts do not take place in a vacuum; their form and structure take shape in specific contexts. The state-level, district-level, and village-level contexts, to an increasing degree, influence who are the parties to the moneylender contracts and the features of these contracts.

While the figures presented in Table 2 provide All-India estimates of the shares of institutional and non-institutional credit agencies in rural household debt, there is considerable state-to-state variation in such shares. Rajasthan, where the moneylender is located, is the largest state in India by area, and seventh largest by population.[50] It is located in the northwest of the country, bordering Pakistan, and has one of the highest shares of rural household debt owed to non-institutional agencies—69.1% in 2012, compared to the All-India average of 44.0%.

In comparison with India as a whole, this state has a rather higher percentage of rural dwellers (75.1% compared to 72.2%) and, more significantly, a much higher proportion of the population classified as Scheduled Tribe (13.5% compared to 8.2%). The tribal communities have traditionally formed a disadvantaged section of India's population. Moreover, in recent years, the Scheduled Tribe population in Rajasthan has remained poorer and made slower progress compared to other disadvantaged social groups in the state.[51] On the supply side, Rajasthan had, and

[49] Jones, 'Good business'.

[50] 68.6 million. Census of India, 2011 (https://censusindia.co.in/states/rajasthan).

[51] World Bank, Rajasthan Playing to its Strengths: A Strategy for Sustained and Inclusive Growth (World Bank, 2018).

no doubt still has, one of the highest state-level concentrations of trading and moneylending communities in India.[52] One of a number of such communities, the Jains, distinguishable in the census records by virtue of their religion, form 0.9% of the state's population compared to 0.4% for the country as a whole.

Such factors assume greater significance in the district-level context. Dungarpur District, where the moneylender's village is located, lies in the south of Rajasthan on the border with the neighboring state of Gujarat and had a population of nearly 1.4 million in 2011. It is traditionally regarded as a poor and "backward" part of Rajasthan, similar to the kind of area described as less commercialized and monetized in the All-India Rural Credit Survey. The district had the lowest human development index of all the 32 districts in the state in the early part of this century.[53] The population is predominantly rural (93.6%) and tribal (70.8%), compared to 75.1% and 13.5%, respectively, for the population in Rajasthan as a whole.[54] The majority of the district's population, the tribal Bhils, live in dispersed rural settlements called *pals*, while the caste Hindu and Jain (see below) households mainly reside in nucleated settlements where government and private sector services, including moneylenders, are concentrated.[55] Moreover, the Bhil tribe, concentrated in this southern part of Rajasthan, is a much more disadvantaged group than the Minas, the other major tribal group in the state.[56]

Chandrapur, the name for the moneylender's village used in this and other publications, comprises both types of settlement. The nucleated part of the village is where the caste Hindu and Jain households reside (and where the moneylender discussed in this chapter lives and works), and where the busy bazaar area is located. In contrast, the village's tribal

[52] Jain, *Indigenous Banking*.

[53] Institute of Development Studies, *Dungarpur District Human Development Report* (Jaipur, 2008).

[54] Census of India, 2011, Rajasthan, Series-09, Part XII-B, District Census Handbook, Dungarpur, Village and Town Wise Primary Census Abstract (PCA), Jaipur, Directorate of Census Operations, Rajasthan (https://censusindia.gov.in/census.website/data/handbooks).

[55] J. Howard M. Jones, 'A child of the City: a Longitudinal Study of Stratification and Migration in a Rajasthan Village', in: *International Review of Social Science Research* 6:3 (2016), 107–117.

[56] Nandini Sunder, 'Rights for forgotten tribes', in: *Hindustan Times*, June 4 (2007).

households are dispersed over an adjacent land area, their houses being constructed in the usual Bhil manner, on individual hillocks or slopes. Together, in 2010/2011, the total number of households in the village was 283, and the total number of individuals living in the village was 1,351.[57] However, the village-level context is significant, not just due to the economy and population of the village itself, but also because this village is surrounded by a huge hinterland of tribal settlements (*pals*), the households of which form the main client group for the shopkeepers and other service providers based in Chandrapur.

8 Parties to the Village Moneylender Contracts

8.1 The Lenders

The link between particular communities and the profession of moneylending was hardly touched upon in the AIRCS (the moneylender interview questionnaire included specification of respondent's caste, though very little use seems to have been made of any such data) and entirely missing from the subsequent AIDIS. But community affiliation of moneylenders was very much a concern of earlier studies, especially when they were considered to be "alien" to the clients, often cultivators, to whom they provided loans. The Report of the Deccan Riots Commission (the riots took place in Poona and Ahmednagar Districts in 1875) referred to the Marwari moneylenders as "foreign immigrants",[58] while Darling, referred to moneylenders in Musaffargarh District as a class "alien in race, religion and trade".[59]

In Chandrapur, those who constitute the "professional" moneylenders in the village, as defined in the AIRCS and in the later All-India Debt and Investment Surveys, are all Jain. The Jains are a distinct religious community, traditionally associated with trade and moneylending.[60] In 2010/2011, 36 of the 283 households in Chandrapur were Jain, outnumbering

[57] Jones, 'A child of the City'.

[58] East India (Deccan Riots Commission), *Report of the Commission appointed in India to inquire into the Causes of the Riots which took place in the Year 1875, in the Poona and Ahmednagar Districts of the Bombay Presidency* (London, 1878), 11.

[59] Darling, *The Punjab Peasant*, 219.

[60] Wendy Doniger, *On Hinduism* (Oxford, 2014).

those of any of the individual Hindu castes in the village.[61] In an urban context, where the Jains and their Hindu-merchant caste counterparts co-exist, the dividing lines between merchant communities can be blurred.[62] In Chandrapur, the Jains formed the only hereditary merchant group in the village and were distinguishable as a business community.[63] Not only did the Jain households operate the greatest number of shops in Chandrapur and ran the widest range of different types of shops (e.g., provision stores, cloth shops, metal goods shops, medical stores), these were generally the most successful retail businesses in the village.[64] Compared to all other religious groups the highest literacy rate in Dungarpur District is reported for the Jains (95.9%).[65]

As of January 2020 there were eighteen Jain moneylenders in Chandrapur, all men; earlier there was a Jain widow who lent money and grain. All eighteen moneylenders combined moneylending with other retail businesses, the latter usually being general provision (*kirana*) stores, sometimes combined with the sale of fabric and clothing. The *kirana* stores are regarded as an "evergreen" business: there is a demand for their goods throughout the year. This is a useful feature of a business run in conjunction with moneylending—clients frequently shop, and profits, which can help finance moneylending, accrue on a regular basis.

Only three of the eighteen Jain shopkeeper/moneylenders held a moneylending license. Ceilings on interest rates, cumbersome procedures, fees, fear of penalties, fear of disclosure of unaccounted money, compulsory periodic reports were the main reasons cited by the Reserve Bank of India for the reluctance of moneylenders to be licensed.[66] Even if a moneylender held such a license, thereby being officially recognized and

[61] Jones, 'A child of the City'.

[62] Christine M. Cottam Ellis, 'The Jain Merchant Castes of Rajasthan: Some Aspects of the Management of Social Identity in a Market Town', in: Michael Carrithers and Caroline Humphrey (eds.), *The Assembly of Listeners: Jains in Society* (Cambridge, 1991), 75–107.

[63] J. Howard M. Jones, 'Jain Shopkeepers and Moneylenders: Rural Informal Credit Networks in south Rajasthan', in: Michael Carrithers and Caroline Humphrey (eds.), *The Assembly of Listeners: Jains in Society* (Cambridge, 1991), 109–138.

[64] Jones, 'Jain shopkeepers'.

[65] Census of India, 2011, Dungarpur District Data (https://etrace.in/census/district/dungarpur-124/).

[66] Reserve Bank of India, *The Report,* 36.

sanctioned, he or she would not be regarded as an institutional credit agent, a point verified during a personal visit to the Central Statistics Office in New Delhi.

While depicting moneylenders as alien to their clients has been a potent component of stereotypes of moneylenders, it is questionable whether this characterization applies to the Jain moneylenders in Chandrapur. Definitions of "alien" include notions of foreignness (in nature, character, origin, allegiance), of not belonging, and of being out of harmony.[67] The "professional" moneylenders in the village are all "Jain", thus being part of a particular community, but this hardly qualifies them as being uniquely "alien". In a country where specific occupations have been associated with distinct hereditary groups for centuries, it would require further research to determine whether those practicing moneylending are any more alien to their clients than the other communities from whom these same clients secure a range of services and about whom, as communities, they may know equally little.

8.2 The Borrowers

Data from the moneylender's records show that the great majority of his clients are tribal Bhils from dispersed settlements within a ten-mile radius of Chandrapur. On average, for the five years 1982/1983, 1988/1989, 2000/2001, 2010/2011, and 2013/2014 (five of the years when additional information was recorded by the moneylender),[68] nearly 90% of loans were advanced to borrowers outside the moneylender's own village. Moreover, of the loans advanced within Chandrapur, nearly 40% of these were to households in the tribal part of the village.

Cultivated land holdings of tribal households, within Chandrapur and in the surrounding settlements, are generally small in size, poor in soil quality, and largely dependent on the very variable monsoon rains. Non-agricultural livelihood activities for these households largely revolve around seasonal migration to secure poorly paid and erratic employment

[67] The New Shorter Oxford English Dictionary on Historical Principles, edited by Lesley Brown (Oxford, 1993).

[68] For all five years the repayment date for each loan was recorded by the moneylender. For three of these five years (1988/89, 2000/01, 2010/11) the purpose for each loan was also recorded by the moneylender.

in Gujarat and Mumbai.[69] Risks are co-variant not just with respect to agriculture, but also with respect to work in the construction and service sectors away from home villages. In contrast to the Jains in Dungarpur district, the tribal population in the district has much lower levels of literacy, 53.7% for males and just 32.2% for females.[70]

The remaining non-tribal clients of the moneylender are largely from Other Backward Classes (OBC) and Scheduled Caste (SC) households, mainly from within Chandrapur, but also including a few such households from surrounding settlements. Like the Scheduled Tribes, the SCs (formerly "untouchable" castes) and the OBCs are historically disadvantaged groups and qualify, to varying degrees, for reservation in government sector education and employment.[71]

While Dungarpur District has traditionally been regarded as a remote, tribal and an "industrially backward" part of Rajasthan, the rural economy of the district is far from simple. It is only with respect to certain farming caste (Patel) communities that livelihoods are based exclusively, or even principally, on the cultivation of land, and even this has been changing for these communities over the years. In Chandrapur, to varying degrees, households engage in an extensive range of both agricultural and non-agricultural livelihood activities. The sources, types, combinations, and locations of these vary, both within and between the different caste households and the tribal Bhil households in the village.[72]

Although the nature of historical disadvantage experienced by the Bhil and lower-caste households is rather different there are aspects of their livelihoods and incomes which these households have in common—uncertainty, unpredictability, irregularity, and small scale of operations. These commonalities can exclude such households from certain forms of "non-institutional finance", such as Rotating Savings and Credit Associations (ROSCAs), which, as Ruthven and Kumar note, are not feasible

[69] Jones, 'A child of the city'.

[70] Census of India, 2011, Rajasthan, Series-09, Part XII-B, District Census Handbook, Dungarpur, Village and Town Wise Primary Census Abstract (PCA), Jaipur, Directorate of Census Operations, Rajasthan (https://censusindia.gov.in/census.website/data/handbooks).

[71] Jones, 'A child of the city'.

[72] Jones, 'A child of the city'.

for those with volatile and seasonal incomes.[73] They also impact on many aspects of these households' credit needs and on the contracts with the Jain moneylender.

9 Features of the Moneylender's Contracts

Given the fragilities, uncertainties, and marginalities of their lives and livelihoods, it is not surprising that credit is needed by Bhil households and the poorer lower caste households in the area. But these same fragilities and uncertainties pose risks for potential lenders. To what extent do the moneylender's contracts meet the financial service needs of such households while at the same time mitigating the risks faced by the lender?

9.1 The Space Where Loans are Secured

There is nothing unfamiliar or intimidating about the space where the moneylender's contracts are undertaken. His shop is like a "corner" shop, visited on a regular basis in the course of everyday shopping. Like other shopkeepers in the village he is approachable, welcoming, and speaks the local language. The moneylender knows each of his clients by name and by village. He weighs the piece of jewelry, usually silver, offered as collateral, and informs the potential borrower how much he is willing to advance. If agreed, the details are written down on a piece of paper which is tied to the jewelry (information later transferred to his account books), and the money is immediately handed to the client. No application forms need to be read and completed, the whole business is over in a matter of minutes. Multiple and concurrent contracts are possible.

When in his shop the moneylender's records are by his side all the time. At the time of repayment, he can refer to these and immediately inform the client the amount to be paid. If there is any disagreement he can point to the information in the records. These details also enable the moneylender to locate the particular pieces of jewelry quickly; these may be stored in the shop or in his house. He can monitor his position by reference to the account books and be easily alerted to loans which have not been repaid after quite some time.

[73] Ruthven and Kumar, *Fine-Grain Finance.*

The taking of collateral has advantages for both the client and the moneylender. Gold and silver are widely owned in India, and even the poorer households will have at least some silver jewelry in their possession. With this security, the moneylender imposes no restrictions on credit use; his clients can do whatever they want with the money. The same collateral, once retrieved, can be used for another rainy day. For the moneylender, collateral puts pressure on the client to repay and can be sold if the client does not do so. Jewelry is convenient as collateral; it is widely owned, easily storable, very portable, and very saleable. While the moneylender knows each client by name and by village and will have some knowledge of their occupational standing, this does not constitute "close ties" as such; cash loans would not be provided on the basis of this knowledge alone.

9.2 *The Certainty and Scale of Loans Secured*

While the policy rhetoric of replacing moneylender credit with institutional alternatives was still strong, from 1982/1983 up to 2012/2013, there was a steady increase in the annual number of loans provided by the moneylender—from 290 loans to 1,429, and this was for just one of the moneylenders in the village. Subsequently, for the next two years there was a substantial decline in his loan provision, 953 loans in 2013/2014 and 636 loans in 2014/2015. But this was not due to growing competition from institutional credit agencies, but because of a personal family mishap that required substantial expenditure.[74] Moreover, the decline in this moneylender's loan provision was not systemic; clients could go to any of the other professional moneylenders in the village if necessary. In recent years, the family's misfortune has been reversed; it is hoped that the impact of this on the moneylender's loan provision can be ascertained in the not too distant future.

For many households in the area the ability to secure small value loans is important. This is impossible with the local bank's "gold loans" (the institutional equivalent of the moneylender's pawn-broking loans), the minimum size of which was 10,000 Indian rupees (INR)—about £99. In contrast, for the five reference years indicated earlier, 43% of the moneylender's loans were for a value of up to just INR 999 (about £10),

[74] Jones, 'Good business'.

and as much as 70% of his loans were for a value of up to a value of INR 1,999—around £20.[75] The smallest of the loans advanced over the five years had a value of just under and just over £1. These may seem "trivial" amounts, a word once used by a reviewer to describe such loans, but they are not trivial amounts for the clients concerned, especially when, at the time, they may have equated to a day's payment for casual work.

9.3 Comparative Measures of Loan Provision

In the AIRCS, AIRDIS, and the AIDIS investigations, the comparative scale of lending for different credit agencies is assessed according to their respective shares in outstanding stock of household debt.

However, the relative importance of institutional and non-institutional credit agencies may be reversed when measured by number of loans, rather than by value of loans. In 1988/1989, while the local bank lent four times the *value* of loans advanced by the moneylender, the latter lent nearly four times the *number* of loans advanced by the bank.[76] Moreover, when loans are of short duration, many are likely to be omitted from periodic one-point-in time stock of debt measures—nearly half of the moneylender loans taken during 2010/2011 were taken for less than a period of three months.[77]

In addition, using stock of debt measures means that the timing and sequencing of loan provision are also invisible. For 1988/1989, a comparison of *flow* of credit over the twelve months, based on the moneylender's and the local bank's records, showed that the seasonality of loan provision was very different for these two credit agencies: the highs of the moneylender's loan provision coincided with the lows of the bank's loan provision, and vice versa.[78] Moreover, immediacy of loan provision, something the moneylender emphasized as an important factor in

[75] Jones, 'Good business'.

[76] J. Howard M. Jones, 'A Changing Financial Landscape in India: Macro-Level and Micro-Level Perspectives', in: F.J.A. Bouman and Otto Hospes (eds.), *Financial Landscapes Reconstructed: The Fine Art of Mapping Development* (Boulder, 1994), 305–324.

[77] Jones, 'Good business'.

[78] Jones, 'A Changing Financial Landscape'.

securing repeat custom, is not just a matter of convenience. His loans were advanced at exactly the time they were needed, for a host of different loan purposes.

9.4 Loan Purposes

With collateral secured, the moneylender is uninterested in the purpose of a loan. There is no need for a client to justify any loan request; the contract provides for a single loan product that can be used for any purpose whatsoever.

When the moneylender did record the purpose of each loan an extensive range of "production" and "consumption" purposes emerged.[79] This was shown by the averages for three of these years: 1988/1989, 2000/2001, and 2010/2011. Agriculture (itself comprising many distinct credit needs), together with non-agricultural business, accounted for 25% of loans (by value), with a similar proportion being taken for social/religious activities, including marriage. Health expenses and house construction/repair each accounted for about 12% of loans by value. The majority of these credit needs could only be financed by a cash loan, something the shopkeeper/moneylender is willing to provide with collateral requirements built into the contracts.

With complete flexibility in use, the contracts provide for changes in livelihood patterns and immediate changes in credit needs over time. For the tribal Bhils, increased migration to Gujarat and Mumbai was reflected in the growing number of loans to finance travel. The diversification of livelihoods for certain Scheduled Caste households, through the purchase and resale of scrap items such as metal utensils and shoes, was reflected in loans used to finance the initial purchases. Changes in loan purposes also related to developments in service provision. Loans to help pay private school fees, for instance, reflected the growth of private schooling in rural India, even in this rather remote and relatively poor part of Rajasthan. Changes in loan purposes also quickly reflected the availability and demand for new technologies, such as loans to help purchase and repair mobile phones.[80]

[79] Jones, 'Good business', 288–289.

[80] Jones, 'Good business'.

9.5 *Interest Rates Charged*

A common justification for replacing moneylenders with institutional credit agencies is the higher interest rates charged by the former in comparison with the latter. Traditionally, the moneylender has charged 3% a month, with particularly small loans incurring an additional fee. In recent years, after Diwali (late October) 2019, his interest charges have increased to 5% monthly for loans of a value of INR 2,000 (around £20) and below. The annualized interest charges are much higher than for those for the bank's gold loans (13%-16.5%).

However, comparison of annualized interest rates can be misleading. A high proportion of the moneylender loans are advanced for less than a year. They are usually of short duration, some even paid back the very next day. For the five years referenced earlier nearly half of the loans the moneylender advanced were repaid within three months, 63% were repaid within six months, and just over 70% were repaid within nine months.[81] Moreover, while interest charges are calculated on a monthly basis, with a minimum of one month's interest being chargeable, gold loans advanced by the bank had a fixed duration of either six months or twelve months, with financial penalties incurred with loan foreclosure.[82] In addition, one-stop (rather than a series of visits) access to moneylender loans makes for low non-interest borrowing costs.

9.6 *Moneylender Loans and Microfinance Liabilities*

Over the years there have been interactions between the moneylender's loan provision and institutional credit agencies. Loans have been taken to help repay a bank loan or to open a bank account in order to receive payments.

In 2017/2018, something new and unexpected appeared in the moneylender's records. A few years earlier, as part of a microfinance livelihoods program, women's Self-Help Groups (SHGs) had been established in many surrounding tribal settlements and in the tribal part of Chandrapur. These groups were linked to a bank, thus constituting, as we have seen in Table 1, the latest form of institutional credit agency meant to compete with moneylenders in the supply of credit. However, in order

[81] Jones, 'Good business'.

[82] Jones, 'Good business'.

to meet financial obligations under the microfinance program, some Self-Help Group members were resorting to moneylender loans, quite the opposite of what this program was designed to achieve.

One of the banking orthodoxies that Self-Help Groups broke from, as noted earlier, was to depart from sporadic individual transactions to regular group-based transactions.[83] But, as indicated when discussing the moneylender's clients, *regularity* is one feature that is conspicuously absent in the livelihoods and incomes of many tribal households. Moreover, while a single client may hold a number of concurrent loans from the moneylender, important when there may be a succession of emergency needs, under the microfinance livelihoods program, once a loan has been taken, no further loan can be sanctioned until the first loan is paid back.

10 Conclusion

While the 1951/1952 All-India Rural Credit Survey distinguished between credit sourced from government and co-operatives, and credit sourced from private credit agencies (including commercial banks), it was not until the 1971/1972 All-India Debt and Investment Survey that the binary division between Institutional Credit Agencies and Non-Institutional Credit Agencies became formalized, and the constituent components of each identified.

Following publication of the AIRCS findings, there was criticism of the survey's approach, conceptual framework, methodology, and of the ways both lenders and their clients were classified. Some of these criticisms have been voiced with respect to the later AIDIS investigations, especially the apportioning of exact shares of debt to credit agencies that may be overlapping and not easily distinguishable.

In addition to definitional issues, the binary division between institutional and non-institutional credit agencies is premised on deep-rooted attitudes and perceptions: the institutional being regarded as morally and technically superior, the non-institutional (especially moneylenders) regarded as the opposite. The AIDIS investigations have included an ever-increasing range of institutional credit agencies, each initiated with the hope of diminishing, if not ending altogether, the role of moneylender

83 Sriram, *Talking Financial Inclusion*.

finance. Such hopes have only been partially fulfilled. After an initial decline, since the 1990s, the share of rural household debt sourced from moneylenders has actually increased.

Whatever the shortcomings of the AIRCS/AIRDIS/AIDIS investigations may be, they *do* show broad trends, at the national level and inter-state levels, and demonstrate that moneylender finance continues to be an important part of the present-day financial landscape in the country, credit that is significant both *before* and *alongside* banks. Moreover, even if recommendations made in the Reserve Bank of India report on Moneylender Legislations have not, as yet, been implemented by individual states in India, these policies would not have been forthcoming in the first place, without the evidence made available through the decennial macro-level surveys.

Micro-level studies enable researchers to question key features of the All-India surveys: the classification of credit agencies, the measurement of their relative importance, and the assumed unsuitability and inferiority of non-institutional lenders (especially moneylenders)—assumptions which are firmly held in the financial inclusion literature. Importantly, micro-level surveys have the potential to provide *reasons* for the trends depicted in their All-India level counterparts, especially when combined with data on the lives and livelihoods of borrower groups.

The Jain shopkeepers/lenders discussed in this chapter are distinguishable as *professional* moneylenders as defined and classified in the national surveys, but their professionalism is not just based on the proportion of income derived from this activity. Being members of a specific merchant community steeped for centuries in the expertise of trade and credit is also significant in this respect. Although such communities have long been charged with being *alien* to their borrowers, it is not clear how this alienness is different, in degree and kind, from the perceptions of *otherness*, attached by these same clients to a range of communities from whom they secure specific services.

Data from the moneylender's records indicate that the one-point-in-time stock of debt measures, as used in the decennial All-India credit surveys, underestimate the relative importance of non-institutional credit agencies. Also, these same stock of debt measures cannot show any differences in the timing and seasonality of loan provision between the institutional and non-institutional agencies.

Poor and traditionally low-status households need credit provision that is convenient, assured, unintimidating, non-judgmental, flexible in use, speedy, multiple, and often small in value. Data from the moneylender's records together with observations from sitting in his shop show that these are exactly the kind of loan contracts that he is able to provide. With moneylenders regarded as unsuitable, expensive, and undesirable, it is all too easy to assume that they can readily be replaced by "lower cost" institutional alternatives. But, effective substitutability is related to multiple features of loan provision, not simply to relative interest rate charges. The "last mile", a notion popular in the financial inclusion literature, relates to much more than simply *physical* proximity. Having a bank on the doorstep is no guarantee of providing effective competition to moneylenders; the same can be said for microfinance programs.

Micro-level investigations, however insightful, cannot, of themselves, provide national level data needed by policymakers. This is the role of macro-level surveys. Moreover, the macro-level surveys in India deserve credit for including non-institutional credit agencies in their enquiries and deliberations. All too often, financial inclusion surveys, national and international, champion institutional (formal) providers, and reduce the non-institutional (informal) financial sector to an unexplored and undifferentiated residual. Treating non-institutional financial agents as an undesirable irrelevance blocks investigation of the very financial agents that *do* reach the poor, and from whom so much can be learnt about the financial service needs, in the broadest sense, of the disadvantaged.

The blanket condemnation of moneylenders is misplaced and unhelpful. The unquestioned approbation of institutional alternatives, and the "therapeutic aura" surrounding these,[84] may well be equally misplaced, but such investigation would be for another study and another chapter.

Archival Sources and Literature

Bell, Clive, 'Interactions between Institutional and Informal Credit Agencies in Rural India', in: Karla Hoff, Avishay Braverman, and Joseph E. Stiglitz (eds.), *The Economics of Rural Organization: Theory, Practice and Policy* (Oxford, 1993), 186–213.

Bouman, F.J.A., 'Informal Rural Finance: An Alladin's Lamp of Information', in: F.J.A. Bouman and Otto Hospes (eds.), *Financial Landscapes Reconstructed: The Fine Art of Mapping Development* (Boulder, 1994), 105–122.

[84] Sultan, 'Malcolm Darling', 1913.

Braverman, Avishay and J. Luis Gausch, *The Theory of Rural Credit Markets*, Department of Economics, Discussion Paper 19 (University of California, 1990).

Census of India, 2011, Office of the Registrar General & Census Commissioner, Ministry of Home Affairs, Government of India. https://censusindia.gov.in/census.website/.

Chandavarkar, Anand G., 'The Non-Institutional Financial Sector in Developing Countries: Macroeconomic Implications for Savings Policies', in: *Savings and Development* 9:2 (1985), 129–141.

Chavan, Pallavi, 'Debt of Rural Households in India: A Note on the All-India Debt and Investment Survey', in: *Review of Agrarian Studies* 2:1 (2012), 151–160.

Cottam Ellis, Christine M., 'The Jain Merchant Castes of Rajasthan : Some Aspects of the Management of Social Identity in a Market Town', in: Michael Carrithers and Caroline Humphrey (eds.), *The Assembly of Listeners: Jains in Society* (Cambridge, 1991), 75–107.

Darling, Malcolm Lyall, *The Punjab Peasant in Prosperity and Debt* (2nd ed.). (Oxford, 1928).

Doniger, Wendy, *On Hinduism* (Oxford, 2014).

East India (Deccan Riots Commission), *Report of the Commission appointed in India to inquire into the Causes of the Riots which took place in the Year 1875, in the Poona and Ahmednagar Districts of the Bombay Presidency* (London, 1878).

Germidis, Dimitri, 'Interlinking the Formal and Informal Financial Sectors in Developing Countries', in: *Savings and Development* 14:1 (1990), 5–21.

Ghate, Prabhu, *Informal Finance: Some Findings from Asia* (Oxford, 1992).

Institute of Development Studies, *Dungarpur District Human Development Report* (Jaipur, 2008).

Jain, Lakshmi Chandra, *Indigenous Banking in India* (London, 1929).

Jeromi, P.D., 'Regulation of Informal Financial Institutions: A Study of Money Lenders in Kerela', in: *Reserve Bank of India Occasional Papers* 28:1 (2007), 1–32.

Jones, J. Howard M., 'Jain Shopkeepers and Moneylenders: Rural Informal Credit Networks in South Rajasthan', in: Michael Carrithers and Caroline Humphrey (eds.), *The Assembly of Listeners: Jains in Society* (Cambridge, 1991), 109–138.

Jones, J. Howard M., 'A Changing Financial Landscape in India: Macro-Level and Micro-Level Perspectives', in: F.J.A. Bouman and Otto Hospes (eds.), *Financial Landscapes Reconstructed: The Fine Art of Mapping Development* (Boulder, 1994), 305–324.

Jones, J. Howard M., 'Informal Finance and Rural Finance Policy in India: Historical and Contemporary Perspectives', in: *Contemporary South Asia* 16:3 (2008), 269–285.

Jones, J. Howard M., 'A child of the City: a Longitudinal Study of Stratification and Migration in a Rajasthan Village', in: *International Review of Social Science Research* 6:3 (2016), 107–117.

Jones, J. Howard M., 'Good Businesses and Good Archives: Perspectives from the Records of a Moneylender in Rural India', in Anna Cantaluppi et al. (eds.), *Social Aims of Finance. Rediscovering Varieties of Credit in Financial Archives* (Frankfurt, 2020), 274–290.

Jones, J. Howard M., Marylin Williams, and Yashwant Thorat , 'Pro-poor Rural Financial Services in India: Institutional Imperatives and Responses', International Conference on Rural Finance Research: Moving Results into Policies and Practice, FAO Headquarters, Rome, Italy, 19–21 March, 2007. https://www.fao.org/ag/rurfinconference/docs/papers_theme_3/rural_financial_institutions.pdf.

Patole, Meenal and Orlanda Ruthven, 'Metro Moneylenders: Microcredit Providers for Delhi's Poor', in: *Small Enterprise Development* 12:2 (2002), 36–45.

Reddy, S.T. Somashekhara, 'Diary of a Moneylender', in: *Economic and Political Weekly* 42:29 (2007), 3037–3043.

Reserve Bank of India, *The General Report of the Committee of Direction, All-India Rural Credit Survey, Abridged Edition* (Bombay, 1955).

Reserve Bank of India, 'All-India Rural Debt and Investment Survey, 1961–2', in: *Reserve Bank of India Bulletin* December (1963), 1512–1520.

Reserve Bank of India, 'All-India Rural Debt and Investment Survey, 1961–62: Outstanding Loans, Borrowings and Repayments of Rural Households', in: *Reserve Bank of India Bulletin* September (1965), 1296–1393.

Reserve Bank of India, *The Report of the Technical Group to Review Legislations on Money Lending* (Mumbai, 2007).

Ruthven, Orlanda, 'Money Mosaics: Financial Choice and Strategy in a West Delhi Squatter Settlement', in: *Journal of International Development* 14:2 (2002), 249–271.

Ruthven, Orlanda and Sushil Kumar, *Fine-Grain Finance: Financial Choice and Strategy Among the Poor in Rural North India*, Working Paper No. 57, IDPM (University of Manchester, 2002).

Sastry, N.S.R., 'The All-India Rural Credit Survey Viewed as a Scientific Enquiry: A Reply', in: *The Economic Weekly* 12:37 (1960), 1379–1380.

Sriram, M.S., *Talking Financial Inclusion in Liberalised India: Conversations with Governors of the Reserve Bank of India* (New Delhi, 2018).

Sultan, Atiyab, 'Malcolm Darling and Developmentalism in Colonial Punjab', in: *Modern Asian Studies*, 51:6 (2017), 1891–1921.

Sunder, Nandini, 'Rights for Forgotten Tribes', in: *Hindustan Times*, June 4 (2007).

The New Shorter Oxford English Dictionary on Historical Principles, edited by Lesley Brown (Oxford, 1993).

Thorner, Daniel, 'The All-India Rural Credit Survey Viewed as a Scientific Enquiry', in: *The Economic Weekly*, Special Number 12:23–25 (1960), 949–963.

World Bank, *Rajasthan Playing to its Strengths: A Strategy for Sustained and Inclusive Growth* (World Bank, 2018). https://openknowledge.worldbank.org/handle/10986/29817 License: CC BY 3.0 IGO.

Sacré Crédit! The Rise and Fall of Ecclesiastical Credit in Early Modern Spain

Cyril Milhaud

1 Solving Market Fragmentation: Flows of Capital Within an Integrated Religious Order[1]

At the end of the sixteenth century, Spain dominated the world and its conquests ensured for the Spaniards a political and economic hegemony within all of Europe. Yet, at the end of the nineteenth century, Spain was the very example of countries usually referred to as "backward" by the historiography. Not only had the country failed its economic and financial integration, but it had also failed to integrate politically. Scholars

[1] This chapter is based on the results of doctoral research carried out at the Paris School of Economics. I would like to thank Jérôme Bourdieu, Regina Grafe, Alejandra Irigoin, Enrique Jorge-Sotelo, Gilles Postel-Vinay, Leandro Prados de la Escosura, Vigyan Ratnoo, Jean-Laurent Rosenthal, Tim White and Bartolomé Yun Casalilla for their constant support and advice.

C. Milhaud (✉)
Paris School of Economics, Paris, France
e-mail: cyril.milhaud@gmail.com

C. van Bochove and J. Levy (eds.), *Beyond Banks*, Palgrave Studies in the History of Finance,
https://doi.org/10.1007/978-3-031-75819-5_9

are unanimous in their observation of Spanish decline after the Golden Age.[2]

This chronology has fueled much work on the economic and financial development of Spain. This body of work can be classified into two categories. The first, which economists particularly like, denounces the centralized and predatory nature of the Spanish monarchy as responsible for its economic decline, even if some ports benefited from the dynamism of Atlantic trade.[3] The absolute power of the king was responsible for a centralized political system based on coercion and likely to organize, unlike the English political model, a tax system siphoning off resources. According to this historiography, the absence of political representation led to a double failure. First, it hindered the development of a financial system capable of propelling Spain onto a path of modern economic growth. Second, it prevented the monarchy from raising the necessary sums for its operations and, above all, its military needs, thus compromising its survival in the concert of nations.

The second category follows Elliott's work in emphasizing the "composite" nature of the kingdom.[4] Far from being a centralized and unified

[2] See Earl J. Hamilton, 'The Decline of Spain', in: *The Economic History Review* 8:2 (1938), 193–211; John H. Elliott, 'The Decline of Spain', in: *Past and Present* 20 (1961), 52–75; Carlos Álvarez-Nogal and Leandro Prados de la Escosura, 'The rise and fall of Spain (1270–1850)', in: *The Economic History Review* 66:1 (2013), 1–37; Carlos Álvarez-Nogal and Leandro Prados de la Escosura, 'The Decline of Spain (1500–1850): conjectural estimates', in: *European Review of Economic History* 11:3 (2007), 319–366.

[3] Douglass C. North and Robert Paul Thomas, *The Rise of the Western World: A New Economic History* (Cambridge, 1973); Douglass C. North, *Structure and Change in Economic History* (London, 1981); Douglass C. North, 'Institutions and Economic Growth: An Historical Introduction', in: *World Development* 17:9 (1989), 1319–1332; Charles Tilly, *Coercion, Capital, and European States, A.D. 990–1990* (Oxford, 1990); Daron Acemoglu, Simon Johnson, and James A. Robinson, 'The Rise of Europe: Atlantic Trade, Institutional Change, and Economic Growth', in: *The American Economic Review* 95:3 (2005), 546–579. On the impact of absolutism in the colonies, see Douglass C. North, William Summerhill, and Barry R. Weingast, 'Order, Disorder, and Economic Change: Latin America versus North America', in: Bruce Bueno de Mesquita and Hilton L. Root (eds.), *Governing for Prosperity* (New York, 2000), 16–58; Daron Acemoglu, Simon Johnson, and James A. Robinson, 'The Colonial Origins of Comparative Development: An Empirical Investigation', in: *The American Economic Review* 91:5 (2001), 1369–1401; Daron Acemoglu, Simon Johnson, and James A. Robinson, 'Reversal of Fortune: Geography and Institutions in the Making of the Modern World Income Distribution', in: *The Quarterly Journal of Economics* 117:4 (2002), 1231–1294.

[4] J.H. Elliott, 'A Europe of Composite Monarchies', in: *Past and Present* 137:1 (1992), 48–71.

state, Spain was rather the result of an assembly of various territories (Castile and León, Aragon, Navarre, and the Basque provinces) which preserved most of their politico-administrative structure and their independence. According to recent studies, this lack of unification may have been a major obstacle to the economic development of some European states during modern times, and Spain would be the best example.[5] The Spanish political system was the result of a series of pacts between territories, cities, corporations, the Church, and a monarchy which played more the role of mediator than that of prescriber.[6] Until the beginning of the nineteenth century, sovereignty remained shared and involved a high degree of decentralization.[7] The result has been the maintenance of an economic and social system which quickly reached the limits of its productive capacity. Recently, Grafe has shown in particular how the constitution of this "composite" state hampered the development of internal markets through jurisdictional obstacles.[8] It was the lack of coordination, and not predation, which slowed down Spanish economic development.

There are many reasons to depart from the first vision. Like many other European nations, the Spanish political system was characterized by the decentralization of power and its fiscal system, not by its absolutism. In previous work, I have shown that Spanish long-term credit markets suffered an endemic fragmentation that was more jurisdictional than geographic.[9] I explored capital flows within and between the various kingdoms of the Spanish monarchy and noted that the composite nature of the monarchy was behind strong local autonomy and privileges, which obstructed the development of long-term credit markets. Within

[5] S.R. Epstein, *Freedom and Growth: The Rise of States and Markets in Europe, 1300–1750* (London, 2000); Mark Dincecco, 'Fiscal Centralization, Limited Government, and Public Revenues in Europe, 1650–1913', in: *The Journal of Economic History* 69:1 (2009), 48–103.

[6] Bartolomé Yun Casalilla, 'The American Empire and the Spanish Economy: an Institutional and Regional Perspective', in: *Revista de Historia Económica—Journal of Iberian and Latin American Economic History* 16:1 (1998), 123–156.

[7] For a bibliography, see Bartolomé Yun Casalilla, 'Cambiamento e continuità. La Castiglia nell'impero durante il secolo d'oro', in: *Studi Storici* 36:1 (1995), 51–101.

[8] Regina Grafe, *Distant Tyranny: Markets, Power, and Backwardness in Spain, 1650–1800* (Princeton, 2012).

[9] Cyril Milhaud, 'Sacré credit! The Rise and Fall of Ecclesiastical Credit in Early Modern Spain' (unpublished dissertation, l'École des Hautes Études en Sciences Sociales, 2017), see Chapter 2.

kingdoms, I showed that belonging to the same jurisdiction increased expected long-term capital flows almost tenfold distance included, *ceteris paribus*. Between kingdoms, even large interest rate differentials did not reverse this pattern.

Second, this narrative of the predatory nature of the Spanish monarchy would imply admitting that before the development of "modern" financial markets, transactions were primarily interpersonal, which would confine credit within narrow limits. From this point of view, the credit situation would be characterized by an endemic scarcity of loans as soon as one ventured outside the circle of personal relationships. But that was not so. Not only were there many financial intermediaries but, among them, one group stood out for the mass of capital it mobilized and the thousands and thousands of loans it granted each year to contractors who a priori did not know each other.

Spanish historiography has long highlighted the crucial role of ecclesiastical institutions in long-term credit markets, especially in religious foundations (pious foundations, chantries among others) administered by the clergy.[10] This role was by no means obvious. Indeed, the participation of the Church in the credit markets in England, France, or the Netherlands, was only limited.[11] However, in catholic societies that were also politically and jurisdictionally fragmented, like Italy, ecclesiastical institutions also lent extensively. It is hard to give an exact estimate of the share of the Church in total credit. In Castile, an exhaustive cadaster recorded in the 1750s all the long-term credit contracts that were secured by a piece of land. These were redeemable annuities called *censos consignativos*; they were the main instrument of long-term credit like in many other regions in Europe. This cadaster indicates that church institutions received 72.9%

[10] For a bibliography, see Cyril Milhaud, 'Interregional Flows of Capital and Information in Spain: A Case Study of the Theresian Carmelite Order', in: *Revista de Historia Económica—Journal of Iberian and Latin American Economic History* 37:1 (2019), 81–110.

[11] Godwin James, Francis, 'Charity Endowments as Sources of Local Credit in Seventeenth- and Eighteenth-Century England', in: *The Journal of Economic History* 8:2 (1948), 153–170; Philip T. Hoffman, Gilles Postel-Vinay, and Jean-Laurent Rosenthal, *Priceless Markets: The Political Economy of Credit in Paris, 1660–1870* (Chicago, 2000); Oscar Gelderblom, Joost Jonker, and Clemens Kool, 'Direct finance in the Dutch Golden Age', in: *The Economic History Review* 69:4 (2016), 1178–1198.

of the total interest generated by the *censos*. In the other parts of the peninsula, they represented broadly the same share.[12]

This considerable role fits in part in a very fragmented credit market. But some ecclesiastical institutions had succeeded in overcoming the jurisdictional obstacles generated by the political and territorial fragmentation of Spain. By developing sophisticated economic governance, some of them facilitated monetary transfers between territories and were able to mobilize large sums while supporting very low transaction costs. The Theresian Carmelites, for example, not only provided credit to a very large number and diverse group of people, from nobility to peasantry, but also managed to integrate a very fragmented market thanks to its internal organization.[13] Like other orders, it counted on a vast network of convents and parishes scattered across all of Spain. It also had at its disposal large financial assets pledged through dowries and other religious dotages, among which pious works and chantries were the most popular.[14] The convent acted like a sort of match-maker between the person who pledged a certain sum to a pious work and the borrower, who could be anyone from a farmer to a noble in need of some cash.

Not only did the Theresian Carmelite order provide credit—as did many other religious organizations—but it also developed a highly sophisticated three-tier system, divided between local convents, provincial houses, and, at its center, the General Curia. The first tier, the local convents, was mainly devoted to rural credit, usually loans under 2,000 *reales* to local farmers bearing a 2.5% interest rate. The second tier, the order's provincial houses, pushed the logic a step further. They addressed upper social layers, local nobility, and consequently lent larger amounts of money.[15] This second level could also pool the excess capital earned by the convents in the province, which was then lent to other ecclesiastical or non-ecclesiastical institutions and all kind of individuals with

12 Milhaud, 'Interregional flows'.

13 Milhaud, 'Interregional flows'.

14 For a good description of the different kind of religious foundations, see Gisela von Wobeser, *El crédito eclesiástico en la Nueva España: Siglo XVIII* (Mexico, 1994).

15 For example, the average loan to members of the high nobility was 74,461 *reales* from the provincial house and ordinary people only represented 2.6% of the capital lent. See Alberto Marcos Martín, 'La actividad crediticia del clero regular castellano en la edad moderna', in: Fiorenzo Landi (ed.), *Accumulation and Dissolution of Large Estates of the Regular Clergy in Early Modern Europe* (Rimini, 1999), 69–103.

sufficient collateral. As opposed to local convents, they lent to people and institutions farther away.

Finally, in Madrid, the General Curia, located in the convent of San Hermenegildo, ruled the entire congregation, and it only lent large amounts of capital. Like the provincial houses, it could pool capital from local convents to meet the demand for larger loans. The example of the Marquis of San Juan de Tasso is particularly interesting.[16] To supply the 400,000 *reales* that the Marquis wanted, the General Curia pooled in Madrid the capital from nine convents throughout Spain and drew on its own funds (see Fig. 1). The organization of the General Curia allowed capital to flow across the whole of Spain and the General Curia lent the expected amount.

Fig. 1 The origin of the money lent by the general curia to the marquis of Tasso (1762) (*Source* Reprinted with permission from Milhaud, 'Interregional flows')

[16] Milhaud, 'Interregional flows'.

One of the most surprising aspects is in the reciprocity guaranteed by this system. Capital flowed from bottom to top, but also from top to bottom. At any moment, the General Curia could send money to local convents when they needed capital to meet local demand. All this was made possible thanks to a constant exchange of information. Local monks had access to their provincial priors, who visited them regularly, and the latter had regular access to the General Curia. A system of notarial proxies also allowed the General Curia in Madrid to lend and borrow on behalf of any of its local convents and to represent them at courts. Figure 2 shows the amounts lent by the General Curia to its local convents. As such, 101 of the 196 convents across Spain borrowed from the Curia.

This network of convents and the constant exchange of information permitted the General Curia to lend in the whole of Spain despite different legal systems and local controls. Indeed, the Curia's omnipresence and proximity to the borrower allowed the order to circumvent jurisdictional obstacles and diminish legal risks and transaction costs.

This long-term credit system, dominated by church institutions and their religious foundations, progressively came to a standstill in the second half of the eighteenth century and finally vanished at the end of the century. The sections below analyze the decline of ecclesiastical institutions in credit markets at the turn of the nineteenth century in Madrid. I analyze the impact of war loans on the volume of private loans (*censos consignativos*) and show the effects of the successive operations of disentailment. Disentailment (*desamortización*) was the progressive appropriation by the monarchy of Church property held in inalienably. The main lenders of these assets, namely the ecclesiastical institutions that held these inalienable entails—were immediately threatened by this policy. It was intended to uphold public finances, but it also led to a spectacular decline in the private long-term credit market. After nearly three centuries of domination over Spanish credit activities, ecclesiastical institutions disappeared in just two decades.

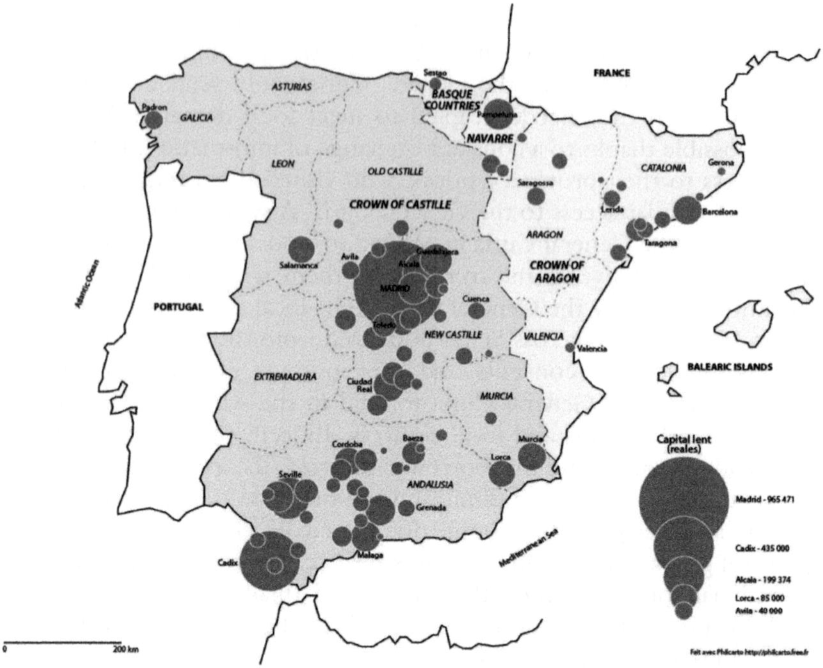

Fig. 2 The general curia's cross-border lending to its local convents, 1700–1807 (*Source* Reprinted with permission from Milhaud, 'Interregional flows')

2 Changes in the Monarchy's Debt Policy and the Decline of Ecclesiastical Lending

The historiography has noted the decline of ecclesiastical institutions in long-term credit activities in various regions of Spain.[17] The disentailment process of church assets, imposed by the Crown during the Bourbon reforms to finance its growing debt, provides a convincing explanation of that decline.[18] In fact, church institutions were the main providers of long-term credit at the time and, as such, they had always lent to public authorities through the religious funds they administered. City councils represented an important outlet for the parishes and convents looking for a good candidate for their funds. Usually, they borrowed

[17] Rosa Congost, 'Enfiteusis y pequeña explotacion campesina en Cataluña, siglos XVIII–XIX', in: Pegerto Saavedra and Ramon Villares (eds.), *Señores y campesinos en la peninsula Ibérica, siglos XVIII–XX*, volume 2 (1991); Julián Pablo Díaz López, 'Transformaciones institucionales del mercado de capitales en un medio agrícola mediterráneo: Almeria (1769–1853)', in: *Chronica Nova* 28:1 (2001), 129–157; Emiliano Fernández de Pinedo, 'Del censo a la obligación: modificaciones en el crédito rural antes de la primera guerra carlista en el País Vasco', in: Ramon Garrabou and Angel García Sanz (eds.), *Historia agraria de la España contemporánea* (Barcelona, 1985), 297–305; Mariano Peset Reig and Yolanda Blasco Gil, 'Redención y extinción de censos en el siglo XIX', in: *Saitabi: Revista de la Facultat de Geografia i Història* 42: (1992), 63–80; Joseba de la Torre, 'Coyuntura económica, crédito agricola y cambio social en Navarra, 1750–1850', in: *Noticiario de Historia Agraria* 7:1 (1994), 109–129; Enric Tello Aragay, 'El papel del crédito rural en la agricultura del Antiguo Régimen: desarrollo y crisis de las modalidades crediticias (1600–1850)', in: *Noticiario de Historia Agraria* 7:1 (1994), 9–37.

[18] Rosa Congost, 'De censatarios de la Iglesia a deudores del Estado. Más reflexiones sobre el proceso desamortizador y la revolución liberal en España', in: Bernard Bodinier, Rosa Congost, and Pablo F. Luna (eds.), *De la Iglesia al Estado: las desamortizaciones de bienes eclesiásticos en Francia, España y América Latina* (Zaragoza, 2009), 377–407. On Spanish America, see Regina Grafe and Alejandra, 'Bounded leviathan: Fiscal Constraints and Financial Development in the Early Modern Hispanic world', in: D'Maris Coffman, Adrian Leonard, and Larry Neal (eds.), *Questioning Credible Commitment: Perspectives on the Rose of Financial Capitalism* (Cambridge, 2013), 188–227; Margaret Chowning, 'The Consolidación de Vales Reales in the Bishopric of Michoacán', in: *The Hispanic American Historical Review* 69:3 (1989), 451–78; Reinhard Liehr 'Endeudamiento Estatal y credito privado: la consolidacion de vales reales en hispanoamerica', in: *Anuario de Estudios Americanos* 41:1 (1984), 553–578; Linda Greenow, *Credit and Socioeconomic Change in Colonial Mexico: Loans and Mortgages in Guadalajara, 1720–1820* (Boulder, 1983); Brian R. Hamnett, 'The Appropriation of Mexican Church Wealth by the Spanish Bourbon Government—The "Consolidación de Vales Reales", 1805–1809', in: *The Journal of Latin American Studies* 1:2 (1969), 85–113.

large sums of capital.[19] These loans financed not only the donations to the king, but also the maintenance and construction of public infrastructure and the provisioning of basic public services. For example, in Elorrio, almost 60% of the amount lent between 1780 and 1789 (367,000 *reales*), was invested in the construction of roads.[20] As for the General Curia of the Theresian Carmelites, 7% of the capital was lent to cities and to the monarchy between 1700 and 1807. The cities were often close to Madrid, such as Vicálvaro or Colmenar Viejo, but some were quite far away such as Rus (province of Jaén) or Salmeroncillos (province of Cuenca). Royal monopolies such as the Tobacco Monopoly and the Mail Monopoly also were the destination of various loans. These were long-term loans provided to the government, like the *censos,* secured on the Tobacco Monopoly, and sold in the late eighteenth century to finance warfare.[21]

This latter example is particularly enlightening to see how the monarchy attempted to attract ecclesiastical institutions funds. The monarchy's entry into the American War of Independence (1779–1783) on the side of France, followed by the French Wars between 1793 and 1808, triggered a period of financial turmoil. The Crown had to turn to new debt markets to raise the necessary funds. In 1780, the Spanish Treasury first launched public redeemable annuities secured on Tobacco Monopoly revenues—the Tobacco *censos*—to attract private funds to royal coffers by offering better guarantees. This instrument was specifically geared to attract funds that were in the hands of ecclesiastical institutions and *mayorazgos* (entails).

Indeed, administrators of ecclesiastical funds had to invest capital in *censos*. The aim was to generate a regular income and accomplish the donor's will, which was an obligation under the terms of the said foundation's contract. As a result, they were expected to keep the funds safe which made them less likely to be invested in risky entrepreneurial ventures. One solution found by the Crown to tap into what it considered the "captive" credit market of private deposits in religious foundations and entails—was to issue public *censos* in which ecclesiastical institutions

[19] In Medina, nearly 14 times the amount lent to the ordinary people. See Marcos Martín, 'La actividad crediticia'.

[20] Fernández de Pinedo, 'Del censo a la obligación', 302.

[21] Rafael Torres Sánchez, *El precio de la guerra. El Estado fiscal-militar de Carlos III (1779–1783)* (Madrid, 2013).

could safely invest their deposits and expect the best possible return, which was 3% at the time (the legal maximum). This operation offered highly advantageous conditions to the administrators of these funds and for the Spanish monarchy. For the king, it was an easy way to raise cheap capital. For the fund administrators, it was a safe and profitable investment. In 1780, the market interest rate for *censos* was much nearer 2.5% than 3% and the Tobacco Monopoly, considered one of the safest sources of income for the monarchy. With a higher rate of return and better guarantees for foundation and entail administrators, Tobacco *censos* could not fail to be successful. Between 1780 and 1786, a total amount of 95.5 million *reales* was raised through Tobacco *censos*.[22] This represented almost 14% of the new Spanish public debt raised between 1779 and 1783.[23] These four years also concentrated 96% of the total capital borrowed by the government through the Monopoly between 1779 and 1786.

But these public *censos* secured on the Tobacco Monopoly were not enough. Confronted with the unprecedented rise in military spending, the Crown created another financial instrument in 1780 to facilitate an increase in public debt. The *vales reales* were long-term annuities with a twenty-year amortization scheme bearing a yield of 4%. They were set to quickly become the main public debt instrument by the end of the eighteenth century.[24] Between 1779 and 1783, they had already grown to represent 68% of total borrowing.[25]

Until the very end of the century, creditors trusted the Crown's capacity to meet its obligations and *vales* were broadly quoted at face value. However, the resumption of hostilities against Great Britain in August 1796 severely undermined the monarchy's creditworthiness and the government had to urgently seek new sources of revenue. The Crown therefore decided to progressively alienate mortmain assets when its fiscal position was particularly dramatic.

This should not have come as a surprise. In 1794, an anonymous memorandum estimated the estates of benefices, confraternities, and

[22] Rafael Torres Sánchez, *Constructing a Fiscal-Military State in Eighteenth-Century Spain* (New York, 2015), 151.

[23] Torres Sánchez, *El precio de la guerra*, 404–405.

[24] Issues of vales are recorded in Pedro Tedde de Lorca, *El Banco de San Carlos* (Madrid, 1988), 171.

[25] Torres Sánchez, *El precio de la guerra*, 405.

pious foundations at 3,000 million *reales*, and those of the churches and religious orders at another 4,500; more than the total public debt reported to Napoleon in 1808 which amounted to 7,198 million *reales*.[26] Indeed, in the face of the gravity of the situation, the Spanish monarchy merely implemented the reformers' ideas which were largely against the supremacy of the Church in the context of the Bourbon reforms. Ecclesiastical assets increasingly came under attack since 1767 with the closure of the Society of Jesus. More generally, these ecclesiastical funds that were tied in perpetuity to ecclesiastical institutions, were being severely criticized by Spanish contemporaries who blamed them for preventing the development of small farms and hugely compromising agriculture.[27]

On September 19, 1798, the king initiated the first step in a long process of disentailment of church property and assets (from hereon I will refer to it by its Spanish term: *desamortización*). He decreed that anytime a mortgage supported pious foundations, chantries, or the like was redeemed, the capital should be loaned to the monarchy. This enabled persons whose properties were encumbered by *censos* with these institutions to redeem them by depositing their capital value in an amortization fund created to extinguish the *vales* debt. The capital was consequently not lent on to a private party, but to the monarchy. The opportunity for the monarchy was clear. Using the amortization fund, on which it paid 3% to the religious foundations, it could clear the *vales* debt bearing a 4% interest rate. The capital pledged on religious foundations was also easier to seize since ecclesiastical institutions did not *own* but *administer* it. These foundations were often small, scattered geographically, and hence less powerful to resist the king's move. A little after, the consolidation took the move a step further with the extension of the process of *desamortización* to secular entails in 1801 and to the whole Spanish Empire in 1804.

It is relatively hard to study the Crown's proceeds from the *desamortización*. The total amount reported to Napoleon in 1808 from the various funds impacted by the new policy was 1,653 million *reales*.[28] This sum

[26] Richard Herr, *Rural Change and Royal Finances in Spain at the End of the Old Regime* (Berkeley, 1989), 91.

[27] Gaspar Melchor de Jovellanos, *Informe sobre el expediente de Ley Agraria* (Madrid, 1795); Vicente Vizcaino Pérez, *Discursos políticos, sobre los estragos que causan los censos, felicidades y medios de su extinción* (Madrid, 1766).

[28] Herr, *Rural change*, 122.

included both money received by the monarchy on the sale of real properties and money received on redeemed *censos*. Herr estimated that 4.5% of all ecclesiastical deposits came from redeemed *censos* totaling 112 million *reales*. However, this percentage masks large regional differences, since the proportion was as high as 61.5% in Catalonia.[29] In Madrid, redeemed *censos* from ecclesiastical deposits and from secular entails represented 6% of deposits in the two funds amounting to 14 million *reales*, which does not point to a clear-cut success for the incentives to redeem *censos* capital considering that Tobacco *censos* signed in Madrid brought in nearly 82 million *reales*.[30] Indeed, debtors were not forced to pay back the capital of their loans.

Grafe and Irigoin argue in their discussion of the Spanish American case that the process of *desamortización*, extended to the whole Spanish Empire in 1804, and most certainly "created severe breaks in lending, mainly because the 'dead hand' had been very much alive and active in banking".[31] Anyhow, this also brought substantial changes in the body of actors in the credit market as church loans changed hands.[32]

3 The Negative Impact of the Monarchy's Debt Policy on Church Lending: Evidence from Madrid

In Madrid changes in the monarchy's debt policy at the end of the eighteenth century and the subsequent disentailment process of mainmort assets led to the withdrawal of ecclesiastical institutions from credit markets and a subsequent drop in mortgage credit. To observe the impact of disentailment on the long-term credit market, I analyze who the actors were and how much they lent across time in the capital. Madrid is a

[29] Herr, *Rural change*, 124.

[30] Herr, *Rural change*, 29. However, Herr estimated that 25% of ecclesiastical properties in Madrid were sold.

[31] Regina Grafe and Alejandra Irigoin, 'Bounded leviathan: Fiscal constraints and financial development in the early modern Hispanic world', in: D'Maris Coffman, Adrian Leonard, and Larry Neal (eds.), *Questioning Credible Commitment: Perspectives on the Rose of Financial Capitalism* (Cambridge, 2013), 188–227, there 221. The "dead hand" in the quote refers to mortmain funds—where "mortmain" literally means "dead hand".

[32] Juliette Levy, *The Making of a Market: Credit, Henequen, and Notaries in Yucatan, 1850–1900* (University Park, 2012), showed that notarial credit actually exploded in México in the second half of the nineteenth century.

good example to explore this hypothesis because, in addition to being the king's capital where all political decisions were made, the concentration of ecclesiastical institutions and capital was tremendous.

To estimate the volume of *censos* across time, the data is extracted from the mortgage registry of Madrid. In 1768, the Bourbons created this first public and universal system of information on mortgages in a move to foster the development of credit markets. In these registries, each mortgage loan had to be registered as soon as it was secured by collateral. In theory, all mortgages had to be recorded in the registry but, in practice, these lien registries were not widely used at first, especially in Castile. However, over time, Spaniards came to increasingly register their mortgaged assets.[33] The registry is divided into 553 blocks, called *manzanas*, which correspond to blocks of properties in the capital. The mortgage registry of Madrid also has a separate section listing all the Tobacco Monopoly *censos* signed in the capital which allows for an analysis of the role played by this particular debt instrument.

We can see from Table 1 that a substantial part of the Tobacco *censos* were signed in Madrid. They accounted for almost 50% of the total amount issued throughout Spain over the years 1780–1786.

Table 1 Tobacco censos signed in Madrid and in Spain, 1780–1786

	Tobacco censos *Spain* (reales)	*Tobacco* censos *Madrid* (reales)	%
1780	**47,430,963**	**16,941,241**	**35.7**
1781	**22,213,763**	**13,419,350**	**60.4**
1782	**15,224,263**	**9,203,350**	**60.5**
1783	**7,160,049**	**3,734,659**	**52.1**
1784	2,752,013	2,238,501	81.3
1785	582,938	118,926	20.4
1786	216,292	54,937	25.4
Total	95,580,281	45,710,964	47.8

Source For column 2, see Torres Sánchez, 'Constructing', 150. Unfortunately, data on Tobacco *censos* in Spain stop in 1786. For column 3, see Archivo del Registro de la Propiedad de Madrid (hereafter ARPM), Contaduría de Hipotecas, inv.nr. 9000
Note War years are in bold

[33] Margarita Serna Vallejo, *La publicidad inmobiliaria en el derecho hipotecario histórico español* (Madrid, 1996).

One of the potential effects of this attempt to attract mainmort funds was most certainly the transfer to the government of resources that might otherwise have been lent in the private credit market. The mortgage registry can be used to trace the buyers of Tobacco *censos* signed in the city of Madrid and compare them with the usual actors in the long-term credit market. Table 2 records the lenders to the Tobacco Monopoly and the lenders in the private market in Madrid.

Ecclesiastical institutions provided almost 50% of the amount lent to the Tobacco Monopoly in Madrid. Within this group, religious foundations were the main sources of capital for public credit, providing 26% of the total amount lent. In second place, the nobility provided another 35% of the amount lent to the Monopoly via its entails.

The records from the Madrid mortgage registry show how the buyers of *censos* behaved in the private market and whether the lenders to the Tobacco Monopoly were the same as the lenders in the long-term credit market. The sample includes 192 *manzanas* for which all new *censos* between 1768 and 1808 were recorded: 64 blocks were located in south-east Madrid where owners were mainly common people (*particulares*)

Table 2 Lenders to the tobacco monopoly in Madrid versus lenders in the private market, 1768–1808

	Ecclesiastical institutions			*Nobility and Don*			*Others******
	*Religious foundations**	*Others***	*Total*	*Entails*	*Nobles*	*Total*	
TOBACCO MONOPOLY (PUBLIC CREDIT)							
% total contracts	47.07	9.57	57.49	34.41	0	34.41	8.10
% capital lent	25.86	21.67	47.53	37.16	0	37.16	15.31
MORTGAGE LOANS—CENSOS (PRIVATE CREDIT)							
% total contracts	42.71	21.45	64.16	24.46	2.85	27.31	8.53
% capital lent	22.70	21.13	43.83	40.47	7.89	48.36	7.81

Source For Tobacco *censos* see ARPM, Contaduría de Hipotecas, inv.nr. 9000 and for private *censos* see footnote 36

Note (*) *Aniversarios*, *beneficios*, *capellanias*, *memorias*, *obras pias*, *patronatos*. (**) Convents and monasteries (men and women), brotherhoods, parishes, bishoprics, and church staff. (***) Other institutions (hospitals, cities), lay individuals, and unknown and 128 blocks were dispersed throughout Madrid where they were inhabited largely by nobles and dons.[34] This sample represents 34% of the entire population. It includes poor and rich areas, and the selected *manzanas* cover south, north, west, east, and central Madrid, making the sample, if not random, fairly representative.[35] As Table 2 records, ecclesiastical institutions and the nobility provided 92% of the capital lent on the long-term private credit market.

Crucially here, Table 2 shows that the lenders to the public authorities were the same as the lenders in the long-term private credit market. From here, it is a short step to the conclusion that, at least in Madrid, capital from religious foundations and entails was diverted to Tobacco coffers instead of being invested in the private credit market. Qualitative evidence supports that hypothesis. Many examples of redemptions of *censos* during those years stipulated that the redeemed capital had been placed in the Tobacco Monopoly. In these cases, we could find the annotation: "said *censo* owned by said Don Ygnacio Buitrago memorial fund considered paid and redeemed, and said house freed, by transfer made by the owner to the General Treasury of Her Majesty, for a new *censo* secured by the Tobacco Monopoly".[36] This shows that once a *censo*'s capital had been redeemed following the years of interest, it was more interesting to invest it in public *censos* (Tobacco Monopoly).

Table 3 shows that the diverted capital was originally geared mainly to private borrowers in Madrid, be they nobles, craftsmen, merchants, civil servants, or other ordinary people who might have used this money to start a new business, buy or build a new house, or pay for repairs. Unfortunately, as is rarely the case, the purposes of these loans were not mentioned in the contracts. There is no way to develop a systematic counterfactual as to how much of the diverted capital would have been used

[34] The prevalence of a social group within a block can be found in Virgilio Pinto Crespo and Santos Madrazo Madrazo, Madrid: Atlas histórico de la ciudad siglos IX–XIX (Madrid, 1995), 113.

[35] ARPM, Contaduría de Hipotecas, *manzanas* 1–64, 120, 123, 126–127, 129–130, 132, 135, 145, 151, 154, 164–183, 185, 188, 190–191, 193–199, 203, 205–208, 211, 214, 217, 227, 238, 249, 254, 264–265, 267–268, 270, 273, 278–279, 285, 290, 298–299, 301, 307, 331, 336, 342–343, 369–370, 372–376, 380–381, 385–386, 391, 393, 397, 399, 401–402, 405–406, 409–410, 414, 417, 420, 425, 428, 431–433, 436–437, 442, 458, 462, 465–467, 469, 474, 485, 490, 492–494, 500, 524–525, 531, 533, 545–546, 556–557.

[36] ARPM, Contaduría de Hipotecas, *manzana* 494, inv.nr. 2,484,277, f18.

Table 3 Borrowers in Madrid (censos), 1768–1808

	Ecclesiastical institutions	*Nobility and Don*	*Ordinary people*	*Others**
% total contracts	14.57	29.98	54.60	0.85
% capital lent	10.86	56.71	24.20	8.23

Source See footnote 36
Note (*) Merchant companies, lay institutions, and unknown

to start new businesses and whether these businesses would have been connected with industrial development.

The annual volume of new *censos* in the mortgage registry also allows me to examine changes in the aggregate volume of long-term credit in Madrid. The sample includes first 64 *manzanas* for which all new *censos* and new obligations backed with a collateral between 1768 and 1853 are included. Figure 3 is particularly enlightening in terms of assessing the considerable impact of the consolidation laws on the volume of long-term private credit. It shows the gradual withdrawal of the *censo* debt instrument starting in the mid-1770s, shortly after the suppression of the Society of Jesus by the Crown in 1767 and the appropriation of its considerable wealth. The 1790s were a dramatic turn of events for the long-term credit market too. With the creation of the first amortization fund in 1794, ecclesiastical institutions and entails started to understand the fate that awaited their funds. Their withdrawal started four years before the first consolidation laws in 1798 and became completely effective in 1800 when the capital amount of new *censos* was almost zero.

Indeed, this drop in the volume of new *censos* was also associated with the complete disappearance of ecclesiastical institutions from the private credit market. The fortune of the *censos* was tied to the ecclesiastical institutions and entails as they represented almost 96% of the market (at least in Madrid). As these institutions stopped lending to private parties because of the consolidation laws, the *censo* gradually died out.

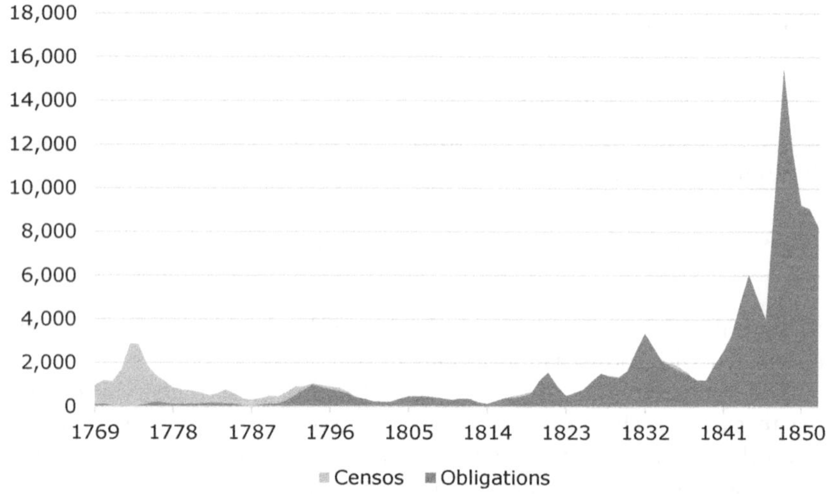

Fig. 3 Real annual volume of new loans in Madrid, 1769–1852 (three-year moving average) (*Source* ARPM, Contaduría de Hipotecas, *manzanas* 1–64 *Note* I used as a deflator the price index computed in David S. Reher and Esmeralda Ballesteros, 'Precios y salarios en Castilla la Nueva: La construcción de un índice de salarios reales, 1501–1991', in: *Revista de Historia Económica—Journal of Iberian and Latin American Economic History*, 11:1 (1993), 101–151)

4 Long-Term Credit Crunch and the Rise of Obligations

At the same time, another type of loan became the leading debt instrument. The use of obligations became systematic (Fig. 3) during the first half of the nineteenth century, as the role of ecclesiastical institutions vanished and the *censo* disappeared. Originally, obligations were short term (less than one year) and mainly used for commercial credit. But as it expanded, its nature changed. As of the mid-1790s, obligations increasingly bore an explicit interest rate, generally between 4 and 6% (theoretically prohibited by the usury laws). In addition, obligations progressively turned into a mid-term instrument and were increasingly used for building and construction, two sectors traditionally addressed by *censos*.

This development was not specific to Madrid. The rise of the obligation to the position of predominant debt instrument was observed in many regions of Spain.[37] In Vizcaya, *censos* were replaced by obligations between 1790 and 1810, as they were in Madrid.[38] Yet the substitution occurred earlier in some regions, in the second half of the eighteenth century, as in Catalonia and Valencia, and later in others such as in Navarra during the Ominous decade (1823–1833).[39]

Can this substitution be related to the changes in public borrowing? Fernández de Pinedo, among others, believed that the *censos* fell out of use because they were not profitable, especially after the usury rate was reduced to 3% in 1705 in Castile and then in Aragon in 1750. Yet, as Tello noticed, if this was the case, why was the *censo* then massively used in Castile during the entire eighteenth century? Tello argued that the "*huelga de pensiones*" ("rent strike") episode was behind the *censos* crisis when borrowers, mainly in rural regions, stopped paying the interest associated with the *censos* and the tithe in the midst of an agrarian crisis at the beginning of the nineteenth century.[40] If so, why can I observe a decline in the use of *censos* years before? These explanations are certainly valuable, but I offer an alternative interpretation. As seen in Madrid, the *censos* started to wane when the Crown started to appropriate church assets, from the 1770s if we take the suppression of the Society of Jesus as a milestone. As religious foundations were owners of over 70% of the *censos*, the withdrawal of the ecclesiastical institutions from the credit market marked the end of their favorite debt instrument. Indeed, this long-term debt instrument was suited to their need to secure a regular stream of income to fund their ceremonies and maintain their member numbers.

The rise of the obligation corresponded to the arrival of new actors in the market with different preferences for debt instruments than church institutions. As these latter withdrew as financial intermediaries, lay individuals, especially merchant bankers, entered the space left by the ecclesiastical institutions. They mainly used obligations with a higher rate of return, since it became common practice from the end of the eighteenth century to stipulate an interest rate on the contracts. In addition,

[37] Congost 'Enfiteusis'; Díaz López 'Transformaciones'; Fernández de Pinedo 'Del censo a la obligación'; Peset Reig and Blasco Gil 'Redención y extinción'; Torre, 'Coyuntura económica'; Tello Aragay 'El papel del crédito'.

[38] Fernández de Pinedo, 'Del censo a la obligación'.

[39] Joachim Cuevas, 'La financiación del desarrollo agrario valenciano, 1750–1914', in: *Historia Agraria* 25:1 (2001), 89–120; Torre, 'Coyuntura económica'.

[40] Tello Aragay, 'El papel del crédito'.

in this period of uncertainty, the shorter maturity of obligations was much appreciated.

The entire private credit market suffered considerably from the withdrawal of the ecclesiastical institutions. Aside from the repeated complaints from landlords finding it hard to access credit, especially in rural areas, the obligation had a much shorter lifetime than the *censo* even though it morphed over time into a mid-term debt instrument.[41] The fact that long-term credit no longer was available, and that short-term credit had to be relied upon instead must have been a problem for borrowers with long-term horizons.

This sample of obligations and *censos* shows the impact of the withdrawal of ecclesiastical institutions on the mortgage credit market in Madrid. The average maturity of an obligation increased from nine months between 1768 and 1777 to one year between 1778 and 1828, and two years between 1828 and 1853. The average lifetime of a *censo*, however, remained roughly stable (14.8 years on average during the whole period). This information can be taken to compute the stock of capital. The stock of capital in year t is defined as the stock of capital in year t-1 plus the capital lent in year t minus the capital paid off in year t. New loans are identified directly by the new *censos* and obligations recorded in the registry. We can deduce the amount of capital paid off each year from the inverse of the theoretical maturity d of each kind of debt instrument ($1/d$).

Figure 4 shows the stock of capital of *censos* and obligations between 1768 and 1853. In keeping with Hoffman et al., for 1768, I took the average volume of new *censos* and obligations of the first five years (that is the period 1768–1772) and multiplied it by their respective maturities.[42] It suggests that the collapse of the *censos* and ecclesiastical institutions started during the late 1770s. The repeated attacks by the monarchy by means of forcing ecclesiastical institutions to deposit religious foundations' funds in its coffers triggered a huge contraction in the long-term private credit market. Over four decades, the stock of private debt was reduced to a fifth of its previous amount. *Censos*, and the Church, almost disappeared from the private credit market and left a gap in long-term lending that no debt instruments or financial institutions could fill initially.

[41] Congost, 'De censatarios'.

[42] Hoffman, Postel-Vinay, and Rosenthal, *Priceless Markets*.

These results may have to be qualified. Although *censos* had to be systematically recorded in the mortgage registry because they were pledged on real properties, not all obligations were secured on real assets. As a result, my sources may underestimate the stock of obligations. One result remains obvious: the collapse of lending by the ecclesiastical institutions occurred alongside the demise of the *censos*, the most popular long-term debt instrument on private credit markets at the time.

The mortgage credit market's stock of capital only returned to its 1770s level in the 1840s. This long and painstaking revival brought significant changes, especially in the average period a person could borrow. Indeed, the stock of obligations in the 1840s did not have the same constraints as the stock of *censos* in the 1770s. Obligations had a shorter maturity than *censos* (two years versus 15 years). As a result, even though the amount of outstanding debt was equivalent in 1770 and in 1840, the outcome was quite different for borrowers. Considering the likelihood of frequent renewals, the stock of obligations, although similar in volume, was much more volatile than the stock of *censos* and entailed uncertainties for borrowers.

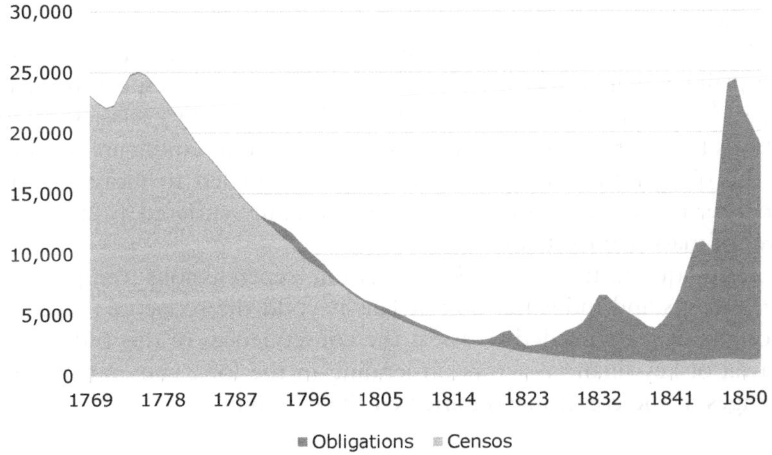

Fig. 4 The real annual stock of private mortgage credit in Madrid, 1769–1852 (*Source* ARPM, Contaduría de Hipotecas, *manzanas* 1–64 *Note* I used as a deflator the price index computed in Reher and Ballesteros, 'Precios y salarios')

5 Conclusion

During the early modern period, ecclesiastical institutions were the most important providers of long-term credit in Spain. Although they only engaged in mortgage lending and benefited from a particular kind of deposits which the depositor could not withdraw, the monks and nuns acted almost like traditional bankers by pooling, lending, and borrowing money. Some of them, thanks to their three-tier structure, managed to solve problems of asymmetric information and circumvent the strong jurisdictional barriers prevalent in Spain.

At the end of the eighteenth century, however, this system came to a standstill as the monarchy diverted the ecclesiastical long-term credit flow to finance its costly wars, thereby shattering a credit system made that had succeeded in integrating the Spanish market.

The effect was enormous: after dominating Spanish long-term credit activities for almost three centuries, the ecclesiastical institutions vanished from the credit market in the space of just two decades. The overall stock of mortgage credit plummeted to a fifth of its previous amount over a period of 40 years, and the volume of mortgage obligations only recovered by the 1840s. Nothing comparable happened elsewhere in Europe.

Prior to the creation of the *Banco Hipotecario* in 1861, many voices complained that it was hard to get access to credit, especially in rural areas.[43] Merchant bankers could not fill the gap left by ecclesiastical institutions that were "close to the consumer", even in remote areas. The rise of the obligation as the major debt instrument led to more expensive, short-term credit. Consumption most certainly suffered from a higher level of market uncertainty.

Many questions remain but showing repercussions on productive investments and industrial output falls beyond the scope of this chapter. More studies are needed to assess the consequences of this sudden withdrawal of key financial actors on lending in the long run and how these changes in the credit market affected the economy.

[43] Congost, 'De censatarios'.

Archival Sources and Literature

Acemoglu, Daron, Simon Johnson, and James A. Robinson, 'The Colonial Origins of Comparative Development: An Empirical Investigation', in: *The American Economic Review* 91:5 (2001), 1369–1401.

Acemoglu, Daron, Simon Johnson, and James A. Robinson, 'Reversal of Fortune: Geography and Institutions in the Making of the Modern World Income Distribution', in: *The Quarterly Journal of Economics* 117:4 (2002), 1231–1294.

Acemoglu, Daron, Simon Johnson, and James A. Robinson, 'The Rise of Europe: Atlantic Trade, Institutional Change, and Economic Growth', in: *The American Economic Review* 95:3 (2005), 546–579.

Álvarez-Nogal, Carlos, and Leando Prados de la Escosura, 'The Decline of Spain (1500–1850): Conjectural Estimates', in: *European Review of Economic History* 11:3 (2007), 319–366.

Álvarez-Nogal, Carlos, and Leando Prados de la Escosura, 'The Rise and fall of Spain (1270–1850)', in: *The Economic History Review* 66:1 (2013), 1–37.

Archivo del Registro de la Propiedad de Madrid, *Contaduría de Hipotecas*.

Chowning, Margaret, 'The Consolidación de Vales Reales in the Bishopric of Michoacán', in: *The Hispanic American Historical Review* 69:3 (1989), 451–478.

Congost, Rosa, 'Enfiteusis y pequeña explotación campesina en Cataluña, siglos XVIII–XIX', in: Pegerto Saavedra and Ramon Villares (eds.), *Señores y campesinos en la peninsula Ibérica, siglos XVIII–XX*, volume 2 (Barcelona, 1991), 63–87.

Congost, Rosa, 'De censatarios de la Iglesia a deudores del Estado: Más reflexiones sobre el proceso desamortizador y la revolución liberal en España', in: Bernard Bodinier, Rosa Congost, and Pablo F. Luna (eds.), De la Iglesia al Estado*: las desamortizaciones de bienes eclesiásticos en Francia, España y América Latina* (Zaragoza, 2009), 377–407.

Cuevas, Joachim, 'La financiación del desarrollo agrario valenciano, 1750–1914', in: *Historia Agraria* 25:1 (2001), 89–120.

Díaz López, Julián Pablo, 'Transformaciones institucionales del mercado de capitales en un medio agrícola mediterráneo: Almería (1769–1853)', in: *Chronica Nova* 28:1 (2001), 129–157.

Dincecco, Mark, 'Fiscal Centralization, Limited Government, and Public Revenues in Europe, 1650–1913', in: *The Journal of Economic History* 69:1 (2009), 48–103.

Elliott, John H., 'The Decline of Spain', in: *Past and Present* 20 (1961), 52–75.

Elliott, J.H., 'A Europe of Composite Monarchies', in: *Past and Present* 137:1 (1992), 48–71.

Epstein, S.R., *Freedom and Growth: The Rise of States and Markets in Europe, 1300–1750* (London, 2000).

Fernández de Pinedo, Emiliano, 'Del censo a la obligación: modificaciones en el crédito rural antes de la primera guerra carlista en el País Vasco', in: Ramon Garrabou and Angel García Sanz (eds.), *Historia agraria de la España contemporánea* (Barcelona, 1985), 297–305.

Gelderblom, Oscar, Joost Jonker, and Clemens Kool, 'Direct finance in the Dutch Golden Age', in: *The Economic History Review* 69:4 (2016), 1178–1198.

Godwin James, Francis, 'Charity Endowments as Sources of Local Credit in Seventeenth- and Eighteenth-Century England', in: *The Journal of Economic History* 8:2 (1948), 153–170.

Grafe, Regina, *Distant Tyranny: Markets, Power, and Backwardness in Spain, 1650–1800* (Princeton, 2012).

Grafe, Regina, and Alejandra Irigoin, 'Bounded Leviathan: Fiscal Constraints and Financial Development in the Early Modern Hispanic World', in: D'Maris Coffman, Adrian Leonard, and Larry Neal (eds.), *Questioning Credible Commitment: Perspectives on the Rose of Financial Capitalism* (Cambridge, 2013), 188–227.

Greenow, Linda, *Credit and Socioeconomic Change in Colonial Mexico: Loans and Mortgages in Guadalajara, 1720–1820* (Boulder, 1983).

Hamilton, Earl J., 'The Decline of Spain', in: *The Economic History Review* 8:2 (1938), 193–211.

Hamnett, Brian R., 'The Appropriation of Mexican Church Wealth by the Spanish Bourbon Government—The "Consolidación de Vales Reales", 1805–1809', in: *The Journal of Latin American Studies* 1:2 (1969), 85–113.

Herr, Richard, *Rural Change and Royal Finances in Spain at the End of the Old Regime* (Berkeley, 1989).

Hoffman, Philip T., Gilles Postel-Vinay, and Jean-Laurent Rosenthal, *Priceless Markets: The Political Economy of Credit in Paris, 1660–1870* (Chicago, 2000).

Jovellanos, Gaspar Melchor de, *Informe sobre el expediente de Ley Agraria* (Madrid, 1795).

Levy, Juliette, *The Making of a Market: Credit, Henequen, and Notaries in Yucatan, 1850–1900* (University Park, 2012).

Liehr, Reinhard, 'Endeudamiento Estatal y credito privado: la consolidacion de vales reales en hispanoamerica', *Anuario de Estudios Americanos* 41:1 (1984), 553–578.

Marcos Martín, Alberto, 'La actividad crediticia del clero regular castellano en la edad moderna', in: Fiorenzo Landi (ed.), *Accumulation and Dissolution of Large Estates of the Regular Clergy in Early Modern Europe* (Rimini, 1999), 69–103.

Milhaud, Cyril, 'Sacré Credit! The Rise and Fall of Ecclesiastical Credit in Early Modern Spain' (unpublished dissertation, l'École des Hautes Études en Sciences Sociales, 2017).
Milhaud, Cyril, 'Interregional Flows of Capital and Information in Spain: a case study of the Theresian Carmelite Order', in: *Revista de Historia Económica—Journal of Iberian and Latin American Economic History* 37:1 (2019), 81–110.
North, Douglass C., *Structure and Change in Economic History* (London, 1981).
North, Douglass C., 'Institutions and Economic Growth: An Historical Introduction', in: *World Development* 17:9 (1989), 1319–1332.
North, Douglass C., William Summerhill, and Barry R. Weingast, 'Order, disorder, and economic change: Latin America versus North America', in: Bruce Bueno de Mesquita and Hilton L. Root (eds.), *Governing for Prosperity* (New York, 2000), 17–58.
North, Douglass C., and Robert Paul Thomas, *The Rise of the Western World: A New Economic History* (Cambridge, 1973).
Peset Reig, Mariano, and Yolanda Blasco Gil, 'Redención y extinción de censos en el siglo XIX', in: Saitabi: R*evista de la Facultat de Geografia i Història* 42:1 (1992), 63–80.
Pinto Crespo, Virgilio, and Santos Madrazo Madrazo, *Madrid: Atlas histórico de la ciudad siglos IX–XIX* (Madrid, 1995).
Reher, David S., and Esmeralda Ballesteros, 'Precios y salarios en Castilla la Nueva: La construcción de un índice de salarios reales, 1501–1991', in: *Revista de Historia Económica—Journal of Iberian and Latin American Economic History* 11:1 (1993), 101–151.
Serna Vallejo, Margarita, *La publicidad inmobiliaria en el derecho hipotecario histórico español* (Madrid, 1996).
Tedde de Lorca, Pedro, *El Banco de San Carlos* (Madrid, 1988).
Tello Aragay, Enric, 'El papel del crédito rural en la agricultura del Antiguo Régimen: desarrollo y crisis de las modalidades crediticias (1600–1850)', in: *Noticiario de Historia Agraria* 7:1 (1994), 9–37.
Tilly, Charles, *Coercion, Capital, and European States, A.D. 990–1990* (Oxford, 1990).
Torre, Joseba de la, 'Coyuntura económica, crédito agrícola y cambio social en Navarra, 1750–1850', in: *Noticiario de Historia Agraria* 7:1 (1994), 109–129.
Torres Sánchez, Rafael, *El precio de la guerra: El Estado fiscal-militar de Carlos III (1779–1783)* (Madrid, 2013).
Torres Sánchez, Rafael, *Constructing a Fiscal-Military State in Eighteenth-Century Spain* (New York, 2015).
Vizcaino Pérez, Vicente, *Discursos políticos, sobre los estragos que causan los censos, felicidades y medios de su extinción* (Madrid, 1766).

Wobeser, Gisela von, *El crédito eclesiástico en la Nueva España: Siglo XVIII* (Mexico, 1994).
Yun Casalilla, Bartolomé, 'Cambiamento e continuità La Castiglia nell'impero durante il secolo d'oro', in: *Studi Storici* 36:1 (1995), 51–101.
Yun Casalilla, Bartolomé, 'The American Empire and the Spanish Economy: An Institutional and Regional Perspective', in: *Revista de Historia Económica—Journal of Iberian and Latin American Economic History* 16:1 (1998), 123–156.

Banking Before Banks in Early Modern Japan: Buddhist Temple Finance

Matthew Mitchell

1 Introduction[1]

"Nothing on earth is more terrifying than the interest which grows from debts", wrote Ihara Saikaku, famed Japanese author, in 1688.[2] The tale this quote is drawn from, "Happiness riding in on the first day of the horse" (***hatsuuma ni nottekuru shiawase*** 初午に乗って来る仕

[1] This chapter developed out of and is an elaboration on research in my dissertation (Matthew Steven Mitchell, 'Beyond the Convent Walls: The Local and Japan-wide Activities of Daihongan's Nuns in the Early Modern Period (c. 1550–1868)' (unpublished dissertation, Duke University, 2016)); further details on the 1793 financial ledger and the financial confraternity of 1816 can be found there.

[2] A note about naming conventions. Below, I have listed Japanese names in Japanese name order, with family name followed by given name (ex. Yokoyama Yuriko, where Yokoyama is her family name and Yuriko is her given name). Exceptions to this are if

M. Mitchell (✉)
Department of Religion and Philosophy, High Point University, High Point, NC, USA
e-mail: mmitche4@highpoint.edu

C. van Bochove and J. Levy (eds.), *Beyond Banks*, Palgrave Studies in the History of Finance,
https://doi.org/10.1007/978-3-031-75819-5_10

合), tells how one man became wealthy and happy by borrowing money from Mizumadera, a Buddhist temple south of Osaka.[4] In Saikaku's tale, pilgrims of all ages and social statuses trekked to petition Mizumadera's chief deity, Avalokitesvara (Japanese: Kannon, Chinese: Guanyin), for wealth despite repeated warnings from it that "there is no easy money in this world".[5] In the tale, these pilgrims borrowed small amounts of money from the deity on the first day of the horse each year,[6] and returned it at 100% interest the following year. This was often in amounts of one to five small copper coins, which today would be around a few US dollars (for the sake of comparison, a bowl of buckwheat noodles in broth from a street vendor was sixteen copper coins at the time), so it was easy to return with interest. Because it was thought of as the deity's money, borrowers used it prudently and returned it without fail. Saikaku says that one year a strangely dressed man in his early twenties came to the temple and asked for 1000 copper coins. The startled priest handed it over without asking any questions, and the young man returned home. The temple priests later agreed to never hand over such a large amount of money again because they had no way of guaranteeing its return. Meanwhile, the young man, a shipping agent from the Koami-chō neighborhood of Edo (now Tokyo), grew prosperous. He attributed this to his loan from Mizumadera. He told all who would listen about this, and began lending copper coins to any who wanted them. Borrowers grew wealthy, and they repaid their loans with interest to the man without fail. Through this, the man's wealth grew, but with each passing year his debt to the Mizumadera's Avalokitesvara did as well. On the thirteenth year, he loaded packhorses with 8,192,000 copper coins, the principal and interest (compounded annually at 100%) on his initial 1000 copper coin loan, and

[4] This is my translation of the title, which captures more of the meaning than Sargent's. Also, a note on terminology: throughout the paper, I follow convention and use "temple" to refer to Buddhist institutions broadly speaking, "monastery" to refer to Buddhist institutions that housed monks, and "convent" to refer to Buddhist institutions that housed nuns.

[5] Saikaku, *The Japanese Family Storehouse,* 14.

[6] This would have been the first day of the horse in the spring, or the seventh day of the second month. Prior to 1872, Japan used a luni-solar calendar, and one way of calculating dates and times in pre- and early modern Japan involved the Chinese zodiac. The first day of the horse is still celebrated at some shrines in Japan, though because it is calculated using the old on a luni-solar calendar, the date varies from year to year with the Gregorian calendar. Now, this typically falls in February or March.

returned to Mizumadera. The astonished priests decided to use the man's payment to rebuild their pagoda, which had been destroyed years before.

Saikaku's tale gives us a snapshot of life in early modern Japan, some of which is backed up by the large number of documents that have survived from the period; fires, floods, paper recycling, and insects were constant threats to documents.[7] Coins, which had been used in Japan for hundreds of years, began to pervade all aspects of life. Official government currencies were in gold, silver, and copper. These came in a variety of denominations with a gold *ryō* coin being the largest in common circulation, and the copper *mon* coin being the smallest. Exchange rates varied with the market, but the government tried to establish a rate of one gold *ryō* to sixty silver *monme* coins to 4,000 copper *mon* coins.[8] To put this in a bit of perspective, in 1769 male employees at the high-end Shirokiya dried goods store could earn annually anywhere from four gold *ryō* for beginning employees up to ten gold *ryō* for a branch manager; in the early nineteenth century, female domestic servants could earn around a hundred silver *monme* coins in wages annually with more given as tips and gifts.[9]

Related to the spread of a monetary economy, a middle class of merchants, artisans, and wealthy land-holding farmers blossomed. Cities, which were some of the largest in the world at the time, surged with people of all statuses and classes, from the poor day laborers and shipping agents to the powerful (yet deeply indebted) samurai/administrators and their merchant-class lenders who were incredibly well-off.[10] To connect these cities, the government invested in highways. The relative peace of

[7] For an engaging and well-written view into early modern Japan through the life of one woman, see Amy Stanley, *Stranger in the Shogun's City: A Japanese Woman and Her World* (New York, 2021).

[8] For more on coinage in Japan, see the Bank of Japan's Currency Museum, which has a very detailed online exhibit www.imes.boj.or.jp/cm/english/. For more on the complexities of exchange between these coins, see Atsuko Suzuki, 'Early Monetary Policies of the Tokugawa Shogunate and Merchants' Coping Strategies: 1695–1736', in: *Discussion Papers in Economics and Business* (discussion paper, 2021).

[9] Gary P. Leupp, *Servants, Shophands, and Laborers in the Cities of Tokugawa Japan* (Princeton, 1992), 100–105.

[10] For more on the merchant lenders of early modern Japan, see Yōtarō Sakudō, 'The Management Practices of Family Business', in: Chie Nakane and Shinzaburo Oishi (eds.), *Tokugawa Japan: The Social and Economic Antecedents of Modern Japan* (Tokyo, 1990), 150–156.

the era meant that people traveled with greater frequency than before, and people could travel with money without worrying too much about being robbed.[11]

More to the point of this chapter, Saikaku's story reveals a few things about borrowing and lending in early modern Japan (roughly 1600–1868) that will be discussed in detail below. Borrowing and lending on interest was common enough that it could become a crucial component of a story written for a wide audience. Indeed, there are records in Japan of interest on loans from at least a millennium before Saikaku penned his tale. In the early modern period, the most famous (and wealthy) lenders were the rice exchangers who serviced the samurai/administrators who worked in the government and who were paid stipends in rice. However, anyone with extra money could be a lender, from shipping agents to Buddhist temples.[12]

Unlike the priests in Saikaku's tale, however, lenders almost always required documentation recording the borrower's information (name and affiliation/address), amount borrowed, interest rate and term of the loan, a guarantor, and often collateral. Mizumadera's open lending policy was also unusual; many loans drew from existing networks or geographical affiliations. From the early 1700s, the shogunal government refused to hear lawsuits about loans, so in many cases, conflicts over repayment were to be resolved between the lender and the borrower. The one exception to this was for official endowments or "entitled funds" run by powerful temples and shrines. For loans from these funds, the government would arbitrate litigation and help enforce payment from delinquent borrowers.[13]

[11] Constantine Nomikos Vaporis, *Breaking Barriers: Travel and the State in Early Modern Japan* (Cambridge, 1994); Constantine Nomikos Vaporis, *Tour of Duty: Samurai, Military Service in Edo, and the Culture of Early Modern Japan* (Honolulu, 2008).

[12] See, for instance, Edward E. Pratt, *Japan's Protoindustrial Elite: The Economic Foundations of the Gōnō* (Cambridge, 2008); Gerald Groemer, 'The Guild of the Blind in Tokugawa Japan', in: *Monumenta Nipponica* 56:3 (2001), 349–380.

[13] For more information, see Yokoyama, Yuriko, 'Expanding and Multilayering Networks in Nineteenth-Century Japan: The Case of the Shin-Yoshiwara Red-Light District', in: Bettina Gramlich-Oka et al. (eds.) *Women and Networks in Nineteenth-Century Japan* (Michigan, 2020), 226; Buyō Inshi, *Lust, Commerce, and Corruption: An Account of What I Have Seen and Heard,* translated by John Breen et al. (New York, 2014), 48, footnote 6.

The 100% interest rate in Saikaku's tale was also unheard of in early modern Japan. The warrior government (the shogunate) set an official cap on interest rates at 20% from the 1600s, 15% in 1736, and 12% in 1842. Interest was compounded, typically annually, though it could be altered by the terms of the loan. We will also see below that some people and institutions could receive interest-free loans.

From this brief overview and Saikaku's story, we can see that in early modern Japan, borrowers could turn to an array of lenders. Buddhist temples and convents were one option out of many, which, like Saikaku, I will focus on here. Following a brief overview of Buddhist lending practices in premodern Japan, I turn to three different types of credit features offered at many Buddhist temples in the period. These were basic loans, temple endowments, and mutual financing associations. I will demonstrate how each one of these drew from, and could strengthen (or if poorly managed, weaken), existing religious, social, or geographic connections between the temple and the laypeople. Additionally, we will see how as with other types of financing available, temple financing could support a spectrum of goals from what we might consider noble (for example disaster relief) to those we would judge to be morally bankrupt (for example the building of brothels). In other words, though there were some differences in the particulars between the two, Buddhist banking was not morally or ethically different from other forms of lending in early modern Japan. Buddhist banking was a way to receive (through interest or borrowing) or distribute money.

2 Buddhist Lending

Buddhist temples have been involved in money lending since the religion's origins in what is now India and Nepal, and they undertook that role throughout East Asia.[14] In twelfth- to sixteenth-century Japan, large Buddhist temples offered loans to each other, to the warrior government (the shogunate), and financed private money lenders. Many of these medieval temple loans were low-interest and had legal protection by the warrior government, but borrowers had to have connections to the temple lenders. They are similar to the *shidōkin* endowment loans I discuss below. These were offered by temples in a variety of sects, from

[14] Matthew Mitchell, 'Borrowing from the Buddha: Buddhist Temples as Financial Centers in Premodern East Asia', in: *Education about Asia* 24:2 (2019), 51–54.

the established Tendai and Shingon sects to the relatively new Zen monasteries.[15] Japanese temples also were indirectly involved in moneylending: Suzanne Gay discusses the lending activities of hundreds of *sake* brewers under the control of the incredibly powerful Enryakuji Temple and its network of temples and shrines.[16]

Of course, financing was not the only role for Buddhist temples in Japan, and by the early modern period, Buddhist temples performed a number of social roles. Their clerics performed funerals, memorials, and rituals for this-worldly benefits. Priests kept the early modern equivalent of census records for the government. Temples were also sites of education, places of refuge for women seeking divorces, and Buddhist priests were conflict mediators. At the same time, and importantly for this chapter, they continued to function as financial centers for those connected to the temple.[17]

Buddhist temples operated in this financial space as a result of a confluence of factors. Temples were often central to their communities—people had a number of existing connections to temples that ranged from ritual to landlord-tenant relationships. Temples were seen as relatively reliable institutions—they had existed in the same location for generations and would most likely continue to do so—so borrowers knew where to find monastic lenders, and vice-versa. Building on this, a number of high-ranking temples had connections with the imperial family, shogunate, and other warlords, all of whom had a deep concern with maintaining and supporting these temples. Temples also had a relatively reliable flow of cash from landholdings, the sponsorship of rituals, and alms from

[15] Martin Colcutt, *Five Mountains: The Rinzai Zen Monastic Institution in Medieval Japan* (Cambridge, 1981), 241–262; Suzanne Gay, *The Moneylenders of Late Medieval Kyoto* (Honolulu, 2001), 2.

[16] Gay, *The Moneylenders of Late Medieval Kyoto.* These brewer-lenders gained social capital and protection of their monopolies through affiliation with Enryakuji Temple, while the temple and its network profited by taxing the lenders. Because they were connected to and backed by the temple, these lenders were highly influential in Kyoto's culture and society.

[17] For more on the roles of early modern temples in Japan, see Alexander M. Vesey, 'Entering the Temple: Priests, Peasants, and Village Contention in Tokugawa Japan', in: *Japanese Journal of Religious Studies* 28:3–4 (2001) 293–328; Alexander Vesey, 'The Buddhist Clergy and Village Society in Early Modern Japan' (unpublished dissertation, Princeton University, 2003).

pilgrims. They could lend from their regular funds, or in some cases, they were allowed to maintain endowments and lend from those.

The analysis of Buddhist credit practices and intermediation in this chapter focuses on the Zenkōji Temple complex from the seventeenth century to the nineteenth century, with a few examples from other locations. Zenkōji is in modern-day Nagano City, Japan, which developed around the temple after its (supposed) founding in the seventh century. The temple has been a popular pilgrimage site for over a thousand years, in part because it has welcomed pilgrims regardless of gender or sectarian affiliation. More recently, it made news when it refused to be the starting point of Japan's leg of the Olympic torch relay in 2008, and instead its clerics held a ceremony in solidarity with Tibetan Buddhists.

Zenkōji is a temple complex made up of a conglomeration of temple buildings. The temple's main hall itself is non-sectarian while the more than forty sub-temples on the grounds have a variety of sectarian affiliations.[18] Two of these sub-temples have administrative and ritual authority over the entire temple complex. These are the Pure Land convent of Daihongan and the Tendai sect monastery of Daikanjin. Only a few other temples in Japan have shared administration between two sub-temples, and no other temple in Japan after the medieval period has had both monks and nuns administering the temple. I mention this complexity because both of these sub-temples offered loans in the seventeenth to nineteenth centuries and both will appear below.[19]

[18] In the early modern period these were Tendai, Pure Land (Jōdo), and Ji sects. There may have been Shingon sect temples there as well. In the modern day, all the temples are affiliated with the Tendai and Pure Land sects.

[19] Gender was not an issue with Buddhist lending. Both Buddhist monks and nuns offered loans if their temples had the funds. Though not studied as much as lending by other institutions, Buddhist convents affiliated with the imperial family such as Reikanji 霊鑑寺, Jijuin 慈受院, and Chūgūji 中宮寺lent money, and their archives hold a number of documents related to loans and other investments. Oka Yoshiko 岡佳子 (ed.), *Nihon no shūkyō to jenda- ni kansuru kokusai sōgō kenkyū: Amadera chōsa no seika wo kiso toshite IV Jijuin monjo mokuroku* 日本の宗教とジェンダーに関する国際総合研究: 尼寺調査の成果を基礎として *IV* 慈受院文書目録 [Comprehensive International Research on Japanese Religions and Gender: Using results from a survey of convents as a base, Vol. IV, a list of Jijuin's archival materials] (Nishinomiya, 2009); Oka Yoshiko 岡佳子 (ed.), *Nihon no shūkyō to jenda- ni kansuru kokusai sōgō kenkyū: Amadera chōsa no seika wo kiso toshite III Chūgūji monjo mokuroku* 日本の宗教とジェンダーに関する国際総合研究: 尼寺調査の成果を基礎として *III* 中宮寺文書目録 [Comprehensive International Research on Japanese Religions and Gender: Using results from a survey of convents as a base, Vol. III, a list of Chūgūji's archival materials] (Nishinomiya, 2009); Oka Yoshiko 岡佳子 (ed.), *Nihon no*

3 Basic Loans

Japanese Buddhist temples were both lenders and borrowers in Japan's early modern period and I will discuss both lending and borrowing in this section.

Money lent by the temple can be divided into different categories based on where the money came from and the regulations (or lack thereof) surrounding them. The basic loans I discuss here came from the temple's regular funds, while the endowments I discuss in the next section came from a separate fund and were subject to additional governmental regulations and backing.

Direct evidence for temple loans survives in loan contracts between the temple and the lender/borrower. However, not all of these contracts survived floods, fires, wars, paper recycling, or bookworms. Fortunately, indirect evidence of loans can be found in other temple records. These include financial ledgers which would list payments made and received, journals or diaries kept by administrators, and other sources. While not providing us with exact details, such as interest rates and terms of loans, these indirect sources indicate the financial activities of temples as lenders and borrowers.

One such indirect source in Zenkōji Daihongan Convent's archives is a financial ledger for the year 1793, which gives us a snapshot of the convent's finances for that year.[20] In it we have indirect evidence of the convent receiving interest on money lent and paying interest for money borrowed. This ledger does not suggest that the convent was acting as a financial middle-person, but rather that it borrowed when it needed to meet its needs and lent to certain people when it could. The only two loans listed in the ledger are not large: 9.5 gold *ryō* and 270 copper *mon* coins to a man named Denpei from the Ganzeki neighborhood of

shūkyō to jenda- ni kansuru kokusai sōgō kenkyū: Amadera chōsa no seika wo kiso toshite II Reikanji monjo mokuroku 日本の宗教とジェンダーに関する国際総合研究: 尼寺調査の成果を基礎として *II* 霊鑑寺文書目録 [Comprehensive International Research on Japanese Religions and Gender: Using results from a survey of convents as a base, Vol. II, a list of Reikanji's archival materials] (Nishinomiya, 2009).

20 The ledger is: Kansei gonen ushidoshichū osamekata narabini watashikata okanjōchō [Ledger of Payments and Receipts for Year of the Ox, the Fifth Year of Kansei Era], 1793. Reprinted in: Nagano Kenshi Kankōkai (ed.), *Nagano Kenshi: Kinsei Shiryō Hen* 長野県史: 近世史料編, vol. 7-1 [Nagano Prefectural History: Early Modern Documents, vol. 7-1] (Nagano-shi: Nagano kenshi kankōkai, 1971).

Zenkōji Town and 3.25 gold *ryō* coins to its own branch temple Jūnenji. That same year, the convent only received slightly more than 1.75 gold *ryō* from interest on money lent. This constituted a small percentage of the temple's income for that year, which was more than 766 gold *ryō*.[21] Unfortunately, there are no surviving loan documents for any of the loans mentioned in this ledger.

Direct evidence of Daihongan's loans can be found in the Nagano City Public Archives (*Nagano shiritsu kōbunshokan*), which holds copies of the convent's archival materials for the early modern period. In its collection are fifty-eight loan documents related to Daihongan. These documents date from 1754 to 1865.[22] Of these, fifty-two documents concern loans administered by the convent, four concern money borrowed by the convent, and two are unclear what type of document they are. These can be further divided. Of the documents concerning money lent by the convent, thirty-six are basic loans from Daihongan's main convent, three are basic loans handled by the convent's jointly administered branch temple (Aoyama Zenkōji) to people in the city of Edo, and six are documents that reaffirm previous loans or discuss payment plans (four documents from Daihongan, and two documents from Aoyama). Seven of the loan documents (three from Daihongan and four from Aoyama) mention the "Tamaya Rebuilding Fund", so these are most likely related to an endowment to rebuild the Tamaya Shrine on Zenkōji's grounds; I discuss endowments in more detail below. The smallest amount lent was one gold *ryō* in 1784.[23] The largest amount lent by the convent that appears in these records was 236.5 gold *ryō* in 1799.[24] The borrower had difficulty making payments, so this loan is discussed in two later documents in 1805.

[21] Mitchell, 'Beyond the Convent Walls', 108.

[22] A large group of those (thirty-eight) documents are bound together. Daihongan Documents fuku 2 65.085.

[23] Daihongan Documents fuku 2 65.085. Here and below, Daihongan Documents refers to the collection of archival documents from the Daihongan Convent held in the Nagano City Archives. In the citations, "fuku" refers to reproductions of the original documents. The "1" or "2" refers to the first or second batch of documents in the archive. The number following that—65.085 in this case—refers to each individual document's archival number.

[24] This appears as two documents in Daihongan Documents fuku 2 65.085.

As mentioned above, Nagano City Public Archives have loan documents for both Daihongan's main convent and the jointly administered branch, Aoyama Zenkōji. Although in his chapter in this volume, Cyril discusses the ways that lending by church networks in Spain could enable access to markets by crossing jurisdictional boundaries, I do not believe that this is the case with Daihongan and Aoyama Zenkōji's basic loans. In other words, I have seen no evidence to indicate that the convent was using its branch as a way to move money between the main temple and the branch for the purpose of offering basic loans. The relationship between these two convents was close; Daihongan's abbess lived at and administered both (thus the title "jointly administered") and this is why there are many documents from Aoyama Zenkōji in Daihongan's documents in the archives. However, evidence that the finances of the two convents were kept separate and the major difference in the number of loan documents from each—forty for Daihongan compared to seven for Aoyama Zenkōji—suggests that most likely, funds for basic loans such as these were not moved between these two temples to gain access to other lending markets. As I discuss below, evidence suggests that unlike basic loans, loans from endowments could in some cases cross jurisdictional boundaries.

Here I will examine three loan documents from the mid-nineteenth century: two where the convent or its branch was a lender, and one where it was a borrower. Most of the extant loan documents from the convent are short. The first example, from the fifth month of 1754, has a title, amount borrowed, six lines of text, the date, borrowers' names, and names of the convent's administrators.[25] In it, Kichikurō and Heishichi from the Daimonchō neighborhood of Zenkōji's town borrowed 25 gold *ryō* coins at 12% annual interest.[26] The loan is addressed to Yoshimura and Karasawa, two of Daihongan convent's administrators. A payment schedule is not mentioned, but a year later, the convent received a request for extension on the loan from two different residents of Daimonchō. These people, writing on Heishichi's behalf, said that he had run into troubles and was having difficulty paying any of the

[25] This is the first loan document transcribed in Daihongan Documents fuku 2 65.085.

[26] The borrowers' names could also be pronounced Yoshikurō and Hirashichi; it is unclear from the document which pronunciation should be used.

loan back.[27] Kichikurō is not mentioned anywhere in the document. This loan does not appear elsewhere in the convent's archives, so it is unclear whether it was eventually repaid or not.

The second example (Fig. 1) is from 1843, and it concerns a loan given by the convent's jointly administered branch temple, Aoyama Zenkōji in Edo.[28] The borrower is Iwamoto Mataemon (dates unknown), a vassal of Matsudaira Yorisato (1809–1865), the ninth leader of the fairly well-off Saijō Matsudaira clan. The document is co-signed by Toyoshima Nagasaburo (dates unknown), also a vassal of Matsudaira. The document was sent to the administrators of Aoyama Zenkōji in the sixth month of 1843.[29] Iwamoto borrowed five gold *ryō* coins, at 1% interest per month. It was to be repaid by the end of 1843. If Iwamoto was unable to repay it, co-signer Toyoshima was to take on responsibility for the loan. Both Iwamoto and Toyoshima have placed their name seals over their names

Mitchell

Translation of figure 1 in Banking before banks

Loan document

Item: Five gold *ryō* [coins] (Iwamoto's seal) Provided that these are coins in common circulation

It is certified that the above [amount] is being borrowed for work purposes. Therefore, regarding interest, 1 *bu* [gold coin, which is ¼ of a gold *ryō*,] will be charged per 25 gold *ryō* borrowed per month [i.e. 1% interest per month]. [The amount due] is to be paid by the 20th day of the 12th month of the year of the rabbit [this year]. If the borrower has difficulty repaying or other [difficulties] arise, the cosigner will take on [the responsibility]. So there is not the slightest discrepancy and principle and interest can be repaid, this serves as a record for later days.

In the Master of the Eastern Offices, Matsudaira [Yorisato's service]

Cosigner: Toyoshima Nagasaburo (Toyoshima's seal)

Tenpō 14 [1843], year of the rabbit, Sixth month

Borrower: Iwamoto Mataemon (Iwamoto's seal)

Shinshū Zenkōji

[Daihongan Convent's] Jointly Held Temple [Aoyama Zenkōji]

The administrators

Fig. 1 The contract for a loan dated 1843 (*Source* Daihongan Documents fuku 2 68.116)

[27] This is the third document transcribed in Daihongan Documents fuku 2 65.085.

[28] Daihongan Documents fuku 2 68.116.

[29] The document says "the administrators of the Zenkōji Temple Jointly Administered Convent", which is one of the names for Aoyama Zenkōji.

at the end of the document and Iwamoto has placed his seal over the amount of the loan, certifying its amount.

Daihongan's loans were to people (or institutions) in proximity to or with a relationship to the convent or its jointly administered branch. From the 1793 ledger, Denpei lived in the neighborhood surrounding the convent and Jūnenji was one of the convent's own branch temples. Similarly, many of the loan documents in the archives, such as the 1754 loan to Kichikurō and Heishichi, concern loans given to people living in the neighborhood surrounding the convent or its Edo branch. This proximity developed out of convenience for the borrower (why borrow from Daihongan if another person or institution offering loans is closer?) and lender (why worry about the administrative headache of pursuing a borrower across jurisdictional boundaries?) but also was a matter of trust on the part of both.

In the case of the 1843 loan, the convent lent money to vassals of warlords who had compounds near their branch temple in Edo. In this case as well, proximity was important, but there were perhaps other benefits that came with lending to the vassals of these warlords. First, the convent could perhaps rely on them for repayment since they were associated with known people whose compounds were nearby. Second, loans such as these may also have aided connections between the convent and these important families. However, this is conjecture since the loans are not explicit on this.

Daihongan Convent was also a frequent borrower of money via direct loans such as these. Indeed, the convent came to rely upon a variety of loans from wealthy commoners and lords of domains, especially toward the end of the early modern period. According to the 1793 financial ledger, Daihongan received roughly 24% of its income from money it borrowed, while 37% of its expenditures were payments related to loans it had previously taken out.[30] Many of these lenders were residents of Zenkōji's lands.

The convent's reliance upon loans only grew over the next thirty years. In the period surrounding Abbess Chishō's visit to the imperial palace in 1808, the convent had accrued over seven thousand gold *ryō* coins in debt, and the convent continued to rely on borrowing in the following

[30] If we count a large, undescribed payment to Koyama Yaemon as a loan payment, then loan payments reach 80% of the convent's expenditures for that year.

decades.[31] As the 1793 financial ledger shows, even in periods where there were no large expenditures for travel or maintenance to temple halls, the convent still took out a number of loans and was involved in mutual aid confraternities to make payments on preexisting loans. Unexpected calamities put a strain on the convent that it was only able to escape by taking out further loans: it received a loan of 500 gold *ryō* coins at 10% annual interest from the nearby Matsushiro domain to rebuild the convent from the ashes of the 1847 Zenkōji Earthquake and provide loans to commoners on temple lands.[32]

A few years later, Abbess Seien took out loans from the Matsushiro domain and 340 *ryō* in interest-free loans from two commoners in 1853 in order to travel to Kyoto to meet with the emperor.[33] Even though the loans from these commoners were interest-free, the convent made payment plans with its lenders. Indeed, in 1859, the convent administrator Akamatsu Moku established a repayment plan with one lender named Fumiemon. This entailed making monthly payments starting in the eleventh month of 1859: for the first nine months they were to pay 2.5 gold *ryō* coins, the following year they were to pay three gold *ryō* coins per month, and following that they were to pay one gold *ryō* coin per month until the debt was finally repaid, ideally fifty months later.[34] Although the repayment plan was signed by the lender and Daihongan's administrator Akamatsu Moku, it was also approved by the two elder nuns Bonjō 梵定 and Risshō 立成, suggesting perhaps that the administrators of the convent did not have autonomous control over its finances or at least that borrowing was monitored by the convent's clergy.

When borrowers such as Daihongan Convent were unable to repay their loans, there were a number of paths they could take. One option to avoid mounting debts was to request a repayment plan, like the one outlined above. Another was to request loan cancellation, usually in return

31 Takatsukasa Seigyoku 鷹司誓玉, 'Zenkōji Chishō Shōnin No Shōgai 善光寺智昭上人の生涯' [The Life of Abbess Chishō of Zenkōji], *Bukkyō Daigaku Kenkyū Kiyō* 佛教大學研究紀要 62 [Research Bulletin of Bukkyō University] (1978), 239.

32 Nagano City Public Archives 長野市立公文書館, Sanadake monjo 3 [Sanada Clan Documents 3] Fuku 2 1548.481.

33 Though both documents date to the eleventh month of 1859, they state that they are for the abbess's travels from "the previous year of the ox", which corresponds to 1853. Daihongan fuku 2 69.139 and 69.140.

34 Daihongan Documents Fuku 2 69.139.

for a title or position with a small stipend within the domain or temple hierarchy. Some of the lenders to Zenkōji Daikanjin (the other administrative sub-temple at Zenkōji) were offered positions as administrators, a significant raise in status. These lenders (who had not been repaid in kind) were no longer commoners, but samurai-administrators during the duration of their service, and they were granted permission to carry swords when acting in an official capacity. It is possible that this happened at Daihongan, too, although there are no surviving records to support this.

Powerful domain governments and the shogunal government often stepped in to relieve their own or their vassals' debts a number of times in the eighteenth and nineteenth centuries, especially as the samurai/administrator class became overburdened by mounting debts when their stipends, which were paid in rice, did not keep pace with market transitions.[35] When faced with massive debts and in need of a way to stem expenditures, Satsuma domain in western Japan canceled their debts to merchants inside the domain by stopping payment and they renegotiated with the rice merchant-lenders based in Osaka to make their existing debts payable over 250 years.[36] The shogunal government occasionally stepped in as well because samurai indebtedness affected the shogun's ability to maintain an effective military. In one instance in 1705, the shogun dissolved the Yodoya house, a wealthy Osaka merchant family, supposedly for ostentatious behavior; this also erased the numerous loans that various domains owed the Yodoya.[37] The shogunate also refused to adjudicate conflicts over simple loans, instead encouraging negotiation between the parties involved, which could often result in more favorable terms for borrowers.[38]

[35] For more on samurai and warlord indebtedness and orders of blanket loan forgiveness, see Stanley, *Stranger in the Shogun's City*, 115–116; Sakudō, 'The Management Practices of Family Business', 153; Conrad Totman, *Early Modern Japan* (Berkeley, 1995), 291–293.

[36] Totman, *Early Modern Japan*, 519.

[37] Totman, *Early Modern Japan*, 139.

[38] Totman, *Early Modern Japan*, 291.

4 Temple Endowments (*Shidōkin*)

Some temples offered loans from their endowments (*shidōkin*). These endowments originated from donations to the temples. Interest from these loans funded memorial services for the departed, or they subsidized physical improvements such as building and maintaining temple halls. Similar practices existed at Buddhist temples in India and China.

In the early modern period, a number of temples throughout Japan offered *shidōkin* endowment loans. These could only be explicitly called "*shidōkin*" if they had official approval to organize an endowment from the shogun's government.[39] This approval was granted only to the highest-ranking temples, and the interest from these funds was intended to be used to maintain temple buildings or perform rituals. According to Buddhist studies scholar Tamamuro Fumio, these funds were often used to expand temples' wealth and influence and so were not always used in a way that the government intended. Temples would receive some money from the shogun's family, warlords, or wealthy commoners as a gift or an investment. They would then offer it as a loan to the temple's parishioners, people living on temple lands, or those nearby. Interest rates varied, but the government ordered that official rates of interest on loans from temple endowments could not exceed those of other loans (20% in the 1600s, 15% in 1736, and 12% in 1842). With the interest, temples could repay their initial investors (if it was an investment and not a donation; see below for more details) and keep the remaining interest income as profits.

The examples discussed here demonstrate that recipients of *shidōkin* loans could vary from wealthy entrepreneurs and farmers to townspeople who were adversely affected by disasters or famines. To protect its loan, temples often required collateral or guarantors, but when those did not work, lenders could pursue litigation against the borrower or decide to

[39] These could take a number of names besides *shidōkin*, including *meimokukin* or *myōmokukin* 名目金; the name of the hall they were supposed to fund (Yakushidōkin for a hall to Yakushi or Kannondōkin for a hall to Kannon); the name of the largest or most prestigious financier (Mito goyōkin for money offered by the head of the Mito domain); or the name of the priest who organized it. Tamamuro Fumio 圭室文雄, *Nihon Bukkyō shi: Kinsei* 日本仏教史近世 [History of Japanese Buddhism: Early Modern Period] (Tokyo, 1987), 320. Kobayashi states that only imperial temples, those with connections to the bakufu, or high-ranking temples could receive bakufu approval to offer *shidōkin* loans. Kobayashi Keiichirō 小林計一郎, *Zenkōjishi Kenkyū* 善光寺史研究 [Research on the History of Zenkōji] (Nagano, 2000), 331.

lose their principal and interest income. If temples had required land as collateral, they could gain lands beyond what they initially possessed when the borrower defaulted; they could then rent out these lands to tenant farmers to earn extra income. However, the shogunal government, hoping to limit the expansion of temple lands, outlawed acquiring land in this way from the second month of 1762, so if a temple received land as collateral, it had to sell it immediately.[40] While the government, as a general rule, did not hear lawsuits concerning private loans such as the basic loans discussed above, the Magistrate of Temples and Shrines could adjudicate disputes involving official temple endowments. The potential for the involvement of the Magistrate when legal arbitration was needed or in cases of default provided an aura of reliability and credibility to these instruments, and Yokoyama Yuriko has discussed how they were seen as a fairly reliable investment for wealthy merchants.[41]

Daihongan Convent seems to have administered the endowment associated with the Tamaya Shrine; and they have seven documents related to it from 1805 to the 1850s. The temple complex that Daihongan was a part of, Zenkōji temple, offered *shidōkin* loans, which were administered by the sub-temple Daikanjin. Though the temple received lands and funds from wealthy courtiers or warriors to set up endowments for memorial rites since at least the thirteenth century, these rites and the endowments that supported them most likely came to an end due to the social and economic changes of the Warring States period (1467–1567). The temple's early modern *shidōkin* loans started in the early eighteenth century. Zenkōji Daikanjin's head Keiun (abbot from 1700 to 1714) provided the original assets for the *shidōkin* account: he set aside 429 gold *ryō* in leftover funds from the rebuilding of Zenkōji's main hall in 1707.[42] The account grew as petitioners made donations for permanent memorial services at the temple, and by the end of the early modern

40 Tamamuro Fumio 圭室文雄, *Nihon Bukkyō shi: Kinsei* 日本仏教史近世 [History of Japanese Buddhism: Early Modern Period], 320–322.

41 Name in Japanese order with family name first (Yokoyama) and given name second (Yuriko). Yokoyama, 'Expanding and Multilayering Networks', 226.

42 There were actually two *shidōkin* accounts at Zenkōji: the first was fund for various expenses (*shoryōmotsukin* 諸料物金), which was founded by Keiun and grew with donations from petitioners, and the second was the sub-temples' *shidōkin* (Sanjichū shidōkin 三寺中祠堂金), which was based on donations given to Zenkōji's various sub-temples. However, in reality, Daikanjin administered both of these jointly. Kobayashi Keiichirō 小林計一郎, *Zenkōjishi Kenkyū* [Research on the History of Zenkōji], 334.

period, it had reached over 7000 *ryō*. A group of monks and their administrators from Zenkōji Daikanjin controlled the account, and recipients were limited to those living on Zenkōji temple's lands.[43] Unfortunately, the public archives remain silent on how many of these loans Daikanjin administered.[44]

Though it grew considerably over the period, the administrators of Zenkōji's endowment were careful with the funds in a number of ways. They usually only lent out half of the funds in the account at a time. Furthermore, to counter difficulties collecting debts or collateral on loans that had been defaulted on, the temple only offered loans to people living on temple lands. This was a double-edged sword. It meant that the temple did not have to cross jurisdictional boundaries (and possibly involve the shogunal government in jurisdictional disputes) to collect loans, but it also meant that the temple could not be too forceful in collecting payments because it could sour relations with locals. Instead, administrators usually offered extensions on loans rather than enforce repayment and risk the ill will of the townspeople. Endowments from main temples seem to have been available at a few branch temples, however, enabling temples to reach across boundaries as long as they had a branch temple approved to handle the endowment (this is one difference from the basic loans discussed above). Daihongan's control of the Tamaya Shrine Endowment is one example. Its documents related to this Endowment show an almost equal number of borrowers from both the area surrounding Daihongan and the Edo area surrounding Aoyama Zenkōji. In this case, the number of borrowers and amounts borrowed were fairly small, so it is difficult to draw too many conclusions about it. The Bukkōji temple endowments that I discuss below similarly demonstrate how endowments could reach across boundaries: Bukkōji was based in Kyoto, but its branch temple in Edo seems to have been used to gain access to distant markets.

43 Or, rather, Daikanjin's abbot was to oversee the operations while the temple's administrators handled day-to-day running of the funds. However, in reality the administrators operated unchecked, according to Kobayashi.

44 There is only one document related to "*shidogin*" endowments in the public archives for Daihongan Convent. This document, dated to 1712, states that Kiuemon from Komatsu Village (location unknown) donated 300 silver coins for continued repetition of the name of Amitabha Buddha at Daihongan's branch temple in Osaka, Wakōji. This was to be administered by the temple's confraternities. Unfortunately, no records remain that indicate exactly how it was used. Daihongan Documents Fuku 2 61.020.

Additionally, and particularly near the end of the period, these loans came to function as a form of assistance to those in need (*kyūsai* 救済)—the temple abolished or reduced interest payments on existing loans following disasters such as the Zenkōji Earthquake of 1847, and in the 1850s and 1860s it offered over a third of its loans interest-free.

The second way that the administrators tried to protect Zenkōji's *shidōkin* account was to not draw from it, even though this was the fundamental purpose of these endowments. The administrative temple usually tried to keep its own accounts separate from the *shidōkin* accounts. It also attempted to pay for temple repairs and cover its expenses by other means, such as traveling displays of temple treasures. However, there were times in the end of the Edo period when it did draw from the *shidōkin* account to cover these expenses.[45]

There are cases where temple endowments were used as an investment by outsiders, and the temple itself was simply the middle-person in this. The work of Yokoyama Yuriko uncovers how a network of wealthy farmer-investors in what is now northern Nagano Prefecture lent money to fund the building and maintenance of brothels in the Shin-Yoshiwara red-light district. They did so by funneling the money through Kyoto temple Bukkōji's endowment, even going so far as to send family members to work with Bukkōji temple's Edo loan office and directly oversee their loans. Due to the requirement that borrowers of temple endowments be connected to the temple in some way, the official loan documents were made out in Bukkōji's name, but on internal ledgers it is made clear that borrowers were a number of people from many locations throughout Edo (now Tokyo). Yokoyama shows how in the two-year period 1858–1860, loans to people in the official red-light district (94 cases) were more than triple loans to people living in other areas (thirty cases). In these documents, brothels acted as guarantors for other brothels, and the brothels listed sex workers owned by the brothels as collateral. This example shows how temple endowments could be used as cover for lending and borrowing by people unaffiliated with the temple itself and how they could be used to shore up businesses unaffiliated with Buddhism. Through the Bukkōji Temple endowment, rural investors were able to participate in and profit from lending in the city. They were able to draw on Bukkōji's prestige to connect with borrowers they could not have

[45] Kobayashi Keiichirō 小林計一郎, *Zenkōjishi Kenkyū* [Research on the History of Zenkōji], 330–349.

otherwise reached, all while interest was collected by Bukkōji's loan office and their investments were protected by the legal backing of the Magistrate of Temples and Shrines. It is unclear how often this occurred at other temples, but the fact that these temple endowments contributed to the maintenance of Edo's mid-nineteenth-century brothels forces us to consider how these temple endowments did not operate in a separate moral or spiritual realm from other loan products of the time.[46] Indeed, Yokoyama states that all parties involved—including the temple and the rural investors—"considered the red-light district finance system to be entirely normal and sought to take advantage of it".[47]

5 Mutual Financing

Another type of loan occasionally organized by Buddhist temples in Japan was mutual financing or financing associations. Though these have their origins in Buddhist practices, by the early modern period, they were used by both Buddhist temples and laypeople for a variety of reasons. In these associations, a group of borrowers came together as association members and agreed to meet a set number of meeting times, pooled their money at each meeting, and distributed the pool of money to a member or members of the association at each meeting. Much like in rotating savings associations and credit cooperatives in Latin America and Africa, the disbursement rotates until everyone has received the pool (or a portion of it). In these mutual financing associations, every member is a borrower and a lender. In many cases, people who received the pool of money earlier would pay more into it over the course of all the meetings, while those who received it later would pay less—this would act as a form of interest paid or interest received.[48]

Financial associations of various kinds were organized in China as early as the fourth century, and were often used to contribute to local festivals,

[46] Yokoyama, 'Expanding and Multilayering Networks'.

[47] Yokoyama, 'Expanding and Multilayering Networks', 242.

[48] For a detailed analysis of the eighteenth-century mutual financing confraternity, see Sakurai Tokutarō 桜井徳太郎, *Kōshūdan seiritsu katei no kenkyū* 講集団成立過程の研究 [Research on the Process of the Formation of Confraternities] (Tokyo, 1962), 396–402. Najita also discusses this confraternity in Tetsuo Najita, *Ordinary Economies in Japan: A Historical Perspective, 1750–1950* (Berkeley, 2009), 80–82.

vegetarian feasts for monks, purchasing Buddhist images, and so on.[49] These groups included Buddhist monks, nuns, and laypeople.

There are records of Japanese organizing these financial confraternities in the twelfth to the fourteenth centuries. As in China, these could be organized for Buddhist purposes, but local communities could also organize them to support local interests and to protect community members. Scholars have argued that they developed as a means to provide financial assistance for community members in need.[50] These were called *tanomoshikō (頼母子講)*, "the confraternity [like the] reliance of a child upon their mother", or *mujinkō (無尽講)*, "the inexhaustible [compassion] confraternity". In practice the *tanomoshi* and *mujin* confraternities did not differ. Furthermore, the terms were used interchangeably in primary and secondary sources, sometimes even when referring to the same confraternity: the financial confraternity active at Daihongan from 1816 to 1826 that I will discuss in detail below was called the Abbess's *mujin* Confraternity or the Abbess's *tanomoshi* Confraternity in different documents, for example. Unless a document I am citing specifically uses one or the other, I will use *mujin* confraternity below for simplicity's sake.

By the eighteenth century, these confraternities had taken on a number of forms: lotteries, mutual aid, and mutual financing/rotating savings associations. For the lottery, many people put money into a pot of money, but only a single person drawn at random could receive those funds. The members of lottery-type *mujin* changed from meeting to meeting. These lottery-style *mujin* faced contemporary critique. Kitamura Nobuyo (1783–1856), also known as Sesshin, wrote of how this type of *mujin* led to people losing their money by seeking greater wealth than they needed. He said that they should be called "contradiction confraternities", *mujun kō*, rather than "unlimited compassion confraternities", *mujin kō* because they caused people to seek more wealth than was natural, causing people to behave contrary to how they should.[51] Alternatively, Kaiho Seiryō

49 Liansheng Yang, *Money and Credit in China, a Short History* (Cambridge, 1952), 71–91; Liansheng Yang, *Studies in Chinese Institutional History* (Cambridge, 1961), 198–215; Najita, *Ordinary Economies in Japan*, 66–67; Jacques Gernet, *Buddhism in Chinese Society: An Economic History from the Fifth to the Tenth Centuries* (New York, 1995), 166–171, 259–277.

50 Sakurai Tokutarō 桜井徳太郎, *Kōshūdan seiritsu katei no kenkyū* 講集団成立過程の研究 [Research on the Process of the Formation of Confraternities].

51 Sesshin's view of *mujin* confraternities is cited in Tetsuo Najita's work. It seems from context that Sesshin was referring to the lottery-type confraternities rather than

(1755–1817) suggested that *mujin* lotteries were harmless entertainments that should be used to gather funds for local governments instead of rice taxes.[52] The prevailing assessment was, however, negative and the shogunal government attempted to ban *mujin* lotteries several times throughout the period.[53]

Another type of *mujin* confraternity was for mutual aid. In this case, a group of people, sometimes whole villages, pooled their money to help during times of famine or other natural disasters. Funds could be drawn from the group's coffers when the group or some of its members faced hardship.[54] In some cases, funds from these groups were lent out at interest for those who wanted loans. This was an effort to grow the group's coffers for the real purpose: support of the community and the group's members in times of famine, disaster, and disease. Relief funds were not to be repaid—indeed, membership in the group was predicated on having given to the group's funds in times of plenty so that people could draw from them in times of need. Economic historian Tetsuo Najita has examined this type of confraternity in detail.[55] He argues that this type of confraternity was an inspiration for, and occasionally the direct ancestor of, modern-day health, life, and travel insurance companies.

One of the most basic forms for the *mujin* confraternities, and the one I will discuss in this section, was the contract cooperative/confraternity (*keiyaku kō*). In this type, a set group of people gathered a set number of times, each putting a predetermined amount of money into the group's money pool. One person received all the money in the pool at each

other financial ones, though Najita is unclear on this. Najita, *Ordinary Economies in Japan*, 74–76.

[52] Najita, *Ordinary Economies in Japan*, 76–77. For more on Seiryō's life and thought, see W.M. Theodore De Bary, Carol Gluck, and Arthur E. Tiedeman (eds.), *Sources of Japanese Tradition volume 2: 1600 to 2000* (Columbia, 2013), 432–436.

[53] *Kojiruien Database* 古事類苑データベース hōritsu bu 3 [Database of the Lexical Encyclopedia of Historical Documents, Legal Sect. 3], 68–70. For more on early modern Japanese lotteries, the critiques leveled at them, and the shogunal government's varied stances toward them, see Matthew Mitchell, 'Regulating chance: Buddhist temple lotteries, government oversight, and anti-Buddhist discourse in early modern Japan', in: *Journal of Cultural Economy* 16:5 (2022), 716–732.

[54] An example of the contract from the mutual aid confraternity founded by Miura Baien (1723–1789) in the village of Tominaga appears in Najita, *Ordinary Economies in Japan*, 95–98.

[55] Najita, *Ordinary Economies in Japan*.

meeting; this was either decided in advance or chosen by drawing, but this occurred in rotation so each person received money once.

These groups were established and managed by a contract, but they were not normally backed by local or national regulations. Najita argues that these confraternities worked because of their "inherent ethical values of trust, promise, and contract", which he traces to the confraternities' origins in "Buddhist and Shinto themes of compassion and mutual aid [that] established a basis of interpersonal trust within the *kō* [confraternity] that allowed for such cooperative action".[56] Despite the elements of "trust, promise, and contract" that Najita examines and these groups' Buddhist and Shintō connections that he alludes to, there was still an element of risk involved in this type: the confraternity could fold or individual members might not be able to continue making their required payments at the meetings, for example, even when drawing from local communities and known associates.

Contract cooperative associations provided an important, quick source of income to early modern temples and shrines. Furthermore, associations did not require navigating the lengthy preapproval process with the shogunate's Magistrate of Temples and Shrines, unlike other forms of fundraising such as displays of temple treasures, fundraising drives, and lotteries. As such, temples could organize these to bring in needed funds and then slowly pay them back.

But not all cooperative associations were successful. One example of a failed confraternity comes from Zenkōji Daihongan.[57] The convent had been involved in several financial associations in the late eighteenth century, however, the only extant detailed records are from a failed one. In other words, detailed records exist precisely because of its failure. The fallout from this failed confraternity demonstrates clearly how these forms of financing affected the local community and how Buddhist temples' influences extended beyond rituals and sutras.

[56] Though Najita states that there was a religious basis for these ethical ideas, he does not provide evidence other than stating that confraternities in general had their start in Buddhist prayer gatherings and sutra lectures in the Nara and Heian periods. Najita, *Ordinary Economies in Japan*, 17 and 83.

[57] I have discussed this briefly in Mitchell, 'Borrowing from the Buddha'.

This financing association existed from 1816 to 1826, and its members were householders, tenants, and priests of Zenkōji's town.[58] The convent received five hundred gold *ryō* coins at its first meeting, which it used for loan payments, travel expenses, repairs to the convent buildings, and for the running of the confraternity itself.[59] The confraternity was to be held over ten years, meeting in the spring and fall, for a total of twenty meetings. However, sometime in the middle of this period, Yoshimura Tomiemon, the convent's administrator in charge of the confraternity, decided to delay payouts to individual participants until the final meeting. When the time for the final meeting came in the fall of 1826, he canceled it without paying the members. Instead, Yoshimura decided to bring in new members, which was not done once a confraternity had started because it essentially diluted and erased each original member's investment.[60] Some members said that the loss of money "caused great difficulty: some went bankrupt or fell into poverty, and one person even hanged himself" as a result.[61] The initial members brought a suit against Daihongan Convent, Yoshimura, and two other managers. The abbess, who had been 240 kilometers away in Edo throughout the entirety of the confraternity's existence, was not held responsible by members. The suit was passed from the local administrative temple, Zenkōji Daikanjin, to the administrative temple in charge of Zenkōji, Kan'eiji Temple in Edo.

[58] Miyazaki used the lawsuits against Daihongan, neighborhood registers, and registers of professions to determine that the investors came from a various economic strata in Zenkōji's neighborhoods. Miyazaki Masaki 宮崎正規, 'Kinsei Kōki Ni Okeru Zenkōji Machi No Shin'yō Jijō – Daihongan Shōninsama Mujinkō o Meguru Shiron – 近世後期における善光寺町の信用事情 —— 大本願上人様無尽講をめぐる試論 ——' [The Situation of Credit in Zenkōji Town in the End of the Early Modern Period: An Essay on the Daihongan Abbess's Mujin Confraternity], in: *Shishi Kenkyū Nagano* 市誌研究ながの [City Research Magazine Nagano] 18 (February 2011), 52–53.

[59] Nagano kenshi [Nagano Prefectural History: Early Modern Documents], vol. 7–1, 699–700; Daihongan Fuku 2 71.167; Miyazaki Masaki 宮崎正規, 'Kinsei Kōki Ni Okeru Zenkōji Machi No Shin'yō Jijō – Daihongan Shōninsama Mujinkō o Meguru Shiron – 近世後期における善光寺町の信用事情 —— 大本願上人様無尽講をめぐる試論 ——' [The Situation of Credit in Zenkōji Town in the End of the Early Modern Period: An Essay on the Daihongan Abbess's Mujin Confraternity], 50.

[60] Miyazaki Masaki 宮崎正規, 'Daihongan Shōninsama Mujinkō' [On the Daihongan Abbess's Mujin Confraternity], 50.

[61] A quote from the suit to Daikanjin cited in Kobayashi Keiichirō 小林計一郎, *Zenkōjishi Kenkyū* [Research on the History of Zenkōji], 328.

Tensions were high in the town surrounding Zenkōji Temple after months without a resolution. However, with the help of an intermediary an agreement was reached in the second month of 1830. The convent was to return 436 gold *ryō* total to the plaintiffs in the lawsuit and dozens of other investors not involved in the suit, even though these 139 investors were owed 3374 *ryō*, according to local historian Kobayashi Keiichirō's calculations. The convent and association managers paid most of this settlement.[62] Though the abbess was not considered responsible for the confraternity's failure by its members, she had to pay a portion of the settlement because she was held responsible for the actions of her convent's administrators. For reasons that do not appear in existing documents, Yoshimura did not receive any punishment.

Not all of the members of this failed *mujin* confraternity took part in the suit, however. Some of these were priests at local temples, who may have had some connection to Daihongan and thus had no reason to sue. Others included shop owners such as Yahei, a clothing store owner. People such as Yahei may have been involved in a number of similar confraternities and thus saw them as an investment opportunity, some of which may not always pay rewards as anticipated—much as an angel investor or a venture capitalist today would. Furthermore, members like Yahei may have seen the loss as the price to pay for the chance to attend the various confraternity gatherings, to eat and drink, and to participate in cultural circles that may have happened at those events.[63] Indeed, this *mujin* confraternity had elements of a cultural circle: the convent put together a collection of "wild poems" (*kyōka*) that had been composed during the confraternity meetings.[64]

Following this failure, Daihongan had difficulties setting up new *mujin* confraternities. The next evidence of its involvement is in a document in 1843, though this document is not very detailed.[65] In 1853, the convent

[62] Kobayashi Keiichirō 小林計一郎, *Zenkōjishi kenkyū* [Research on the History of Zenkōji], 328.

[63] Miyazaki Masaki 宮崎正規, '*Daihongan Shōninsama mujinkō*' [On the Daihongan Abbess's Mujin Confraternity], 53.

[64] The poems are collected in a hand-written book entitled *Wild poems and scribbles composed during Daihongan Abbess's mujin confraternity* (*Daihongan Shōninsama gomujin no setsu rakugaki kyōka nari* 大本願上人様御無尽之節落書狂歌也) Daihongan 1 Fuku 2 1153.056.

[65] Daihongan Documents Fuku 2 68.115.

relied on the neighborhood elders (*machidoshiyori*) to persuade people to invest in another *mujin*. It is unclear why the elders had to become involved; people may have been careful with their funds because of a recent disastrous earthquake in 1847, or they were wary to participate because they remembered the failed 1816–1826 confraternity. In any case, because of the involvement of the elders, it is difficult to determine whether people joined to invest money, to participate in a cultural group, or if they were coerced.[66]

In his examination of *mujin* and *tanomoshi* confraternities, Tetsuo Najita rather optimistically had stated that they were based on "trust, promise, and contract". The case of Daihongan's 1816–1826 confraternity demonstrates what happens when those are broken. This case further demonstrates that even confraternities managed by supposedly trustworthy and stable institutions such as large temples or shrines could fail, resulting in the loss of money or even the loss of lives for investors.

Najita argues that these mutual financing associations organized by a contract did not have the legal backing of outside authorities, yet investors in Daihongan's relied on several levels of outside authority when the confraternity's contract was breached. When discussions with Daihongan's administrators failed, the investors called upon Daikanjin as the local authority, Matsushiro as a neighboring domainal power, and Kan'eiji as Daihongan and Daikanjin's administrative/sectarian headquarters in an attempt to reach some form of agreeable conclusion to the situation. They turned to threats of violence when these means failed.

In Najita's analysis, samurai, aristocrats, and other members of the ruling classes were not involved in the running of these confraternities—he even goes so far as to say that "the *kō* [confraternity] is significant precisely because of the absence of aristocratic influence and participation".[67] That being said, as Daihongan's confraternity demonstrates, these confraternities were not always controlled by commoners. These confraternities were sometimes organized and controlled by administrators in charge of the rulers' coffers. That the convent's 1816–1826 confraternity's funds were mismanaged or misappropriated demonstrates that these administrators did not always have the financial knowhow to

[66] Kobayashi Keiichirō 小林計一郎, *Zenkōjishi kenkyū* [Research on the History of Zenkōji], 328.

[67] Najita, *Ordinary Economies in Japan*, 83.

manage the group and distribute the funds responsibly. Furthermore, the heavy-handed manner in which Yoshimura attempted to restart the confraternity without paying its current members demonstrates that these administrators did not always have the best interests of the investors in mind; rather, they were concerned with the well-being of the ruler's coffers or their own pockets. Finally, that membership in the later 1853 confraternity may have been coerced, rather than voluntary, brings home the point that some of these "mutual" financing confraternities may have existed not for the benefit of the groups' members, but for the rulers who organized them.

6 Conclusions

The cases above show the intricate world of Buddhist lending and borrowing in Japan's early modern period. This went beyond borrowing a few coins from a temple's deity in the hopes that it would bring luck, as discussed in Saikaku's story. As we have seen, some temples and convents offered direct loans to trusted borrowers, but also borrowed extensively. Temples organized financial confraternities that provided funding and investment opportunities for themselves and those in their neighborhoods. Some high-ranking temples were allowed to manage endowments and could use those to fund the restoration of their own temple buildings, but they also used them to give no-interest loans in support of locals affected by disasters. Since lawsuits on loans from these endowments could be brought before shogunal government, they were used as low-risk investment opportunities by wealthy commoners. In other words, Buddhist lending could be used to refurbish temple structures, support local residents, or as an investment (regardless of our views of the immorality of the borrowers). In this way, they mirrored other forms of lending and investment practices in early modern Japan.

In each of these cases, temples either lent their own capital out, or they were intermediaries (who may have received a cut of the deal) between borrowers and lenders (investors). Their connections were the bedrock of their function. These connections were formed within pre-defined clerical networks (Daihongan lending to its own branch temple), or within the territory and geographic boundaries of a temple (Zenkōji's endowment being lent to people within its own lands). Beyond clerical networks and territory, temples would work directly with people or entities that had solid, reliable credentials (Daihongan lending to the vassals of important warlords). In cases where these connections were non-existent, they could be forged (in both senses of the word: faked and created), linking distant borrowers and lenders through two sets of loan documents, as happened at Bukkōji Temple.

Buddhist credit activity existed in flux between formal and informal lending. Many supporting documents may not have survived, but it was common practice for all loans to and from Buddhist temples to be recorded in loan documents and financial ledgers. These included name seals by the borrowers on the amount borrowed and the signature portion of the document. However, if issues arose with direct loans or financial confraternities, they were to be resolved between the lender and the borrower. Public authorities only rarely intervened, allowing temples to establish and (often) strengthen their connections not just because they were the conduit to and from credit, but because they also shaped the social and communal fabric that held these relationships together.

Archival Sources and Literature

Buyō Inshi, *Lust, Commerce, and Corruption: An Account of What I Have Seen and Heard*, translated by John Breen et al. (New York, 2014).

De Bary, W.M. Theodore, Carol Gluck, and Arthur E. Tiedeman (eds.), *Sources of Japanese Tradition* volume 2: *1600 to 2000* (Columbia, 2013).

Colcutt, Martin, *Five Mountains: The Rinzai Zen Monastic Institution in Medieval Japan* (Cambridge, 1981).

Gay, Suzanne, *The Moneylenders of Late Medieval Kyoto* (Honolulu, 2001).

Gernet, Jacques, *Buddhism in Chinese Society: An Economic History from the Fifth to the Tenth Centuries* (New York, 1995).

Groemer, Gerald, 'The Guild of the Blind in Tokugawa Japan', in: *Monumenta Nipponica* 56:3 (2001), 349-380.

Ihara, Saikaku, *The Japanese Family Storehouse, or, The Millionaire's Gospel Modernised (Cambridge, 1959).*

Keiichirō, Kobayashi 小林計一郎. *Zenkōjishi Kenkyū* 善光寺史研究 [Research on the History of Zenkōji] (Nagano, 2000).

Kojiruien Database 古事類苑データベース hōritsu bu 3 [Database of the Lexical Encyclopedia of Historical Documents, Legal Section 3] http://base1.nijl.ac.jp/~kojiruien/.

Leupp, Gary P., *Servants, Shophands, and Laborers in the Cities of Tokugawa Japan* (Princeton, 1992).

Mitchell, Matthew Steven, 'Beyond the Convent Walls: The Local and Japan-wide Activities of Daihongan's Nuns in the Early Modern Period (c. 1550–1868)' (unpublished dissertation, Duke University, 2016).

Mitchell, Matthew, 'Borrowing from the Buddha: Buddhist Temples as Financial Centers in Premodern East Asia', in: *Education about Asia* 24:2 (2019), 51-54.

Mitchell, Matthew, 'Regulating Chance: Buddhist Temple Lotteries, Government Oversight, and Anti-Buddhist Discourse in Early Modern Japan', in: *Journal of Cultural Economy* 16:5 (2022), 716-732.

Miyazaki, Masaki 宮崎正規. 'Kinsei Kōki Ni Okeru Zenkōji Machi No Shin'yō Jijō – Daihongan Shōninsama Mujinkō o Meguru Shiron - 近世後期における善光寺町の信用事情 — 大本人様無尽講をめぐる試論 —' [The Situation of Credit in Zenkōji Town in the End of the Early Modern Period: An Essay on the Daihongan Abbess's Mujin Confraternity], in: *Shishi Kenkyū Nagano* 市誌研究ながの [City Research Magazine Nagano] 18 (February 2011), 49–55.

Nagano City Public Archives 長野市立公文書館. Daihongan Documents fuku 2 61.020.

Nagano City Public Archives 長野市立公文書館. Daihongan Documents fuku 2 65.085.

Nagano City Public Archives 長野市立公文書館. Daihongan Documents fuku 2 68.115.

Nagano City Public Archives 長野市立公文書館. Daihongan Documents fuku 2 68.116.

Nagano City Public Archives 長野市立公文書館. Daihongan Documents fuku 2 69.139.

Nagano City Public Archives 長野市立公文書館. Daihongan Documents fuku 2 69.140.

Nagano City Public Archives 長野市立公文書館. Daihongan Documents fuku 2 71.167.

Nagano City Public Archives 長野市立公文書館. *Wild poems and scribbles composed during Daihongan Abbess's mujin confraternity* (*Daihongan Shōninsama gomujin no setsu rakugaki kyōka nari* 大本願上人様御無尽之節落書狂歌也) Daihongan 1 Fuku 2 1153.056.

Nagano City Public Archives 長野市立公文書館. Sanadake monjo [Sanada Clan Documents] 3 Fuku 2 1548.481.

Nagano Kenshi Kankōkai (ed.), *Nagano Kenshi : Kinsei Shiryō Hen* 長野県史 : 近世史料編 [Nagano Prefectural History: Early Modern Historical Documents] Vol. 7–1 (Nagano-shi, 1971).

Najita, Tetsuo, *Ordinary Economies in Japan: A Historical Perspective, 1750–1950* (Berkeley, 2009).

Oka, Yoshiko, 岡佳子, *Nihon no shūkyō to jenda- ni kansuru kokusai sōgō kenkyū: Amadera chōsa no seika wo kiso toshite II Reikanji monjo mokuroku* 日本の宗教とジェンーに関する国際総合研究: 尼寺調査の成果を基礎として *II* 霊鑑寺文書目録 [Comprehensive International Research on Japanese Religions and Gender: Using results from a survey of convents as a base, Vol. II, a list of Reikanji's archival materials] (Nishinomiya, 2009).

Oka, Yoshiko, *Nihon no shūkyō to jenda- ni kansuru kokusai sōgō kenkyū: Amadera chōsa no seika wo kiso toshite III Chūgūji monjo mokuroku* 日本の宗教とジェンダーに関す国際総合研究: 尼寺調査の成果を基礎として *III* 中宮寺文書目録 [Comprehensive International Research on Japanese Religions and Gender: Using results from a survey of convents as a base, Vol. III, a list of Chūgūji's archival materials] (Nishinomiya, 2009).

Oka Yoshiko (ed.), *Nihon no shūkyō to jenda- ni kansuru kokusai sōgō kenkyū: Amadera chōsa no seika wo kiso toshite IV Jijuin monjo mokuroku* 日本の宗教とジェンダーに関する 際総合研究: 尼寺調査の成果を基礎として *IV* 慈受院文書目録 [Comprehensive International Research on Japanese Religions and Gender: Using results from a survey of convents as a base, Vol. IV, a list of Jijuin's archival materials] (Nishinomiya, 2009).

Pratt, Edward E., *Japan's Protoindustrial Elite: The Economic Foundations of the Gōnō* (Cambridge, 2008).

Sakudō, Yōtarō, 'The Management Practices of Family Business', in: Chie Nakane and Shinzaburo Oishi (eds.), *Tokugawa Japan: The Social and Economic Antecedents of Modern Japan* (Tokyo, 1990), 147–166.

Sakurai, Tokutarō 桜井徳太郎, *Kōshūdan seiritsu katei no kenkyū* 講集団成立過程の研究 [Research on the Process of Formation of Confraternities] (Tokyo, 1962).

Stanley, Amy, *Stranger in the Shogun's City: A Japanese Woman and Her World* (New York, 2021).

Suzuki, Atsuko, 'Early Monetary Policies of the Tokugawa Shogunate and Merchants' Coping Strategies: 1695–1736', in: *Discussion Papers in Economics and Business* (discussion paper, 2021).

Takatsukasa, Seigyoku 鷹司誓玉, 'Zenkōji Chishō Shōnin No Shōgai 善光寺智昭上人の生涯' [The Life of Abbess Chishō of Zenkōji], in: *Bukkyō Daigaku Kenkyū Kiyō* 佛教大學研究紀要 [Research Bulletin of Bukkyō University] 62 (1978), 190–263.

Tamamuro, Fumio 圭室文雄, *Nihon Bukkyō shi: Kinsei* 日本仏教史近世 [History of Japanese Buddhism: Early Modern Period] (Tokyo, 1987).

Totman, Conrad, *Early Modern Japan* (Berkeley, 1995).

Vaporis, Constantine Nomikos, *Breaking Barriers: Travel and the State in Early Modern Japan* (Cambridge, 1994).

Vaporis, Constantine Nomikos, *Tour of Duty : Samurai, Military Service in Edo, and the Culture of Early Modern Japan* (Honolu, 2008).

Vesey, Alexander M., 'Entering the Temple: Priests, Peasants, and Village Contention in Tokugawa Japan', in: *Japanese Journal of Religious Studies* 28:3-4 (2001), 293-328.

Vesey, Alexander M., 'The Buddhist Clergy and Village Society in Early Modern Japan' (unpublished dissertation, Princeton University, 2003).

Yang, Lien-Sheng, *Money and Credit in China, a Short History* (Cambridge, 1952).

Yang, Lien-Sheng, *Studies in Chinese Institutional History* (Cambridge, 1961).

Yokoyama, Yuriko, 'Expanding and Multilayering Networks in Nineteenth-Century Japan: The Case of the Shin-Yoshiwara Red-Light District', in: Bettina Gramlich-Oka et al. (eds.) *Women and Networks in Nineteenth-Century Japan* (Michigan, 2020).

Ottoman Guilds as Credit-Providing Institutions from the Late 17th to the Early 19th Century

Konstantinos Giakoumis

1 Introduction

This chapter explores how, in the absence of banks, guilds in the Ottoman Empire formed capital and lent it in the form of credit to its members. In this way, Ottoman guilds established credit markets and what might be called a proto-bank financial environment. Guilds as credit suppliers and financers of public debt are better studied in Western Europe than the eastern Mediterranean.[1] This is also due to the fact that, to my knowledge, only two guild registers from the Ottoman Balkans have been fully

[1] Oscar Gelderblom and Joost Jonker, 'With a View to Hold: The Emergence of Institutional Investors on the Amsterdam Securities Market during the Seventeenth and Eighteenth Centuries', in: Jeremy Atack and Larry Neal (eds.), *The Origins and Development of Financial Markets and Institutions from the Seventeenth Century to the Present* (Cambridge, 2009), 71–98; Vanessa Harding, 'The Crown, the City, and the Orphans: The City of London and its Finances, 1400–1700', in: Marc Boone, C.A. Davids, and Paul Janssens (eds.), *Urban Public Debts: Urban Government and the Market for Annuities in Western Europe (fourteenth-eighteenth centuries)* (Turnhout, 2003), 51–60.

K. Giakoumis (✉)
LOGOS University College, Tirana, Albania
e-mail: konstantinos.giakoumis@kulogos.edu.al

C. van Bochove and J. Levy (eds.), *Beyond Banks*, Palgrave Studies in the History of Finance,
https://doi.org/10.1007/978-3-031-75819-5_11

published to date: the register of the Plovdiv *abadjis* (tailors, weavers, or vendors of *aba*, a sort of coarse fabric)[2] and the register of the guild of tailors[3] of Voskopoja. Although research on the Ottoman guilds is quite substantial, our understanding of their capital formation before the rise of banks in the Ottoman Empire remains very limited, as I shall demonstrate in the literature review below. This chapter aspires to fill this gap by looking into the Ottoman guilds as cash *vakıfs*.

After providing a general outline of their origins, legal framework, and organization, the chapter will explore capital formation through fixed contributions by newly certified masters of the guild and payments of interest. The chapter analyzes guild lending operations and control mechanisms, such as avoiding hoarding (and misuse) of financial resources; lending patterns and risk management strategies by profiling loan applicants; as well as a checks and balances to avoid corruption and abuse of communal funds. This chapter concludes that community-controlled credit markets prevented a few companies from establishing credit supply monopolies or oligopolies, which in turn helped avoid usury and helped finance public and private debt.

This chapter illuminates the role of guilds as local suppliers of credit in the Ottoman world based on research in a variety of primary sources from well-preserved but rarely used archival sources primarily from modern-day Albania. I illuminate practices spanning from as early as 1645 to as late as 1900 by focusing in particular on five registers, which at different times belonged to six different guilds: four from the city of Elbasan (goldsmiths, furriers, boilermakers, and dyers) and two (tailors and grocers) from the city of Voskopoja (alternatively known as Moschopolis in Greek and Moscopole in Romanian).

The registers are invaluable as sources about the various functions and operations of Ottoman guilds from the 17th to the 19th centuries. Apart

[2] Kosmas Apostolidis and Aleksandr Peev, 'Кондика на пловдивския абаджийски еснаф [The Codex of the Guild of Plovdiv Abadjis]', in: *Годишник на Народната библиотека в Пловдив* 1:2 and 3:1 (1931–1932), 1–170 and 1–186.

[3] Konstantinos Giakoumis, 'Glimpses from the Activities of Ottoman Guilds. The Register AQSH. F. 141, D. 2 of the Central Archives of the State, Tirana, Albania', in: *Historiography in Ottoman Europe* (Working Paper No. 4, 2022).

from the guilds' social, cultural, and pedagogical functions,[4] the registers also recorded numerous credit acts along with relevant accounting symbols (for example the strikethrough denoting the repayment of a loan) or notes related to their repayment and annual interest payment when the funds were lent for another year. The statistical analysis of these acts recorded in the last of these registers, used by the tailors of Voskopoja,[5] along with other evidence such as lists of journeymen acquiring tailor-master certification and cap-makers obtaining a second master certification, highlights the contributions of the guild of tailors and their risk management mechanisms.[6] The understanding of the guilds in society is impossible without the study of its economic life.[7] Yet, although research on the guilds is more than a century old[8], our knowledge on

[4] Konstantinos Giakoumis, 'The Social, Cultural and Pedagogical Activities of the Moschopolitan Guild of Tailors (1714–1749)', in: Floresha Dado et al. (eds.), *Qytetërimi i Voskopojës dhe shekulli i iluminizmit në Balkan: Konferencë shkencore ndërkombëtare* (Tirana, 2018), 294–304.

[5] Central Archive of the State (=C.A.S.), Archive of the Metropolic of Korcë 1716–1791, fond 141, dossier 2, ff 1r–37v.

[6] Konstantinos Giakoumis, '"The Voskopoja Guild of Tailors" Credit Lending Operations and Risk Management (1716–27)', *Turkish Historical Review* 9:2 (2018), 242–277; Konstantinos Giakoumis and Juna Miluka, 'The Voskopoja Guild of Tailors' Credit-Lending Operations and Risk Management (1716–1727)', in: *Money and Banking in Albania, from Antiquity to Modern Times, First Conference of the Museum of the Bank of Albania Proceedings, 14–15 June 2017* (Tirana, 2018), 99–110.

[7] Evangelos Hekimoglou, 'Των Ρουφετίων, Μεγάλων και Μικρών. Χριστιανικές Συντεχνίες της Θεσσαλονίκης στα Τέλη του 18ου Αιώνα [Of Big and Small Guilds. Christian Guilds in Thessaloniki at the End of the 18th Century]', in: *Πρακτικά Ε΄ Επιστημονικού Συμποσίου, Χριστιανική Θεσσαλονίκη: Οθωμανική Περίοδος 1430–1912* (Thessaloniki, 1993), 115–136, there 115–116.

[8] Ergin Osman Nuri, *Mecelle-i Umûr-ı Belediyye [The Code of Municipal Affairs]* (Istanbul, 1914–1922); Dimitris Salamangas, 'Τα Ισνάφια και τα Επαγγέλματα επί Τουρκοκρατίας στα Γιάννινα [The Guilds and Crafts in Ioannina during the Turkish Rule]', in: *Epeirotiki Estia* 82:1 (1959) 136–140; continues in 83:1 214–218; 84:1 311–315; 86:1 482–486; 87:1 565–9; Hilal Inalcık, 'Capital Formation in the Ottoman Empire', in: *The Journal of Economic History* 29:1 (1969), 113–119; Gabriel Baer, 'The Administrative, Economic and Social Functions of Turkish Guilds', in: *International Journal of Middle East Studies* 1:1 (1970), 28–50; Georgios Papageorgiou, 'Οι Συντεχνίες στα Γιάννενα κατά το 19ο και τις Αρχές του 20ού Αιώνα (Αρχές 19ου ως 1912) [The Guilds in Ioannina During the 19th and the Beginning of the 20th Century (Beginning of 19th to 1912]' (unpublished PhD dissertation, University of Ionnina, 1982); Hamdija Kreševljaković, 'Esnafi i obrti u Bosni i Hercegovini (1463–1878) [Guilds and crafts in Bosnia and Herzegovina (1463–1878)]', in: *Izabrana Djela* 2 [Selected works 2] (Sarajevo, 1991),

guilds' capital formation, circulation, and management remains limited, especially before the establishment of banking institutions in the Ottoman Empire with the Imperial Ottoman Bank in 1863[9] and the Agricultural Bank in 1888.[10] It is also very recently that we have acquired a deeper understanding of the conditions of decline and abolition of the institution of guilds in the late Ottoman Empire.[11]

The financing of business and trade operations was not impeded by the absence of credit and banking instruments, or Islamic prohibitions of interest and usury.[12] The understudied institution of cash *vakıfs*, which were pious foundations established with the explicit purpose of lending cash and using the interest income to fulfill their goals, constituted an important source of loans in Istanbul, the Balkans, and the Anatolian

991; Amnon Cohen, *The Guilds of Ottoman Jerusalem* (Leiden, 2001); Suraiya Faroqhi, 'Understanding Ottoman Guilds', in: Suraiya Faroghi and Randi Deguilhem (eds.), *Crafts and Craftsmen of the Middle East. Fashioning the Individual in the Muslim Mediterranean* (London, 2005), 3–40; Eunjeong Yi, *Guilds Dynamics in Seventeenth Century Istanbul. Fluidity and Leverage* (Leiden, 2004); Onur Yildirim, 'Ottoman Guilds in the Early Modern Era', in: Jan Lucassen, Tine De Moor, and Jan Luiten van Zanden (eds.), *The Return of the Guilds* (Cambridge, 2008), 73–93; Suraiya Faroqhi, *Bread from the Lion's Mouth: Artisans Struggling for a Livelihood in Ottoman Cities* (New York, 2015); Giakoumis, '"The Voskopoja Guild of Tailors"'; Giakoumis and Miluka, '"The Voskopoja Guild of Tailors"'; Ines Aščerić-Todd, 'Religious Diversity in Ottoman Guilds', in: David Thomas and John Chesworth (eds.), *Christian-Muslim Relations: A Bibliographical History* volume 12: *Asia, Africa and the Americas (1700–1800)* (Leiden, 2018), 29–41.

[9] Christopher Clay, 'The Origins of Modern Banking in the Levant: The Branch Network of the Imperial Ottoman Bank, 1890–1914', in: *The International Journal of Middle East Studies* 26:4 (1994), 589–614; André Autheman, *La Banque impérial ottoman* (Paris, 1996).

[10] D. Quataert, 'Dilemma of Development: The Agricultural Bank and Agricultural Reform in Ottoman Turkey, 1888–1908', in: *The International Journal of Middle East Studies* 6:2 (1975), 210–227.

[11] Pinar Süt, 'The Transformation of the Istanbul Artisans and Traders (Esnaf) in the Late Ottoman Empire: 1839–1922' (unpublished PhD dissertation, Middle East Technical University, 2022).

[12] Şevket Pamuk, 'Institutional Change and the Longevity of the Ottoman Empire, 1500–1800', in: *The Journal of Interdisciplinary History* 35:2 (2004), 225–247, there 231–233; Jared Rubin, 'The Lender's Curse: A New Look at the Origin and Persistence of Interest Bans in Islam and Christianity', in: *The Journal of Economic History* 68:2 (2008), 575–579; Jared Rubin, 'Institutions, the Rise of Commerce and the Persistence of Laws: Interest Restrictions in Islam and Christianity', in: *The Economic Journal* 121:557 (2011), 1310–1339.

urban centers.[13] The reality portrayed above suggests that credit was embedded in the market in Ottoman society.[14]

This picture of market embeddedness will be explored through the Ottoman guilds and their credit operations before the establishment of Ottoman banking institutions. After discussing the principal sources and methodology of this chapter, I focus on the Ottoman guilds as an institution, specifically their capital formation, lending operations and

[13] Şevket Pamuk, *A Monetary History of the Ottoman Empire* (Cambridge, 2000), 76–82 and 89–95; Pamuk, 'Institutional Change', 231–233; Şevket Pamuk, 'The Evolution of Financial Institutions in the Ottoman Empire, 1600–1914', in: *The Financial History Review* 11:1 (2004), 7–32, there 10–12; Abraham L. Udovitch, 'Credit as a Means of Investment in Medieval Islamic Trade', in: *The Journal of the American Oriental Society* 87:3 (1967), 260–264; Baer, 'The Administrative, Economic and Social Functions', 44–46; Ronald C. Jennings, 'Loans and Credit in Early Seventeenth Century Ottoman Judicial Records: The Sharia Court of Anatolian Kayseri', in: *The Journal of the Economic and Social History of the Orient* 16:2–3 (1973), 168–216; Zija Shkodra, *Esnafet Shqiptare (Shekujt XV–XX) [Albanian Guilds (15th–20th Centuries)]* (Tirana, 1973), 89–95; J.E. Mandaville, 'Usurious Piety: The Cash Waqf Controversy in the Ottoman Empire', in: *The International Journal of Middle East Studies* 10:3 (1979), 289–308; Haim Gerber, *Economy and Society in an Ottoman City: Bursa, 1600–1700* (Jerusalem, 1988); Murat Çizakça, 'Cash Waqfs of Bursa, 1555–1823', in: *The Journal of the Economic and Social History of the Orient* 38:3 (1995), 313–354; Murat Çizakça, *A Comparative Evolution of Business Partnerships: The Islamic World and Europe, with Specific Reference to the Ottoman Archives* (Leiden, 1996); Bogdan Murgescu, 'Romanian Information regarding the Ottoman Capital Market: Prince Constantin Brancoveanu's Debt Payments (1694–1703)', in: *Toplum ve Ekonomi* 10:1 (1997), 39–51; Timur Kuran, 'The Provision of Public Goods under Islamic Law: Origins, Impact, and Limitations of the Waqf System', in: *Law & Society Review* 35:4 (2024), 841–897; Eduart Caka, 'Vakefët dhe Funksioni i Tyre në Qytetin e Elbasanit gjatë Shekullit XVII [The Role and Function of Waqf's in the City of Elbasan during the XVII Century]', in: *Studime Historike* 1–2:1 (2016), 99–113, there 110–111; Mehmet Bulut and Cem Korkut, 'A Comparison Between Ottoman Cash Waqfs (CWs) and Modern Interest-Free Financial Institutions', in: *Vakıflar Dergisi* 46:1 (2016), 23–45; Gürer Karagedikli and Ali Coşkun Tunçer, 'Microcredit in the Ottoman Empire: A Review of Cash Waqfs in Transition to Modern Banking', in: Marcella Lorenzini, Cinzia Lorandini, and D'Maris Coffman (eds.), *Financing in Europe: Evolution, Coexistence and Complementarity of Lending Practices from the Middle Ages to Modern Times* (London, 2018), 237–266.

[14] Nicholas J. Theocarakis, 'The Market as Default Mechanism: A History of Economic Thought Perspective', in: Christina Agriantoni, Maria Christina Chatziioannou, and Leda Papastefanaki (eds.), *Markets and Politics. Private Interest and Public Authority, Eighteenth-20th Centuries* (Volos, 2016), 35–49; Michael A. Kallinderis, *Αἱ Συντεχνίαι καὶ ἡ Ἐκκλησία ἐπὶ Τουρκοκρατίας [The Guilds and the Church During the Ottoman Rule]* (Athens, 1973), 22–23; Eleutherios A. Karakitsios, 'Ο Ελληνισμός στην Μητροπολιτική Περιφέρεια Κορυτσάς [Hellenism in the Metropolitan Region of Korça]' (unpublished PhD dissertation, University of Thessaloniki, 2010), 106–107.

application of interest, as well as management of credit risk by profiling borrowers. This chapter does not extend to the period of banking in the Ottoman state, when guild-based lending operations declined from the end of the 19th century and eventually faded out and were ousted from the market at the beginning of the 20th century.

2 Sources and Methods

The primary sources used in this chapter are record-keeping products by the bureaucracies of guilds. Often referred to as social documents, these sources provide information of economic, social, political, and juridical nature, containing accounts of the particular charges or agencies, of meetings and collective business policies pursued by the guilds under consideration.[15] I used descriptive statistics to provide a measurement of the phenomena under consideration.[16] The data, though not always continuous, are homogeneous, and allow the calculation of means, trends, comparisons in particular points of time and incidence of correlation. On the other hand, the mostly unpublished character of these sources[17] prevents good statistical work requiring long runs of data.

The first of the registers[18] belongs to the guild of goldsmiths of the city of Elbasan; it is made of paper and contains multiple acts recording the guild's deliberations extending in 98 folia covering a broad period of time between 1645 and 1900. Some of the acts of this register, together with a few other 18th- and 19th-century acts, have been copied in folios from another, unknown register (the second register used in this chapter) which are currently part of the miscellaneous contents of another dossier which once belonged to the guild of goldsmiths (Gk. *χρυσολάδες*, *χρυσικοί*, or *χρυσικάδες*) of Elbasan[19]; in spite of the small size of the archival fond (fourteen folios), its acts cover a considerable breadth of time, from 1645 to 1824.

[15] Martha Howell and Walter Prevenier, *From Reliable Sources: An Introduction to Historical Methods* (New York, 2001), 22.

[16] Howell and Prevenier, *From Reliable Sources*, 50–55.

[17] Perhaps except for Giakoumis, '"The Voskopoja Guild of Tailors"'.

[18] C.A.S., fond 80, dossier 5.

[19] C.A.S., fond 80, dossier 7.

The third register[20] was found in the archival collection of a local intellectual from Elbasan named Lef Nosi. Its 51 folios provide valuable information about the activities of the guild of Elbasan furriers (Gk. *γουναράδες*). Its acts, copied from the older register (codex, as the guild called it) of the guild some time toward the end of the 19th century or the beginning of the 20th century, span a significant period of time between 1669 until the end of World War I (1918).

A fourth register[21] was retrieved from an Elbasan savant named Simon Kazanxhiu. Its 21 folios contain acts of the guild of boilermakers (*καζαντζίδες* from the Turkish word *kazançi*) of Elbasan dating from 1775 to 1886,[22] while a small part of the remainder[23] contains acts copied from the guild of dyers (*μπογιατζίδες* from the Turkish word *boyaci*) of Elbasan, spanning a great deal of time, from 1689 to 1745. The remaining folios of the dossier are of a mixed nature and content, as they include a 12th- to 13th-century folio, cut in rips,[24] with parts of sermons by Saint John Scholasticus and Saint John Chrysostome, as well as a prayer in Hebrew.

The fifth register considered[25] contains acts from the guild of tailors (Gk. *ραφτάδες*) and grocers (Gk. *μπακαλάδες*) of Voskopoja. The register has been published as a source[26] and broadens our understanding of how the local guild members interacted among themselves in terms of their credit activities. The most part of the register encompasses a range of activities related to the administration, functions, and operations of Voskopoja's guild of tailors. It spans from the foundational act of the register, dated June 10, 1714,[27] to March 15, 1749, when the guild determined the fees for journeymen to open market stalls and addressed various issues regarding members' conduct and the technical standardization of their production.[28] As of May 10, 1750[29] the manuscript was

[20] C.A.S., fond 32, dossier 143.

[21] C.A.S., fond 65, dossier 67.

[22] C.A.S., fond 65, dossier 67, ff 1r–9r.

[23] C.A.S., fond 65, dossier 67, ff 10r–11r.

[24] C.A.S., fond 65, dossier 67, ff 13r–18v.

[25] C.A.S., fond 141, dossier 2.

[26] Giakoumis, 'Glimpses from the Activities of Ottoman Guilds'.

[27] C.A.S., fond 141, dossier 2, f 1r.

[28] C.A.S., fond 141, dossier 2, f 37v.

[29] C.A.S., fond 141, dossier 2, f 46r.

used to record various donations to churches (not confined to the guild of tailors' members) and a few acts of the guild of grocers up to August 7, 1791, when the last entry on the guild's new members was recorded.[30]

All of these manuscripts were written in Greek. Greek was overall the *lingua franca* of business for the Orthodox subjects of the Ottoman Empire, not only in Bulgaria until the late nineteenth century,[31] but also in other culturally, ethnically, and linguistically mixed regions such as Epiros and Albania,[32] although the archive of the guilds of Elbasan also contains some documents in Ottoman Turkish. As to why all of the manuscripts have been unbound, it is possible that they were detached from their binding once they were no longer functional as accounting registers.

Only assumptions can be made as to why the third and fourth registers were not only unbound but also changed hands and why past records were not retained by the guild's administration before passing the register on to another guild. It is likely that the manuscripts were given out to churches or another guild only when their contents had been duly copied in neat registers, as was usual practice in codices,[33] including guild registers.[34] Zija Shkodra accounts that "from the 18th–19th century rich guilds created special registers, on top of a general register or evidence, such as the register of capitals, of loans delinquent, of interests and the small register".[35] It is therefore evident that what we have at hand are

[30] C.A.S., fond 141, dossier 2, f 60r.

[31] R.J. Crampton, *A Concise History of Bulgaria* (Cambridge, 1997), 67; M. Gürbüz, 'Emergence of Bulgarian Nationalism', in: *Güneydoğu Avrupa Araştırmaları Dergisi* 0:16 (2009), 27–51, there 31.

[32] Konstantinos Giakoumis, 'Fourteenth-Century Albanian Migration and the 'relativeautochthony' of the Albanians in Epeiros: The Case of Gjirokastër', in: *Byzantine and Modern Greek Studies* 27:1 (2003), 171–83; Konstantinos Giakoumis, 'Self-Identifications by Himarriots, Sixteenth to Nineteenth Centuries', in: *Erytheia* 37:1 (2016), 205–246; Giakoumis, 'Glimpses from the Activities of Ottoman Guilds'.

[33] Vasilis Katsaros, and Christos Papastathis, 'Προδρομικά Αποσημειώματα. Βραχέα Χρονικὰ Σημειώματα Τεσσάρων Καταστίχων τῆς Μονῆς Τιμίου Προδρόμου Σερρῶν τῶν Ἐτῶν 1730–1806 μετὰ «Παραρτήματος» δύο Γραμμάτων: «Ζητείας» καὶ Ἐπικυρώσεως [Preliminary Annotations. Brief Chronicle Notes of Four Registers of the Monastery of the Holy Forerunner in Serres of the years 1730–1806 together with an Annex of two letters, of *zitiye* and validation]', in: *Serraika Symmikta* 2 (2013), 21–86, there 24.

[34] Shkodra, *Esnafet Shqiptare*, 170–177.

[35] Shkodra, *Esnafet Shqiptare*, 171, author's translation.

folios from casual (or general) registers, in which facts and information of interest to the guilds were kept. This explains why some of their folios remained blank in anticipation of later completions.[36]

3 The Ottoman Guilds

To understand the ways in which the Ottoman guilds organized their business and hierarchy, formed capital and engaged in credit operations, it is indispensable to delve into the very institution of the guild and its internal structure. Prior to the acquisition of the form and organization of guilds in the 17th to 19th centuries, merchant and craft guilds developed in stages since the Byzantine Empire.[37] Leo VI the Wise's *Book of the Prefect* records a great number of crafts and craftsmen organized in guilds known with names of associative organizations supervised by local authorities.[38] Despite local variations, the general form of guild organization during the Byzantine state[39] can be traced throughout the Empire, including cities like Ioannina. The transition of Ioannina to the Ottoman Empire did not result in large-scale destruction or population displacements.[40] Hence, in many parts of the Balkans, the guilds managed to adapt their pre-Ottoman practices to the new political, religious, and legal

[36] See, for instance, C.A.S., fond 141, dossier 2, ff 11r 26v.

[37] Papageorgiou, 'Οι Συντεχνίες', 17–25.

[38] Papageorgiou, 'Οι Συντεχνίες', 17; Vaso Nerantzi-Varmazi, 'Συντεχνίες Εμπόρων στην Κωνσταντινούπολη τον 10° αιώνα [Commercial Guilds in Constantinople in the 10th Century]', in: Christine Angelidis (ed.), *Πρακτικά του Α' Διεθνούς Συμποσίου, Η Καθημερινή Ζωή στο Βυζάντιο, Τομές και Συνέχειες στην Ελληνιστική και Ρωμαϊκή Παράδοση, Αθήνα 15–17 Σεπτεμβρίου 1988* (Athens, 1989), 353–361; Dimitrios G. Mavridis and Konstantinos I. Vatalis, 'Best and Bad Practices—The Imperial Guilds of Constantinople', in: *Procedia Engeneering* 84:1 (2014), 689–697, there 425–434.

[39] George C. Maniatis, 'The Domain of Private Guilds in the Byzantine Economy, Tenth to Fifteenth Centuries', in: *The Dumbarton Oaks Papers* 55: (2001), 339–369.

[40] Angeliki Hadjimichali, 'Μορφές από τη Σωματειακή Οργάνωση των Ελλήνων στην Οθωμανική Αυτοκρατορία: Οι συντεχνίες—τα Ισνάφια [Forms of the Corporate Organisation of the Greeks in the Ottoman Empire: Guilds—the *Esnaf*]', in: *L' Hellénisme Contemporain*: *"Η Πεντακοσιοστή Επέτειος από της Αλώσεως της Κων/πόλεως», 29 Μαΐου 1453–1953* (Athens, 1953), 297–303.

frame as indicated by the early Ottoman organization of the guilds of Edirne, conquered by the Ottomans in 1361.[41]

Corporate forms of craft organization modeled after medieval institutions existed since the 13th century not only in Venice and other Italian city states, but also in the Ottoman Balkans. For example, there are records pertaining to the guild of notaries of Durrës, and the guild of shoemakers of Prizren. The latter of these was headed by a headmaster named Rajko in 1348. We also know that in the course of the 15th century there were guilds (organized under the name *scuola*) in Shkodra (1416) and Drisht (1442), northern Albania.[42] Shortly before the capitulation of two very important urban centers for the region, Ioannina and Berat, Sultan Mehmet II extended a special *firman*[43] guaranteeing free markets to the corporations of both cities in recognition of their importance to the supply needs of the Ottoman army.[44] The guilds of Berat were granted tax breaks in return for their contributions to the protection of the castle of Vlora, a port city of paramount importance to the Ottomans as the westernmost port of Via Egnatia.[45] Egro has published a copy of a *kanunname*[46] for the registration of a *vilayet*, an administrative division in the late Ottoman Empire corresponding to a province, for which a special *berat* (edict or privilege title) was drafted dating from the time of Mehmet II. It orders the registration of rice farmers holding

[41] Eleni Vourazeli-Marinakou, *Αἱ ἐν Θράκῃ Συντεχνίαι τῶν Ἑλλήνων κατὰ τὴν Τουρκοκρατίαν [The Guilds of Greeks in Thrace during the Ottoman Rule]* (Thessaloniki, 1950), 58–9.

[42] Shkodra, *Esnafet Shqiptare*, 82–84.

[43] The *firman* is a royal decree issued by a ruler in an Islamic state, the Ottoman sultan in this occasion.

[44] Dritan Egro, 'Christianity Versus Islam in the Early Stages of the Ottoman Domination in Albanian Lands (14th–16th Centuries)' (unpublished PhD dissertation, Bilkent University, 2003), 268.

[45] Shkodra, *Esnafet Shqiptare*, 83–84; Papageorgiou, 'Οι Συντεχνίες', 25; Egro, 'Christianity versus Islam', 266–272.

[46] The *kannuname* is a genre of government documents containing legal regulations combining "sultanic edicts with passages describing regional conditions". See: Heather L. Ferguson, *The Proper Order of Things. Language, Power, and Law in Ottoman Administrative Discourses* (Stanford, 2018), 66–105.

the seeds of the rice farmers' guild.[47] This normative document is a good indication of the continuation of guilds from pre-Ottoman to Ottoman times. As a highly pragmatic state, the Ottoman Empire had no reason to interrupt lucrative trade, but it did establish some state control over it.

Since the 16th century, the guilds of the Ottoman Empire had experienced remarkable growth and shouldered a fair portion of their communities' economic obligations. A city council of seven notables in the 16th century (to increase to 12th in the 17th century), governed the city, the communal economic affairs[48] and oversaw the activities of the guilds. Their head—the "grand archon"—was nominated by the sultan by way of a *firman*.[49] A statute of 36 articles, issued in 1713, regulated the relations between the community, the Church, and the guilds. It stipulated that the guilds were to maintain their superior status over any other form of associative corporate organization and was awarded judicial decision-making rights. The guild's council led by its headmaster exerted judicial jurisdictions as a court of first instance, the higher court being the guilds' grand council.[50] We do not have precise information about what the early 18th-century economic development in the Ottoman Balkans meant for guilds; however, we can make some assumptions by looking at towns such as Voskopoja. Shkodra writes that in the second half of the 18th century Voskopoja had fourteen guilds, a number that is probably not representative of Voskopoja's guilds in the entire course of the 18th century.[51]

[47] Dritan Egro, *Ligji Osman ndër Shqiptarët e Mesjetës së Vonë (Gjysma e Dytë e Shekullit XV—Fillimshekulli XVII) [The Ottoman Law Among Late Medieval Albanians (second half of fifteenth century—beginning of 18th Century)]* (Tirana, 2012), 275–286.

[48] Socrates Petmezas, 'Διαχείριση των Κοινοτικών Οικονομικών και Κοινωνική Κυριαρχία. Η Στρατηγική των Προυχόντων: Ζαγορά 1784–1822 [The Administration of Communal Economics and Social Domination. The Archons' Strategy: Zagora 1784–1822]', in: *Mnemon* 13:1 (1991), 77–102; Socrates D. Petmezas, 'Communities in Eighteenth- and Early Nineteenth-Century Ottoman Greece: Their Fiscal Functions', in: *The Princeton Papers: Interdisciplinary Journal of Middle Eastern Studies* 12:1 (2005), 71–127.

[49] Papageorgiou, 'Οι Συντεχνίες', 128–38; Hilal Inalcık, 'The Appointment Procedure of a Guild Warden', in: *Wiener Zeitschrift für die Kunde des Morgenlandes* 76:1 (1986), 135–142.

[50] Nikolaos Pantazopoulos, 'Community Laws and Customs of Western Macedonia under Ottoman Rule', in: *Balkan Studies* 2:1 (1961), 1–22; Egro, 'Christianity versus Islam', 270–271.

[51] Shkodra, *Esnafet Shqiptare*, 84.

The same act also is indicative of the ways in which the Ottoman state carefully regulated and monitored the corporate environment, as well as how the guilds would resort to higher-level instances to resolve disputes when they were not convinced that a solution could be found and enforced locally: "On 20 July 1733 the furriers, the tanners, the merchants and all of the guilds quarreled with the *ulama*,[52] went to Constantinople and brought the *Kapıcıbaşı*,[53] while the *beylerbey*[54] sent Yahya ağa and were charged with a fine in Elbasan [at the value of] 32 sacks, that is 16,000 *akçe* that is sixteen thousand and we, the guild of furriers, paid 17,000 *akçe*, that is seventeen thousand".[55]

The period from the 17th century until the disintegration of guilds in the 19th century was the heyday of this form of corporate organization. The guilds were governed by written statutes and regulations[56] which were reviewed at times by their assembly. This happened for example on November 29, 1829 when the guild of furriers decided not to allow any apprentices to acquire a second specialization, unless in the craft of their fathers.[57] The guild members were meticulously recorded in special registers, often with their guarantors, as indicated in an act of the Elbasan furriers dated September 17, 1683 recording all of the masters alongside their guarantors.[58]

Decision-making was based on communitarian principles. Every guild held at least one general assembly meeting per year in various places[59] such as in the house of a master,[60] in a church held under the protection of the guild[61] or in a monastery. For example, on September 10,

[52] Name for the group of interpreters of Islam in a city.

[53] The term initially referred to the chief warder of the Porte, but during the period under consideration denoted an office in the sultan's court.

[54] Title for the region's commander-in-chief.

[55] C.A.S., fond 32, dossier 143, f 11r, author's translation.

[56] See, for instance: Nikolaos Veis, 'Εκ του Καταστίχου της Συντεχνίας των Παντοπωλών της Μοσχοπόλεως [A Register of the Voskopoja Guild of Grocers]', in: *Byzantinisch-Neugriechische Jahrbücher* 7:3–4 (1930), 527–528, for the guild of grocers of Voskopoja.

[57] C.A.S., fond 32, dossier 143, f 17r.

[58] C.A.S., fond 32, dossier 143, f 3r–v.

[59] Shkodra, *Esnafet Shqiptare*, 161; Papageorgiou, 'Οι Συντεχνίες', 97.

[60] C.A.S., fond 141, dossier 2, f 12v.

[61] C.A.S., fond 141, dossier 2, f 10v, 22r and 12v.

1812 the Elbasan boilermakers held an assembly in the nearby monastery of Saint John-Vladimir under the auspices of its abbot.[62] Meetings were often long so as to optimize the communal obligation—and the meeting included certification testing of qualifying journeymen. Evidence from expenses incurred for food items indicates that these meetings also served as social events. The sources provide information on the food items consumed in such meetings where one observed remarkable continuity from the 17th until the 19th century.[63] Food items included meat, wine, bread, and *raki*, while such food items as octopus, certainly a delicacy for continental Balkans, were also provided at times, as we learn from the list of expenses recorded in the minutes of the 1716 assembly of the guild of tailors of Voskopoja.[64]

The guild bureaucracy was very serious about keeping records and archives. The introductory note of the guild of the Elvasan boilermakers' register (entered on December 15, 1775) was written over the course of the 19th century, and includes an explanation that the older acts were copied because the old "codex" was "burnt" (in reality damaged, as folios of the manuscript were still readable to copy).[65] The deliberations made in such assemblies were painstakingly recorded in minutes, as shown in the April 22, 1662 assembly of the Elbasan goldsmiths' guild,[66] a practice that continued well into the 19th century. The minutes and records also included follow-ups to ensure implementation; other deliberations of the guild's council were also recorded in registers dedicated to particular sorts of acts.[67]

The guild was governed by an annually elected council (*lonca*). The Voskopoja guild of tailors' register[68] from 1711 to 1715, states that the guild of Voskopoja tailors was headed by Father Theodore the *Skeuophylax* (church title for vestry-keeper) in the quality of headmaster (Gk.

62 C.A.S., fond 65, dossier 67, f 6v.

63 For an example for the assembly of the furriers of Elbasan of May 22, 1677, see: C.A.S., fond 32, dossier 143, f 1r.

64 Giakoumis, 'Glimpses from the Activities of Ottoman Guilds', 18; C.A.S., fond 141, dossier 2, f 12v.

65 C.A.S., fond 65, dossier 67, f 1r, author's translation.

66 C.A.S., fond 80, dossier 5, f 12v.

67 Shkodra, *Esnafet Shqiptare*, 171; Papageorgiou, 'Οι Συντεχνίες'.

68 C.A.S., fond 141, dossier 2, f 10r–v.

Πρωτομάστουρας or *κεχαϊάς'*),[69] whose guild accounts were cleared in a public meeting held on January 10, 1715. Another term used for the headmaster is *müteveli* (Gk. *μουτεβελής*), as we learn from the minutes of a meeting of the Elbasan guild of goldsmiths to audit the accounts of their head.[70] An act of the register of tailors from Voskopoja dated July 7, 1743 provides some insight into the structure of the guild's council.[71] At the time, the guild of Voskopoja's tailors was governed by a council of seven, headed by Theodore Mantoukas, son of Giankos, in his quality as headmaster (Gk. *πρωτομαΐστωρ*) and protector of the guild. Other members of the governing council included five administrators (Tr. *Kâhya*; Gk. *κιχαϊάδες*): Andrias Ouria; Giankos Kota, son of Pousia; Mitros Pokia; Kostis Giannousiou; and Simos Chrysikou. The seventh council member came from the ranks of the journeymen, the head-journeyman (Tr. *Kalfabaşı*; Gk. *καλφαπάσης*) Konstis Kostika.[72] The act records the names of the sons of masters, servant journeymen, and cap-makers, who, in the process of getting certified as master tailors by the craft's guild, kissed the hand of the guild's archons (that is headmasters).

The competences of the guild's council were broad. First and foremost, the council was expected to plead and safeguard the guild's common causes. An act of the guild of furriers of Elbasan dated June 11, 1740 informs us of the impact of widespread famine on the temporary deterioration of the quality of their products.[73] They exercised price controls in raw materials, as indicated by an earlier act of the same guild, dated October 4, 1705, whereby the furriers decided in their assembly that they should get the fox fur at no more than 90 *akçe* and the marten fur for no more than 60 *akçe* upon threat of a 600 *akçe* fine.[74] It was relatively easy to establish price and quality controls, since Ottoman craftsmen, especially in the 18th century, used to work next to one another in the same

[69] C.A.S., fond 141, dossier 2, f 18v.

[70] C.A.S., fond 80, dossier 5, f 20v.

[71] C.A.S., fond 141, dossier 2, f 32v.

[72] C.A.S., fond 141, dossier 2, f 32v.

[73] C.A.S., fond 32, dossier 143, f 17r.

[74] C.A.S., fond 32, dossier 143, f 7v.

streets.[75] Some masters, however, had their workshops in their home.[76] Yet, the guild's council checked and controlled violations, occasionally imposing fines as administrative measures, and holding plenary assemblies of the guild's members on an as-needed basis.[77]

The maintenance of the guild's cohesion and discipline was of paramount importance. On July 22, 1728, the assembly of furriers decided to set a fine for those of its members who swear at their mothers, at each other, or who spit on each other. The penalty imposed over the perpetrators did not only apply to the guild of furriers, but also to the guild of tanners, perhaps due to the damage such behavior brought to all involved in the fur industry. Perhaps the most interesting provision was that the penalty was in the form of rams,[78] whose slaughter would supply meat for socializing events and bonding. The establishment of strong communitarian bonds was not limited to the living members of the guild, but also extended to their deceased peers, as evidenced by lists of names of deceased masters compiled for the purpose of commemoration in religious services sponsored by the guilds. The July 21, 1698 and July 15, 1781 lists of the guild of furriers of Elbasan are evidence of the continuity of this practice.[79]

Fines were also imposed upon infringement of competition rules, at least as per the guild's understanding.[80] The Elbasan furriers, for example, decided on October 6, 1746 that they would charge a fine to all business associates with two workshops, instead of one.[81] The council was also responsible for implementing the guild's regulatory framework and its

[75] Shkodra, *Esnafet Shqiptare*, 67–87; Maria Tsikaloudi, 'Η Αγορά στο Χάνδακα, 1669–1765: Συντεχνίες και Καθορισμός των Τιμών [The Market in Candy, 1669–1765: Guilds and Price Determination]', in: *Ta Istorika* 12:22 (1995), 49–84; Suraiya Faroqhi et al., *An Economic and Social History of the Ottoman Empire* volume 2: *1600–1914* (Cambridge, 1997), 696.

[76] Shkodra, *Esnafet Shqiptare*, 65.

[77] Papageorgiou, 'Οι Συντεχνίες', 20–21; Petraq Pepo, 'Materiale Dokumentare mbi Veprimtarinë e Zanatçinjve të Korçës e të Voskopojës në shek. XVIII dhe XIX [Documentary Materials on the Activity of Korça and Voskopoja Craftsmen in the 18th and 19th Century]', in: *Studime Historike* 1:1 (1967), 165–181.

[78] C.S.A., fond 32, dossier 143, f 10v.

[79] C.A.S., fond 32, dossier 143, f 10r.

[80] Giakoumis, '"The Voskopoja Guild of Tailors"', 257–258.

[81] C.A.S., fond 32, dossier 143, f 11v.

periodic revisions, particularly concerning quality assurance. For instance, the guild of Elbasan goldsmiths decided in an assembly on July 27, 1802, to impose an additional regulatory condition on the standard purity of gold used in the decoration of arms, with violations subject to fines or exclusion.[82] An interesting case of pleading the interests of the guild of tailors from Voskopoja in rapport with the interests of other guilds and formulating new regulations vis-à-vis its operations has been presented in another study.[83]

4 Capital Formation and the Ottoman Guilds

The Ottoman guilds, through their councils, also ensured capital formation for the accomplishment of the guild's social welfare mandate and managed the uninterrupted supply of their products in the markets. The Ottoman guild's stratification mirrored the stratification of Ottoman society. The guild's council members belonged to the guild's higher social class. The lower ranks of the guild consisted of the masters, the journeymen, and the apprentices.[84] The lowest rank of the apprentice (Tr. *çırak*) is also referred to by the term used for the title: "children for the craft" (Gk. *παιδιὰ διὰ τὴν τέχνην*) or servicemen (Tr. *Hizmetli*; Gk. *Χουσμετλής*)[85]; the apprenticeship period is likewise called *χουσμέτι* (Tr. *Hizmet*),[86] that is service. The same rank in the 1779 register of Voskopoja's grocers is found with the even more belittling term of "servant" (Tr. *hizmet-kâr*; Gk. *χουσμικιάρης*) or even "slave".[87] The second-lowest rank of the guild's hierarchy was that of a journeyman, called "student" (Tr. *Kalfa*; Gk. *μαθητής* or *κάλφας*),[88] whose head, as noted above, was member of the guild's administration council. The

[82] C.S.A., fond 80, dossier 7, f 5r–v.

[83] Giakoumis, '"The Voskopoja Guild of Tailors"', 255–257.

[84] Papageorgiou, 'Οι Συντεχνίες', 26 and 38–39; Georgios Papageorgiou, *Η Μαθητεία στα Επαγγέλματα (16ος-20ός αι.) [The Apprenticeship (16th–20th c.)]* (Athens, 1986); Photeini Karlaphti-Mouratidi,'Η Μαθητεία στα Επαγγέλματα στην Κέρκυρα [Apprenticeship in Corfu]', in: *Εώα και Εσπέρια* 6:1 (2006), 133–148.

[85] C.A.S., fond 141, dossier 2, f 22r, author's translation.

[86] C.A.S., fond 141, dossier 2, f 11v.

[87] Veis, 'Εκ του Καταστίχου, 527. "Slave" in this context does not necessarily mean "enslaved person", but serf or otherwise indentured worker.

[88] C.A.S., fond 141, dossier 2, f 37r, v, author's translation.

guild's middle class consisted of masters, whose position was strengthened after Sultan Mustafa III's *firman* regarding guild matters.[89] The duration of apprenticeship and training was two to three years per stage of apprenticeship and varied from place-to-place following customary norms.[90] Two acts recorded in the register of the guild of Voskopoja's tailors make clear that the apprenticeship cycle was three years in total,[91] although an additional three years' service was required from journeymen who were not sons of masters, before being granted the right to open a workshop on their own or with a partner.[92]

Completion of apprenticeship was marked with a certificate issued upon testing of journeymen before the guild, an occasion also functioning as a major socializing event.[93] The registers studied in this chapter record in a painstaking fashion the administration of testing and the names of newly certified masters. Although it is uncertain whether or not the registers at hand include all testing administrations or only some, Fig. 1, in conjunction with similar data presented in a previous study,[94] reveal patterns. First, in spite of the dataset's fragmentation, it is possible to determine a pattern of testing periodicity that varied from guild to guild. The most preferred season for assembling, testing, and certification was the summer, followed by the autumn and, more rarely in spring, while there was clear avoidance of winter, due to weather conditions not favoring great gatherings that needed open space. Second, as might be expected, the testing frequency highly depended on the needs of each guild. Likewise, the guild's needs and local market demand also determined the number of journeymen tested and certified. The Elbasan dyers, for example, appeared to admit one newly certified member per year in their guild, thereby indicating strict control of the members and rather

[89] Papageorgiou, *Η Μαθητεία στα Επαγγέλματα*, 70–72, 125–38; Diamanti A. Ihčiev, 'Esnafski Documenti i Esnafski Organizacii v Tursko Vreme [Guild Documents and Guild Organizations in the Turkish Time]', in: *Spisanie na Balgarskoto Ikonomicesko Druzestvo* 3:1 (1907), 345–452.

[90] Papageorgiou, *Η Μαθητεία στα Επαγγέλματα*, 38–39, and 77–79, who also mentions that the duration of training was not legally sanctioned; Papageorgiou, *Η Μαθητεία στα Επαγγέλματα*, 78; Karlaphti-Mouratidi,'Η Μαθητεία στα Επαγγέλματα, 137–138.

[91] C.A.S., fond 141, dossier 2, ff 11v and 22r.

[92] C.A.S., fond 141, dossier 2, f 22r.

[93] Papageorgiou, *Η Μαθητεία στα Επαγγέλματα*, 109–111.

[94] Giakoumis, '"The Voskopoja Guild of Tailors"', 261.

small market demand. On the contrary, the guild of boilermakers of Elbasan appeared to admit between eighteen and 76 new members from 1776 to 1866, though at a periodicity of four to ten years, if the register considered[95] is the sole one used and is complete. Figure 1 indicates an increase of the number of newly tested and certified masters from the late eighteenth century to the third decade of the nineteenth century, which should be viewed as increased market demand for the respective products in the city of Elbasan.

The meetings took place in a church, monastery or at the house of the headmaster[96] and they were used as an opportunity for socialization and in-group bonding. A note in the register of the guild of furriers of

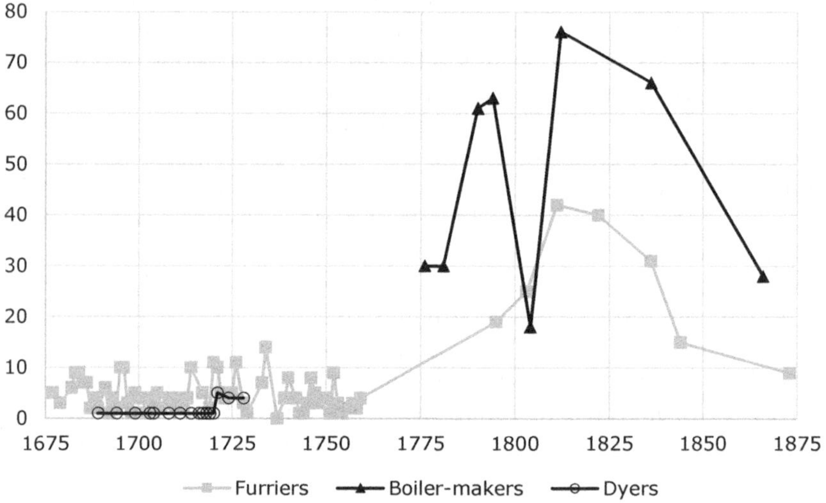

Fig. 1 Certified new masters in Elbasan, 1671–1873 (*Source* Data extracted and elaborated from C.A.S., Archive of Lef Nosi 1669–1918 (fond 32), dossier 143—register of the guild of furriers; C.A.S., Archive of Simon Kazanxhiu 1775–1866 (fond 65), dossier 67—register of the guild of boilermakers and dyers)

[95] C.A.S., fond 65, dossier 67.

[96] Giakoumis, '"The Voskopoja Guild of Tailors"', 259.

Elbasan dated May 22, 1677[97] records that the expenses incurred for the consumption of food in a meeting held in the house of a certain Jon Hala amounted to 230 *akçe*.[98] Similar practices from Voskopoja, about half a century later, indicate that such practices were regular.[99]

The certificates were awarded during a ceremony. According to the *firman* by Sultan Mustafa III, the conferment ceremony involved the master placing a special belt on the candidates in the presence of other masters and journeymen.[100] It was also customary for the newly certified masters to kiss the hand of their guild's headmaster,[101] a practice that is already mentioned in an act of the guild of goldsmiths of Elbasan dated April 22, 1662, which also records the names of the sons of the masters who got tested and certified on the very day,[102] as well as another act, dated July 17, 1671, from the guild of furriers of Elbasan.[103] It has been suggested that this custom carried over from ancient religious practices, as well as *futuwwa* ceremonies.[104]

Once admitted as new guild members, all masters were entitled and subject to the sundry privileges and obligations dictated by the guild's diverse functions. Guilds often served as "links between the government and the urban population".[105] There are instances where guilds imposed administrative fines for various breaches. For instance, the guild of tailors of Voskopoja imposed a 600 *akçe* fine to Giankos Larou "because he does not get convinced to register at the guild, but he hides himself

[97] C.A.S., fond 32, dossier 143, f 1r: "On 22 May 1677, we, the furriers, assembled in the house of Jon Hala and we expended altogether 230 *akçe* for bread, meat, wine and *raki* from the fund of the guild" (author's translation).

[98] C.A.S., fond 32, dossier 143, f 1r.

[99] Giakoumis, '"The Voskopoja Guild of Tailors"', 259.

[100] Papageorgiou, *Η Μαθητεία στα Επαγγέλματα*, 71–72; Yi, *Guilds Dynamics*, 86–87.

[101] Shkodra, *Esnafet Shqiptare*, 113–28; Papageorgiou, 'Οι Συντεχνίες', 109; Papageorgiou, 1986, 71–2; Karlaphti-Mouratidi, 2006, 138; Faroqhi, 'Understanding Ottoman Guilds', 87; Giakoumis, '"The Voskopoja Guild of Tailors"', 259.

[102] C.A.S., fond 80, dossier 5, 12r.

[103] C.A.S., fond 32, dossier 143, 1v.

[104] Giakoumis, '"The Voskopoja Guild of Tailors"', 259. "Futuwwa ceremonies" refer to initiation or ritual ceremonies associated with a traditional code of conduct and "chivalric" values in medieval Islamic societies. These ceremonies were often linked to youth organizations or guilds and emphasized qualities such as bravery, generosity, and loyalty.

[105] Baer, 'The Administrative, Economic and Social Functions', 33–35.

and because he did not reveal some [individuals] to the Turks".[106] Likewise, Mitros Georgousiou was fined "because he did not accept to take an oath upon excommunication for the case of Giannos Niskou Nitza".[107] Similar records of fines imposed on guild members in Elbasan are evidence that the guilds under consideration were not exceptions. Other functions of the guilds includes fixing prices for raw and processed products and wages. The registers considered do not reveal any evidence of supplying government services and labor, as has been recorded in Ottoman Syria.[108]

There is little doubt that the guild operated as a cash *vakıf*, that is charitable organizations created to lend money and use the interest earned to achieve their social mandate.[109] The Ottoman state did not tax such institutions, in spite of suspicions for tax evasion and corruptive practices,[110] because their services substituted for the absence of state and social welfare. Hence, the guilds could afford to donate cash to churches and monasteries—the guild of tailors of Voskopoja, for instance, provides

[106] Giakoumis, '"The Voskopoja Guild of Tailors"', 59–60; Giakoumis, 'Glimpses from the Activities of Ottoman Guilds', 52–53.

[107] C.A.S., fond 139, dossier 2, f 31r, author's translation.

[108] Baer, 'The Administrative, Economic and Social Functions', 36–38; Abdul-Karim Rafeq, 'Craft Organization, Work Ethics, and the Strains of Change in Ottoman Syria', in: *The Journal of the American Oriental Society* 11:3 (1991), 495–511.

[109] Pamuk, *A Monetary History*, 76–82 and 89–95; Pamuk, 'Institutional Change', 231–233; Pamuk, 'The Evolution of Financial Institutions', 10–12; Udovitch, 'Credit as a Means of Investment', 260–264; Baer, 'The Administrative, Economic and Social Functions', 44–46; Jennings, 'Loans and Credit'; Shkodra, *Esnafet Shqiptare*, 89–95; Mandaville, 'Usurious Piety'; Gerber, *Economy and Society*; Çizakça, 'Cash Waqfs'; Çizakça, *A Comparative Evolution*; Murgescu, 'Romanian Information'; Caka, 'Vakefët dhe Funksioni', 110–111.

[110] Mandaville, 'Usurious Piety'. In the context of religious *vakıfs*, such as monasteries, land acquisitions through donations or disguised sales fostered a sense of communal ownership over monastic properties. This sense of communal ownership might have contributed to the corrupt leasing of monastic lands to private individuals from nearby villages. See Konstantinos Giakoumis, 'Η Οικονομική Κατάσταση των Ηπειρωτικών Μοναστηριών κατά τα τέλη του 19ου αιώνα: Η περίπτωση της Ι.Μ. Σπηλαίου Λιούντζης [The Economic Situation of Epirotan Monasteries at the end of the nineteenth century]', in: *Ηπειρωτικό Ημερολόγιο* 19:1 (1998), 303–320 (English synopsis on pp. 318–320); Konstantinos Giakoumis, 'Monastic Financial Management in the Provinces of the Patriarchate of Constantinople (1867–1873): The Case of the Metropolis of Dryinoupolis and Gjirokastra', in: Roumen Avramov, Aleksandar Fotić and Elias Kolovos (eds.), *Monastic Economy Across Time: Wealth Management, Patterns, and Trends* (Sofia, 2021), 130–152, there 149–150.

ample evidence thereof, for example the 1718 cash donation of 3,200 *akçe* for the painting of the church of the Dormition of the Virgin in Voskopoja or the 150 *akçe* donation to the church of St. Dimitrios in Voskopoja in the same year.[111] The same guild also figures sponsoring the *raki* offered for needy persons on social occasions like the funeral of children, betrothals, and marriages.[112]

To engage in such activities, guilds formed capital for the purpose of establishing and sustaining a provident fund.[113] Interpreting the *Chronicle of Serres*, Papageorgiou suggested that the primary means of capital formation were the fees collected for the testing of journeymen and their certification by the guilds as masters.[114] In my study on the capital formation and credit providing operations of the guild of tailors of Voskopoja (1716–1727), I find that, while there is ample evidence to suggest that levying testing fees was one of the ways to form capital, it was not the most important,[115] a conclusion that seems to be corroborated, at least for some guilds, by the combined reading of Fig. 1 with Table 1. The following note of the guild of dyers of the city of Elbasan, dating from ca. 1745, indicates that testing fees were also differentiated on the basis of whether or not a newly certified master continued the family workshop: "Here we record for memory that when the children of the masters get tested, they should give as fees one *kuruş (i.e., 1500 akçe)*, two *okas* of *raki* and ten *akçe* for the [local] sergeant, while interns, whose fathers are

[111] Giakoumis, '"The Voskopoja Guild of Tailors"', 260; Giakoumis, 'The Social, Cultural and Pedagogical Activities'; Konstantinos Giakoumis, 'Nektarios Terpos and the Iconographic Programme of Ardenica Monastery', in: *Byzantine and Modern Greek Studies* 41:1 (2017), 81–102, there 88 and n. 3; Konstantinos Giakoumis and Dritan Egro, 'Ottoman Pragmatism in Domestic Inter-Religious Affairs: The Legal Framework of Church Construction in the Ottoman Empire and the 1741 Firman of Ardenica Monastery', in: *Ηπειρωτικά Χρονικά* 44:1 (2010), 73–127, there 96 and n. 87; Konstantinos Giakoumis, 'Dialectics of Pragmatism in Ottoman Domestic Interreligious Affairs. Reflections on the Ottoman Legal Framework of Church Confiscation and Construction and a 1741 Firman for Ardenica Monastery', in: *Balkan Studies* 47:1 (2012), 73–132, there 101–102 and n. 97.

[112] C.A.S., fond 141, dossier 2, f 12v.

[113] Inalcık, 'Capital Formation in the Ottoman Empire', 113–119; Baer, 'The Administrative, Economic and Social Functions', 44–6; Jennings, 'Loans and Credit'; Shkodra, *Esnafet Shqiptare*, 162–167 and 221–251; Papageorgiou, *Η Μαθητεία στα Επαγγέλματα*, 109; Yi, *Guilds Dynamics*, 57–65 and 106–103.

[114] Papageorgiou, *Η Μαθητεία στα Επαγγέλματα*, 107–113.

[115] Giakoumis, '"The Voskopoja Guild of Tailors"', 261–265.

not dyers, they should pay a testing fee of 500 *akçe*, two *okas* of *raki* and ten *akçe* for the [local] sergeant".[116]

The comparison is very telling, as the newly certified masters without family links to dyers would pay almost four times larger fees than newly certified masters continuing their father's business (500 *akçe* vs. 150 *akçe*).[117]

A number of additional income streams existed for the Ottoman guilds. The collection of fees, other than testing fees, from all members of the guild was another way of capital formation. In 1718, for instance, the guild of tailors from Voskopoja collected a total of 1,875 *akçe* by its 121 members.[118] An important act of the same guild's register, dated May 20, 1743, however, reveals the diversity of income sources for the guild: " + May 20 1743 We signal here what we received this year from interests and capitals of the guild's fund, on top of the names

Table 1 Testing fees (in akçe) in Elbasan and Voskopoja, 1677–1743

Year(s)/Period	*Guild*	*Elbasan*	*Voskopoja*
1684	Furriers	400	–
seventeenth-eighteenth centuries	Goldsmiths	300–500	–
1689	Goldsmiths	450	–
1689	Dyers	160–500	–
1721–1733	Tailors	–	120–600
1733–1743	Tailors	–	800–4,000
Later in 1743	Tailors	–	360–2,400

Source C.A.S., fond 32, dossier 143; Shkodra, *Esnafet Shqiptare*, 125; Giakoumis, 'Glimpses from the Activities of Ottoman Guilds'

116 C.A.S., fond 65, dossier 67, f 10r, author's translation.

117 As per Liata's equivalency tables. Eutychia Liata, *Φλωρία Δεκατέσσερα Στένουν Γρόσια Σαράντα. Η Κυκλοφορία των Νομισμάτων στον Ελλαδικό Χώρο, 15ος–19ος Αι [Fourteen Florins Equal Forty Kuruş. The Circulation of Coins in the Hellenic Territory, 15th to nineteenth century]* (Athens, 1996), 95–114. For an idea about the purchasing power of the *akçe* toward the end of the eighteenth century, see Table 6.2 of Konstantinos Giakoumis, '"For a Christian Ending to Our Life": Church Endowments, Commemoration, and Tomb Purchases in Albania and the West Balkans (Thirteenth-Nineteenth Centuries)', in: Angela Jianu and Gheorghe Lazăr (eds.), *Pro Refrigerio Animae: Death and Memory in East-Central Europe, Fourteenth-Nineteenth Centuries* (London, 2024), 114–141, there 124.

118 Giakoumis, '"The Voskopoja Guild of Tailors"', 262.

of apprentices, sons of masters and cap-makers, who pay *akçe* [fees], journeymen [cited] name by name".[119]

As Table 2 shows, the credit and the interest collected from them was the most important income stream for the guild, accounting for almost half of the guild's annual income (48%). Papageorgiou's assertion that "this monetary [testing] fee was one of the most basic income streams of the guild",[120] thus appears not to be supported. Hence, at first sight, it seems that the capital and interests collected from the credit operations were the most significant income stream for the guild of tailors from Voskopoja for the economic year audited in 1743. On a closer inspection, however, although the credit operations of guilds have been viewed as a mechanism of social differentiation within the guild,[121] considering that in the Table repayments of loans and payments of interest are combined into one amount, even if we take into account a 20% interest rate (i.e., the maximum interest rate found later in the chapter), the relative importance of the sources of income will change quite significantly, making income from interest less crucial.

The mutual help function of the Ottoman guilds also included lending from the capital formed by the guilds to their members. The fullest and most formal recording of credit transactions is as follows: "1726. + Vrousias Katesia received 1,000, that is one thousand *akçe* from the [fund] of the guild of tailors; [the annual interest rate is] eleven and a half for [every] ten [*akçe*, that is an interest at the rate of 15%]. I should repay them without opposition. Guarantor is Kostis Katesia".[122] In earlier times the recording was significantly more cursory, as evidenced in a June 16, 1669 act from the register of the guild of furriers of Elbasan: " + Kola Simoni owes 800 *akçe*".[123] Equally interesting is the formulation of a repayment failure in the register of the same guild: " + Thanasi Hadji owes 400 *akçe* also on account of the child who got

[119] C.A.S., fond 141, dossier 2, f 37r, author's translation; Giakoumis, '"The Voskopoja Guild of Tailors"', 262–264.

[120] Papageorgiou, *Η Μαθητεία στα Επαγγέλματα*, 107.

[121] Shkodra, *Esnafet Shqiptare*, 136–161.

[122] C.A.S., fond 141, dossier 2, f 17v, author's translation.

[123] C.A.S., fond 32, dossier 143, f 1r, author's translation.

Table 2 Diversity of income streams for the Voskopoja guild of tailors

Description in the source	*Amount of income (akçe)*	*Share of income (%)*
From the sons of the masters		
From the cap-makers	21,000	29%
From capitals and interests we received	34,580	48%
From capitals we received		
From Michos Papandria for the debt he had	3,329	5%
We further sold the cow skins and received	1,500	2%
Additionally, from sheep skins	3,144	4%
Sub total	63,553	
Furthermore, from the vessels left over from the testing ceremony and then from the wine barrels	3,772	
In addition, from the soap we bought for the needs of our guild whose left-over was provisioned in the budget to sell, we received	850	5%
We also received Timtzo Tzangara's fine	720	1%
We also received the fine of Thanasis Papagianni Biakou	1,200	1%
We also received from Tondo Kotzio for the *bayrak* [flag] he held	400	2%
We also received the fine of Thanasis Pizios	1,200	1%
And from Giorgis of Alexos Tzitzinika	480	2%
Total	71,375	100%

Source C.A.S., fond 141, dossier 2, f 37r; Giakoumis, '"The Voskopoja Guild of Tailors"', 262–264
Note The summation in the source is incorrect as it should have added up to 72,175 *akçe*

tested and he swindled [the guild]".[124] On account of the communitarian form of organization of a guild, which significantly reduced the transaction costs of risk management, instances of non-repayment were very rare. Hence, the existence of a guarantor on a credit contract is not typical[125] and even more unusual are notes of full repayment by the guarantor: "He [Vrousias Katesia] has to give 150 *akçe* for the interest; Kostis gave these for Vrousias and he [also] gave 1,050 aspres and [the loan] was entirely repaid".[126] Yet, practices of masters recording each other as guarantors, as the Elbasan furriers were asked to do as we learn from an act

[124] C.A.S., fond 32, dossier 143, f 1r, author's translation.

[125] Giakoumis, '"The Voskopoja Guild of Tailors"', 265, 268–270, 271–274.

[126] Giakoumis, '"The Voskopoja Guild of Tailors"', 265.

dated September 17, 1683, must have provided additional risk mitigation assurances.[127]

5 Lending and Interest Rates

Regrettably, detailed comparative perspectives are impossible at this stage, as there are not enough published records of the lending practices recorded in the Muslim courts of major Balkan cities, while the lending practices mentioned for Berat[128] have been insufficiently studied. Some insight from the standpoint of only one guild (of tailors) from one city (Voskopoja) is available, however, thanks to the publication of the guild's register[129] and the study of its lending operations and risk management.[130] The absence of similar systematic data and analysis from the registers of other guilds, makes a detailed comparison impossible, but comparative observations can be made, with data from the guilds of goldsmiths and furriers of Elbasan.

First, thanks to the existence of two acts we can calculate interest rates and complement data published earlier on the guild of tailors of Voskopoja. The first act dates July 21, 1684 and its content is as follows: "On 9 April 1680. Today the goldsmiths were assembled in the house of Tria Kola and made accounts of the sums held by the *müteveli* with interest rate. These were 5,840 *akçe* which, with interest rate, summed up to 6890 with saints Peter and Paul's feast being set as repayment deadline—may he return them next year. I wrote this, Dēmētrēs, son of Komini Nika and also testify as for the above".[131] The interest rate calculated on the basis of this data is ca. 18%.

The second act reads: "Thanas Balabani received 817 *akçe* from the guild [on top of 350 *akçe* he already had]; all of the above sum up in 1767[132] *akçe*, among which expenses (not burdening the debtor, but the

[127] C.A.S., fond 32, dossier 143, f 3r–3v.

[128] Ferit Duka, *Berati në Kohën Osmane (shek. XVI–XVIII) [Berat in the Ottoman Times (16th–18th Centuries)]* (Tirana, 2001), 117.

[129] Giakoumis, 'Glimpses from the Activities of Ottoman Guilds'.

[130] Giakoumis, '"The Voskopoja Guild of Tailors"'.

[131] C.A.S., fond 80, dossier 5, f 20v, author's translation.

[132] The summation of 817 and 350 is 1,167 *akçe* and not 1,767, as the register records. It is impossible for me to explain why this difference is, other than assuming that he had also obtained a credit at the value of 600 *akçe*, which corresponds to the amount he was

guild) were 1,200 *akçe*; hence, Thanas remains in debt and should repay 600 *akçe* to the guild by the feast of saint George, next year".[133] For a loan of 567 *akçe*, Thanas Balabani was asked to pay 600 *akçe* for a period of nine months. This would lead us to an interest at the annual rate of ca. 7.8%, if the source were not so confusing as to prevent me from drawing unequivocal conclusions. With the help of this data, we are now in the position of extending the range of interest rates from 1680 to 1727 and present them in Fig. 2. For the above reason I excluded the second source from Fig. 2.

Figure 2 confirms earlier findings that interest rates were volatile in the period under study (1680–1727)[134] and not only in the Ottoman

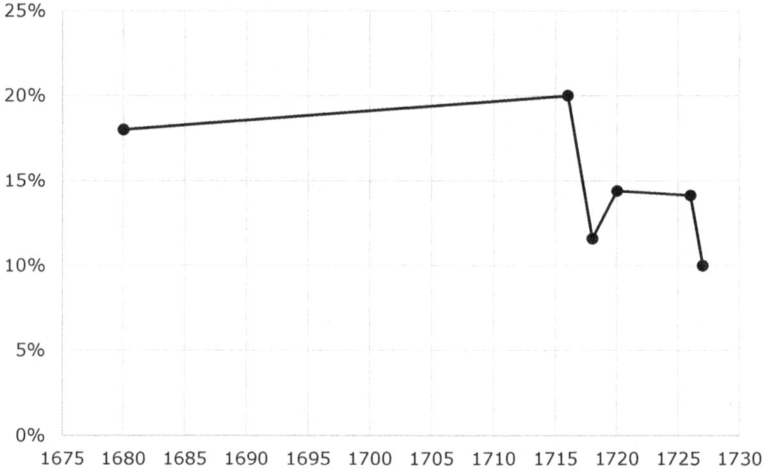

Fig. 2 Interest rates on loans provided by the guilds of furriers and goldsmiths of Elbasan (1680) and of the tailors of Voskopoja (1716–1727) (*Source* C.A.S., fond 80, dossier 5, f 20v; C.A.S., fond 32, dossier 143, f 2v; Giakoumis, '"The Voskopoja Guild of Tailors"', 266 [Graph 1])

called to repay. But then, if, out of a 1,767 *akçe* credit the debtor paid 1,200 *akçe* in favor of the guild, then, his credit's remainder would amount to 567 *akçe*.

[133] C.A.S., fond 32, dossier 143, f 2v, author's translation.

[134] Giakoumis, '"The Voskopoja Guild of Tailors"', 265.

Balkans.[135] In 1680 the annual interest rate was at the rate of 18% dropping to 5.4% in 1684. It should be noted, however, that the scarce number of transactions from the guild of Elbasan goldsmiths in this early period does not promise any safe conclusions.

Safer conclusions can be drawn on the basis of data from the guild of tailors from Voskopoja, where, in 1716, the mean annual interest was 20%, while in 1718 it dropped to 12%. In 1720 the mean annual interest rate increased to 14%, at the same rate as it was found in 1726. On the second half of the year 1726 an unexplained change of the interest was observed which continued until 1727, a year in which the data again showed a decrease of the annual interest rate which now was 10%. The interest rates may be set in order to recover costs and to discount the risk for exercising this activity.[136] The guild of tailors in Voskopoja had the tendency to lower the interest rate from 1716 to 1727. What seems to have driven changes in interest rates is that in this period the number of guilds increased, which may have made the market more competitive, thereby leading to a decrease in interest rates. As a point of comparison, it is interesting to note that in 1792 the Orthodox community of Thessaloniki got credit at interest rates ranging from 12 to 15%.[137] In the case of the guild of tailors from Voskopoja, the interest rates for loans in the period from 1716 to 1728 fluctuated between 10 and 20%.[138] However, compared to the similar data from various contemporary states in Europe,[139] the interest rates of the guilds were overall not competitive.

The amount of capital lent by the guild of Voskopoja tailors increased considerably from 1716 until 1726,[140] followed by a decrease in the respective interest rates, evidence that was interpreted as indication of economic growth. Still, the credit flows were usually fixed and strictly controlled, thereby avoiding hoarding. The guild did not merely hoard

[135] Marc Flandreau et al., 'The Bell Jar: Commercial Interest Rates between Two Revolutions, 1688–1789', in: Jeremy Atack and Larry Neal (eds.), *The Origins and Development of Financial Markets and Institutions from the Seventeenth Century to the Present* (Cambridge, 2009), 161–208, there 163–165 and 200–201.

[136] Ibrahim Mert, 'A Historical Overview of Accounting in Turkey', in: *Internal Auditing and Risk Management* 3:31 (2013), 15–25.

[137] Hekimoglou, 'Των Ρουφετίων, Μεγάλων και Μικρών', 119.

[138] Giakoumis, '"The Voskopoja Guild of Tailors"', 265–267.

[139] Flandreau et al., 'The Bell Jar', 200–201, Appendix A.

[140] Giakoumis, '"The Voskopoja Guild of Tailors"', 265–268.

their funds; instead, they actively invested their capital to generate income.[141] The limited flows of credit for several years and in different guilds (for example in 1727 for the guild of tailors of Voskopoja), should not be viewed as a sign of economic decline, but rather as a response to limited availability of capital on account of maturing loans or temporary circumstances, such as the July 20, 1733 extraordinary payment of the guild of furriers of Elbasan mentioned above. Other indirect evidence of economic development has been correlated to this discussion in another study.[142]

The comparison of the volumes of capital available to lend to the tailors of Voskopoja and the silversmiths of Elbasan indicates that at the peak activity, the Voskopoja guild of tailors was able to provide more loans than the guild of Elbasan silversmiths.[143] Since we cannot know the number of members of each guild, the fee and fine levels, and the dependency of each profession on loans, it is impossible to draw conclusions on the overall economic situation of these cities in comparison. In line with modern understanding of economics, had the growth of money (credit) supply in the market been due to inflation, it would have called for higher interest rates to control it.[144] In a previous study[145] I have demonstrated that economic growth and activity in Voskopoja were also evident in church construction. Indeed, increasing volumes of loans during the first three decades of the eighteenth century coincide with increasing intensity of church construction. This indicates that higher credit volumes are evidence of a growing economy, rather than the consequence of inflationary pressures. It can thus be inferred that the median loan value of 1,000 *akçe* per transaction would have been rather significant.

[141] Hoarding is defined as the practice of accumulating big sums of money, which can slow down the circulation of money.

[142] Giakoumis, '"The Voskopoja Guild of Tailors"', 267.

[143] Shkodra, *Esnafet Shqiptare*, 139; Fig. 3.

[144] Mark A. Thoma, 'The Effects on Money Growth on Inflation and Interest Rates Across Spectral Frequency Bands', in: *The Journal of Money Credit and Banking* 26:2 (1994), 218–231.

[145] Giakoumis, '"The Voskopoja Guild of Tailors"', 267–277.

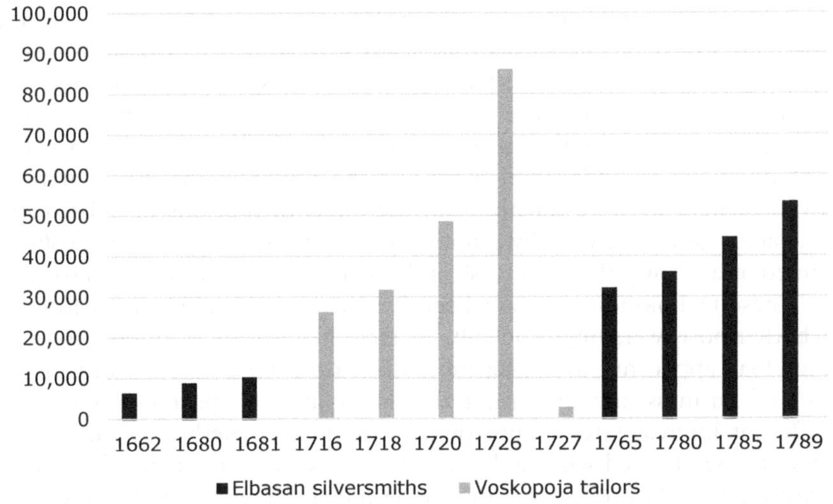

Fig. 3 Loan volumes (in akçe) (*Source* Shkodra, *Esnafet Shqiptare*, 139; C.A.S., fond 141, dossier 2; Giakoumis, '"The Voskopoja Guild of Tailors"', 266 [Graph 2])

6 Borrowers

The tailor's guild of Voskopoja determined and managed the risk of its members.[146] Evidence shows that only the most experienced masters could expect to get a loan after becoming apprenticed and getting certified. It was very rare to see a young master receive a loan to help develop a business.[147]

On the other hand, there is ample evidence that, similar to the guilds of Ioannina,[148] masters often bequeathed tools and possibly a modest sum to help young masters from their ranks in their initial professional steps. The guild of tailors of Voskopoja[149] also shows that masters registered as guarantors to the new master, ensuring the transfer of the craft's tools.

[146] Çizakça, *A Comparative Evolution.*

[147] Konstantinos, '"The Voskopoja Guild of Tailors"', 268.

[148] Papageorgiou, *Η Μαθητεία στα Επαγγέλματα*, 112–113; Shkodra, *Esnafet Shqiptare*, 107, 125 and 128.

[149] Giakoumis, '"The Voskopoja Guild of Tailors"', 268–269.

In a list of the names of master furriers of the city of Elbasan alongside the names of their guarantors, one reads several names of masters whose guarantors were their former teachers.[150] It is reasonable to conclude that credit was given for the development of new businesses, whether by experienced masters or by new masters. When the application for a loan was not on these grounds, then there was the requirement of a guarantor. Even guarantors were mostly from the ranks of previous or subsequent recipients of credit, thereby pointing to some task of guarantor profiling aimed at assessing the credit risk and calculating the transaction costs.

These techniques may have been used to control, prevent, or forecast whether borrowers might default.[151] First, loans were given only to qualified loan applicants, as a measure of decreasing the possibility of running out of business and increasing the possibility of repayment. Charging different interest rates to borrowers was another method of mitigating risk. Those charged with higher interest rates were either new borrowers without record of repayment or borrowers who might have defaulted and were thus charged a higher interest rate in a subsequent credit.[152] The creditworthiness of family members seems to have been another factor analyzed when the guild decided about the interest rate to be charged on a loan. In the case of Voskopoja, three out of four borrowers who were recent and new masters and received lower interest rates, were sons of priests.[153] While the lower mean interest rates for priests compared to lay individuals may not show statistically significant differences, although one would rationally expect higher interest rates due to increased risk levels accompanying a secondary vocation, their clerical status could have been perceived as an additional guarantee to lenders. Perhaps, priests might have received preferential treatment, resulting in lower interest rates than the ones expected due to their religious vocation. The above techniques indicate an entire range of tools engaged by the guild to manage credit risk.

[150] C.A.S., fond 32, dossier 143, f 3r–v.

[151] Robert C. Merton and Zvi Bodie, 'On the Management of Financial Guarantees', in: *Financial Management* 21:4 (1992), 87–109.

[152] Giakoumis, '"The Voskopoja Guild of Tailors"', 269.

[153] Giakoumis, '"The Voskopoja Guild of Tailors"', 269.

Other evidence points to some connection between the creditworthiness of borrowers and the sums the guild approved to lend them.[154] The previous documents and registers were used to analyze the creditworthiness of the loan applicants. The control mechanism also assessed the total amount of credit for each calendar year and scrutinized the funds from previous years that seemed not to have been repaid. Relations of trust among partners were a key part of risk mitigation and these were often built on marital and kin relations. The guilds used formalization, ritualization, and publicity of ties to establish trust among their members, especially when information was asymmetrical and when there were no central institutions to guarantee mutually good behavior.[155] All these methods were helpful for controlling the performance of credit.

7 Conclusion

Assessing the creditworthiness of loan applicants at a local level was a risk management tactic and it provided a remedy to balance the asymmetries of information in pre-industrial societies of the Ottoman Balkans. Considering that taxation was at fixed rates and that keeping accounting books was not obligatory, it would have been impossible for a bank to collect ample data about the financial capacity of a credit applicant. In addition, the lifestyle and law abidance of each applicant were privileged information that could not easily be obtained to profile loan applicants, unless from peers, who could also enforce repayments, if necessary, through peer pressure. It is tempting to read this long survival of lending by the Ottoman guilds as another aspect of "the strength of weak ties", to use the classical study of Mark Granovetter.[156] Be this as it may, Ottoman guilds were capable of capitalizing on access to superior

[154] Timothy W. Guinnane, 'Cooperatives as Information Machines: German Rural Credit Cooperatives, 1883–1914', in: *The Journal of Economic History* 61:2 (2001), 366–389.

[155] For similar practices of the families of merchants, see: Ikaros Mantouvalos, 'Greek Immigrants in Central Europe: A Concise Study of Migration Routes from the Balkans to the Territories of the Hungarian Kingdom (From the Late 17th to the Early 19th Centuries)', in: Olga Katsiardi-Hering and Maria A. Stassinopoulou (eds.), *Across the Danube. Southeastern Europeans and Their Travelling Identities (17th–19th C.)* (Leiden, 2017), 25–53, there 32–33.

[156] Mark S. Granovetter, 'The Strength of Weak Ties', in: *The American Journal of Sociology* 78:6 (1973), 1360–1380.

information about their members and imposing inexpensive and effective sanctions on defaulters. In this respect, they resembled German rural credit cooperatives, also characterized as "information machines".[157]

This chapter cast additional light on small-scale credit institutions providing funds for in-group members at affordable terms. In particular, funds clustering in guilds were used on a private credit market to generate income. The fact that the funding needs of the Ottoman state were met in other ways, for example loans from pious foundations,[158] meant that there was no external outlet for guilds' capital. They were consequently able, or necessitated, to invest this internally between their members. Hence, what I hope to have demonstrated is that capital created within such clusters does not seem to have been generated for the purpose of capital investments. Instead, it seems likely that capital formation and its use was aimed at serving the social mandate of the guild as some sort of mutual aid fund for the guilds' members.

The Ottoman guilds governed their activities by following a strict framework of business operations. They used inside information to tackle information asymmetries, evaluate current performance, and make decisions for the future, in some ways similar to how modern banks operate to assess loan applicants operating in an economic environment with information asymmetries. The key profit driver for them was interest rates so it was the only variable through which they made assumptions for increasing profits. Credit through these institutions was overall lent at locally competitive interest rates.[159]

I do not know whether or not guild members could obtain loans from capital suppliers outside the guild, yet I suspect that even if there was such access, its terms would certainly not have been conducive to genuine economic development. This suspicion is reinforced by some indirect evidence. We do know that the absence of reliable privileged access to personal financial data, combined with information asymmetries, compelled Ottoman financial institutions, such as the Agricultural Bank, "to concentrate resources in areas of proven productivity, where lending

157 Guinnane, 'Cooperatives as Information Machines'.

158 Linda T. Darling, *Revenue-Raising and Legitimacy: Tax Collection and Finance Administration in the Ottoman Empire 1560–1660* (Leiden, 1996), 26; Wantje Fritschy, *Public Finance of the Dutch Republic in Comparative Perspective. The Viability of an Early Modern Federal State (1570 s–1795)* (Leiden, 2017), 315 and 350.

159 Pamuk, *A Monetary History*, 181.

risks were minimized".[160] It is therefore hardly surprising that the Balkan provinces of the Ottoman Empire benefitted very little from this bank's capital[161]; absence of privileged information enabling effective creditor profiling made the lending risk unmanageable. It was precisely to tackle this issue that Mit'hat Pasha, the Ottoman governor of Niš, of Albanian descent and an expert on the economic challenges of the wider region, established the Homelands Funds.[162] This was a cooperative system with farmer-based resources, similar to the ones formed by guilds, to meet the credit needs of rural farmers and counter high interest charged by moneylenders.[163] Still, although this fund was collectively resourced by all farmers by offering voluntary work in designated common lands managed by a council of farmers, guarantees were solicited in the form of collateral, which could be confiscated in case of default.[164]

It is reasonable to see the Ottoman guilds as precursor forms of cooperatives in the Balkans. Their communal credit operations resembled those of institutional investors in Europe.[165] Though different in mission,

[160] Quataert, 'Dilemma of Development', 218–220; Zhulieta Daja, 'Banka Bujqësore Otomane, kreditë dhe borxhet në sanxhakun e Elbasanit [The Ottoman Agricultural Bank, Credits and Loans in the Sancak of Elbasan]', in: *Buletini Shkencor, Universiteti i Elbasanit "Aleksandër Xhuvani". Seria e Shkencave Shoqërore dhe Edukimit* 1:45 (2020), 217–231, there 222–223.

[161] Daja, 'Banka Bujqësore Otomane'.

[162] Literally "Hometown Coffers". See: Sertaç Dokuzlu, 'The Agricultural Credit System in the Ottoman Empire between 1863 and 1888', in: *The Rural History* 28:2 (2017), 177–188.

[163] Dhimitri P. Pasko, *Shqipëria e Re Ekonomike. Bankat Bujqësore të Shteteve të Ballkanit [The Code of Municipal Affairs]* (Constanza, 1933), 8–9; Necdet Bilgin and Şaban Tanıyıcı, 'Türkiye'de Kooperatif ve Devlet Ilişkilerinin Tarihi Gelişimi [Historical Development of Cooperative and State Relations in Turkey]', in: *Karamanoğlu Mehmetbey Üniversitesi Sosyal Ve Ekonomik Araştırmalar Dergisi* 15:2 (2008), 136–159; Cabir Doğan and Ferhat Güngör, 'Midilli Memleket Sandiklari (Osmanlı Devleti Hâkimiyetindeki Midilli Adası'nda Zirai Kredi Teskilatı Kurma Konusunda Ðlk Tesebbüs) [Midilli Homeland Coffers (Under The Rule of The Ottoman Empire in The Island of Lesbos. The First Attempt for an Agricultural Credit Organization)]', in: *Elektronik Sosyal Bilimler Dergisi* 14:53 (2015), 298–309.

[164] Ermal Nurja, *Elbasani në Dokumentet Osmane të Arkivit të Stambollit [Elbasan in Ottoman Documents of the Istanbul Archive]* (Elbasan, 2019), 446; Daja, 'Banka Bujqësore Otomane', 23.

[165] Jean-Laurent Rosenthal and R. Bin Wong, *Before and Beyond Divergence: The Politics of Economic Change in China and Europe* (London, 2011), 144–145; Harm Zwarts, 'Institutional Investors in the Countryside of the Dutch Republic. An Analysis of the

scope, framework, and operations, Balkan guilds bear some similarities to certain urban non-cooperative counterparts.[166] Yet, in the Ottoman context, institutional investments of the sort explored here seem not to have developed with an eye on capital investments but rather for the purpose of serving an inner and mutual aid mandate of the guilds.

Archival Sources and Literature

Apostolidis, Kosmas, and Aleksandr Peev, 'Кондика на пловдивския абаджийски еснаф [The Codex of the Guild of Plovdiv Abadjis]', in: *Годишник на Народната библиотека в Пловдив* 1:2 and 3:1 (1931–1932), 1–170 and 1–186.

Aščerić-Todd, Ines, 'Religious Diversity in Ottoman Guilds', in: David Thomas and John Chesworth (eds.), *Christian-Muslim Relations: A Bibliographical History* volume 12: *Asia, Africa and the Americas (1700–1800)* (Leiden, 2018), 29–41.

Autheman, André, *La Banque impérial ottoman* (Paris, 1996).

Baer, Gabriel, 'The Administrative, Economic and Social Functions of Turkish Guilds', in: *International Journal of Middle East Studies* 1:1 (1970), 28–50.

Bilgin, Necdet, and Şaban Tanıyıcı, 'Türkiye'de Kooperatif ve Devlet Ilişkilerinin Tarihi Gelişimi [Historical Development of Cooperative and State Relations in Turkey]', in: *Karamanoğlu Mehmetbey Üniversitesi Sosyal Ve Ekonomik Araştırmalar Dergisi* 15:2 (2008), 136–159.

Bulut, Mehmet, and Cem Korkut, 'A Comparison Between Ottoman Cash Waqfs (CWs) and Modern Interest-Free Financial Institutions', in: *Vakıflar Dergisi* 46:1 (2016), 23–45.

Caka, Eduart, 'Vakefët dhe Funksioni i Tyre në Qytetin e Elbasanit gjatë Shekullit XVII [The Role and Function of Waqf's in the City of Elbasan during the XVII Century]', in: *Studime Historike* 1–2:1 (2016), 99–113.

Central Archive of the State, Archive of Lef Nosi 1669–1918 (fond 32), dossier 143.

Central Archive of the State, Archive of Simon Kazanxhiu 1775–1866 (fond 65), dossier 67.

Central Archive of the State, Archive of Elbasan Guilds (fond 80), dossiers 5 and 7.

Central Archive of the State, Archive of the Metropolic of Korcë 1716–1791 (fond 141), dossier 2.

Investment Portfolios of Reformed Deaconries in the Countryside of the Dutch Republic, c.1750–1800' (unpublished PhD dissertation, Utrecht University, 2015).

166 Guinnane, 'Cooperatives as Information Machines'.

Çizakça, Murat, 'Cash Waqfs of Bursa, 1555–1823', in: *The Journal of the Economic and Social History of the Orient* 38:3 (1995), 313–354.

Çizakça, Murat, *A Comparative Evolution of Business Partnerships: The Islamic World and Europe, with Specific Reference to the Ottoman Archives* (Leiden, 1996).

Clay, Christopher, 'The Origins of Modern Banking in the Levant: The Branch Network of the Imperial Ottoman Bank, 1890–1914', in: *The International Journal of Middle East Studies* 26:4 (1994), 589–614.

Cohen, Amnon, *The Guilds of Ottoman Jerusalem* (Leiden, 2001).

Crampton, R. J., *A Concise History of Bulgaria* (Cambridge, 1997).

Daja, Zhulieta, 'Banka Bujqësore Otomane, kreditë dhe borxhet në sanxhakun e Elbasanit [The Ottoman Agricultural Bank, credits and loans in the Sancak of Elbasan]', in: *Buletini Shkencor, Universiteti i Elbasanit "Aleksandër Xhuvani". Seria e Shkencave Shoqërore dhe Edukimit* 1:45 (2020), 217–231.

Darling, Linda T., *Revenue-Raising and Legitimacy: Tax Collection and Finance Administration in the Ottoman Empire 1560–1660* (Leiden, 1996).

Dokuzlu, Sertaç, 'The Agricultural Credit System in the Ottoman Empire between 1863 and 1888', in: *The Rural History* 28:2 (2017), 177–188.

Doğan, Cabir, and Ferhat Güngör, 'Midilli Memleket Sandiklari (Osmanlı Devleti Hâkimiyetindeki Midilli Adası'nda Zirai Kredi Teskilatı Kurma Konusunda Đlk Tesebbüs) [Midilli Homeland Coffers (Under The Rule of The Ottoman Empire in The Island of Lesbos. The First Attempt for an Agricultural Credit Organization)]', in: *Elektronik Sosyal Bilimler Dergisi* 14:53 (2015), 298–309.

Duka, Ferit, *Berati në Kohën Osmane (shek. XVI–XVIII) [Berat in the Ottoman Times (16th–18th Centuries)]* (Tirana, 2001).

Egro, Dritan, 'Christianity versus Islam in the Early Stages of the Ottoman Domination in Albanian Lands (14th–16th Centuries)' (unpublished PhD dissertation, Bilkent University, 2003).

Egro, Dritan, *Ligji Osman ndër Shqiptarët e Mesjetës së Vonë (Gjysma e Dytë e Shekullit XV—Fillimshekulli XVII) [The Ottoman Law Among Late Medieval Albanians (second half of 15th century—beginning of 18th Century)]* (Tirana, 2012).

Faroqhi, Suraiya et al., *An Economic and Social History of the Ottoman Empire* volume 2: *1600–1914* (Cambridge, 1997).

Faroqhi, Suraiya, 'Understanding Ottoman Guilds', in: Suraiya Faroghi and Randi Deguilhem (eds.) *Crafts and Craftsmen of the Middle East. Fashioning the Individual in the Muslim Mediterranean* (London, 2005), 3–40.

Faroqhi, Suraiya, *Bread from the Lion's Mouth: Artisans Struggling for a Livelihood in Ottoman Cities* (New York, 2015).

Ferguson, Heather L., *The Proper Order of Things. Language, Power, and Law in Ottoman Administrative Discourses* (Stanford, 2018).

Flandreau, Marc et al., 'The Bell Jar: Commercial Interest Rates between Two Revolutions, 1688–1789', in: Jeremy Atack and Larry Neal (eds.), *The Origins and Development of Financial Markets and Institutions from the Seventeenth Century to the Present* (Cambridge, 2009), 161–208.

Fritschy, Wantje, *Public Finance of the Dutch Republic in Comparative Perspective. The Viability of an Early Modern Federal State (1570s–1795)* (Leiden, 2017).

Gelderblom, Oscar, and Joost Jonker, 'With a View to Hold: The Emergence of Institutional Investors on the Amsterdam Securities Market during the Seventeenth and Eighteenth Centuries', in: Jeremy Atack and Larry Neal (eds.), *The Origins and Development of Financial Markets and Institutions from the Seventeenth Century to the Present* (Cambridge, 2009), 71–98.

Gerber, Haim, *Economy and Society in an Ottoman City: Bursa, 1600–1700* (Jerusalem, 1988).

Giakoumis, Konstantinos, and Dritan Egro, 'Ottoman Pragmatism in Domestic Inter-Religious Affairs: The Legal Framework of Church Construction in the Ottoman Empire and the 1741 Firman of Ardenica Monastery', in: *Ηπειρωτικά Χρονικά* 44:1 (2010), 73–127.

Giakoumis, Konstantinos, 'Η Οικονομική Κατάσταση των Ηπειρωτικών Μοναστηριών κατά τα τέλη του 19ου αιώνα: Η περίπτωση της Ι.Μ. Σπηλαίου Λιούντζης [The Economic Situation of Epirotan Monasteries at the end of the 19th century]', in: *Ηπειρωτικό Ημερολόγιο* 19:1 (1998), 303–320 (English synopsis on pp. 318–320).

Giakoumis, Konstantinos, 'Fourteenth-Century Albanian Migration and the 'relativeautochthony' of the Albanians in Epeiros: The Case of Gjirokastër', in: *Byzantine and Modern Greek Studies* 27:1 (2003), 171–183.

Giakoumis, Konstantinos, 'Dialectics of Pragmatism in Ottoman Domestic Interreligious Affairs. Reflections on the Ottoman Legal Framework of Church Confiscation and Construction and a 1741 Firman for Ardenica Monastery', in: *Balkan Studies* 47:1 (2012), 73–132.

Giakoumis, Konstantinos, 'Self-Identifications by Himarriots, Sixteenth to Nineteenth Centuries', in: *Erytheia* 37:1 (2016), 205–246.

Giakoumis, Konstantinos, 'Nektarios Terpos and the Iconographic Programme of Ardenica Monastery', in: *Byzantine and Modern Greek Studies* 41:1 (2017), 81–102.

Giakoumis, Konstantinos, 'The Social, Cultural and Pedagogical Activities of the Moschopolitan Guild of Tailors (1714–1749)', in: Floresha Dado et al. (eds.), *Qytetërimi i Voskopojës dhe shekulli i iluminizmit në Balkan: Konferencë shkencore ndërkombëtare* (Tirana, 2018), 294–304.

Giakoumis, Konstantinos, '"The Voskopoja Guild of Tailors" Credit Lending Operations and Risk Management (1716–27)', *Turkish Historical Review* 9:2 (2018), 242–277.

Giakoumis, Konstantinos, 'Monastic Financial Management in the Provinces of the Patriarchate of Constantinople (1867–1873): The Case of the Metropolis of Dryinoupolis and Gjirokastra', in: Roumen Avramov, Aleksandar Fotić and Elias Kolovos (eds.), *Monastic Economy Across Time: Wealth Management, Patterns, and Trends* (Sofia, 2021), 130–152.

Giakoumis, Konstantinos, 'Glimpses from the Activities of Ottoman Guilds. The Register AQSH. F. 141, D. 2 of the Central Archives of the State, Tirana, Albania', in: *Historiography in Ottoman Europe* (Working Paper No. 4, 2022).

Giakoumis, Konstantinos, '"For a Christian Ending to Our Life": Church Endowments, Commemoration, and Tomb Purchases in Albania and the West Balkans (Thirteenth-Nineteenth Centuries)', in: Angela Jianu and Gheorghe Lazăr (eds.), *Pro Refrigerio Animae: Death and Memory in East-Central Europe, Fourteenth-Nineteenth Centuries* (London, 2024), 114–141.

Giakoumis, Konstantinos, and Juna Miluka, 'The Voskopoja Guild of Tailors' Credit-Lending Operations and Risk Management (1716–1727)', in: *Money and Banking in Albania, from Antiquity to Modern Times, First Conference of the Museum of the Bank of Albania Proceedings, 14–15 June 2017* (Tirana, 2018), 99–110.

Granovetter, Mark S., 'The Strength of Weak Ties', in: *The American Journal of Sociology* 78:6 (1973), 1360–1380.

Guinnane, Timothy W., 'Cooperatives as Information Machines: German Rural Credit Cooperatives, 1883–1914', in: *The Journal of Economic History* 61:2 (2001), 366–389.

Gürbüz, M., 'Emergence of Bulgarian Nationalism', in: *Güneydoğu Avrupa Araştırmaları Dergisi* 0:16 (2009), 27–51.

Hadjimichali, Angeliki, 'Μορφές από τη Σωματειακή Οργάνωση των Ελλήνων στην Οθωμανική Αυτοκρατορία: Οι συντεχνίες—τα Ισνάφια [Forms of the Corporate Organisation of the Greeks in the Ottoman Empire: Guilds—the *Esnaf*]', in: *L' Hellénisme Contemporain: «Η Πεντακοσιοστή Επέτειος από της Αλώσεως της Κων/πόλεως», 29 Μαΐου 1453–1953* (Athens, 1953), 297–303.

Harding, Vanessa, 'The Crown, the City, and the Orphans: The City of London and its Finances, 1400–1700', in: Marc Boone, C.A. Davids, and Paul Janssens (eds.), *Urban Public Debts: Urban Government and the Market for Annuities in Western Europe (14th–18th centuries)* (Turnhout, 2003), 51–60.

Hekimoglou, Evangelos, 'Των Ρουφετίων, Μεγάλων και Μικρών. Χριστιανικές Συντεχνίες της Θεσσαλονίκης στα Τέλη του 18ου Αιώνα [Of Big and Small Guilds. Christian Guilds in Thessaloniki at the End of the 18th Century]', in: *Πρακτικά Ε΄ Επιστημονικού Συμποσίου, Χριστιανική Θεσσαλονίκη: Οθωμανική Περίοδος 1430–1912* (Thessaloniki, 1993), 115–136.

Howell, Martha, and Walter Prevenier, *From Reliable Sources: An Introduction to Historical Methods* (New York, 2001).

Ihčiev, Diamanti A., 'Esnafski Documenti i Esnafski Organizacii v Tursko Vreme [Guild Documents and Guild Organizations in the Turkish Time]', in: *Spisanie na Balgarskoto Ikonomicesko Druzestvo* 3:1 (1907), 345–452.

Inalcık, Hilal, 'Capital Formation in the Ottoman Empire', in: *The Journal of Economic History* 29:1 (1969), 113–119.

Inalcık, Hilal, 'The Appointment Procedure of a Guild Warden', in: *Wiener Zeitschrift für die Kunde des Morgenlandes* 76:1 (1986), 135–142.

Jennings, Ronald C., 'Loans and Credit in Early Seventeenth Century Ottoman Judicial Records: The Sharia Court of Anatolian Kayseri', in: *The Journal of the Economic and Social History of the Orient* 16:2–3 (1973), 168–216.

Kallinderis, Michael A., *Αἱ Συντεχνίαι καὶ ἡ Ἐκκλησία ἐπὶ Τουρκοκρατίας [The Guilds and the Church During the Ottoman Rule]* (Athens, 1973).

Karagedikli, Gürer, and Ali Coşkun Tunçer, 'Microcredit in the Ottoman Empire: A Review of Cash Waqfs in Transition to Modern Banking', in: Marcella Lorenzini, Cinzia Lorandini, and D'Maris Coffman (eds.), *Financing in Europe: Evolution, Coexistence and Complementarity of Lending Practices from the Middle Ages to Modern Times* (London, 2018), 237–266.

Karakitsios, Eleutherios A., 'Ο Ελληνισμός στην Μητροπολιτική Περιφέρεια Κορυτσάς [Hellenism in the Metropolitan Region of Korça]' (unpublished PhD dissertation, University of Thessaloniki, 2010).

Katsaros, Vasilis, and Christos Papastathis, 'Προδρομικά Αποσημειώματα. Βραχέα Χρονικὰ Σημειώματα Τεσσάρων Καταστίχων τῆς Μονῆς Τιμίου Προδρόμου Σερρῶν τῶν Ἐτῶν 1730–1806 μετὰ «Παραρτήματος» δύο Γραμμάτων: «Ζητείας» καὶ Ἐπικυρώσεως [Preliminary Annotations. Brief Chronicle Notes of Four Registers of the Monastery of the Holy Forerunner in Serres of the years 1730–1806 together with an Annex of two letters, of *zitiye* and validation]', in: *Serraika Symmikta* 2 (2013), 21–86.

Karlaphti-Mouratidi, Photeini, 'Η Μαθητεία στα Επαγγέλματα στην Κέρκυρα [Apprenticeship in Corfu]', in: *Εώα και Εσπέρια* 6:1 (2006), 133–148.

Kreševljaković, Hamdija, 'Esnafi i obrti u Bosni i Hercegovini (1463–1878) [Guilds and crafts in Bosnia and Herzegovina (1463–1878)]', in: *Izabrana Djela* 2 [Selected works 2] (Sarajevo, 1991).

Kuran, Timur, 'The Provision of Public Goods under Islamic Law: Origins, Impact, and Limitations of the Waqf System', in: *Law & Society Review* 35:4 (2024), 841–897.

Liata, Eutychia, *Φλωρία Δεκατέσσερα Στένουν Γρόσια Σαράντα. Η Κυκλοφορία των Νομισμάτων στον Ελλαδικό Χώρο, 15ος–19ος Αι [Fourteen Florins Equal Forty Kuruş. The Circulation of Coins in the Hellenic Territory, 15th to 19th century]* (Athens, 1996).

Mandaville, J.E., 'Usurious Piety: The Cash Waqf Controversy in the Ottoman Empire', in: *The International Journal of Middle East Studies* 10:3 (1979), 289–308.

Maniatis, George C., 'The Domain of Private Guilds in the Byzantine Economy, Tenth to Fifteenth Centuries', in: *The Dumbarton Oaks Papers* 55: (2001), 339–369.

Mantouvalos, Ikaros, 'Greek Immigrants in Central Europe: A Concise Study of Migration Routes from the Balkans to the Territories of the Hungarian Kingdom (From the Late 17th to the Early 19th Centuries)', in: Olga Katsiardi-Hering and Maria A. Stassinopoulou (eds.), *Across the Danube. Southeastern Europeans and Their Travelling Identities (17th–19th C.)* (Leiden, 2017), 25–53.

Mavridis, Dimitrios G., and Konstantinos I. Vatalis, 'Best and Bad Practices—The Imperial Guilds of Constantinople', in: *Procedia Engeneering* 84:1 (2014), 689–697.

Mert, Ibrahim, 'A Historical Overview of Accounting in Turkey', in: *Internal Auditing and Risk Management* 3:31 (2013), 15–25.

Merton, Robert C., and Zvi Bodie, 'On the Management of Financial Guarantees', in: *Financial Management* 21:4 (1992), 87–109.

Murgescu, Bogdan, 'Romanian Information Regarding the Ottoman Capital Market: Prince Constantin Brancoveanu's Debt Payments (1694–1703)', in: *Toplum ve Ekonomi* 10:1 (1997), 39–51.

Nerantzi-Varmazi, Vaso, 'Συντεχνίες Εμπόρων στην Κωνσταντινούπολη τον 10^{ο} αιώνα [Commercial Guilds in Constantinople in the 10th Century]', in: Christine Angelidis (ed.), *Πρακτικά του Α' Διεθνούς Συμποσίου, Η Καθημερινή Ζωή στο Βυζάντιο, Τομές και Συνέχειες στην Ελληνιστική και Ρωμαϊκή Παράδοση, Αθήνα 15–17 Σεπτεμβρίου 1988* (Athens, 1989), 353–361.

Nuri, Ergin Osman, *Mecelle-i Umûr-ı Belediyye [The Code of Municipal Affairs]* (Istanbul, 1914–1922).

Nurja, Ermal, *Elbasani në Dokumentet Osmane të Arkivit të Stambollit [Elbasan in Ottoman Documents of the Istanbul Archive]* (Elbasan, 2019).

Pamuk, Şevket, *A Monetary History of the Ottoman Empire* (Cambridge, 2000).

Pamuk, Şevket, 'Institutional Change and the Longevity of the Ottoman Empire, 1500–1800', in: *The Journal of Interdisciplinary History* 35:2 (2004), 225–247.

Pamuk, Şevket, 'The Evolution of Financial Institutions in the Ottoman Empire, 1600–1914', in: *The Financial History Review* 11:1 (2004), 7–32.

Pantazopoulos, Nikolaos, 'Community Laws and Customs of Western Macedonia under Ottoman Rule', in: *Balkan Studies* 2:1 (1961), 1–22.

Papageorgiou, Georgios, 'Οι Συντεχνίες στα Γιάννενα κατά το 19^{ο} και τις Αρχές του 20^{ού} Αιώνα (Αρχές 19^{ου} ως 1912) [The Guilds in Ioannina During the 19th and the Beginning of the 20th Century (Beginning of 19th to 1912]' (unpublished PhD dissertation, University of Ionnina, 1982).

Papageorgiou, Georgios, *Η Μαθητεία στα Επαγγέλματα (16^{ος}–20^{ός} αι.) [The Apprenticeship (16th–20th c.)]* (Athens, 1986).

Pasko, Dhimitri P., *Shqipëria e Re Ekonomike. Bankat Bujqësore të Shteteve të Ballkanit [The Code of Municipal Affairs]* (Constanza, 1933).
Pepo, Petraq, 'Materiale Dokumentare mbi Veprimtarinë e Zanatçinjve të Korçës e të Voskopojës në shek. XVIII dhe XIX [Documentary Materials on the Activity of Korça and Voskopoja Craftsmen in the 18th and 19th Century]', in: *Studime Historike* 1:1 (1967), 165–181.
Petmezas, Socrates, 'Διαχείριση των Κοινοτικών Οικονομικών και Κοινωνική Κυριαρχία. Η Στρατηγική των Προυχόντων: Ζαγορά 1784–1822 [The Administration of Communal Economics and Social Domination. The Archons' Strategy: Zagora 1784–1822]', in: *Mnemon* 13:1 (1991), 77–102.
Petmezas, Socrates D., 'Communities in Eighteenth- and Early Nineteenth-Century Ottoman Greece: Their Fiscal Functions', in: *The Princeton Papers: Interdisciplinary Journal of Middle Eastern Studies* 12:1 (2005), 71–127.
Quataert, D., 'Dilemma of Development: The Agricultural Bank and Agricultural Reform in Ottoman Turkey, 1888–1908', in: *The International Journal of Middle East Studies* 6:2 (1975), 210–227.
Rafeq, Abdul-Karim, 'Craft Organization, Work Ethics, and the Strains of Change in Ottoman Syria', in: *The Journal of the American Oriental Society* 11:3 (1991), 495–511.
Rubin, Jared, 'The Lender's Curse: A New Look at the Origin and Persistence of Interest Bans in Islam and Christianity', in: *The Journal of Economic History* 68:2 (2008), 575–579.
Rubin, Jared, 'Institutions, the Rise of Commerce and the Persistence of Laws: Interest Restrictions in Islam and Christianity', in: *The Economic Journal* 121:557 (2011), 1310–1339.
Rosenthal, Jean-Laurent, and R. Bin Wong, *Before and Beyond Divergence: The Politics of Economic Change in China and Europe* (London, 2011).
Salamangas, Dimitris, 'Τα Ισνάφια και τα Επαγγέλματα επί Τουρκοκρατίας στα Γιάννινα [The Guilds and Crafts in Ioannina during the Turkish Rule]', in: *Epeirotiki Estia* 82:1 (1959) 136–140; continues in 83:1 214–218; 84:1 311–315; 86:1 482–486; 87:1 565–569.
Shkodra, Zija, *Esnafet Shqiptare (Shekujt XV–XX) [Albanian Guilds (15th–20th Centuries)]* (Tirana, 1973).
Süt, Pinar, 'The Transformation of the Istanbul Artisans and Traders (Esnaf) in the Late Ottoman Empire: 1839–1922' (unpublished PhD dissertation, Middle East Technical University, 2022).
Theocarakis, Nicholas J., 'The Market as Default Mechanism: A History of Economic Thought Perspective', in: Christina Agriantoni, Maria Christina Chatziioannou, and Leda Papastefanaki (eds.), *Markets and Politics. Private Interest and Public Authority, Eighteenth-20th Centuries* (Volos, 2016), 35–49.

Thoma, Mark A., 'The Effects on Money Growth on Inflation and Interest Rates Across Spectral Frequency Bands', in: *The Journal of Money Credit and Banking* 26:2 (1994), 218–231.

Tsikaloudi, Maria, 'Η Αγορά στο Χάνδακα, 1669–1765: Συντεχνίες και Καθορισμός των Τιμών [The Market in Candy, 1669–1765: Guilds and Price Determination]', in: *Ta Istorika* 12:22 (1995), 49–84.

Udovitch, Abraham L., 'Credit as a Means of Investment in Medieval Islamic Trade', in: *The Journal of the American Oriental Society* 87:3 (1967), 260–264.

Veis, Nikolaos, 'Εκ του Καταστίχου της Συντεχνίας των Παντοπωλών της Μοσχοπόλεως [A Register of the Voskopoja Guild of Grocers]', in: *Byzantinisch-Neugriechische Jahrbücher* 7:3–4 (1930), 527–528.

Vourazeli-Marinakou, Eleni, *Αἱ ἐν Θράκῃ Συντεχνίαι τῶν Ἑλλήνων κατὰ τὴν Τουρκοκρατίαν [The Guilds of Greeks in Thrace during the Ottoman Rule]* (Thessaloniki, 1950).

Yi, Eunjeong, *Guilds Dynamics in Seventeenth Century Istanbul. Fluidity and Leverage* (Leiden, 2004).

Yildirim, Onur, 'Ottoman Guilds in the Early Modern Era', in: Jan Lucassen, Tine De Moor, and Jan Luiten van Zanden (eds.), *The Return of the Guilds* (Cambridge, 2008), 73–93.

Zwarts, Harm, 'Institutional Investors in the Countryside of the Dutch Republic. An Analysis of the Investment Portfolios of Reformed Deaconries in the Countryside of the Dutch Republic, c.1750–1800' (unpublished PhD dissertation, Utrecht University, 2015).

Index

C. van Bochove and J. Levy (eds.), *Beyond Banks*, Palgrave Studies in the History of Finance, https://doi.org/10.1007/978-3-031-75819-5

9783031758188